Econometric Society Monographs No. 19

Applied nonparametric regression

Econometric Society Monographs

Editors:

Avinash K. Dixit   *Princeton University*
Alain Monfort   *Institut National de la Statistique et des Etudes Economiques*

The Econometric Society is an international society for the advancement of economic theory in relation to statistics and mathematics. The Econometric Society Monograph Series is designed to promote the publication of original research contributions of high quality in mathematical economics and theoretical and applied econometrics.

Other titles in the series:

Werner Hildenbrand, Editor   *Advances in economic theory*
Werner Hildenbrand, Editor   *Advances in econometrics*
G. S. Maddala   *Limited-dependent and qualitative variables in econometrics*
Gerard Debreu   *Mathematical economics*
Jean-Michel Grandmont   *Money and value*
Franklin M. Fisher   *Disequilibrium foundations of equilibrium economics*
Bezalel Peleg   *Game theoretic analysis of voting in committees*
Roger Bowden and Darrell Turkington   *Instrumental variables*
Andreu Mas-Colell   *The theory of general economic equilibrium*
James J. Heckman and Burton Singer   *Longitudinal analysis of labor market data*
Cheng Hsiao   *Analysis of panel data*
Truman F. Bewley, Editor   *Advances in economic theory – Fifth World Congress*
Truman F. Bewley, Editor   *Advances in econometrics – Fifth World Congress (Volume I)*
Truman F. Bewley, Editor   *Advances in econometrics – Fifth World Congress (Volume II)*
Hervé Moulin   *Axioms of cooperative decision making*
L. G. Godfrey   *Misspecification tests in econometrics*
Tony Lancaster   *The econometric analysis of transition data*
Alvin E. Roth and Marilda A. Oliviera Sotomayor, Editors   *Two-sided matching: A study in game-theoretic modeling and analysis*

Applied nonparametric regression

Wolfgang Härdle
Fakultät Rechts- und Staatswissenschaften
Wirtschaftstheoretische Abteilung II
Adenauerallee 24-26
Rheinische-Friedrich-Wilhelms Universität
D-5300 Bonn
15.6. 1989

CAMBRIDGE
UNIVERSITY PRESS

Published by the Press Syndicate of the University of Cambridge
The Pitt Building, Trumpington Street, Cambridge CB2 1RP
40 West 20th Street, New York, NY 10011-4211, USA
10 Stamford Road, Oakleigh, Melbourne 3166, Australia

First published 1990
First paperback edition 1991
Reprinted 1993

Printed in Great Britain

Library of Congress Cataloging-in-Publication Data available.

A catalogue record for this book is available from the British Library.

ISBN 0-521-38248-3 hardback
ISBN 0-521-42950-1 paperback

Für Renate, Nora, Viola, und Adrian

Contents

Preface

The theory and methods of smoothing have been developed mainly in the past ten years. The intensive interest in smoothing over this past decade had two reasons: Statisticians realized that pure parametric thinking in curve estimations often does not meet the need for flexibility in data analysis and the development of hardware created the demand for theory of now computable nonparametric estimates.

Smoothing techniques have a long tradition. In the nineteenth century the nonparametric approach had been used as a major tool for empirical analysis: In 1857 the Saxonian economist Engel found the famous Engelsches Gesetz by constructing a curve which we would nowadays call a regressogram. Since then, the nonparametric smoothing approach has then long been neglected and the mathematical development of statistical theory in the first half of this century has mainly suggested a purely parametric approach for its simplicity in computation, for its compatibility with model assumptions and also for its mathematical convenience.

This book concentrates on the statistical aspects of nonparametric regression smoothing from an applied point of view. The methods covered in this text can be used in biometry, econometrics, engineering and mathematics. The two central problems discussed are the choice of smoothing parameter and the construction of confidence bands in practice. Various smoothing methods, among them splines and orthogonal polynomials, are presented and discussed in their qualitative aspects. To simplify the exposition, kernel smoothers are investigated in greater detail. It is argued that all smoothing methods are in an asymptotic sense essentially equivalent to kernel smoothing. So it seems legitimate to expose the deeper problems of smoothing parameter selection and confidence bands for that method which is mathematically convenient and can be most easily understood on an intuitive level.

Most of the results are stated in a rather compact form and proved only in the simplest situations. On purpose I have tried to avoid being as general and precise as possible since I believe that the essential ideas which are relevant to practical data analysis can be understood without too much mathematical background. Generalizations and specializations, as well as additional results, are deferred to an "Exercises" part at the end of each section. I am aware that this decision might discourage most theoretical and some practical statisticians. However, I am sure that for the average reader this is a convenient presentation of a collection of tools and mathematical concepts for the application of smoothing methods.

I would like to express my deepest gratitude to Theo Gasser and to Werner Hildenbrand. Theo Gasser introduced me to the subject I treat in this book. Without his feeling for smoothing problems in practice I could have never developed the viewpoint of an applied mathematician. I have certainly taken up many of his ideas without explicit reference. Werner Hildenbrand opened my eyes to smoothing techniques in economics, especially in connection with the "law of demand." Without his constant encouragement and very constructive criticism I would not have written this book.

In the past years I have had particularly close collaboration with Adrian Bowman, Ray Carroll, Jürgen Franke, Jeff Hart, Enno Mammen, Michael Nussbaum, David Scott, Alexander Tsybakov and Philippe Vieu. Their influence and contributions essentially determined the shape of the book. I would like to thank all of them for their extremely helpful cooperation.

During the past two years I have taught on smoothing techniques at the Rheinische–Friedrich–Wilhelms Universität Bonn; Universität Dortmund; Université de Sciences Sociales, Toulouse; G.R.E.Q.E., Marseille and Universidad de Santiago de Compostela. It was a pleasure to teach at these places and to converse with colleagues and students.

I am especially grateful to Steve Marron, who helped a lot in focusing the book on the central themes. Peter Schönfeld pointed out some errors in earlier versions and advised me in the presentation of the smoothing problem. I would also like to thank Charles Manski, who helped me in sharpening my view toward the economic themes. Nick Fisher, Kurt Hildenbrand, John Rice, Heinz-Peter Schmitz, Ritei Shibata, Bernard Silverman and Rob Tibshirani read the manuscript at different stages and helped improve the exposition. Their help and comments are gratefully acknowledged. The text was carefully typed in a non–WYSIWYG environment by Christiane Beyer, Irenäus Drzensla, Elisabeth Fetsch, Katka Kukul and Rüdiger Plantiko. Sigbert Klinke and Berwin Turlach provided efficient algorithms and assisted in computing. Their help was essential and I would like to thank them.

Finally, I gratefully acknowledge the financial support of the Air Force Office of Scientific Research, the Koizumi Foundation and the Deutsche Forschungsgemeinschaft (Sonderforschungsbereiche 123 und 303).

Bonn   Wolfgang Härdle

Symbols and notation

X predictor variable in $\mathbb{R}^d$
Y response variable in $\mathbb{R}$
$f(x)$ marginal density of X
$f(x,y)$ joint density of X and Y
$f(y|x) = f(x,y)/f(x)$ conditional density of Y given $X = x$
$F(y|x)$ conditional distribution function Y given $X = x$
$\hat{f}(x)$ estimator of $f(x)$
$m(x) = E(Y|X = x)$ regression curve of Y on X
$\hat{m}(x)$ estimator of $m(x)$
$\sigma^2(x) = E(Y^2|X = x) - m^2(x)$ conditional variance of Y given $X = x$
$\hat{\sigma}^2(x)$ estimator of $\sigma^2(x)$
$\Phi(x)$ standard normal distribution function
$\varphi(x)$ density of the standard normal distribution
$I(\mathcal{M})$ indicator function, i.e. $I = 1$ on $\mathcal{M}$, $I = 0$ otherwise
$x = \operatorname{argmax} g(u)$ iff $g(\cdot)$ has a unique maximum at x
$x = \operatorname{argmin} g(u)$ iff $g(\cdot)$ has a unique minimum at x

Distributions

$N(0,1)$ standard normal distribution
$U(a,b)$ uniform distribution on (a,b)

$\{(X_i, Y_i)\}_{i=1}^n$ sample of n observations
$\{X_{(i)}\}_{i=1}^n$ the order statistic of $\{X_i\}_{i=1}^n$ in $\mathbb{R}$
$\{(X_{(i)}, Y_{(i)})\}_{i=1}^n$ the ordered sample with $\{X_{(i)}\}_{i=1}^n$ sorted according to X

$\mathcal{F}_1^n = \sigma((X_1, Y_1), ..., (X_n, Y_n))$ the σ-algebra generated by $\{(X_i, Y_i)\}_{i=1}^n$
$\mathcal{F}_n^\infty = \sigma((X_n, Y_n), ...)$ the σ-algebra generated by $\{(X_n, Y_n), ...\}$

Mean squared error
$MSE = E[\hat{m}_h(X) - m(X)]^2.$

Mean integrated squared error
$MISE = d_M(h) = E \int [\hat{m}_h(x) - m(x)]^2 w(x) dx$.
Integrated squared error
$ISE = d_I(h) = \int [\hat{m}_h(x) - m(x)]^2 f(x) w(x) dx$.
Averaged squared error
$ASE = d_A(h) = \sum_{i=1}^{n} [\hat{m}_h(X_i) - m(X_i)]^2 w(X_i)$.
Mean averaged squared error
$MASE = d_{MA}(h) = E d_A(h)$.

Kernel constants
$c_K = \int K^2(u) du$.
$d_K = \int u^2 K(u) du$.

Let α_n and β_n be sequences of real numbers.
$\alpha_n = O(\beta_n)$ iff $\alpha_n / \beta_n \to$ constant, as $n \to \infty$.
$\alpha_n = o(\beta_n)$ iff $\alpha_n / \beta_n \to 0$, as $n \to \infty$.
$\alpha_n \sim \beta_n$ iff $\alpha_n / \beta_n = c + o(1), c \neq 0$, as $n \to \infty$.

Let A_n and B_n be sequences of real random variables.
$A_n = O_p(B_n)$ iff $\forall \varepsilon > 0 \; \exists M, \; \exists N$ such that $P\{|A_n / B_n| > M\} < \varepsilon, \forall n >$
   N.
$A_n = o_p(B_n)$ iff $\forall \varepsilon > 0 \; \lim_{n \to \infty} P\{|A_n / B_n| > \varepsilon\} = 0$.
$A_n \approx B_n$ iff $A_n = B_n + o_p(B_n)$.
$A_n \overset{a.s.}{\to} A$ iff $P\{lim_{n \to \infty} A_n = A\} = 1$.
$A_n \overset{p}{\to} A$ iff $A_n - A = o_p(1)$, as $n \to \infty$.
$A_n \overset{r}{\to} A$ iff $E[A_n - A]^r = o(1)$, as $n \to \infty$.
$A_n \overset{\mathcal{L}}{\to} A$ iff $P\{A_n < x\} \to P\{A < x\} = F(x)$, at every point of continuity
   of $F(x)$ as $n \to \infty$.

For comparison of these convergence concepts see Schönfeld (1969,
   Chapter 6).
$g : \mathbb{R}^d \to \mathbb{R}$ is called Hölder continuous if there exist constants C and
   $0 \le \xi \le 1$ such that $|g(u) - g(v)| \le C \|u - v\|^\xi \; \forall u, v$.

PART I

Regression smoothing

CHAPTER 1

Introduction

> As regards problems of specification, these are entirely a matter
> for the practical statistician, for those cases where the quali-
> tative nature of the hypothetical population is known do not
> involve any problems of this type.
>
> Sir R. A. Fisher (1922)

A regression curve describes a general relationship between an explanatory variable X and a response variable Y. Having observed X, the
average value of Y is given by the regression function. It is of great
interest to have some knowledge about this relation. The form of the
regression function may tell us where higher Y-observations are to be
expected for certain values of X or whether a special sort of dependence
between the two variables is indicated. Interesting special features are,
for instance, monotonicity or unimodality. Other characteristics include
the location of zeros or the size of extrema. Also, quite often the regression curve itself is not the target of interest but rather derivatives
of it or other functionals.

If n data points $\{(X_i, Y_i)\}_{i=1}^n$ have been collected, the regression relationship can be modeled as

$$Y_i = m(X_i) + \varepsilon_i, \qquad i = 1, \ldots, n,$$

with the unknown regression function m and observation errors ε_i. A
look at a scatter plot of X_i versus Y_i does not always suffice to establish
an interpretable regression relationship. The eye is sometimes distracted
by extreme points or fuzzy structures. An example is given in Figure 1.1,
a scatter plot of X_i = rescaled net income versus Y_i = expenditure for
potatoes from the Family Expenditure Survey (1968–1983). The scatter
of points is presented in the form of a sunflower plot (see Cleveland and
McGill, 1984, for construction of sunflower plots).

In this particular situation one is interested in estimating the mean
expenditure as a function of income. The main body of the data covers
only a quarter of the diagram with a bad "signal to ink ratio" (Tufte
1983): it seems therefore to be difficult to determine the average expenditure for given income X. The aim of a regression analysis is to produce
a reasonable approximation to the unknown response function m. By

3

POTATOES VS. NET INCOME

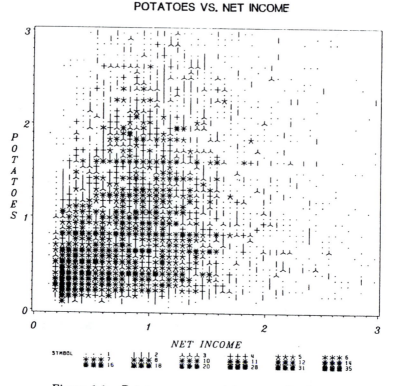

Figure 1.1. Potatoes versus net income. Sunflower plot of $Y =$ expenditure for potatoes versus $X =$ net income of British households for year 1973, $n = 7125$. Units are multiples of mean income and mean expenditure, respectively. The number of petals of the sunflower indicates the frequency of observations falling in the cell covered by the sunflower. Family Expenditure Survey (1968–1983).

reducing the observational errors it allows interpretation to concentrate on important details of the mean dependence of Y on X. This curve approximation procedure is commonly called "smoothing."

  This task of approximating the mean function can be done essentially in two ways. The quite often used *parametric* approach is to assume that the mean curve m has some prespecified functional form, for example, a line with unknown slope and intercept. As an alternative one could try to estimate m *nonparametrically* without reference to a specific form. The first approach to analyze a regression relationship is called parametric since it is assumed that the functional form is fully described by a finite

set of parameters. A typical example of a parametric model is a polynomial regression equation where the parameters are the coefficients of the
independent variables. A tacit assumption of the parametric approach
though is that the curve can be represented in terms of the parametric
model or that, at least, it is believed that the approximation bias of the
best parametric fit is a negligible quantity. By contrast, nonparametric
modeling of a regression relationship does not project the observed data
into a Procrustean bed of a fixed parametrization, for example, fit a line
to the potato data. A preselected parametric model might be too restricted or too low-dimensional to fit unexpected features, whereas the
nonparametric smoothing approach offers a flexible tool in analyzing
unknown regression relationships.

The term *nonparametric* thus refers to the flexible functional form of
the regression curve. There are other notions of "nonparametric statistics" which refer mostly to distribution-free methods. In the present
context, however, neither the error distribution nor the functional form
of the mean function is prespecified.

The question of which approach should be taken in data analysis was
a key issue in a bitter fight between Pearson and Fisher in the twenties.
Fisher pointed out that the nonparametric approach gave generally poor
efficiency whereas Pearson was more concerned about the specification
question. Tapia and Thompson (1978) summarize this discussion in the
related setting of density estimation.

*Fisher neatly side-stepped the question of what to do in case one did
not know the functional form of the unknown density. He did this by
separating the problem of determining the form of the unknown density
(in Fisher's terminology, the problem of "specification") from the problem of determining the parameters which characterize a specified density
(in Fisher's terminology, the problem of "estimation").*

Both viewpoints are interesting in their own right. Pearson pointed
out that the price we have to pay for pure parametric fitting is the
possibility of gross misspecification resulting in too high a model bias.
On the other hand, Fisher was concerned about a too pure consideration
of parameter-free models which may result in more variable estimates,
especially for small sample size n.

An example for these two different approaches is given in Figure 1.2,
where the straight line indicates a linear parametric fit (Leser 1963,
eq. 2a) and the other curve is a nonparametric smoothing estimate.
Both curves model the market demand for potatoes as a function of
income from the point cloud presented in Figure 1.1. The linear parametric model is unable to represent a decreasing demand for potatoes
as a function of increasing income. The nonparametric smoothing ap-

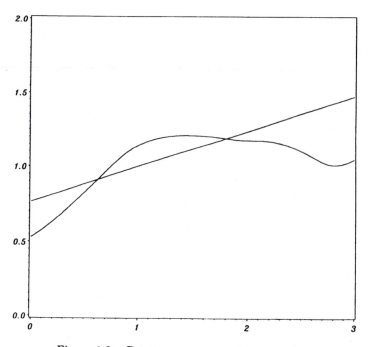

Figure 1.2. Potatoes versus net income. A linear parametric fit of Y = expenditure for potatoes versus X = net income (straight line) and a nonparametric kernel smoother (bandwidth = 0.4) for the same variables, year 1973, n = 7125. Units are multiples of mean income and mean expenditure, respectively. Family Expenditure Survey (1968–1983).

proach suggests here rather an approximate U-shaped regression relation between income and expenditure for potatoes. Of course, to make this graphical way of assessing features more precise we need to know how much variability we have to expect when using the nonparametric approach. This is discussed in Chapter 4. Another approach could be to combine the advantages of both methods in a semiparametric mixture. This line of thought is discussed in Chapters 9 and 10.

1.1   Motivation

The nonparametric approach to estimating a regression curve has four main purposes. First, it provides a versatile method of exploring a general relationship between two variables. Second, it gives predictions of observations yet to be made without reference to a fixed parametric model. Third, it provides a tool for finding spurious observations by studying the influence of isolated points. Fourth, it constitutes a flexible method of substituting for missing values or interpolating between adjacent X-values.

The *flexibility* of the method is extremely helpful in a preliminary and exploratory statistical analysis of a data set. If no a priori model information about the regression curve is available, the nonparametric analysis could help in suggesting simple parametric formulations of the regression relationship. An example is depicted in Figure 1.3. In that study of human longitudinal growth curves the target of interest was the first (respectively, second) derivative of the regression function (Gasser et al. 1984; Jørgensen et al. 1985).

The nonparametric regression smoothing method revealed an extra peak in the first derivative, the so-called mid-growth spurt at the age of about eight years. Other approaches based on ad hoc parametric modeling made it extremely difficult to detect this extra peak (dashed line Figure 1.3).

An analogous situation in the related field of density estimation was reported by Hildenbrand (1986) for the income density income of British households. It is important in economic theory, especially in demand and equilibrium theory, to have good approximations to income distributions. A traditional parametric fit – the Singh–Madalla model – resulted in Figure 1.4.

The parametric model class of Singh–Madalla densities can only produce unimodal densities per se. By contrast, the more flexible nonparametric smoothing method produced Figure 1.5. The nonparametric approach makes it possible to estimate functions of greater complexity and suggests instead a bimodal income distribution. This bimodality is present over the thirteen years from 1968 to 1981 and changes its shape: More people enter the "lower income range" and the "middle class" peak becomes less dominant.

An example which once more underlines this flexibility of modeling regression curves is presented in Engle et al. (1986). They consider a nonlinear relationship between electricity sales and temperature using a parametric–nonparametric estimation procedure. Figure 1.6 shows the result of a spline smoothing procedure that nicely models a kink in the electricity sales.

Another example arises in modeling alcohol concentration curves. A commonly used practice in forensic medicine is to approximate ethanol reduction curves with parametric models. More specifically, a linear regression model is used which in a simple way gives the so-called β_{60} value, the ethanol reduction rate per hour. In practice, of course, this

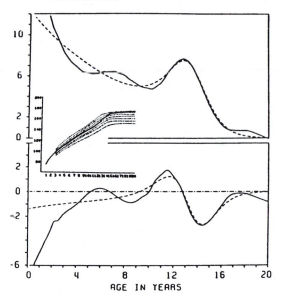

Figure 1.3. Human height growth versus age. The small graph gives
raw data of height connected by straight lines (solid line) with cross-
sectional sample quantiles (dashed lines). Velocity of height growth of
a girl (above) and acceleration (below) modeled by a nonparametric
smoother (solid line) and a parametric fit (dashed line). Units are cm
(for height), cm/year (for velocity) and cm/year^2 (for acceleration).
From Gasser and Müller (1984 figure 1) with the permission of the
Scandinavian Journal of Statistics.

model can be used only in a very limited time interval; an extension
into the "late ethanol reduction region" would not be possible. A nonparametric analysis based on splines suggested a mixture of a linear and
exponential reduction curve. (Mattern et al. 1983).

The *prediction* of new observations is of particular interest in time
series analysis. It has been observed by a number of people that in certain applications classical parametric models are too restrictive to give
reasonable explanations of observed phenomena.   The nonparametric
prediction of times series has been investigated by Robinson (1983) and
Doukhan and Ghindes (1985). Ullah (1987) applies kernel smoothing to
a time series of stock market prices and estimates certain risk indexes.
Deaton (1988) uses smoothing methods to examine demand patterns
in Thailand and investigates how knowledge of those patterns affects
the assessment of pricing policies. Yakowitz (1985b) applies smoothing
techniques for one-day-ahead prediction of river flow. Figure 1.7 be-

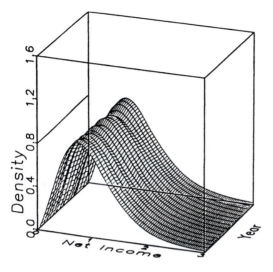

Figure 1.4.   Net income densities over time. A Singh–Madalla fit to the densities of $X =$ net income from 1969 to 1983. Units are mean income for each year. Family Expenditure Survey (1968–1983).

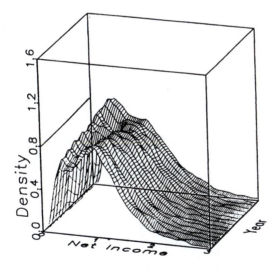

Figure 1.5.   Net income densities over time. A nonparametric kernel fit (bandwidth $h = 0.2$) to the densities of $X =$ net income from 1969 to 1981. Units are mean income for each year. Family Expenditure Survey (1968–1983).

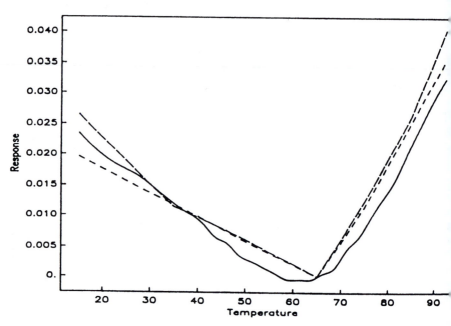

Figure 1.6.   Temperature response function for Georgia. The nonparametric estimate is given by the solid curve and two parametric estimates by the dashed curves. From Engle et al. (1986) with the permission of the American Statistical Association.

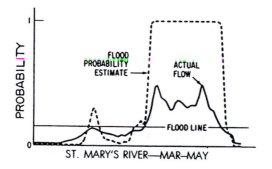

Figure 1.7.   Nonparametric flow probability for the St. Mary's river. From Yakowitz (1985b) with permission of the Water Resources Research.

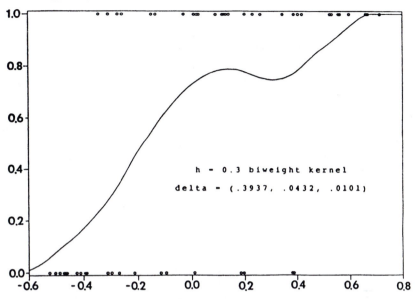

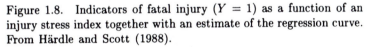

Figure 1.8.   Indicators of fatal injury $(Y = 1)$ as a function of an injury stress index together with an estimate of the regression curve. From Härdle and Scott (1988).

low shows a nonparametric estimate of the flow probability for the St. Mary's river.

A treatment of *outliers* is an important step in highlighting features of a data set. Extreme points affect the scale of plots so that the structure of the main body of the data can become invisible. There is a rich literature on robust parametric methods in which different kinds of outlier influence are discussed. There are a number of diagnostic techniques for parametric models which can usually cope with outliers. However, with some parametric models one may not even be able to diagnose an implausible value since the parameters could be completely distorted by the outliers. This is true in particular for isolated (leverage) points in the predictor variable X. An example is given in Rousseeouw and Yohai (1984) in which a linear regression line fitted a few outliers but missed the main body of the data. Nonparametric smoothing provides a versatile pre-screening method for outliers in the x-direction without reference to a specific parametric model. Figure 1.8 shows a nonparametric smoother applied to analysis of simulated side impact studies. The curve shown is an approximation to the probability of a fatal injury as a function of anthropometric and biokinetic parameters. The Y-ordinates are binary in this case ($Y = 1$ denoting fatal injury). The curve shows visually what could also be derived from an influence analysis: it makes a dip at the isolated x-points in the far right. The points could be identified as observations from young persons which had a rather unnormal reaction behavior in these experiments; see Kallieris and Mattern (1984). This example is discussed in more detail in Section 10.4.

Missing data is a problem quite often encountered in practice. Some response variables may not have been recorded since an instrument broke down or a certain entry on an inquiry form was not answered. Nonparametric smoothing bridges the gap of missing data by interpolating between adjacent data points, whereas parametric models would involve all the observations in the interpolation. An approach in spatial statistics is to interpolate points by the "kriging" method. This method is used by statisticians in hydrology, mining, and petroleum engineering and is related to predicting values of noisy data in a nonparametric fashion; see Yakowitz and Szidarovszky (1986). Schmerling and Peil (1985) use local polynomial interpolation in anatomy to extrapolate missing data.

1.2   Scope of this book

This book takes the viewpoint of an applied statistician who is interested in a flexible regression analysis of exploratory character. In this spirit, I shall concentrate on simple smoothing techniques and analyze problems that typically arise in applications. Important practical questions are:

> *What is the right amount of smoothing?*
>
> *How close is the estimated curve to the underlying curve?*
>
> *How can we effectively estimate curves in dimensions higher than three?*

One of the simplest smoothing techniques is kernel estimation. It is straightforward to implement without further mathematical knowledge and it is understandable on an intuitive level. It is argued in Chapter 2 that kernel smoothing is a suitable tool in many ways. A variety of alternative smoothing techniques such as splines are discussed as well. In Chapter 3 it is seen that they are, in an asymptotic sense, equivalent to kernel smoothing.

The decision about the right amount of smoothing is crucial. Every smoothing method has to be tuned by some smoothing parameter which balances the degree of fidelity to the data against the smoothness of the estimated curve. A choice of the smoothing parameter has to be made in practice and controls the performance of the estimators. This *smoothing parameter selection problem* will be discussed in great detail and will be a centerpiece of this book (Chapters 4 and 5). The user of a nonparametric smoothing technique should be aware that the final decision about an estimated regression curve is partly subjective since even asymptotically optimal smoothers contain a considerable amount of noise that leaves space for subjective judgment. It is therefore of great importance to make such a decision in interaction with the data, which means that ideally one should have computer resources with some sort of interactive graphical display. Bearing this in mind, a great deal of the discussion will be devoted to algorithmic aspects of nonparametric smoothing.

In Chapters 6 and 7 I discuss smoothing in the presence of outliers and correlation, respectively. In Chapter 8 smoothing under qualitative constraints, such as monotonicity or more general piecewise monotonicity, is presented. Smoothing in dimensions higher than three creates problems on the computational and on the statistical side of the estimator. It takes longer to compute the estimators and the accuracy decreases exponentially as the dimension grows. Chapter 9 presents some semiparametric approaches to incorporate parametric components into nonparametric smoothing. Chapter 10 discusses additive models and gives some heuristics as to why these models achieve better accuracy and in this sense reduce the dimension problem.

The great flexibility of nonparametric curve estimation makes a precise theoretical description of the accuracy of the smoothers for finite sample sizes extremely difficult. It is therefore necessary to achieve some sort of simplification. This is done here in two ways. First, the mathematical arguments are of asymptotic character, that is, the accuracy of the nonparametric smoothing method will be evaluated as the sample size n tends to infinity. Second, the class of smoothers that is mainly considered here is of very simple structure (kernel estimators).

The reader interested in the applied aspects should not be too disappointed about the asymptotic mathematical results. I have tried to present them in the spirit aptly described by Murray Rosenblatt:

The arguments ... have been of an asymptotic character and it is a mistake to take them too literally from a finite sample point of view. But even asymptotic arguments if used and interpreted with care can yield meaningful ideas.

Technical details of the mathematical theory are kept simple or else deferred to exercises and complements. I believe that each chapter provides stimulation to work out some of the mathematical arguments. Some practically oriented readers might find themselves encouraged to try the methods in practice. This can be done, for instance, with graphically oriented computing environments and systems such as GAUSS (1987), ISP (1987), S (1988) or XploRe (1989).

CHAPTER 2

Basic idea of smoothing

If m is believed to be smooth, then the observations at X_i near
x should contain information about the value of m at x. Thus
it should be possible to use something like a local average of the
data near x to construct an estimator of $m(x)$.

R. Eubank (1988, p. 7)

Smoothing of a dataset $\{(X_i, Y_i)\}_{i=1}^{n}$ involves the approximation of the
mean response curve m in the regression relationship

$$Y_i = m(X_i) + \varepsilon_i, \quad i = 1, \ldots, n. \tag{2.0.1}$$

The functional of interest could be the regression curve itself, certain
derivatives of it or functions of derivatives such as extrema or inflection
points. The data collection could have been performed in several ways.
If there are repeated observations at a fixed point $X = x$ estimation
of $m(x)$ can be done by using just the average of the corresponding Y-
values. In the majority of cases though repeated responses at a given x
cannot be obtained. In most studies of a regression relationship (2.0.1),
there is just a single response variable Y and a single predictor variable X
which may be a vector in $\mathbb{R}^d$. An example from biometry is the height
growth experiment described in Chapter 1. In a frequently occurring
economic example the variable Y is a discrete variable (indicating some
choice) and the vector X denotes an influential variable; see Manski
(1989).

There are other restrictions on the possibility of multiple data record-
ing. An experimental setup may not be repeatable since the object under
consideration gets demolished. This is often the case in biomechanical experiments. Kallieris and Mattern (1984) describe a side impact
study where acceleration curves from postmortal test objects have been
recorded in simulated crashes. Also, budget restrictions and ethical considerations may force the experimenter to adopt a single experimental
setup. One can certainly imagine situations in which it is too expen-
sive to carry out more than one experiment for a specific level of the
influential variable X. This raises the following question:

*If there are no repeated observations how can we possibly gather in-
formation about the regression curve?*

14

In the trivial case in which $m(x)$ is a constant, estimation of m reduces to the point estimation of location, since an average over the response variables Y yields an estimate of m. In practical studies though it is unlikely (or not believed, since otherwise there is not quite a response to study) that the regression curve is constant. Rather the assumed curve is modeled as a smooth continuous function of a particular structure which is "nearly constant" in small neighborhoods around x. It is difficult to judge from looking even at a two-dimensional scatter plot whether a regression curve is locally constant. Recall for instance the binary response example as presented in Figure 1.8. It seems to be hard to decide from just looking at this data set whether the regression function m is a smooth function. However, sometimes a graphical inspection of the data is helpful. A look at a two-dimensional histogram or similar graphical enhancements can give support for such a smoothness assumption. One should be aware though that even for large data sets small jumps in m may occur and a smooth regression curve is then only an approximation to the true curve.

In Figure 2.1 a scatter plot of a data set of expenditure for food (Y) and income (X) is shown. This scatter plot of the entire data looks unclear, especially in the lower left corner.

It is desirable to have a technique which helps us in seeing where the data concentrate. Such an illustration technique is the *sunflower plot* (Cleveland and McGill 1984): Figure 2.2 shows the food versus net income example.

The sunflower plot is constructed by defining a net of squares covering the (X, Y) space and counting the number of observations that fall into the disjoint squares. The number of petals of the sunflower blossom corresponds to the number of observations in the square around the sunflower: It represents the empirical distribution of the data. The sunflower plot of food versus net income shows a concentration of the data around an increasing band of densely packed "blossoms." The shape of this band seems to suggest smooth dependence of the average response curve on x.

Another example is depicted in Figure 2.3, where heights and ages of a group of persons are shown.

The lengths of the needles in Figure 2.3 correspond to the counts of observations that fall into a net of squares in (X, Y) space. The relation to the sunflower plot is intimate: the needle length is equivalent to the number of petals in the sunflower. In this height versus age data set, the average response curve seems to lie in a band that rises steeply with age (up to about 10,000–15,000 days) and then slowly decreases as the individuals get older.

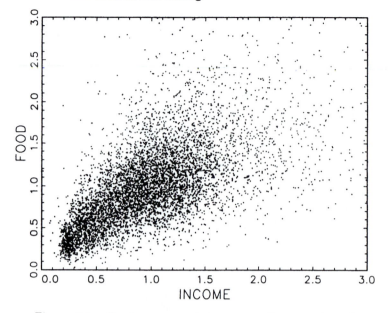

Figure 2.1. Food versus net income.   Scatter plot of $Y =$ expenditure for food versus $X =$ net income (both reported in multiples of mean expenditure, resp. mean income), $n = 7125$. (See Figure 1.1 for the corresponding plot of potatoes versus net income). Family Expenditure Survey (1968–1983).

For the illustrations (Figs. 2.2 and 2.3), the food versus income and height versus age scatter plots our eyes, in fact, smooth: The data look more concentrated in a smooth band (of varying extension). This band has no apparent jumps or rapid local fluctuations. A reasonable approximation to the regression curve $m(x)$ will therefore be any representative point close to the center of this band of response variables. A quite natural choice is the mean of the response variables near a point x. This "local average" should be constructed in such a way that it is defined only from observations in a small neighborhood around x, since Y-observations from points far away from x will have, in general, very different mean values. This *local averaging procedure* can be viewed as the basic idea of smoothing. More formally this procedure can be defined as

$$\hat{m}(x) = n^{-1} \sum_{i=1}^{n} W_{ni}(x)Y_i,$$

(2.0.2)

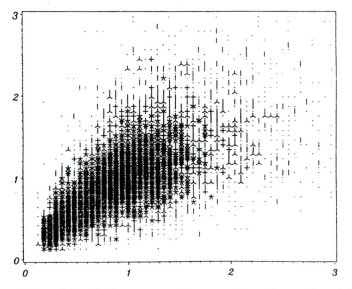

Figure 2.2. Food versus net income. A sunflower plot of $Y =$ expenditure for food versus $X =$ net income (both reported in multiples of mean expenditure, resp. mean income), $n = 7125$. The data shown are from the year 1973 (see Figure 1.1 for the corresponding plot of potatoes versus net income). Family Expenditure Survey (1968–1983).

where $\{W_{ni}(x)\}_{i=1}^{n}$ denotes a sequence of weights which may depend on the whole vector $\{X_i\}_{i=1}^{n}$.

Every smoothing method to be described here is, at least asymptotically, of the form (2.0.2). Quite often the regression estimator $\hat{m}(x)$ is just called a *smoother* and the outcome of the smoothing procedure is simply called the *smooth* (Tukey 1977). A smooth of the potato data set has already been given in Figure 1.2. A very simple smooth can be obtained by defining the weights as constant over adjacent intervals. This procedure is similar to the histogram; therefore Tukey (1961) called it the *regressogram*. A regressogram smooth for the potato data is given in Figure 2.4. The weights $\{W_{ni}(x)\}_{i=1}^{n}$ have been defined here as constant over blocks of length 0.6 starting at 0. Compared to the sunflower plot (Figure 1.1) of this data set a considerable amount of noise reduction has been achieved and the regressogram smooth is again quite different from the linear fit.

Special attention has to be paid to the fact that smoothers, by definition, average over observations with different mean values. The amount

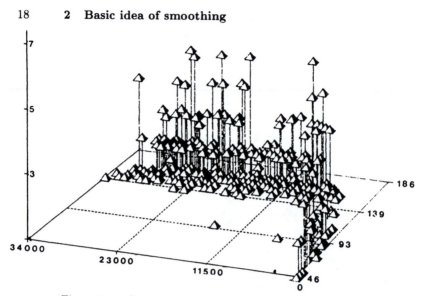

Figure 2.3. Height versus age. Histogram of the two-dimensional distribution of Y = height (in cm) versus X = age (in days) for $n = 500$ female persons. Bin size for age=2 years, for height = 2 cm. The needles give the counts of how many observations fall into a cell of the bin-net. Source: Institute of Forensic Medicine, University of Heidelberg.

of averaging is controlled by the weight sequence $\{W_{ni}(x)\}_{i=1}^{n}$ which is tuned by a *smoothing parameter*. This smoothing parameter regulates the size of the neighborhood around x. A local average over too large a neighborhood would cast away the good with the bad. In this situation an extremely "oversmooth" curve would be produced, resulting in a biased estimate $\hat{m}$. On the other hand, defining the smoothing parameter oo that it oorroopondo to a vory omall noighborhood would not oift the chaff from the wheat. Only a small number of observations would contribute nonnegligibly to the estimate $\hat{m}(x)$ at x making it very rough and wiggly. In this case the variability of $\hat{m}(x)$ would be inflated. Finding the choice of smoothing parameter that balances the trade-off between *oversmoothing* and *undersmoothing* is called the *smoothing parameter selection problem*.

To give insight into the smoothing parameter selection problem consider Figure 2.5. Both curves represent nonparametric estimates of the Engel curve, the average expenditure curve as a function of income. The more wiggly curve has been computed using a kernel estimate with

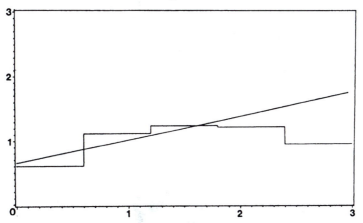

Figure 2.4. Potatoes versus net income. The step function is a non-parametric smooth (regressogram) of the expenditure for potatoes as a function of net income. For this plot the data are normalized by their mean. The straight line denotes a linear fit to the average expenditure curve, $n = 7125$, year=1973. Family Expenditure Survey (1968–1983).

a very low smoothing parameter. By contrast, the more flat curve has been computed using a very big smoothing parameter. Which smoothing parameter is correct? This question will be discussed in Chapter 5.

There is another way of looking at the local averaging formula (2.0.2). Suppose that the weights $\{W_{ni}(x)\}$ are positive and sum to one for all x, that is,

$$n^{-1} \sum_{i=1}^{n} W_{ni}(x) = 1.$$

Then $\hat{m}(x)$ is a *least squares estimate* at point x since we can write $\hat{m}(x)$ as a solution to the following minimization problem:

$$\min_{\theta} n^{-1} \sum_{i=1}^{n} W_{ni}(x)(Y_i - \theta)^2$$

$$= n^{-1} \sum_{i=1}^{n} W_{ni}(x)(Y_i - \hat{m}(x))^2. \quad (2.0.3)$$

This formula says that the residuals are weighted quadratically. In other words:

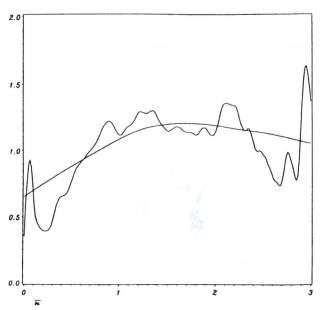

Figure 2.5.   Potatoes versus net income. The wiggly and the flat curve is a nonparametric kernel smooth of the expenditure for potatoes as a function of net income. For this plot the data are normalized by their mean. The kernel was quartic and $h = 0.1$, 1.0, $n = 7125$, year $= 1973$. Family Expenditure Survey (1968–1983).

The basic idea of local averaging is equivalent to the procedure of finding a local weighted least squares estimate.

It is well known from the theory of robustness that a wild spike in the raw data affects the small sample properties of local least squares estimates. When such outliers (in Y-direction) are present, better performance can be expected from *robust smoothers*, which give less weight to large residuals. These smoothers are usually defined as nonlinear functions of the data and it is not immediately clear how they fit into the framework of local averaging. In large data sets, however, they can be approximately represented as a weighted average with suitably nonlinearly transformed residuals; see Chapter 6. The general basic idea of weighted averaging expressed by formula (2.0.2) thus applies also to these nonlinear smoothing techniques.

2.1   The stochastic nature of the observations

I shall consider two scenarios on how the data $\{(X_i, Y_i)\}_{i=1}^n$ have been generated. The first setting is concerned with independent, identically distributed random variables $\{(X_i, Y_i)\}_{i=1}^n$. The regression curve is defined as

$$m(x) = E(Y|X = x). \tag{2.1.1}$$

The regression curve is well defined if $E|Y| < \infty$. If a joint density $f(x, y)$ exists, then $m(x)$ can be calculated as

$$m(x) = \int yf(x, y)dy/f(x), \tag{2.1.2}$$

where $f(x) = \int f(x, y)dy$ denotes the marginal density of X. For a more technical discussion of this formula see Feller (1971, p. 71). It is common terminology to refer to this setting as the *random design model*. By contrast, the *fixed design model* is concerned with controlled, nonstochastic X-variables, so

$$Y_i = m(X_i) + \varepsilon_i, \qquad 1 \le i \le n,$$

where the $\{\varepsilon_i\}_{i=1}^n$ denote zero-mean random variables with variance σ^2. In many experiments the predictor variables $\{X_i\}_{i=1}^n$ are taken to be equidistributed on an interval $[a, b]$; without loss of generality it can be assumed that $[a, b] = [0, 1]$ and $X_i = i/n$.

An example for the fixed design model is the study of human growth curves. The X-variable has been determined well in advance by a team of pediatricians (Gasser et al. 1984). By contrast, the data of Figure 2.4, a sample of heights and ages, do not have this feature of a controlled X-variable since both X and Y are random. Although the stochastic mechanism is different, the basic idea of smoothing is the same for both random and nonrandom X-variables. In both cases one would like to average over neighboring observations and in both cases one would tailor the *span* and the size of the weights to the relative frequency of the X-variables.

Most results in this book are presented for the stochastic design case, since especially the economic applications I consider are in a random design model. For some questions the amount of technical mathematics for the random design model can be enormous. Therefore I sometimes present statistical ideas only for the fixed design model. These ideas carry over to the random design model but require mostly more tedious mathematics. Some of the mathematical arguments I sketch only for the fixed design case, which is easier to analyze theoretically. A possible way of seeing similarities between both models is given in the complements of this section.

2.2   Hurdles for the smoothing process

As does every statistical method the smoothing procedure has to clear some hurdles that require special thought and coordination. It has already been mentioned that compared to a parametric approach there is, in an asymptotic sense, an increase in variability. From a pure quantitative point of view one could justify the statement that the loss in statistical accuracy is "only in an asymptotic sense" and therefore no major difficulties for the data at hand are to be expected. Indeed, for moderate sample size, the confidence intervals will not be much larger than for a parametric model. However, it seems natural to ask what the smoothing process does – in a qualitative sense – to the data at hand. In other words, what are the "qualitative hurdles," for example, shape distortions, that we expect when smoothing a finite data set? The simplest way to answer this question is to assume that no noise is present, for example, the best strategy would be not to smooth at all.

One scenario is concerned with the behavior at peaks of m. Since averaging is performed over neighboring observations, clearly an estimate of m at the peak point will flatten this maximum to some extent. This behavior is an indication that we have to expect a finite sample bias which depends on the local curvature of m. Of course an "asymptotic remedy" is to let the neighborhood around x shrink but when just one data set is at hand we have to do some adjustments; see Section 5.3.

At the boundary of the observation interval the local averaging process gets asymmetric, that is, half of the weights $W_{ni}(x)$ are nondefined and outside the boundary. This will also create a bias: The smooth will depend on the tangential behavior at the boundary. Boundary modifications are discussed in Section 4.4. Another situation is the case where we have regions of sparse data. If the weights $W_{ni}(x)$ do not adapt for that case it can happen that the weights are undefined since there are no observations to average. A safe way of ensuring that observations fall into the averaging window is to design the weights with variable span. Problems of this kind are discussed in Chapter 3.

What computational effort do we expect? At any point x the weights define a neighborhood into which a certain fraction of the X-variables fall. A naive way of computing the smooth $\{\hat{m}(X_j)\}_{j=1}^n$ consists of calculating for $i = 1, \ldots, n$ the weights $W_{ni}(X_j)$ for all $j = 1, \ldots, n$. This unfortunately results in $O(n^2)$ operations. If such an algorithm is implemented in some interactive device, then the calculations can take so long that the process is not really interactive. It is therefore necessary to take great care of the numerical efficiency of smoothing methods. Computational aspects for different weighting schemes are discussed in Chapter 3.

Complements

This complement to Section 2.1 can be omitted by a reader not so interested in mathematical details. Suppose that an experimenter has chosen the X-variables at locations $\{X_i\}_{i=1}^n$ in the fixed interval $[0, 1]$. Is there a way to express the local density of the X-observations? Define the empirical distribution function F_n as

$$F_n(u) = n^{-1} \# \{i : X_i \leq u\}.$$

Assume that there exists an absolutely continuous distribution function F on $[0, 1]$ such that $F_n \to F$ uniformly in $[0, 1]$. An example of a nonstochastic X-variable that is regularly distributed with density $f = F'$ on $[a, b] = [0, 1]$ is

$$X_i = F^{-1}\left(\frac{i - 1/2}{n}\right), \qquad i = 1, \ldots, n.$$

Clearly

$$F_n(u) = n^{-1}[nF(u) + 1/2],$$

and therefore

$$\sup_{0 \leq u \leq 1} |F_n(u) - F(u)| = (1/2)n^{-1}.$$

In the case of stochastic X-variables a slightly slower rate is attained. By the Glivenko–Cantelli Theorem (see Serfling 1980, Th. 2.1.4b)

$$\sup_u |F_n(u) - F(u)| = O(n^{-1/2}(\log \log n)^{1/2}) \quad a.s.$$

Thus in both cases one could speak of a marginal distribution F of X, although in the case of controlled X-variables the randomness of the response only enters through the observation errors $\{\varepsilon_i\}_{i=1}^n$.

CHAPTER 3

Smoothing techniques

The overriding problems are the choice of what method to use in
any given practical context and, given that a particular method
is being used, how to choose the various parameters needed by
the method.

Silverman (1986, p. 32)

In this chapter a survey of the major regression smoothing methods is
given. The kernel estimator will be discussed in more detail in later chapters, but it is helpful to elucidate some common structures of the main
smoothing methods before examining a particular technique. In particular, I present the specific weight sequences $\{W_{ni}(x)\}_{i=1}^{n}$ for kernel,
splines, k-NN and orthogonal series smoothing. These weight sequences
will be related to each other and it is argued that one of the simplest
ways of computing a weight sequence is kernel smoothing. The summary
of the commonly used methods given here is concentrated on univariate
regression estimation. This is done for two reasons. First, the notation
gets rather complicated for higher dimensional X-variables. Second, the
additive model fitting discussed in Chapter 10 uses univariate smoothing
algorithms as elementary building blocks. The different methods will be
compared for a simulated data set and the motor cycle data set, which
are presented in Table 1 and Table 2 in Appendix 2.

3.1   Kernel smoothing

A conceptually simple approach to a representation of the weight sequence $\{W_{ni}(x)\}_{i=1}^{n}$ is to describe the shape of the weight function
$W_{ni}(x)$ by a density function with a scale parameter that adjusts the
size and the form of the weights near x. It is quite common to refer to
this shape function as a *kernel* K. The *kernel* is a continuous, bounded
and symmetric real function K which integrates to one,

$$\int K(u)du = 1. \tag{3.1.1}$$

24

The weight sequence for kernel smoothers (for one-dimensional x) is defined by

$$W_{ni}(x) = K_{h_n}(x - X_i)/\hat{f}_{h_n}(x), \qquad (3.1.2)$$

where

$$\hat{f}_{h_n}(x) = n^{-1} \sum_{i=1}^{n} K_{h_n}(x - X_i) \qquad (3.1.3)$$

and where

$$K_{h_n}(u) = h_n^{-1} K(u/h_n)$$

is the kernel with scale factor h_n. Suppressing the dependence of $h = h_n$ on the sample size n, the kernel weight sequence (3.1.2) is conveniently abbreviated as $\{W_{hi}(x)\}_{i=1}^{n}$. The function $\hat{f}_h(\cdot)$ is the *Rosenblatt–Parzen kernel density estimator* (Rosenblatt 1956; Parzen 1962) of the (marginal) density of X. The form (3.1.2) of kernel weights $W_{hi}(x)$ has been proposed by Nadaraya (1964) and Watson (1964) and therefore

$$\hat{m}_h(x) = \frac{n^{-1} \sum_{i=1}^{n} K_h(x - X_i)Y_i}{n^{-1} \sum_{i=1}^{n} K_h(x - X_i)}$$

is often called the *Nadaraya–Watson estimator*. The *shape* of the kernel weights is determined by K, whereas the *size* of the weights is parameterized by h, which is called the *bandwidth*.

The normalization of the weights $\hat{f}_h(x)$ makes it possible to adapt to the local intensity of the X-variables and, in addition, guarantees that the weights sum to one. A variety of kernel functions are possible in general, but both practical and theoretical considerations limit the choice. For instance, kernel functions that take on very small values can cause numerical underflow on a computer, so one might restrict attention to kernel functions that are zero outside some fixed interval. A commonly used kernel function, which enjoys some optimality properties to be discussed in Section 4.5, is of parabolic shape (Epanechnikov 1969; Bartlett 1963):

$$K(u) = 0.75(1 - u^2)I(|u| \le 1). \qquad (3.1.4)$$

A plot of this so-called *Epanechnikov kernel* is given in Figure 3.1.

Note that this kernel is not differentiable at $u = \pm 1$. The kernel smoother is not defined for a bandwidth with $\hat{f}_h(x) = 0$. If such a "0/0" case occurs one defines $\hat{m}_h(x)$ as being 0. Suppose that the kernel estimator is only evaluated at the observations $\{X_i\}_{i=1}^{n}$. Then, as $h \to 0$,

$$\hat{m}_h(X_i) \to K(0)Y_i/K(0) = Y_i;$$

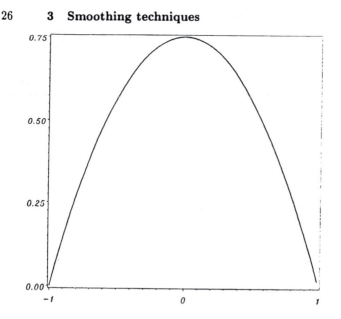

Figure 3.1. The Epanechnikov kernel. This kernel $K(u) = 0.75(1 - u^2)I(|u| \le 1)$ is of parabolic shape and has support $[-1, 1]$.

small bandwidths thus reproduce the data. Let us now investigate what happens as $h \to \infty$. Suppose that K has support $[-1, 1]$ as in Figure 3.1. Then $K(\frac{x-X_i}{h}) \to K(0)$ and thus

$$\hat{m}_h(x) \to n^{-1} \sum_{i=1}^{n} K(0)Y_i / n^{-1} \sum_{i=1}^{n} K(0)$$

$$= n^{-1} \sum_{i=1}^{n} Y_i;$$

very large bandwidths thus result in an oversmooth curve, the average of the response variables.

How does this Epanechnikov kernel act on real data and what is the shape of the weights $\{W_{hi}(x)\}_{i=1}^n$? To obtain some insight, consider the food versus net income data again (see Figures 2.1 and 2.2). The economist is interested in estimating the so-called statistical Engel curve, the average expenditure for food given a certain level of income. Kernel smoothing is a possible procedure for estimating this curve. The kernel weights $\{W_{hi}(x)\}$ depend on the values of the X-observations through the density estimate $\hat{f}_h(x)$. In Figure 3.2 the effective weight function for estimating this Engel curve for food in 1973 is shown centered at

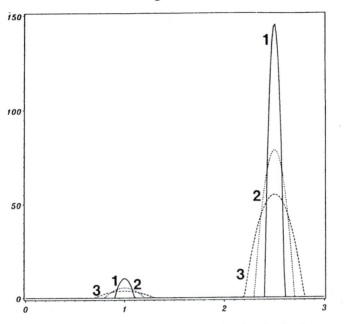

Figure 3.2. The effective kernel weights for the food versus income data set. $K_h(x - \cdot)/\hat{f}_h(x)$ at $x = 1$ and $x = 2.5$ for $h = 0.1$ (label 1), $h = 0.2$ (label 2), $h = 0.3$ (label 3) with Epanechnikov kernel $K(u) = 0.75(1 - u^2)I(|u| \leq 1)$ and density estimate as in Figure 1.5, year $= 1973$, $n = 7125$. Family Expenditure Survey (1968–1983).

$x = 1$ for the bandwidths $h = 0.1$, 0.2, 0.3. Note that the effective weight function depends only on the X-values.

One can learn two things from this picture. First, it is obvious that the smaller the bandwidth, the more concentrated are the weights around x. Second, in regions of sparse data where the marginal density estimate $\hat{f}_h$ is small, the sequence $\{W_{hi}(x)\}$ gives more weight to observations around x. Indeed, around $x = 1$ the density estimate $\hat{f}_h(x)$ reaches its maximum and at $x = 2.5$ the density is roughly a tenth of $\hat{f}_h(1)$. (See Figure 1.5 for the year $= 1973$, which is the fourth density contour counting from the front.)

For multidimensional predictor variables $X_i = (X_{i1}, \ldots, X_{id})$ one can use a multidimensional product kernel function

$$K(u_1, \ldots, u_d) = \prod_{j=1}^{d} K(u_j).$$

The kernel weights for this case are then defined as

$$W_{hi}(x) = \frac{\prod_{j=1}^{d} K_h(x_j - X_{ij})}{\hat{f}_h(x)},$$

where in the definition of the Rosenblatt–Parzen density estimator a product kernel is used as well.

There are cases of applications for which the density $f(x) = F'(x)$ of the X-variables is known. The kernel weights that have been investigated for this sampling scheme are (Greblicki 1974; Johnston 1979, 1982; Greblicki and Krzyzak 1980 and Georgiev 1984a, 1984b)

$$W_{hi}^{(1)}(x) = K_h(x - X_i)/f(x). \tag{3.1.5}$$

Often the X-observations are taken at regular distances and form an equidistant grid of points of some interval. Examples are observations from longitudinal data or discretized analog processes; see Müller (1987). Without loss of generality we can assume that the X-observations have been taken in the unit interval $[0,1]$. In this case, one could use the modified kernel weights $\{W_{hi}^{(1)}(x)\}$ with $f = I_{[0,1]}$, the density of the uniform distribution on $[0,1]$. In the fixed design model of nearly equispaced, nonrandom $\{X_i\}_{i=1}^{n}$ on $[0,1]$, Priestley and Chao (1972) and Benedetti (1977) considered the weight sequence

$$W_{hi}^{(2)}(x) = n(X_i - X_{i-1})K_h(x - X_i), \quad (X_0 = 0). \tag{3.1.6}$$

An interpretation of this weight sequence in terms of (3.1.2) is possible by setting $\hat{f}(x) = [n(X_i - X_{i-1})]^{-1}$ for $x \in (X_{i-1}, X_i]$. Gasser and Müller (1979) defined a related weight sequence

$$W_{hi}^{(3)}(x) = n \int_{S_{i-1}}^{S_i} K_h(x - u)du, \tag{3.1.7}$$

where $X_{i-1} \leq S_{i-1} \leq X_i$ is chosen between the ordered X-data. The special case of $S_i = X_i$ has been investigated by Cheng and Lin (1981). A notion of an asymptotic equivalence of the weight sequences $\{W_{hi}^{(2)}\}$ and $\{W_{hi}^{(3)}\}$ is deferred to the Exercises. Note that $\{W_{hi}^{(1)}\}$ and $\{W_{hi}^{(2)}\}$ do not necessarily sum up to one, but $\{W_{hi}^{(3)}\}$ does.

The weights $W_{hi}^{(3)}(x)$ are related to the so-called *convolution smoothing* as defined by Clark (1980); see Exercise 3.1.1. The weight sequences $\{W_{hi}^{(2)}(x)\}$ and $\{W_{hi}^{(3)}(x)\}$ have been mostly used in the fixed design model. Theoretical analysis of this stochastic behavior in the random design model indicates that they have different variance compared to the Nadaraya–Watson kernel smoother; see Section 3.6.

The consistency of the kernel smoother $\hat{m}_h$ with the Nadaraya–Watson weights $W_{hi}(x)$ defined by (3.1.2) is shown in the following proposition. The proof of consistency of the other weight sequences is very similar and is deferred to exercises.

Proposition 3.1.1 Assume the stochastic design model with a one-dimensional predictor variable X and

(A1) $\int |K(u)|\, du < \infty,$

(A2) $\lim_{|u|\to\infty} uK(u) = 0,$

(A3) $EY^2 < \infty,$

(A4) $n \to \infty, \quad h_n \to 0, \quad nh_n \to \infty.$

Then, at every point of continuity of $m(x)$, $f(x)$ and $\sigma^2(x)$, with $f(x) > 0$,

$$n^{-1} \sum_{i=1}^{n} W_{hi}(x)Y_i \xrightarrow{P} m(x).$$

The proof of this proposition is in the Complements of this section. The above result states that the kernel smoother converges in probability to the true response curve $m(x)$. It is natural to ask how fast this convergence is going to happen. The mean squared error

$$d_M(x, h) = E[\hat{m}_h(x) - m(x)]^2$$

at a point x is one way of quantifying this convergence. The following theorem gives the speed of $d_M(x, h)$ as a function of h and n. For simplicity it is stated for the fixed design model. The rate of convergence for the more complicated random design is the same. The constants are different though and are presented in Section 4.1.

Theorem 3.1.1(Gasser and Müller 1984) Assume the fixed design model with a one-dimensional predictor variable X and define

$$c_K = \int K^2(u)du,$$

$$d_K = \int u^2 K(u)du.$$

Take the kernel weights $\{W_{hi}^{(3)}\}$ and assume

(A0) K *has support* $[-1, 1]$ *with* $K(-1) = K(1) = 0,$

(A1) $m \in C^2,$

(A2) $max_i|X_i - X_{i-1}| = O(n^{-1}),$

(A3) $var(\varepsilon_i) = \sigma^2, \ i = 1,\dots,n,$

(A4) $n \to \infty, \quad h \to 0, \quad nh \to \infty.$

Then

$$d_M(x, h) \approx (nh)^{-1}\sigma^2 c_K + h^4 d_K^2 [m''(x)]^2/4.$$

The mean squared error splits up into the two parts, variance and bias^2. The above theorem says that the bias, as a function of h, is increasing whereas the variance is decreasing. By this qualitative behavior one gets a feeling of what the smoothing problem is about:

Balance the variance versus the bias^2.

We will come back to this task in Chapter 4.

Kernel estimators are local polynomial fits

The kernel weights define a neighborhood of points around a grid point x. Let us investigate the question of fitting a polynomial in such a neighborhood.

The simplest polynomial to fit in such a neighborhood is a constant. There is a striking similarity between local polynomial fitting and kernel smoothing. For fixed x, the kernel estimator $\hat{m}_h(x)$ with positive weights $W_{hi}(x)$ is the solution to the following minimization problem

$$\min_t \sum_{i=1}^n K_h(x - X_i)(Y_i - t)^2 = \sum_{i=1}^n K_h(x - X_i)(Y_i - \hat{m}_h(x))^2.$$

(3.1.8)

In this sense, the kernel smoother can be understood as a local constant polynomial fit: It minimizes, in a neighborhood around x determined in shape and span by the sequence K_h, the sum of squared residuals. How are more complex polynomials related to kernel smoothing?

This question is investigated in the fixed design model. Consider equispaced $X_i = i/n$, and a local parabolic fit. Let us take a point x that is not too close to the boundary of the observation interval. (The behavior of kernel smoothers at the boundary is discussed in Section 4.4.) Consider a uniform kernel $K^U(u) = 1/2 \, I(|u| \le 1)$, which parameterizes the neighborhood around x. We have then to minimize

$$n^{-1} \sum_i K_h^U(x - X_i)(Y_i - a - b(X_i - x)^2)^2$$

with respect to a and b. The linear term is not present here, since it is "orthogonal" to the symmetric, uniform kernel. The normal equations for this problem are

$$n^{-1} \sum_i K_h^U(x - X_i)(Y_i - a - b(X_i - x)^2) = 0,$$

(3.1.9)

$$n^{-1} \sum_i K_h^U(x - X_i)(Y_i - a - b(X_i - x)^2)(X_i - x)^2 = 0.$$

$$(3.1.10)$$

Define $\hat{Y}$ as $n^{-1} \sum_i K_h^U(x - X_i)Y_i$ and approximate $n^{-1} \sum_i K_h^U(x - X_i)$ by one. For large n, the sum

$$n^{-1} \sum_i K_h^U(x - X_i)(x - X_i)^2$$

can be replaced by

$$\int K_h^U(x - u)(x - u)^2 \, du.$$

Integration by substitution shows that this is equal to $h^2/3$. Using similar arguments for $n^{-1} \sum_i K_h^U(x - X_i)(x - X_i)^4$ shows that the normal equations (3.1.9–3.1.10) can be rewritten as

$$\hat{Y} - a - (h^2/3)\, b = 0,$$
$$A - (h^2/3)\, a - (h^4/5)\, b = 0,$$

where

$$A = n^{-1} \sum_i K_h^U(x - X_i)(x - X_i)^2 \, Y_i.$$

Elementary algebraic calculations show that a satisfies the equation

$$3h^2 \, \hat{Y} - 5A + (-3 + 5/3)\, h^2 a = 0,$$

which is solved by

$$\hat{a} = 3/4 \left(n^{-1} \sum_i K_h^U(x - X_i) \left(3 - 5 \left(\frac{x - X_i}{h} \right)^2 \right) Y_i \right).$$

$$(3.1.11)$$

Similarly, an estimate $\hat{b}$ can be computed which leads to the "local parabola" $\hat{a} + \hat{b}(x - u)^2$ in a small neighborhood around x. At the point x itself the regression curve $\hat{m}$ is estimated by $\hat{a}$. A closer look at (3.1.11) reveals that $\hat{a}$ can be written as

$$\hat{a} = \hat{m}(x) = n^{-1} \sum_i K_h^*(x - X_i) \, Y_i,$$

where

$$K_h^*(u) = 3/8 \, (3 - 5u^2) I(|u| \le 1)$$

is a kernel with vanishing first, second and third moment. In this setting of equispaced predictor variables a kernel estimate with kernel K^* is essentially a local parabolic fitting procedure. Figure 3.3 shows some

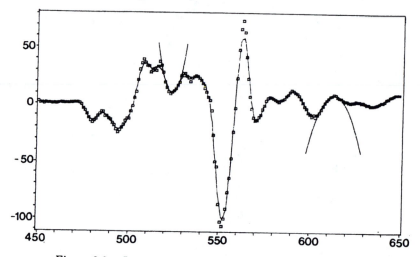

Figure 3.3.   Local parabolic fits. The kernel smooth for acceleration versus time data (see Section 8.1). The kernel smooth is compared to the local parabolic fits at $x = 525$ and 620.

of the "local parabolas" together with a kernel estimate based on the kernel K_h^*. The data set is a stretch from the acceleration versus time data as discussed later in Section 8.1.

The equivalence of local polynomial fitting and kernel smoothing has been studied in great detail by Müller (1987). Some numerical comparison has been done by Schmerling and Peil (1985, figure 1). They used a Gaussian kernel weight sequence with kernel

$$K(u) = (2\pi)^{-1/2} \exp(-u^2/2)$$

and compared locally constant, linear and parabolic fits in an agricultural example.

Kernel estimators of derivatives

The technique of kernel estimation can also be used to estimate derivatives of the regression function. *Kernel derivative estimators* are defined by differentiating the weight function sequence with respect to x. If the weights are sufficiently smooth and the bandwidth sequence is correctly tuned then these estimators will converge to the corresponding derivatives of m. This can be easily illustrated in the equidistant design setting with the kernel smoother, using the Priestley–Chao weights $\{W_{hi}^{(2)}(x)\}$.

Taking the kth derivative with respect to x gives

$$\hat{m}_h^{(k)}(x) = n^{-1}h^{-(k+1)} \sum_{i=1}^{n} K^{(k)} \left(\frac{x - X_i}{h}\right) Y_i. \qquad (3.1.12)$$

The kernel estimate of the kth derivative of m is thus a local average of the response variables in which the kth derivatives of the kernel weights have been used as weights.

Proposition 3.1.2   Assume the fixed design model with a one-dimensional predictor variable X and define

$$c_K^{(k)} = \int [K^{(k)}]^2(u)du,$$

$$d_K^{(k)} = \int u^{k+2}K^{(k)}(u)du.$$

Take the Priestley–Chao kernel weights $\{W_{hi}^{(2)}(x)\}$ and assume
(A0) $K \in C^{(k)}$ has support $[-1,1]$ with $K^{(j)}(-1) = K^{(j)}(1) = 0$,
        $j = 0,\dots,k-1$,
(A1) $m^{(k)}(x) \in C^2$,
(A2) $X_i = i/n$, $i = 1,\dots,n$,
(A3) $var(\varepsilon_i) = \sigma^2$, $i = 1,\dots,n$,
(A4) $n \to \infty$, $h_n \to 0$, $nh_n^{k+1} \to \infty$.
Then

$$d_M(x, h) \approx (nh^{2k+1})^{-1}\sigma^2 c_K^{(k)} + h^4 d_K^{(k)^2}[m^{(k+2)}(x)]^2/(k+2)!^2.$$

A sketch of the proof of this proposition is given in the Complements to this section. Gasser and Müller (1984) studied slightly different weights based on derivatives of $\{W_{hi}^{(3)}(x)\}$. In view of the asymptotic equivalence of the weight functions $\{W_{hi}^{(2)}(x)\}$ and $\{W_{hi}^{(3)}(x)\}$ (see Exercise 3.1.10) it is not surprising that the Gasser–Müller kernel estimator has the same mean squared error expansion as given in Proposition 3.1.2. Figure 3.4 is taken from an application of the Gasser–Müller method, in which they compute the velocity and acceleration of height growth. The upper graphs compare the growth velocity (first derivative) of boys to that of girls. The graphs below depicts the growth accelerations (second derivatives) for the two sexes.

In the case of nonequally spaced and random X-variables the weight sequence becomes more complicated. The principle of differentiating the kernel weights to obtain kernel estimates for derivatives of the regression function also works here. For instance, the first derivative $m'(x)$ could

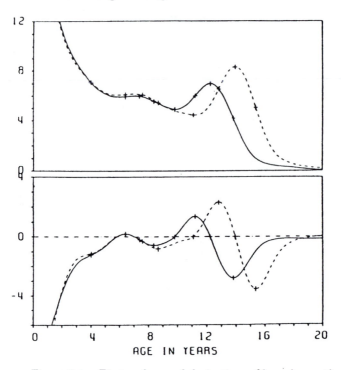

Figure 3.4.   First and second derivatives of kernel smoothers. Average velocity curves (above) and acceleration curves (below) for boys (dashed line) and girls (solid line). From Gasser et al. (1984) with permission of the Institute of Mathematical Statistics.

be estimated using the effective weight sequence

$$W_{hi}(x) = \frac{K_h^{(1)}(x - X_i)}{\hat{f}_h(x)} - \frac{K_h(x - X_i)\hat{f}_h'(x)}{(\hat{f}_h(x))^2}, \qquad (3.1.13)$$

where

$$K_h^{(1)}(u) = h^{-2} K^{(1)}(u/h)$$

and

$$\hat{f}_h'(x) = n^{-1} \sum_{i=1}^{n} K_h^{(1)}(x - X_i)$$

is an estimate of the first derivative of the marginal density $f(x)$.

Computational aspects of kernel smoothing

Suppose that it is desired to compute the Nadaraya–Watson kernel estimate at N distinct points. A direct application of formula (3.1.2) for a kernel with unbounded support would result in $O(Nn)$ operations for determination of the estimator at N gridpoints. Some computer time can be saved by using kernels with bounded support, say $[-1, 1]$. Local averaging is then performed only in a neighborhood of size h around the gridpoints. The number of operations would then be $O(Nnh)$ since about $2nh$ points fall into an interval of length $2h$. Since $h = h_n$ tends to zero, the introduction of kernels with bounded support looks like a drastic improvement.

For optimization of the smoothing parameter one needs to repeat kernel smoothing several times and so even for moderate sample size the algorithm would still be extremely slow. More efficient kernel smoothing algorithms can be defined by first discretizing the data into *bins* of the form

$$B(x; x_0, h) = [x_0 + kh, x_0 + (k + 1)h]$$

for some integer k. This means that one replaces the response variables by a step function with heights equal to the average of the response in the bins. Similarly the predictor variable is replaced by its frequency in the respective bins. This discretization step takes $O(n)$ operations.

The computational advantage comes from building a *weighted average of rounded points (WARP)*. In particular, consider the set of "origins"

$$\left\{ x_{0,k} = \frac{kh}{M} \right\}, k = 0, \ldots, M - 1,$$

and estimate, for example, the marginal density by an average over histograms with origin $x_{0,k}$,

$$\hat{f}_{h,m}(x) = m^{-1} \sum_{k=0}^{M-1} \#\{i : X_i \in B(x; x_0, h)\}/(nh)$$

$$= (Mnh)^{-1} \sum_{k=1-M}^{M-1} (M - |k|)\#\{i : X_i \in B(x; x_0, h)\}/(nh).$$

The triangular weights $(1 - |k|/M)$ can be generalized in an obvious way to other weight sequences. For example, the quartic kernel

$$K(u) = (15/16)(1 - u^2)^2 I(|u| \le 1)$$

corresponds to the weights

$$W_M(k) = (15/16)(1 - k^2/M^2)^2, \quad |k| \le M.$$

Using this generalization we can rewrite the above formula in the general form

$$\hat{f}(x) = M^{-1} \sum_{|k| \le M} W_M(k) RP_{i(x)+k},$$

where $i(x)$ is the bin in which x falls and where in the above case of density smoothing, RP_l is the frequency of rounded points ($= RP$) in the lth bin. Applying this idea to regression smoothing gives

$$\hat{m}(x) = M^{-1} \sum_{|k| \le M} W_M(k) \bar{Y}_{i(x)+k} / \hat{f}(x),$$

where $\bar{Y}_l$ is the average of the response variable over the lth bin. Estimates of this kind are discussed in Härdle and Scott (1988). After discretization of the data the operations are $O(NM)$.

Another technique uses Fourier transforms

$$\tilde{g}(t) = \int g(x) \exp(-itx) dx.$$

Observe that for $g(x) = n^{-1} \sum_{i=1}^{n} K_h(x - X_i) Y_i$, the denominator of the Nadaraya–Watson estimator, one has the Fourier transform

$$\tilde{g}(t) = \tilde{K}(th) \sum_{i=1}^{n} \exp(-itX_i) Y_i.$$

If one uses the Gaussian kernel

$$K(u) = \exp(-u^2/2)/\sqrt{2\pi}$$

one has for example $\tilde{K}(t) = \exp(-t^2/2)$. The numerical efficiency comes from decoupling the smoothing operation from the Fourier transform of the data. The Fourier transform of the data

$$\sum_{i=1}^{n} \exp(-itX_i) Y_i$$

can be computed via the Fast Fourier Transform. If the data is discretized into N bins as above, the operation will be $O(N \log N)$. Note that for computing several smoothers only the rescaled Fourier transform of the kernel function has to be multiplied with the Fourier transform of the data which can be retained in the memory of the computer. An algorithm for this technique is presented in Härdle (1987a).

Exercises

3.1.1 Recall the setting for the weight sequence $\{W_{hi}^{(2)}(x)\}$. Consider linear interpolation between two successive observations (X_{i-1}, Y_{i-1}) and (X_i, Y_i) with $(X_0, Y_0) = (0, Y_1)$,

$$g_i(u) = \frac{Y_i - Y_{i-1}}{X_i - X_{i-1}}(u - X_{i-1}) + Y_{i-1}, \quad i = 1, \ldots, n.$$

A piecewise linear function through the data can be written as

$$G_n(u) = \sum_{i=1}^{n} g_i(u) \, I(X_{i-1} \le u < X_i).$$

Clark (1980) suggested convolving this linear interpolant with a kernel function with bandwidth h,

$$\hat{m}(x) = \int K_h(x - u) G_n(u) du$$

$$= \sum_{i=1}^{n} \int_{X_{i-1}}^{X_i} K_h(x - u) g_i(u) du$$

$$= \sum_{i=1}^{n} \int_{X_{i-1}}^{X_i} K_h(x - u) du \, Y_{i-1}$$

$$+ \sum_{i=1}^{n} \int_{X_{i-1}}^{X_i} K_h(x - u)(u - X_i) du \frac{Y_i - Y_{i-1}}{X_i - X_{i-1}}.$$

Show that if the x-variables are equispaced on $[0, 1]$, that is, $X_i = \frac{i}{n}$, then the last term converges in probability to zero.

3.1.2 Discuss the behavior of the kernel estimator when a single observation moves to a very large value, that is, study the case $(X_i, Y_i) \to (X_i, Y_i \pm c)$ with $c \to \infty$ for a fixed i. How does the curve change under such a distortion? What will happen for a distortion in X-direction $(X_i, Y_i) \to (X_i \pm c, Y_i)$?

3.1.3 When we had the situation of equispaced $X_i = \frac{i}{n}$ we said that a local linear fit would not make much sense with a symmetric kernel weight. Consider now the situation of random Xs. Would you expect a gain in using a local linear fit now?

3.1.4 Prove in analogy to Proposition 3.1.1 the asymptotic mean squared error decomposition of kernel smoothers with weight sequences $\{W_{hi}^{(2)}\}$ and $\{W_{hi}^{(3)}\}$, respectively.

3.1.5 Recall the weighted local fitting of polynomials. If the order of the approximating polynomial $\varphi_0 \equiv 1$ is $p = 0$, then $\hat{m}_h(x)$ is just the ordinary kernel estimate with weights $W_{hi}^*(x) =$

$W_{hi}(x)/\hat{f}_h(x)$. For a local linear approximation one has
$\varphi_0(u) = 1$,
$\varphi_1(u) = (u - x_0) - M_{11}(x_0)/M_{10}(x_0)$,
where

$$M_{1j}(x) = \sum_{i=1}^{n}(X_i - x)^j W_{hi}(x), \quad j = 0, \ldots, p.$$

This results in

$$\hat{m}_h(x) = \frac{M_{20}(x)M_{12}(x) - M_{21}(x)M_{11}(x)}{M_{10}(x)M_{12}(x) - [M_{11}(x)]^2},$$

where

$$M_{2j}(x) = \sum_{i=1}^{n}(X_i - x)^j W_{hi}(x)Y_i, \quad j = 0, \ldots, p.$$

Try this method in practice. (Schmerling and Peil, 1977, present the ALGOL code for this procedure.) Comment on the difference from ordinary kernel smoothing.

3.1.6 Verify that the kernel K^* from the local parabolic fit (see 3.1.13) is indeed a kernel and has vanishing first, second and third moments.

3.1.7 Consider the positive food versus net income data set. Suppose you are asked to do a kernel smooth at the right end. What can happen if the kernel K has negative "sidelobes", that is, the tails of K are allowed to take on negative values?

3.1.8 Give a rigorous proof of Proposition 3.1.2. (A sketch of the proof is in the Complements of this section.) Compare the remainder terms of the bias approximations for the weight sequence $\{W_{hi}^{(2)}(x)\}$ with those of the weight sequence $\{W_{hi}^{(3)}(x)\}$.

3.1.9 Derive that the rate of convergence of $d_M(x, h)$ from Theorem 3.1.1 if h is chosen optimally, that is,

$$h = h_{opt} = \arg\min_h d_M(x, h).$$

3.1.10 Show the asymptotic equivalence of the weight sequences $\{W_{hi}^{(2)}(x)\}$ and $\{W_{hi}^{(3)}(x)\}$ in the following sense

$$W_{hi}^{(2)}(x) = W_{hi}^{(3)}(x) + O(n^{-1}).$$

3.1.11 Give reasons why $\hat{f}(X_{(i)}) = n(X_{(i)} - X_{(i-1)})$, as in the weight sequence (3.1.6), is a reasonable choice for a density estimate. [*Hint*: Consider the asymptotic distribution of the spacings $X_{(i)} - X_{(i-1)}$.]

Complements

Proof of Proposition 3.1.1

The proof of this proposition follows a technique used by Parzen (1962) in the setting of density estimation. Recall the definition of the kernel weights,

$$W_{hi}(x) = K_h(x - X_i)/\hat{f}_h(x).$$

Consider the denominator and numerator separately. I show that

$$\hat{r}_h(x) = n^{-1} \sum_{i=1}^{n} K_h(x - X_i)Y_i \xrightarrow{P} m(x)f(x) = r(x), \qquad (3.1.14)$$

$$\hat{f}_h(x) = n^{-1} \sum_{i=1}^{n} K_h(x - X_i) \xrightarrow{P} f(x). \qquad (3.1.15)$$

From (3.1.9) and (3.1.15) it follows by Slutzky's Theorem (Schönfeld 1969, chapter 6) that

$$\hat{r}_h(x)/\hat{f}_h(x) \xrightarrow{P} r(x)/f(x) = \frac{m(x)f(x)}{f(x)} = m(x).$$

Only (3.1.14) is shown; the statement (3.1.15) can be proved very similarly. Note that

$$E\hat{r}_h(x) = \int\int K_h(x - u)yf(u, y)du\,dy,$$

where $f(u, y)$ denotes the joint density of the distribution of (X, Y). Conditioning on u gives

$$\int K_h(x - u)r(u)du,$$

since

$$m(u) = \int yf(y|u)dy = \int yf(u, y)dy / \int f(u, y)dy.$$

Using integration by substitution it can be shown (see Lemma 3.1.1 in these Complements) that for $\delta > 0$

$$|E\hat{r}_h(x) - r(x)| \leq \sup_{|s| \leq \delta} |r(x - s) - r(x)| \int |K(s)|\,ds$$

$$+ \delta^{-1} \sup_{|s| \geq \delta/h} |sK(s)| \int |r(s)|\,ds.$$

$$+ |r(x)| \int_{|s| \geq \delta/h} |K(s)|\,ds.$$

The last two terms of this bound tend to zero, by (A1) and (A2), as $n \to \infty$. Now let δ tend to zero; then the first term by continuity of $r(\cdot)$ will tend to zero. This proves that $E\hat{r}_h(x) - r(x) = o(1)$, as $n \to \infty$. Now let $s^2(x) = E(Y^2|X = x)$. Use integration by substitution and the above asymptotic unbiasedness of $\hat{r}_h(x)$ to see that the variance of $\hat{r}_h(x)$ is

$$\mathrm{var}(\hat{r}_h(x)) = n^{-2} \sum_{i=1}^{n} \mathrm{var}(K_h(x - X_i)Y_i)$$

$$= n^{-1} \left\{ \int K_h^2(x - u)s^2(u)f(u)du \right.$$

$$\left. - \left(\int K_h(x - u)r(u)du \right)^2 \right\}$$

$$\approx n^{-1}h^{-1} \int K^2(u)s^2(x + uh)f(x + uh)du.$$

This is asymptotically equal to $n^{-1}h^{-1} \int K^2(u)du \ s^2(x)f(x)$ using the techniques of splitting up the same integrals as above. Observe now that the variance tends to zero as $nh \to \infty$. This completes the argument since the mean squared error $E(\hat{r}_h(x) - r(x))^2 = \mathrm{var}(\hat{r}_h(x)) + [E\hat{r}_h(x) - r(x)]^2 \to 0$ as $n \to \infty$, $nh \to \infty$, $h \to 0$. Thus we have seen that

$$\hat{r}_h(x) \xrightarrow{2} r(x).$$

This implies

$$\hat{r}_h(x) \xrightarrow{p} r(x);$$

see Schönfeld (1969, chapter 6). This proof can be adapted to kernel estimation with higher dimensional X. If X is d-dimensional, change K_h to $h^{-d}K(x/h)$, where $K: \mathbb{R}^d \to \mathbb{R}$ and the ratio in the argument of K has to be understood coordinatewise.

Lemma 3.1.1 *The estimator $\hat{r}_h(x)$ is asymptotically unbiased as an estimator for $r(x)$.*

Use integration by substitution and the fact that the kernel integrates to one to bound

$$|E\hat{r}_h(x) - r(x)| = \int K_h(x - u)(r(u) - r(x))du$$

$$= \int K_h(s)(r(x - s) - r(x))ds$$

$$\leq \int_{|s| \leq \delta} |K_h(s)| \, |r(x - s) - r(x)| \, ds$$

$$+ \int_{|s|>\delta} |K_h(s)| \, |r(x-s)| \, ds$$

$$+ \int_{|s|>\delta} |K_h(s)| \, |r(x)| \, ds$$

$$= T_{1n} + T_{2n} + T_{3n}.$$

The first term can be bounded in the following way:

$$T_{1n} \leq \sup_{|s|\leq\delta} |r(x-s) - r(x)| \int |K(s)| \, ds.$$

The third term

$$T_{3n} \leq |r(x)| \int |K(s)| \, ds.$$

The second term can be bounded as follows:

$$T_{2n} = \int_{|s|>\delta} |sK_h(s)| \, |r(x-s)| \, / \, |s| \, ds$$

$$\leq \sup_{|s|>\delta} |sK_h(s)| \int_{|s|>\delta} |r(x-s)| \, / \, |s| \, ds$$

$$= \delta^{-1} \cdot \sup_{|s|\geq\delta/h} |sK(s)| \int |r(s)| \, ds.$$

Note that the last integral exists by assumption (A3) of Proposition 3.1.1.

Sketch of Proof for Proposition 3.1.2

The derivative estimator $\hat{m}_h^{(k)}(x)$ is asymptotically unbiased.

$$E\hat{m}_h^{(k)}(x) = n^{-1}h^{-(k+1)} \sum_{i=1}^{n} K^{(k)} \left(\frac{x - X_i}{h} \right) m(X_i)$$

$$\approx h^{-k} \int K^{(k)}(u) \, m(x - uh) du \qquad (3.1.16)$$

$$= h^{-k+1} \int K^{(k-1)}(u) \, m^{(1)}(x - uh) du$$

$$= \int K(u) \, m^{(k)}(x - uh) du$$

$$\sim m^{(k)}(x) + h^{d_K^{(k)}} m^{(k+2)}(x)/(k+2)!, \quad h \to 0,$$

using partial integration, (A0) and (A4).

The variance of $\hat{m}_h^{(k)}(x)$ tends to zero if $nh^{2k+1} \to \infty$, as the following calculations show:

$$\text{var}\{\hat{m}_h^{(k)}(x)\} = n^{-1}h^{-2(k+1)} \sum_{i=1}^n \left[K^{(k)}\left(\frac{x-X_i}{h}\right)\right]^2 \sigma^2$$

$$\approx n^{-1}h^{-2k-1} \int [K^{(k)}(u)]^2 du \; \sigma^2. \qquad (3.1.17)$$

3.2   k-nearest neighbor estimates

The construction of nearest neighbor estimates differs from that of kernel estimates. The kernel estimate $\hat{m}_h(x)$ was defined as a weighted average of the response variables in a fixed neighborhood around x, determined in shape by the kernel K and the bandwidth h. The *k-nearest neighbor (k-NN)* estimate is a weighted average in a varying neighborhood. This neighborhood is defined through those X-variables which are among the k-nearest neighbors of x in Euclidean distance. The k-NN weight sequence has been introduced by Loftsgaarden and Quesenberry (1965) in the related field of density estimation and has been used by Cover and Hart (1967) for classification purposes. In the present regression setting the k-NN smoother is defined as

$$\hat{m}_k(x) = n^{-1} \sum_{i=1}^n W_{ki}(x) Y_i, \qquad (3.2.1)$$

where $\{W_{ki}(x)\}_{i=1}^n$ is a weight sequence defined through the set of indexes

$$J_x = \{i : X_i \text{ is one of the } k \text{ nearest observations to } x\}.$$

With this set of indexes of neighboring observations the k-NN weight sequence is constructed:

$$W_{ki}(x) = \begin{cases} n/k, & \text{if } i \in J_x; \\ 0 & \text{otherwise.} \end{cases} \qquad (3.2.2)$$

To give some insight into the construction of weights consider the following example. Let $\{(X_i, Y_i)\}_{i=1}^5$ be $\{(1,5),(7,12),(3,1),(2,0),(5,4)\}$ and let us compute the k-NN estimate $\hat{m}_k(x)$ for $x = 4$ and $k = 3$. The k observations closest to x are the last three data points, therefore $J_x = J_4 = \{3,4,5\}$ and thus

$$W_{k1}(4) = 0, W_{k2}(4) = 0, W_{k3}(4) = 1/3,$$
$$W_{k4}(4) = 1/3, W_{k5}(4) = 1/3,$$

which results in $\hat{m}_3(4) = (1+0+4)/3 = 5/3$.

In an experiment in which the X-variable is chosen from an equidistant grid the k-NN weights are equivalent to kernel weights. Let $k = 2nh$ and compare $\{W_{ki}(x)\}$ with $\{W_{hi}(x)\}$ for a uniform kernel $K(u) = \frac{1}{2}I(|u| \le 1)$ for an x not too close to the boundary. Indeed for $i \in J_x$:

$$W_{ki}(x) = \frac{n}{(2nh)} = \frac{1}{2}h^{-1} = W_{hi}(x).$$

The smoothing parameter k regulates the degree of smoothness of the estimated curve. It plays a role similar to the bandwidth for kernel smoothers. The influence of varying k on qualitative features of the estimated curve is similar to that observed for kernel estimation with a uniform kernel.

Consider for fixed n the case that k becomes larger than n. The k-NN smoother then is equal to the average of the response variables. The other limiting case is $k = 1$ in which the observations are reproduced at X_i, and for an x between two adjacent predictor variables a step function is obtained with a jump in the middle between the two observations. Again a smoothing parameter selection problem is observed: k has to be chosen as a function of n or even of the data. As a first goal one might like to reduce the noise by letting $k = k_n$ tend to infinity as a function of the sample size. The second goal is to keep the approximation error (bias) low. The second goal is achieved if the neighborhood around x shrinks asymptotically to zero. This can be done by defining $k = k_n$ such that $k_n/n \to 0$. Unfortunately, this condition conflicts with the first goal. In order to keep the variance as small as possible one would like to choose k as large as possible.

So again we face a *trade-off problem* between a "good approximation" to the regression function and a "good reduction" of observational noise. This trade-off problem can be expressed formally by an expansion of the mean squared error of the k-NN estimate.

Proposition 3.2.1 (Lai 1977) Let $k \to \infty$, $k/n \to 0$, $n \to \infty$. *Bias and variance of the k-NN estimate $\hat{m}_k$ with weights as in (3.2.2) are given by*

$$E\hat{m}_k(x) - m(x) \approx \frac{1}{24f(x)^3} \left[(m''f + 2m'f')(x) \right] (k/n)^2,$$

$$\text{var}\{\hat{m}_k(x)\} \approx \frac{\sigma^2(x)}{k}.$$

The trade-off between bias^2 and variance is thus achieved in an asymptotic sense by setting $k \sim n^{4/5}$. A consequence is that the mean squared error itself converges to zero at a rate of $k^{-1} \sim n^{-(4/5)}$.

Other weight sequences $W_{ki}(x)$ have been proposed by Stone (1977). In addition to the "uniform" weights (3.2.1) he defined "triangular and quadratic k-NN weights." Generally speaking, the weights can be thought of as being generated by a kernel function K,

$$W_{Ri}(x) = \frac{K_R(x - X_i)}{\hat{f}_R(x)},\qquad(3.2.3)$$

where

$$\hat{f}_R(x) = n^{-1} \sum_{i=1}^{n} K_R(x - X_i)$$

is a kernel density estimate of $f(x)$ with kernel sequence

$$K_R(u) = R^{-1} K(u/R)$$

and $R = R_n$ is the distance between x and its kth nearest neighbor. In the example given above with $x = 4$ and $k = 3$, the distance R would be equal to 2 since the observation $(2,0)$ is the furthest away among the three neighbors of $x = 4$.

To give insight into this weight sequence consider the potato example again. In Figure 3.5 the effective k-NN weights $W_{Ri}(x)$ are shown analogous to the kernel weights $W_{hi}(x)$ in Figure 3.5.

One can see quite clearly the difference in the kernel weights. At the right end of the data, where the observations get sparser, the k-NN weights spread out more than the kernel weights, as presented in Figure 3.2. Mack (1981) computes bias and variance for this parameterization of the weights $\{W_{Ri}\}_{i=1}^{n}$.

Proposition 3.2.2 (Mack 1981)   *Let $k \to \infty$, $k/n \to 0$, $n \to \infty$ and let c_K, d_K be defined as in Theorem 3.1.1. Then*

$$E\hat{m}_R(x) - m(x) \approx \left(\frac{k}{n}\right)^2 \frac{(m''f + 2m'f')(x)}{8f(x)^3} d_K,\qquad(3.2.4)$$

$$\mathrm{var}(\hat{m}_R(x)|X = x) \approx 2\frac{\sigma^2(x)}{k} c_K.\qquad(3.2.5)$$

A consequence of this proposition is that a balance between the bias[2] and the variance contribution to the mean squared error is as for the uniform k-NN weights (3.2.2) achieved by letting $k = k_n$ be proportional to $n^{4/5}$. Thinking of the bandwidth parameter h for kernel smoothers as being roughly equivalent to $\frac{1}{2}nk^{-1}$ it is seen that the bias and variance rates of $\hat{m}_R$ are completely equivalent to those for kernel smoothers, only the constants differ. The bias of $\hat{m}_R$ tends to be large in the tail of the

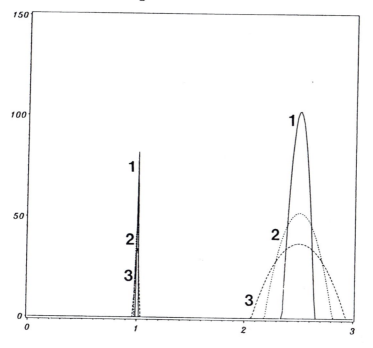

Figure 3.5. The effective k-NN weights for the food versus net income data set. $K_R(x - .)/\hat{f}_R(x)$ at $x = 1$ and $x = 2.5$ for $k = 100$ (label 1), $k = 200$ (label 2), $k = 300$ (label 3) with Epanechnikov kernel $K(u) = 0.75(1 - u^2)I(|u| \leq 1)$ and density estimate as in Figure 1.3, year $= 1973$, $n = 7125$. Family Expenditure Survey (1968–1983).

marginal distribution. The kernel estimators show a different behavior: There the variance is a multiple of $f(x)^{-1}$ and the bias turns out not to be a function of $f(x)^{-3}$. A comparison of kernel and k-NN smoother's mean squared error properties can be found in Table 3.2.1.

The entries of Table 3.2.1 show the asymptotic dependence of bias and variance on f, k and h. The essential equivalence of the row entries of Table 3.2.1 can be seen by using the relation

$$k = 2nhf(x). \qquad (3.2.6)$$

Using this k leads to the same (asymptotic) mean squared error (at x) for the k-NN and the kernel smoothers. The accuracy of $\hat{m}_R$ can be stated in terms of a central limit theorem, which was given by Mack (1981, theorem 3). Rates of convergence for this k-NN smoother have also been derived by Devroye (1978a) and Györfi (1981).

Table 3.2.1   *Bias and variance of k-NN and kernel smoother*

	kernel	k-NN
bias	$h^2 \dfrac{(m''f + 2m'f')(x)}{2f(x)} d_K$	$\left(\dfrac{k}{n}\right)^2 \dfrac{(m''f + 2m'f')(x)}{8f^3(x)} d_K$
variance	$\dfrac{\sigma^2(x)}{nhf(x)} c_K$	$\dfrac{2\sigma^2(x)}{k} c_K$

Source: Mack (1981, table 1).

A third kind of k-NN smoothers are *symmetrized nearest neighbor estimators*. Let F_n denote the empirical distribution of the sample from X. Let h be a bandwidth tending to zero. The estimate proposed by Yang (1981) and studied by Stute (1984) is

$$\hat{m}_{k(h)}(x) = (nh)^{-1} \sum_{i=1}^{n} K\left(\frac{F_n(X_i) - F_n(x)}{h}\right) Y_i. \qquad (3.2.7)$$

The estimate (3.2.7) is also a nearest neighbor estimate, but now neighbors are defined in terms of distance based on the empirical distribution function of the $\{X_i\}_{i=1}^{n}$. Thus a weight sequence (symmetric in $F_n(X)$ space)

$$W_{k(h)}(x) = K_h(F_n(X_i) - F_n(x))$$

is used.

Note that $\hat{m}_R$ always averages over a symmetric neighborhood in the X-space, but may have an asymmetric neighborhood of $F_n(X)$. By contrast, $\hat{m}_{k(h)}$ always averages over the same amount of points left and right of x, but may in effect average over an asymmetric neighborhood in the X-space. The estimate $\hat{m}_{k(h)}$ has an intriguing relationship with the k-NN estimator used by Friedman (1984). The variable span smoother (supersmoother) proposed by Friedman uses the same type of neighborhood as does $\hat{m}_{k(h)}$; see Section 5.3. The estimate (3.2.7) also looks appealingly like a kernel regression estimate of Y against not X but rather $F_n(X)$. Define the expected value

$$\bar{m}_{k(h)}(x) = h^{-1} \int m(u) K\left(\frac{F(u) - F(x)}{h}\right) du.$$

Then Stute (1984) shows that as $n \to \infty$, $h \to 0$ and $nh^3 \to \infty$,

$$(nh)^{1/2}(\hat{m}_{k(h)}(x) - \bar{m}_{k(h)}(x)) \overset{\mathcal{L}}{\to} N(0, c_K \sigma^2(x)).$$

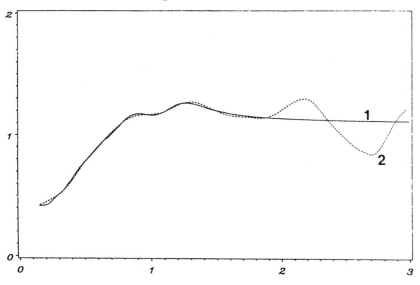

Figure 3.6. The symmetrized nearest neighbor estimator together with the kernel estimator for the potato versus income data set. From Carroll and Härdle (1988) with permission of Elsevier Science Publishers.

With this choice of $h, \hat{m}_{k(h)}(x)$ has the same limit properties as a kernel or ordinary nearest neighbor estimate as long as its bias term is of order $O(h^2)$. It is in fact not hard to show that the bias satisfies to order $O(h^2)$:

$$h^2 d_K \frac{(m''f - m'f')(x)}{2f^3(x)}. \qquad (3.2.8)$$

Carroll and Härdle (1988) compare (3.2.8) with the bias for kernel smoothers and *k-NN* smoothers. They show that even when the variances of all three estimates are the same (the case $h = hf(x)$), the bias properties differ unless

$$m'(x)f'(x) = 0.$$

Otherwise, the smoothing parameter balancing variance versus bias^2 for the kernel and ordinary nearest neighbor estimates will lead to a different mean squared error than what one obtains for the symmetrized nearest neighbor estimate. An example is given in Figure 3.6.

For these data, we used the quartic kernel

$$K(u) = (15/16)(1 - u^2)^2 I(|u| \le 1).$$

We computed the ordinary kernel estimate $\hat{m}_h(x)$ and the symmetrized nearest neighbor estimate $\hat{m}_{k(h)}(x)$, the bandwidths being selected by cross-validation, see Chapter 4. The data driven bandwidths were $h = 0.25$ for the kernel smoother on the scale $[0, 3]$ of Figure 3.6 and $h = 0.15$ on the $F_n(X)$ scale. The resulting regression curves are similar for $x \leq 1$, which is where most of the data lie. There is a sharp discrepancy for larger values of x, the kernel estimate showing evidence of a bimodal relationship and the symmetrized nearest neighbor estimate indicating either an asymptote or even a slight decrease as income rises. In the context, the latter seems to make more sense economically and looks quite similar to the curve in Hildenbrand and Hildenbrand (1986). Statistically, it is the range of the data where the density $f(x)$ takes on small values; see Figure 2.1, for example. This is exactly when we expect the biggest differences in the estimates, that is, the kernel estimate should be more variable but less biased.

Computational aspects of k-NN smoothing

A great advantage of the k-NN estimate (3.2.1) is that its computation can be updated quite easily when x runs along the sorted array of X-variables. The algorithm requires essentially $O(n)$ operations to compute the smooth at all X_i, as compared to $O(n^2 h)$ operations for direct computation of the kernel estimate.

Let us construct k-NN smoothers as weighted averages over a fixed number of observations with uniform weights as used as in (3.2.2). Suppose that the data have been presorted, so that $X_i \leq X_{i+1}, i = 1, \ldots, n - 1$. Then if the estimate has already been computed at some point X_i the k-NN smoother at X_{i+1} can be recursively determined as

$$\hat{m}_k(X_{i+1}) = \hat{m}_k(X_i) + k^{-1}(Y_{i+[k/2]+1} - Y_{i-[k/2]}),$$

where $[u] = \sup\{i : i \leq u\}$.

This updating formula is also applicable for local polynomial fits. For simplicity only the local linear fit is described. The slope β and intercept α of the least squares line through the neighborhood determined by uniform weights (3.2.2) are given by

$$\alpha_{X_i} = \hat{m}_k(X_i) - \beta\bar{\mu}_{X_i},$$

$$\beta_{X_i} = \frac{C_{X_i} - \bar{\mu}_{X_i} \cdot \hat{m}_k(X_i)}{V_{X_i} - \bar{\mu}_{X_i}^2},$$

with

$$\bar{\mu}_x = k^{-1} \sum_{i \in J_x} X_i,$$

$$C_x = \sum_{i \in J_x} X_i Y_i,$$

$$V_x = \sum_{i \in J_x} X_i^2.$$

If an observation $(X_{i+[k/2]+1}, Y_{i+[k/2]+1})$ is added and $(X_{i-[k/2]}, Y_{i-[k/2]})$ falls out of the window over which to average, the following formulas can be used:

$$\overline{\mu}_{X_{i+1}} = \overline{\mu}_{X_i} + k^{-1}(X_{i+[k/2]+1} - X_{i-[k/2]}),$$

$$\hat{m}_k(X_{i+1}) = \hat{m}_k(X_i) + k^{-1}(Y_{i+[k/2]+1} - Y_{i-[k/2]}),$$

$$C_{X_{i+1}} = C_{X_i} + X_{i+[k/2]+1}Y_{i+[k/2]+1} - X_{i-[k/2]}Y_{i-[k/2]},$$

$$V_{X_{i+1}} = V_{X_i} + X_{i+[k/2]+1}^2 - X_{i-[k/2]}^2.$$

This recursive algorithm is a component of the *supersmoother* to be described in Section 5.3.

The principal idea of updating also applies to the *k-NN* estimate $\hat{m}_R(x)$ if a discrete approximation to the kernel K is used. Suppose that for fixed k the effective kernel weight is sufficiently well approximated by a sum of indicator functions

$$(2[k/2])^{-1} \sum_{j=0}^{[k/2]} I(|x - X_i| \le R_n(k - 2j)),$$

where $R_n(k)$ is the distance of x to its kth nearest neighbor. Then $\hat{m}_R(x)$ can be represented as a sum of simple *k-NN* estimates,

$$\hat{m}_R(x) \approx (2[k/2])^{-1} \sum_{j=0}^{[k/2]} \hat{m}_{k-2j}(x).$$

Every term in this sum can be updated as before. The computational costs are linear in n.

Exercises

3.2.1 Show that the bias and variance of $\hat{m}_R$ are identical to the bias and variance of $\hat{m}_k$ if a uniform kernel is used.

3.2.2 Define $d_M(k) = \text{variance}(k) + \text{bias}^2(k)$. Compute

$$k_{opt} = \arg\min_k d_M(k)$$

as a function of m, f and K. Also compute $d_M(k_{opt})$. Compare with the speed of convergence for kernel smoothers. Interpret the constants occurring in these expressions.

3.2.3 Implement the k-NN algorithm on a computer and compare with a brute force programming of the kernel smoother. Where do you see numerical advantages or disadvantages of the recursive updating algorithm?

3.2.4 Compare kernel and k-NN smoothers subjectively. At what regions of the data would you prefer the one before the other?

3.2.5 Verify the bias formula (3.2.8) for the symmetrized nearest neighbor estimator. Compare with the bias for the ordinary k-NN smoother and the kernel smoother.

3.3   Orthogonal series estimators

Suppose that the regression function can be represented as a Fourier series,

$$m(x) = \sum_{j=0}^{\infty} \beta_j \varphi_j(x), \qquad (3.3.1)$$

where $\{\varphi_j\}_{j=0}^{\infty}$ is a known basis of functions and $\{\beta_j\}_{j=0}^{\infty}$ are the unknown Fourier coefficients. Szegö (1959) gives conditions under which such a representation of m is possible. Well-known examples for basis functions are the Laguerre and the Legendre polynomials. Once a basis of functions is fixed, the problem of estimating m can be tackled by estimating the Fourier coefficients $\{\beta_j\}$. There is, of course, the restriction that there may be infinitely many non-zero β_j in (3.3.1). So, given the finite sample size n, only a subset of the coefficients can be effectively estimated.

For simplicity of presentation let us assume that the X-variable is confined to the interval $[-1, 1]$ and that observations $\{Y_i\}_{i=1}^{n}$ have been taken at equidistant points $\{X_i\}_{i=1}^{n}$ over this interval. Suppose that the system of functions $\{\varphi_j\}$ constitute an orthonormal basis on $[-1, 1]$,, that is,

$$\int_{-1}^{1} \varphi_j(x)\varphi_k(x)dx = \delta_{jk} = \begin{cases} 0, & \text{if } j \neq k; \\ 1, & \text{if } j = k. \end{cases}$$

Then the Fourier coefficient β_j can be computed as

$$\begin{aligned} \beta_j &= \sum_{k=0}^{\infty} \beta_k \delta_{jk} \\ &= \sum_{k=0}^{\infty} \beta_k \int_{-1}^{1} \varphi_k(x)\varphi_j(x)dx \end{aligned} \qquad (3.3.2)$$

$$= \int_{-1}^{1} m(x)\varphi_j(x)dx.$$

The last integral in this line involves not only the known basis functions but also the unknown function $m(x)$. If it can be estimated in a reasonable way it automatically gives an estimate of β_j. Recall that the observations are taken at discrete points in $[-1, 1]$. Let $\{A_i\}_{i=1}^{n}$ be a set of disjoint intervals such that

$$\sum_{i=1}^{n} A_i = [-1, 1]$$

and

$$X_i \in A_i, \qquad i = 1, \ldots, n.$$

Now the formula for the Fourier coefficients from (3.3.2) can be written as

$$\begin{aligned}
\beta_j &= \sum_{i=1}^{n} \int_{A_i} m(x)\varphi_j(x)dx \\
&\approx \sum_{i=1}^{n} m(X_i) \int_{A_i} \varphi_j(x)dx,
\end{aligned} \qquad (3.3.3)$$

if the intervals A_i are concentrated around X_i. By plugging in the response variable Y_i for $m(X_i)$ we obtain an estimate for β_j of

$$\hat{\beta}_j = \sum_{i=1}^{n} Y_i \int_{A_i} \varphi_j(x)dx. \qquad (3.3.4)$$

Since only a finite number of observations are available not all Fourier coefficients can be estimated at a time. If $N(n)$ terms in the representation (3.3.1) are considered, the regression function is approximated by

$$\hat{m}_N(x) = \sum_{j=0}^{N(n)} \hat{\beta}_j \varphi_j(x). \qquad (3.3.5)$$

This estimator is called an *orthogonal series estimator* of m. It is a weighted average of the Y-variables with weights

$$W_{Ni}(x) = n \sum_{j=0}^{N(n)} \int_{A_i} \varphi_j(u)du \, \varphi_j(x). \qquad (3.3.6)$$

The smoothing parameter here is $N(n)$, the number of Fourier coefficients that enter (3.3.5).

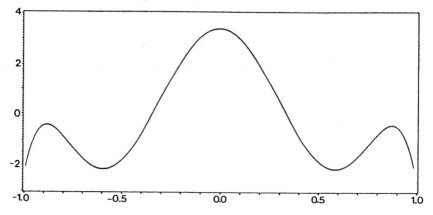

Figure 3.7.   The effective weight function of the Legendre system.
The weight function $W_{Ni}(x)$ from (3.3.6) for $N(n) = 5$, $n = 100$,
$A_i = [X_{i-1}, X_i]$, $X_0 = 1$ evaluated at $X_i = -1 + 2(i/n)$.   The
normalized Legendre polynomial system was chosen as the system of
basis functions $\{\varphi_j\}_{j=0}^{\infty}$.

In Figure 3.7 an effective weight function $W_{Ni}(x)$ evaluated at

$$X_i = -1 + 2(i/n), \qquad n = 100, \ A_i = [X_{i-1}, X_i], \qquad X_0 = 1$$

is shown for estimation at the point $x = 0$. For this effective weight
function the first six normalized Legendre polynomials are used

$$P_0(x) = 1/\sqrt{2},$$
$$P_1(x) = x/\sqrt{2/3},$$
$$P_2(x) = \frac{1}{2}\ (3x^2 - 1)/\sqrt{2/5},$$
$$P_3(x) = \frac{1}{2}\ (5x^3 - 3x)/\sqrt{2/7},$$
$$P_4(x) = \frac{1}{8}\ (35x^4 - 30x^2 + 3)/\sqrt{2/9},$$
$$P_5(x) = \frac{1}{8}\ (63x^5 - 70x^3 + 15x)/\sqrt{2/11}.$$

The Legendre polynomials constitute an orthogonal system of functions on $[-1, 1]$. They can be quite easily computed by the following
recurrence relation

$$(m + 1)P_{m+1}(x) = (2m + 1)\ x\ P_m(x) - mP_{m-1}(x).$$

The statistical aspects of orthogonal series estimation have been investigated mainly in the field of density estimation; see Cenzov (1962), Wahba (1975), Walter (1977). From the few applications in the field of nonparametric regression, I report only two results, concerning consistency and exact rate of convergence, and one application from an agricultural experiment. The consistency of $\hat{m}_N(x)$ follows from the next proposition.

Proposition 3.3.1   If for some $0 < s < 1$

$$n^{s-1} \sum_{j=0}^{N(n)} \sup_x \left|\varphi_j(x)\right|^2 \; < \infty \qquad (3.3.7)$$

and

$$E\left|\varepsilon_i\right|^{\frac{s+1}{s}} \; < \infty$$

then as $N(n) \to \infty$

$$\hat{m}_N(x) \xrightarrow{p} m(x).$$

A sketch of the proof is given in the Complements of this section. A detailed proof of consistency of $\hat{m}_N$ can be found in Rutkowski (1982). Szegö (1959) shows that

$$\sup_x \left|\varphi_j(x)\right| \sim j^\rho, \qquad j = 1,2,3\ldots,$$

with $\rho = -1/4$ for the Hermite and the Laguerre systems, and $\rho = 0, 1/2$ respectively for the Fourier and Legendre systems. The assumption (3.3.7) takes then the form of a growth condition on $N(n)$

$$N(n)^{2\rho+1}/n^{1-s} \le C < \infty \qquad \text{as n} \to \infty. \qquad (3.3.8)$$

The smoothing parameter $N(n)$ has to tend to infinity to ensure consistency, but not too fast as (3.3.8) suggests. Precise convergence rates of orthogonal series smoothers are given by Härdle (1984b) in the setting of stochastic X-variables. In that paper Legendre polynomials and the weight sequence

$$W_{Ni}(x) = K_N(x; X_i)/n^{-1} \sum_{j=1}^{n} K_N(x; X_i)$$

have been used, where

$$K_N(x; X_i) = \sum_{j=0}^{N(n)} \varphi_j(x)\varphi_j(X_i).$$

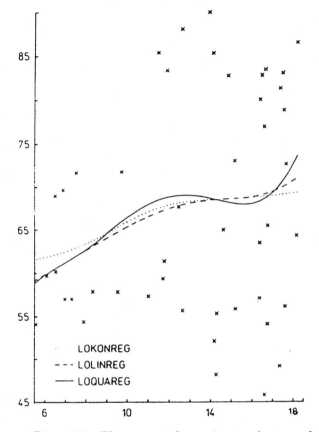

Figure 3.8.   The amount of sugar in sugar-beet as a function of temperature. Three orthogonal series estimators $(N = 0, 1, 2)$ of the functional relationship between temperature and the amount of sugar in sugar-beet. The dotted line is the (local) constant fit, the fine dashed line involves a linear term and the dashed curve is a fit involving three orthogonal polynomials. From Schmerling and Peil (1985) with permission of Gegenbaurs Morphologisches Jahrbuch.

An orthogonal series estimate could also be applied in a local neighborhood around x by rescaling the interval $[-1, 1]$. This approach was pursued by Schmerling and Peil (1986). An application of (local) orthogonal series estimates to real data was given by Schmerling and Peil (1985). In Figure 3.8, the fits with $N(n) = 0, 1, 2$, respectively, are shown. One sees that increasing the degree of approximation $N(n)$ makes the smooth follow the data more closely.

Exercises

3.3.1 Establish that the Legendre polynomials are indeed orthonormal, that is, show that

$$\int_{-1}^{1} P_j(x)P_k(x)dx = \delta_{jk}.$$

3.3.2 Show that if m is Lipschitz continuous then $E\beta_j \to \beta$.

3.3.3 Compute the variance of $\hat{m}_N$ and show that it tends to zero under the condition (3.3.7).

3.3.4 How many terms $N(n)$ should be used for $\hat{m}_N$ in order to achieve a trade-off between variance and bias^2?

3.3.5 Investigate the approximation occurring in (3.3.3). How close is β_j to

$$\sum_{i=1}^{n} m(X_i) \int_{A_i} \varphi_j(x)dx?$$

[*Hint*: Use the mean value theorem and the fact that $X_i - X_{i-1} = O(n^{-1})$.]

3.3.6 Consider $\{W_{Ni}(x)\}$, as given in (3.3.6), more closely. If we exchange summation with integration we see that

$$W_{Ni}(x) = n \int_{A_i} \left(\sum_{j=0}^{N(n)} \varphi_j(u)\varphi_j(x) \right) du.$$

This looks very much like the weight sequence $W_{hi}^{(3)}(x)$. Can you make this more precise?

Complements

Sketch of proof of Proposition 3.3.1
The bias $E\hat{m}_N(x) - m(x)$ tends to zero if m is Lipschitz continuous. This can be seen from the inequalities

$$|E\hat{m}_N(x) - m(x)|$$
$$\leq \left| \sum_{j=0}^{N(n)} \varphi_j(x) \sum_{i=1}^{n} \int_{A_i} (m(x_i) - m(u))\varphi_j(u) \, du \right|$$
$$+ \left| \sum_{j=0}^{N(n)} \varphi_j(x) \sum_{i=1}^{n} \int_{A_i} \varphi_j(u) \, m(u)du - m(x) \right|$$

$$\leq Cn^{-1} \sum_{j=0}^{N(n)} \sup_x \left|\varphi_j(x)\right|^2 + \left|\sum_{j=N(n)+1}^{\infty} \beta_j\varphi_j(x)\right|.$$

The variance calculation is left to the reader. [*Hint*: Use the assumption (3.3.7), essentially a condition on the growth rate of $N(n)$.]

3.4   Spline smoothing

A common measure of "fidelity to the data" for a curve g is the residual sum of squares

$$\sum_{i=1}^{n}(Y_i - g(X_i))^2.$$

If g is allowed to be any curve – unrestricted in functional form – then this distance measure can be reduced to zero by any g that interpolates the data. Such a curve would not be acceptable on the grounds that it is not unique and that it is too wiggly for a structure-oriented interpretation. The spline smoothing approach avoids this implausible interpolation of the data by quantifying the competition between the aim to produce a good fit to the data and the aim to produce a curve without too much rapid local variation.

There are several ways to quantify local variation. One could define measures of roughness based, for instance, on the first, second, and so forth derivative. In order to explicate the main ideas the integrated squared second derivative is most convenient, that is, the *roughness penalty*

$$\int (g''(x))^2 \, dx$$

is used here to quantify local variation. Using this measure, define the weighted sum

$$S_\lambda(g) = \sum_{i=1}^{n}(Y_i - g(X_i))^2 + \lambda \int (g''(x))^2 \, dx, \qquad (3.4.1)$$

where λ denotes a smoothing parameter. The smoothing parameter λ represents the rate of exchange between residual error and roughness of the curve g. The problem of minimizing $S_\lambda(\cdot)$ over the class of all twice differentiable functions on the interval $[a, b] = [X_{(1)}, X_{(n)}]$ has a unique solution $\hat{m}_\lambda(x)$ which is defined as the *cubic spline*; see Schoenberg (1964), Reinsch (1967), Good and Gaskins (1971) and Boneva et al. (1972). The basic idea dates back at least to Whittaker (1923) who called

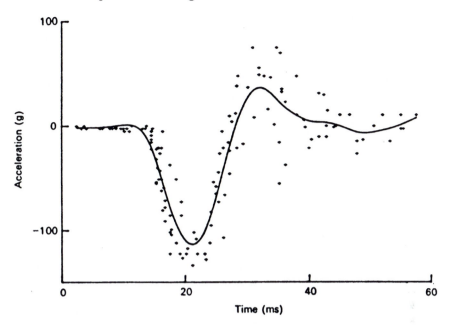

Figure 3.9.   A spline smooth of the motorcycle data set. From Silverman (1985) with permission of the Royal Statistical Society.

this smoothing process a *graduation* or *adjustment* of the observations.
The estimated curve $\hat{m}_\lambda(\cdot)$ has the following properties:

$\hat{m}_\lambda(x)$ is a *cubic polynomial* between two successive X-values;

at the observation points X_i, the curve $\hat{m}_\lambda(\cdot)$ and its first two
derivatives are continuous but there may be a discontinuity in
the third derivative;

at the boundary points $X_{(1)}$ and $X_{(n)}$ the second derivative of
$\hat{m}_\lambda(x)$ is zero.

It should be noted that these properties follow from the particular choice
of the roughness penalty. It is possible to define, say, quintic splines by
considering a roughness penalty that involves higher-order derivatives.

   An example of a spline smooth is given in Figure 3.9, a spline smooth
of the so-called motorcycle data set, see Table 1 in Appendix 2 for a
complete listing of this data set.

   Recall that the spline is a cubic polynomial between the knot points.
The "local cubic polynomial" property is illustrated in Figure 3.10 where
at three significant points the (local) cubic polynomial fit is superim-

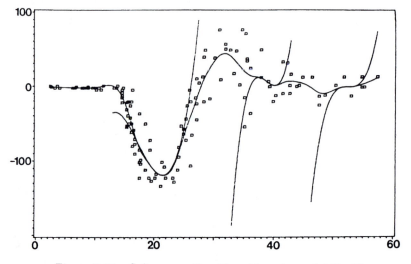

Figure 3.10.   Spline smooth with cubic polynomial fit. The motor-cycle data (Table 1 in Appendix 2) with a spline smooth ($\lambda = 2$) and three (local) cubic polynomial approximations. The raw data $\{(X_i, Y_i)\}_{i=1}^{n}$, $n = 150$, are shown as squares. The smooth as a solid line, local fits at $x = 21, 40, 55$. Units are g (earth-acceleration) for Y and ms (milliseconds after impact in a simulated experiment) for X.

posed on the spline smooth, computed from the motorcycle data set. The curve shown is computed at the points $\{X_i\}_{i=1}^{n}$ itself using the IMSL routine ICSSCU. The motorcycle data set is listed in Table 1 in Appendix 2.

A conceptual difficulty in spline smoothing is the fact that $\hat{m}_\lambda$ is defined implicitly as the solution to a functional minimization problem. This makes it hard to judge the behavior of the estimate and to see what $\hat{m}_\lambda$ is actually doing to the data values. The following argument shows that $\hat{m}_\lambda$ is, in fact, a weighted average of the Y-observations.

The minimum of $S_\lambda(g)$ is unique, so we must have $S_\lambda(\hat{m}_\lambda + \alpha g) \geq S_\lambda(\hat{m}_\lambda)$ for any $g \in C^2$ and $\alpha \in R$. This means that the real function $T(\alpha) = S_\lambda(\hat{m}_\lambda + \alpha g)$ has a local minimum at $\alpha = 0$. In particular, the Euler–Lagrange condition (Hadley and Kemp 1971, p. 30–31),

$$T'(0) = \sum_{i=1}^{n}(Y_i - \hat{m}_\lambda(X_i))\, g(X_i) + \lambda \int \hat{m}_\lambda''(x)\, g''(x)\, dx = 0,$$

(for all twice differentiable g) must be satisfied. Consider now two splines $\hat{m}_\lambda^{(1)}, \hat{m}_\lambda^{(2)}$ for the data $\{(X_i, Y_i^{(1)})\}_{i=1}^{n}, \{(X_i, Y_i^{(2)})\}_{i=1}^{n}$. Using the above

Euler–Lagrange condition one sees that $\hat{m}_\lambda^{(1+2)} = \hat{m}_\lambda^{(1)} + \hat{m}_\lambda^{(2)}$ is the spline for the data set $\{(X_i, Y_i^{(1)} + Y_i^{(2)})\}_{i=1}^n$. If the data vector $\{Y_i\}_{i=1}^n$ is written as a linear combination of the n coordinate vectors it is easily seen that there exist weights $W_{\lambda i}(x)$ such that

$$\hat{m}_\lambda(x) = n^{-1} \sum_{i=1}^n W_{\lambda i}(x) Y_i. \qquad (3.4.2)$$

The spline is thus linear in the Y-observations. The weight function can be plotted by applying the spline smoothing method to Y-values which are all zero, except one response variable which is set equal to the sample size n. However, the functional form of $\{W_{\lambda i}(x)\}_{i=1}^n$ is hard to write down explicitly and the dependence on the smoothing parameter λ and the design points is extremely complicated. Recall that $W_{\lambda i}(\cdot)$ is the spline for the data $(X_1, 0), \ldots, (X_i, n), \ldots, (X_n, 0)$. More generally, define the spline at point t as $W_\lambda(\cdot, t)$. Silverman (1984, theorem A) showed that the effective weight function $W_\lambda(\cdot, t)$ looks like a kernel K_s, where the *kernel function* K_s is given by

$$K_s(u) = 1/2 \ \exp(- |u| / \sqrt{2}) \sin(|u| / \sqrt{2} + \pi/4).$$

Theorem 3.4.1 (Silverman 1984)   Assume the fixed design model with a design density as in Section 2.1. Apart from very technical conditions the smoothing parameter λ depends on n in such a way that $\lambda n^{1-\varepsilon} \to \infty$ for some $\varepsilon > 0$. Choose any fixed t such that $a < t < b$. Then

$$\lambda^{1/4} n^{-1/4} f(t)^{-1/4} W_\lambda(t + \lambda^{1/4} n^{-1/4} f(t)^{-1/4} x, t) \to K_s(x)/f(t)$$

as $n \to \infty$, uniformly over all x for which $t + \lambda^{1/4} n^{-1/4} f(t)^{-1/4} x$ lies in $[a, b]$.

The approximation of $W_{,\lambda}(X_i) = W_{\lambda i}(\cdot)$ in the above theorem says that for large n and small λ and X_i not too close to the boundary,

$$W_{\lambda i}(\cdot) \approx f(X_i)^{-1} h(X_i)^{-1} K_s\left(\frac{\cdot - X_i}{h(X_i)}\right) \qquad (3.4.3)$$

and the *local bandwidth* $h(X_i)$ satisfies

$$h(X_i) = \lambda^{1/4} n^{-1/4} f(X_i)^{-1/4}.$$

Indeed, setting $t = X_i$ and using the variable substitution $u = X_i + xh(X_i)$ in Theorem 3.4.1 yields formula (3.4.3). A plot of the effective kernel function K_s is given in Figure 3.11.

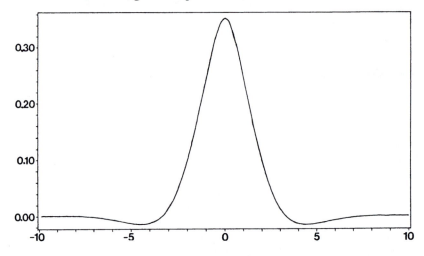

Figure 3.11.   Silverman's approximation to the effective spline kernel.   The asymptotic spline kernel function, $K_s = 1/2 \exp(-|u|/\sqrt{2}) \sin(|u|/\sqrt{2} + \pi/4)$.

One sees that K_s is a symmetric kernel function with negative side lobes and that K_s has vanishing second moment, that is, $\int u^2 \, K_s(u) \, du = 0$. A graphical comparison of the exact weight function $W_{\lambda i}(x)$ and its asymptotic form K_s is given in Silverman (1984, figure 2, p. 902).

The kernel form of this weight function changes as x approaches the boundary of the observation interval. Engle et al. (1986) computed the effective spline weight function for the temperature response example (see Figure 1.6). Figure 3.12 is a reproduction from their article where they show the equivalent kernel function for an x roughly in the middle of the observation interval.

As the observation point moves to the right the weight function becomes more asymmetric as Figure 3.13 indicates.

The question of how much to smooth is of course also to be posed for spline smoothing. A survey of the literature on the mean squared error properties of spline smoothing can be found in Eubank (1988). The smoothing parameter selection problem for this class of estimators has been mainly investigated by Grace Wahba. From her rich collection of results I would like to mention those which are directly connected with the optimization of λ. In Wahba (1975, 1979) convergence rates of splines are considered. The pioneering article on cross-validation in this context is Wahba and Wold (1975), which was extended later to

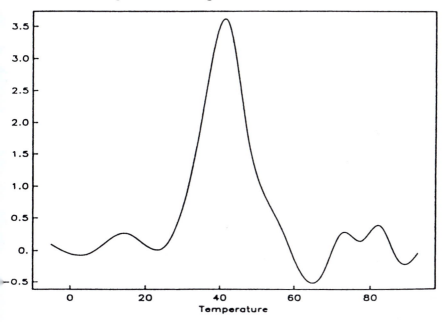

Figure 3.12.   Equivalent kernel function for the temperature range
$40°$ to $45°$ Fahrenheit. From Engle et al. (1986, figure 6) with permission of the American Statistical Association.

the smoothing of the log periodogram; see Wahba (1980). The term
generalized cross-validation (GCV) was coined by Wahba (1977). A
minimax type approach to the question of rates of convergence was done
by Nussbaum (1985), who obtained exact bounds for the integrated
squared error under a normality assumption on the error variables.

Some statistical software packages that compute the spline coefficients
of the local cubic polynomials require a bound Λ on the residual sum of
squares $\sum_{i=1}^{n}(Y_i - g(X_i))^2$. These programs solve the equivalent problem

$$\int [g''(x)]^2 dx = \min$$

under the constraint $\sum_{i=1}^{n}(Y_i - g(X_i))^2 \leq \Lambda$. The parameters λ and Λ
have similar meanings. A very small λ gives a very rough curve, as does
a small Λ since the spline curve is allowed to stay very close to the data.
On the other hand, a large value of Λ allows g'' to be nearly zero and
the same holds true for the parameter λ. A connection between the two
parameters can be derived as follows.

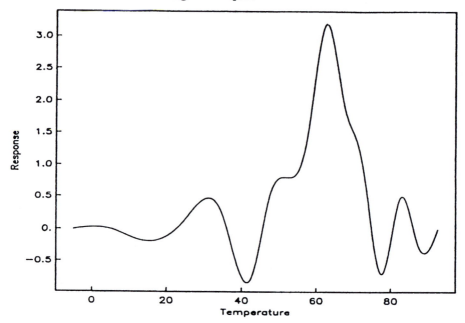

Figure 3.13.   Equivalent kernel function for the temperature range 60° to 65° Fahrenheit. From Engle et al. (1986, figure 7) with permission of the American Statistical Association.

Proposition 3.4.2   Let $G(\Lambda) = \int (\hat{m}''_\Lambda(x))^2 dx$, where $\hat{m}_\Lambda(x)$ solves the above minimization problem. Then the equivalent λ is given by

$$\lambda = -[G'(\Lambda)]^{-1}.$$

This correspondence is derived explicitly for the example given in Section 3.6. The same methods can be used to derive an equivalent Λ for a given smoothing parameter λ.

The effective weights of spline smoothing can be more easily computed for equispaced uniform $X_i = i/n$. In this situation the k-NN estimator $\hat{m}_k$ and the kernel estimator $\hat{m}_h$ coincide for k roughly equal to $2nh$. Huber (1979) showed under a periodicity assumption on m that the spline smoother is exactly equivalent to a weighted kernel-type average of the Y-observations. He considers the following function of $Z = (Z_1, \ldots, Z_n)$

$$\tilde{S}_\delta(Z) = \sum_{i=1}^{n} \{(Y_i - Z_i)^2 + \delta \ (n^2 \Delta^2 Z_i)^2\},$$

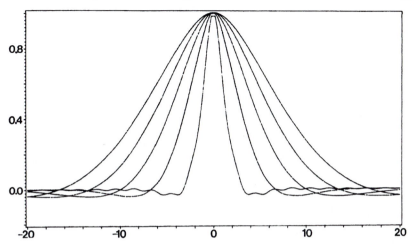

Figure 3.14. Huber's approximation to the effective spline weight function, $\tilde{W}_{\delta j} = \pi^{-1} \int_0^\pi \frac{\cos(\omega j)}{1+\delta(2\sin\omega/2)^4} d\omega$. Shown are the weights $\tilde{W}_{\delta j}$ for $\delta = 0.5, 8, 40.5, 128, 312.5$.

where $\Delta^2 Z_i = Z_{i+1} - 2Z_i + Z_{i-1}$ denotes the second difference quotient. Note that $\tilde{S}_\delta$ is different from S_λ in two respects. First, the roughness penalty is defined by a sum of second difference quotients rather than an integral of second derivatives. Second, δ corresponds to $n^3\delta$ since $n^{-1}\sum_{i=1}^n (n^2\Delta^2 Z_i)^2$ is analogous to $\int_0^1 [g''(x)]^2 dx$. Huber showed that the minimization of $\tilde{S}_\delta(Z)$ for circular data $\{Y_i\}$ yields the weighted average

$$Z_i = \sum_j \tilde{W}_{\delta j}\, Y_{i-j},$$

where the weights $\tilde{W}_{\delta j}$ have the asymptotic form

$$\tilde{W}_{\delta j} = \frac{1}{\pi} \int\limits_0^\pi \frac{\cos(\omega j)}{1 + \delta(2\,\sin\omega/2)^4}\, d\omega. \qquad (3.4.4)$$

This asymptotic holds for fixed j and δ as $n \to \infty$. It is interesting to compare this form of the weights with the approximation given by Silverman (1984). Figure 3.14 gives the form of the weights $\tilde{W}_{\delta j}$ for different values of δ. The weights $\tilde{W}_{\delta j}$ are more concentrated around zero if δ is small.

The curves in Figure 3.14 look indeed very similar to the one in Figure 3.10.

Exercises

3.4.1 Use the spline smoothing algorithm to plot the exact weight function $\{W_{\lambda i}(x)\}$. Compare with the approximate function given by K_s. How does the approximation change when x moves to the boundary?

3.4.2 Show that the kernel K_s is a kernel in the sense of Section 3.1 and prove that

$$\int u^j K_s(u)du = 0, \quad 1 \le j \le 3,$$

$$\int u^4 K_s(u)du = -1.$$

Complements

Proof of Proposition 3.4.2

The proof follows from a slight generalization of Pourciau (1980, section 1), (John multiplier rule). There exist nonzero μ_1, μ_2 such that the pair $(\Lambda, \hat{m}_\Lambda)$ minimizes

$$\mu_1 \left[\int (g''(x))^2 dx - G(\Lambda) \right] + \mu_2 \left[\sum_{i=1}^n (Y_i - g(X_i))^2 - \Lambda \right].$$

A consequence of this is that

$$0 = \frac{\partial}{\partial \Lambda} G(\Lambda) = -\mu_1 G'(\Lambda) - \mu_2$$

or

$$G'(\Lambda) = -\mu_2/\mu_1.$$

Therefore the spline curve with parameter λ can be derived by setting $\lambda = \mu_1/\mu_2 = -(G'(\Lambda))^{-1}$.

Proof of equivalence of the Silverman and Huber approximation

This can be quantified by yet another approximation to the integral (3.4.4). For fixed u and $\delta \to \infty$, put $j = u\delta^{1/4}$. After a change of variables $\omega = t/\delta^{1/4}$ and a first-order Taylor approximation $2\sin(\omega/2) \sim$

ω we obtain

$$\delta^{1/4}\ \tilde{W}_{\delta,u\delta^{1/4}}\ \to\ \frac{1}{2\pi}\int_{-\infty}^{\infty}\frac{e^{iut}}{1+t^4}\,dt.$$

To evaluate the integral, consider $f(z)=e^{iuz}/(1+z^4)$. The denominator has zeros at $\eta_k=e^{i\frac{2k-1}{4}\pi}$, $k=1,\ldots,4$. Integrating over a semicircle in the complex plane using the residue theorem yields

$$\frac{1}{2\pi}\oint f(z)dz=i\{\mathrm{res}[f(z);\eta_1]+\mathrm{res}[f(z);\eta_2]\}$$

$$=\frac{1}{2}e^{-u/\sqrt{2}}\cos(u/\sqrt{2}-\pi/4)$$

which is the effective weight function K_s as given by Silverman (1984). To establish the connection to the approximation in Theorem 3.4.1, remember that δ corresponds to λn^3 and $\tilde{W}_{\delta j}$ corresponds to $n^{-1}W_{\lambda(i-j)}(X_i)$.

3.5   An overview of various smoothers

Not all smoothing techniques have received equal attention. The kernel, k-NN, orthogonal series and spline estimators which have been presented up to this point are widely known and there is a well-developed mathematical theory for them. There are two reasons for this. First, these estimators are simple in structure and therefore easy to compute and easy to analyze mathematically. Second, these estimators have a wide field of applicability and are not designed for estimating special features.

The smoothing techniques to be presented in this section have not received as much theoretical treatment but are of interest in their own right, since they exemplify how the nonparametric smoothing method might be adapted to specific contexts. The list of smoothers presented here is far from being complete; the interested reader should consult the review article by Collomb (1981) for more references.

Recursive techniques

Suppose that the data $\{(X_i,Y_i)\}_{i\geq1}$ are not observed as a sample of fixed size n but rather as an ongoing sequence $(X_1,Y_1),(X_2,Y_2),\ldots$ from some observational mechanism. Such mechanisms occur in surveillance problems, control operations or intervention problems. More generally, one can think of a time series of data. Since nonparametric smoothers are typically defined from the whole sample, for every newly arriving data point the estimator has to be recomputed. It could therefore be of computational advantage if the regression estimator based on $(n+1)$ points could be evaluated from the $(n+1)$-th observation (X_{n+1}, Y_{n+1}) and from the estimator based on the first n points without recalling the previous data points from a computer memory. In this spirit Revesz (1976, 1977) proposed estimating $m(x)$ recursively by

$$\hat{m}_{n+1}(x) = \hat{m}_n(x)$$
$$+ n^{-1} K_{h_{n+1}} (x - X_{n+1})(Y_{n+1} - \hat{m}_n(x)), \qquad (3.5.1)$$

where $\hat{m}_0 \equiv 0$ and K_h is a kernel sequence. He showed convergence of this sequentially defined estimator in different norms and derived the asymptotic normal distribution.

This technique can also be applied to a very general form of time-varying systems which can be modeled by the regression relationship

$$Y_i = m_i(X_i) + \varepsilon_i$$

with a slowly varying mean function $m_i(x)$. Rutkowski (1985a, 1985b) considered an algorithm very similar to (3.5.1) which asymptotically identified the regression functions. Greblicki, Rutkowska and Rutkowski (1983) defined an orthogonal series estimate in this time-varying regression setting and derived the rate of convergence of their estimator. The simpler setting of non-time-varying functions was considered by Rutkowski (1981) by construction of orthogonal series estimates of sequential type.

Ahmad and Lin (1976) studied sequential estimates of the numerator and the denominator of the Nadaraya–Watson estimator

$$\hat{m}_h(x) = \frac{N_n(x)}{D_n(x)},$$

with

$$N_{n+1}(x) = N_n(x) + Y_{n+1} K_{h_{n+1}}(x - X_{n+1}),$$
$$D_{n+1}(x) = D_n(x) + K_{h_{n+1}}(x - X_{n+1}). \qquad (3.5.2)$$

Stochastic approximation methods for estimating a zero or an extremum of $m(x)$ in this setting were proposed by Härdle and Nixdorf (1987). Tsybakov (1988) embedded this recursive scheme into the framework of passive stochastic approximation (PSA). Consider, for instance, the estimation of a zero of m. The sequential scheme

$$Z_{n+1} = Z_n - a_n K_{h_n}(Z_n - X_n)Y_n, \qquad (3.5.3)$$

(Z_1 arbitrary, $\{a_n\}$ a sequence tending to zero) will converge under some conditions to that zero. More details about these techniques are contained in Chapter 8.

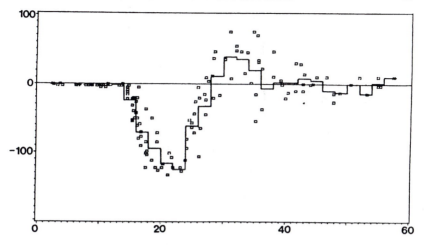

Figure 3.15. A regressogram smooth of the motorcycle data. The raw data are indicated by squares, the regressogram (solid line) has bin-size 4 and bin-edge 0.

The regressogram

This name was coined by Tukey (1961) to accentuate the relationship of this smoother to the histogram. The regressogram is an average of those response variables of which the corresponding Xs fall into disjoint bins spanning the X-observation space (Tukey 1947). It can be thought of as approximating $m(x)$ by a step function and is in fact a kernel estimate (with uniform kernel) evaluated at the midpoints of the bins. Convergence in mean squared error has been shown by Collomb (1977) and Lecoutre (1983, 1984). Figure 3.15 shows the motorcycle data set together with a regressogram of bin size 4.

Although the regressogram is a special kernel estimate it is by definition always a discontinuous step function which might obstruct the perception of features that are "below the bin-size." Recall Figures 1.2 and 2.5. Both show the average expenditures for potatoes. The regressogram (Figure 2.5) captures the general unimodal structure but cannot resolve a slight second mode at $x \approx 2$, the double income level. This slight mode was modeled by the kernel smoother in Figure 1.2.

A k-NN analogue of the regressogram has also been proposed. Instead of averaging the response variables in bins of fixed width, the *statistically equivalent block regressogram* is constructed by averaging always over k neighbors. The result is again a step function but now with different lengths of the windows over which averaging is performed. Bosq and

Lecoutre (1987) consider consistency and rates of convergence of this estimator.

Convolution smoothing

The idea of convolution smoothing was proposed by Clark (1977) and has strong relations to kernel smoothing (see Section 3.1). The CS-estimator (CS for convolution-smoothing) is defined as

$$\hat{m}_{CS}(x) = \int G_n(t)\, K_h(x - t)\, dt,$$

where $G_n(t)$ is the linear interpolant of the data $\{(X_i, Y_i)\}_{i=1}^n$ and K_h is a kernel sequence as in Section 3.1. Clark (1980) studied prediction and calibration of carbon–14 curves and presented Monte Carlo simulations in which the smoothing parameter h had been selected by cross-validation, a method to be analyzed in detail in Section 5.1. It is easy to see that the CS-estimator has also the form of a weighted average:

$$\hat{m}_{CS}(x) = n^{-1} \sum_{i=1}^n W_{ni}^{(CS)}(x)\, Y_i, \tag{3.5.4}$$

where

$$W_{ni}^{(CS)}(x) = \int v_i(t)\, K_h(x - t)\, dt$$

and $v_i(t)$ is the linear interpolant of the points $\{(X_j, \delta_{ij})\}_{j=1}^n$, δ_{ij} being the Kronecker delta.

Delta function sequence estimators

A delta function sequence (DFS) is a sequence of smooth weighting functions $\{\delta_n(x)\}$, approximating the Dirac δ-function for large n. These DFSs were used by Johnston (1979) in forming the following type of regression estimator,

$$\hat{m}_\delta(x) = n^{-1} \sum_{i=1}^n \delta_n(x - X_i)\, Y_i / n^{-1} \sum_{i=1}^n \delta_n(x - X_i). \tag{3.5.5}$$

This estimator, in fact, generalizes the Nadaraya–Watson kernel estimator with the DFS $K_h(u)$. Watson and Leadbetter (1963, 1964) formulated the conditions

(a) $\quad \sup_{n} \int |\delta_n(u)| \ du < \infty,$

(b) $\quad \int \delta_n(u) \ du = 1,$

(c) $\quad \sup_{|u| \geq \alpha} |\delta_n(u)| \to 0 \quad$ for all $\alpha > 0$ $\qquad$ (3.5.6)

(d) $\quad \int_{|u| \geq \alpha} \delta_n(u) \ du \to 0 \quad$ for all $\alpha > 0.$

Under these general conditions on $\{\delta_n\}$ and continuity assumptions on m and f it can be shown that

$$\hat{m}_\delta(x) \xrightarrow{p} m(x).$$

Further restrictions on the speed of convergence of the DFSs permit formulation of a central limit theorem for $\hat{m}_\delta$ (Johnston 1979). There is a richer literature on DFS estimation of densities (see e.g. Walter and Blum 1979).

Median smoothing

Suppose that the aim of approximation is the conditional median curve $\text{med}(Y|X = x)$ rather than the conditional mean curve. A sequence of "local medians" of the response variables defines the *median smoother*. This estimator and related robust smoothers are considered more theoretically in Chapter 6, but it makes sense to present it here since median smoothing played a dominant role in the historical evolution of smoothing techniques. More formally, it is defined as

$$\hat{m}(x) = \text{med}\{Y_i : i \in J_x\},$$

where

$$J_x = \{i: X_i \text{ is one of the } k\text{-nearest neighbors of } x\}.$$

It has obvious similarities to the k-NN estimate (3.2.1) but differs in at least two aspects: Median smoothing is highly resistant to outliers and it is able to model unexpected discontinuities in the regression curve $\text{med}(Y|X = x)$. A comparison of both smoothing techniques is given in Figure 3.16, which shows the motorcycle data set (Table 1 in Appendix 2) with a median smooth and a k-NN smooth.

Note that the robustness aspect of median smoothing becomes visible here. The median smooth is not influenced by a group of possible outliers near $x \approx 35$ and it is a little bit closer to the main body of the data in

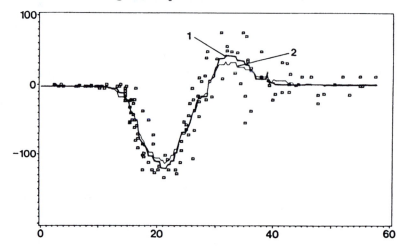

Figure 3.16.   Running median and a k-NN smooth. The squares indicate the raw data (motorcycle data set, Table 3.2.1), the curve with label 1 is the running median, the curve with label 2 denotes the k-NN smooth, $k = 15$.

the two "peak regions" ($x = 20, 32$). A slight disadvantage is that by its nature, the median smooth is a rough function.

Median smoothing seems to require more computing time than the k-NN estimate (due to sorting operations). The simplest algorithm for running medians would sort in each window. This would result in $O(nk \log(k))$ operations using a fast sorting routine. Using the fast median algorithm by Bent and John (1985) this complexity could be reduced to $O(nk)$ operations. Härdle and Steiger (1988) have shown that by maintaining a double heap structure as the window moves over the span of the X-variables, this complexity can be reduced to $O(n \log(k))$ operations. Thus running medians are only by a factor of $\log(k)$ slower than k-NN smoothers.

Split linear fits

A useful assumption for the mathematical analysis of the nonparametric smoothing method is the continuity of the underlying regression curve m. In some situations a curve with steps, abruptly changing derivatives or even cusps might be more appropriate than a smooth regression function. McDonald and Owen (1986) give several examples: These include Sweazy's kinked demand curve (Lipsey, Sparks and Steiner 1976)

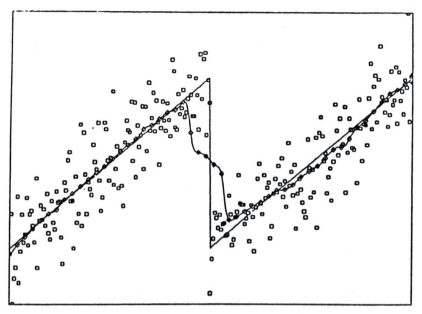

Figure 3.17.   A kernel smooth applied to a sawtooth function. From McDonald and Owen (1986) with permission of the American Statistical Association.

in microeconomics and daily readings of the sea surface temperature. Figure 3.17 shows a sawtooth function together with a kernel estimator.

The kernel estimation curve is qualitatively smooth but by construction must blur the discontinuity. McDonald and Owen (1986) point out that smoothing by running medians has no trouble finding the discontinuity, but appears to be very rough. They proposed, therefore, the *split linear smoother*. Suppose that the X-data are ordered, that is, $X_j \le X_{j+1}$. The split linear smoother begins by obtaining at x a family of linear fits corresponding to a family of windows. These windows are an ensemble of neighborhoods of x with different spans centered at x or having x as their left boundary or right boundary. The split linear smoother at point x is then obtained as a weighted average of the linear fits there. These weights depend on a measure of quality of the corresponding linear fits. In Figure 3.18 the sawtooth data are presented together with the split linear fit. This smoother found the discontinuous sawtooth curve and is smooth elsewhere. Theoretical aspects (confidence bands, convergence to m) are described in Marhoul and Owen (1984).

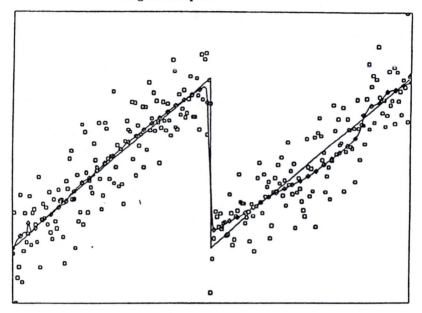

Figure 3.18. The split linear fit applied to a sawtooth function. From McDonald and Owen (1986) with permission of the American Statistical Association.

Empirical regression

Schmerling and Peil (1985) proposed to estimate the unknown joint density $f(x, y)$ of (X, Y) and then to estimate $m(x)$ by the standard formula. In particular, they proposed to use the mixture

$$\hat{f}(x, y) = n^{-1} \sum_{i=1}^{n} f_{XY}(x, y; X_i, Y_i),$$

where $f_{XY}(x, y; X_i, Y_i)$ are known densities. The evaluation of the conditional expectation on the basis of this estimate results in a curve which they call the *empirical regression curve*. There are many possibilities for a choice of f_{XY}. From

$$f_{XY}(x, y; X_i, Y_i) = K_h(x - X_i)K_h(y - Y_i),$$

for instance, follows

$$\hat{m}_h(x) = \frac{n^{-1} \sum_{i=1}^{n} K_h(x - X_i) Y_i}{n^{-1} \sum_{i=1}^{n} K_h(x - X_i)}.$$

This is the Nadaraya–Watson estimator. It is also possible to take a special two-dimensional Gaussian density

$$f_{XY}(x, y; X_i, Y_i) = \frac{1}{2\pi\sigma^2(\det(S))^{1/2}} \exp\left(-\frac{Q_i(x, y)}{2\sigma^2 \det(S)}\right),$$

with S a matrix with components

$$S_{xx} = n^{-1} \sum_{i=1}^{n} (X_i - \bar{X})^2,$$

$$S_{yy} = n^{-1} \sum_{i=1}^{n} (Y_i - \bar{Y})^2,$$

$$S_{xy} = S_{yx} = n^{-1} \sum_{i=1}^{n} (Y_i - \bar{Y})(X_i - \bar{X}),$$

and the quadratic form

$$Q_i(x, y) = n^{-1}(S_{yy}(X_i - \bar{X})^2 - 2S_{xy}(Y_i - \bar{Y})(X_i - \bar{X}) + S_{yy}(Y_i - \bar{Y})^2).$$

Then the empirical regression curve for a Gaussian kernel is given by

$$\hat{m}_h(x) = \frac{\sum_{i=1}^{n}(Y_i + \frac{S_{xy}}{S_{xx}}(x - X_i))\exp(-\frac{n(X_i - \bar{X})^2}{2\sigma^2 S_{xx}})}{\sum_{i=1}^{n} \exp(-\frac{n(X_i - \bar{X})^2}{2\sigma^2 S_{xx}})}. \tag{3.5.7}$$

Figure 3.19 gives an impression of how this empirical regression curve works with real data. For more details I refer to Schmerling and Peil (1985).

Exercises

3.5.1 Vary the "origin" of the regressogram, that is, define the bins over which to average the response variable as

$$((j - 1 + l/m)h, (j + l/m)h),$$
$$l = 0, \ldots, m - 1, \ j = \ldots - 2, -1, 0, 1, 2 \ldots.$$

Study qualitatively the behavior of the regressogram as you compare different regressograms over l.

3.5.2 Average the m regressograms as defined in Exercise 3.5.1. Do you see any connection with the kernel technique? [*Hint:* In Section 3.1 we called this Weighted Averaging over Rounded Points the WARPing technique.]

3.5.3 Find a correspondence between the conditions (3.5.6) and the assumptions needed for the kernel consistency Proposition 3.1.1.

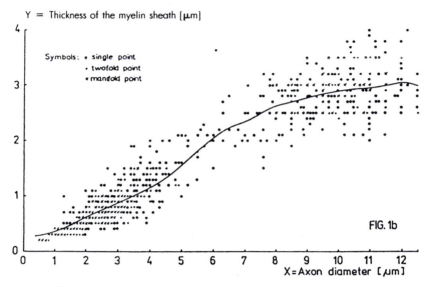

Figure 3.19. Empirical regression for the thickness of the myelin sheath as a function of the axon diameter. From Schmerling and Peil (1985) with permission of Gegenbaurs Morphologisches Jahrbuch.

Complements

Schmerling and Peil also considered more general polynomial fits than there introduced in Section 3.1. These local polynomial fits can be obtained by approximating polynomials of higher order or by using other kernels than the uniform kernel in (3.1.13); see also Katkovnik (1979, 1983, 1985) and Lejeune (1985).

Suppose that $m(x)$ is to be approximated by a polynomial

$$\sum_{j=0}^{p} \alpha_j(x)\varphi_j(u - x), \quad p + 1 < n,$$

where $\varphi_j(\cdot)$ are polynomials of order j and $\alpha_j(x)$ are some weighting coefficients. If the weight sequence $W_{hi}(x) = K_h(x - X_i)$ with a positive symmetric kernel K is used, the least squares problem

$$\sum_{i=1}^{n} W_{hi}(x) \left[Y_i - \sum_{j=0}^{p} \alpha_j(x)\varphi_j(X_i - x) \right]^2 \stackrel{!}{=} \min$$

gives coefficients $\{\hat{\alpha}_j(x)\}_{j=0}^p$. A necessary and sufficient condition is

$$2 \sum_{i=1}^n W_{hi}(x) \left[Y_i - \sum_{j=0}^p \alpha_j(x)\varphi_j(X_i - x) \right] \varphi_k(X_i - x) = 0,$$

$$h = 1, \ldots, n.$$

This linear system of equations can be solved easily if the φ_js are orthogonal polynomials, that is, for some constant C_x

$$\sum_{i=1}^n W_{hi}(x)\varphi_j(X_i - x)\varphi_k(X_i - x) = C_x I(j = k).$$

Hence the least squares coefficients $\{\hat{\alpha}_j(x)\}$ can be written as

$$\hat{\alpha}_j(x) = \frac{\sum_{i=1}^n [W_{hi}(x)\varphi_j(X_i - x)]Y_i}{\sum_{i=1}^n W_{hi}(x)\varphi_j^2(X_i - x)}, \quad j = 0, \ldots, p,$$

and the local polynomial fit can be written as

$$\hat{m}_h(x) = n^{-1} \sum_{i=1}^n W_{hi}^*(x)Y_i$$

with effective weight sequence

$$W_{hi}^*(x) = \sum_{j=0}^p \left[\frac{W_{hi}(x)\varphi_j(X_i - x)}{n^{-1}\sum_{k=1}^n W_{hk}(x)\varphi_j^2(X_k - x)} \right] \varphi_j(0).$$

So here again the local polynomial fitting leads to a weight sequence $\{W_{hi}^*(x)\}$, but this weight sequence is slightly more complicated than that for the ordinary kernel estimator.

3.6   A comparison of kernel, k-NN and spline smoothers

The purpose of this section is to present a comparative study of the three most commonly used and easy-to-implement smoothers: the kernel, the k-nearest neighbor and the cubic spline smoothers. The comparison is performed theoretically and empirically. The practical comparison is based on a simulated data set, which is presented in Table 2 in Appendix 2.

The theoretical comparison is presented for the two design models – fixed equidistant and random design. Kernel estimators $\hat{m}_h$ with weight functions $\{W_{hi}^{(3)}\}$ and $\{W_{hi}\}$ (see Section 3.1) and the k-NN smoother $\hat{m}_R$ are compared. Although the spline estimator also makes sense for

Table 3.6.1   *Pointwise bias and variance of k-NN and kernel smoothers for the fixed design case*

	bias	variance
kernel weights $\{W_{hi}\}$	$h^2 \dfrac{m''(x)}{2} d_K$	$\dfrac{\sigma^2(x)}{nh} c_K$
kernel weights $\{W_{hi}^{(3)}\}$	$h^2 \dfrac{m''(x)}{2} d_K$	$\dfrac{\sigma^2(x)}{nh} c_K$
k-NN weights	$\left(\dfrac{k}{n}\right)^2 \dfrac{m''(x)}{8} d_K$	$\dfrac{2\sigma^2(x)}{k} c_K$

Source: Jennen-Steinmetz and Gasser (1988, table 1).

stochastic predictor variables its statistical properties have been studied mostly for the fixed design case. We have found in Section 3.4 that the fixed design spline almost acts like a kernel smoother with design dependent bandwidth. Recall the kernel-spline equivalence theorem, Theorem 3.4.1. It says that the spline estimator $\hat{m}_\lambda$ for regularly distributed $X_i = F^{-1}((i - 1/2)/n)$ behaves like a Priestley–Chao kernel smoother with effective local bandwidth

$$h(x) = \lambda^{1/4} f(x)^{1/4}.$$

The effective local bandwidth is thus a power of the density of the X variables, $f^\alpha(x)$.

From Table 3.2.1 we saw that the k-NN estimator $\hat{m}_R$ has mean squared error properties comparable to the kernel estimator if the bandwidth $R(x) \sim f(x)^{-1}$. It therefore makes sense to consider kernel smoothers with bandwidths proportional to $f(x)^{-\alpha}$, $\alpha \in [0, 1]$.

Bias and variance behaviors of kernel smoothers with weights $\{W_{hi}^{(3)}\}$ and bandwidth $h \sim f^\alpha$ have been studied by Jennen-Steinmetz and Gasser (1988). The bias and variance of the above three estimators for the fixed equidistant design $(d = 1, X_i = i/n, \alpha = 0)$ are listed in Table 3.6.1. For the correct interpretation of this table recall the definition of c_K, d_K as given in Section 3.1. Table 3.6.1 shows clearly that the two kernel sequences $\{W_{hi}^{(3)}\}$ and $\{W_{hi}\}$ have the same mean squared error properties for the fixed equidistant design case. As noted before the k-NN weight sequence can be seen as a kernel sequence if we make the identification $h = \frac{k}{2n}$.

The bias and variance for the random design case is drastically different, as Table 3.6.2 shows. Pointwise bias and variance are complicated functionals not only of the regression curve m but also of the marginal density f.

Table 3.6.2   *Pointwise bias and variance of k-NN and kernel smoothers for the random design case*

	bias	variance
kernel weights $\{W_{hi}\}$	$h^2 \dfrac{(m''f + 2m'f')(x)}{2f(x)} d_K$	$\dfrac{\sigma^2(x)}{nhf(x)} c_K$
kernel weights $\{W_{hi}^{(3)}\}$	$h^2 \dfrac{m''(x)}{2f(x)^{2\alpha}} d_K$	$\dfrac{2\sigma^2(x)}{nhf(x)^{1-\alpha}} c_K$
k-NN weights	$\left(\dfrac{k}{n}\right)^2 \dfrac{(m''f + 2m'f')(x)}{8f^3(x)} d_K$	$\dfrac{2\sigma^2(x)}{k} c_K$

Source: Jennen-Steinmetz and Gasser (1988, table 1).

Note that essentially all three estimators coincide for the fixed design case when choosing $k = 2nh$ as indicated already in Section 3.2. This is not true for the random design. For $\alpha = 0$ the variance of the kernel with weights $\{W_{hi}^{(3)}\}$ is twice as big as for the Nadaraya–Watson estimator. By contrast, the bias of the Nadaraya–Watson smoother is a complicated expression of m and f. The same is true when comparing the bias of the k-NN smoother for $\alpha = 1$.

The empirical study is based on the simulated data from Figure 3.20. It shows $n = 100$ data points simulated from the regression curve

$$m(x) = 1 - x + e^{-200\ (x-1/2)^2}.$$

The X-variate is uniformly stochastically distributed over the unit interval and the observation errors ε_i have standard normal distributions. (Pseudo-random number generators based on Marsaglia's shuffling method for uniforms and the polar-Marsaglia method for normals were used for this plot; see Morgan 1984.)

A list of the values $\{(X_i, Y_i)\}_{i=1}^n$ is given in Table 2 in Appendix 2. After looking at Figure 3.20 one might say that this example is somewhat extreme since most of "the signal seems to be buried in the noise." By contrast, I consider it as realistic since it shows what can happen in practice. The sunflower plot of the food versus net income example in Chapter 2 gave an impression of such a "realistic data set." Note that the pattern of observation errors in the region around $x \approx 0.25$ seems to be skewed toward positive errors. Any smoother must therefore have a tendency to lie slightly above the true regression curve in this region. This can be seen immediately from the plot of the kernel smoother (Figure 3.21).

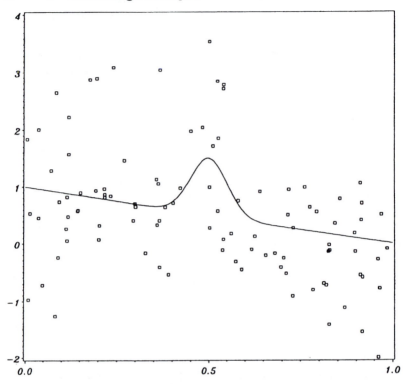

Figure 3.20. A simulated data set. The raw data $\{(X_i, Y_i)\}_{i=1}^{n}$, $n = 100$ were constructed from $Y_i = m(X_i) + \varepsilon_i, \varepsilon_i \sim N(0,1), X_i \sim U(0,1)$ and $m(x) = 1 - x + e^{-200\,(x-1/2)^2}$.

The kernel weights

$$W_{hi}(x) = K_h(x - X_i)/\hat{f}_h(x)$$

of the Nadaraya–Watson estimator have been used here with a Gaussian kernel $K(u) = (2\pi)^{-1/2} \exp(-u^2/2)$ and bandwidth $h = 0.05$. Note that this bandwidth does not mean that the observations are averaged in an interval of length 0.1. Rather, the kernel weights based on the above K extend over the whole interval but downweight observations that are away from the center of the kernel. In this example, $\hat{f}_h \approx 1$ since the X-distribution is uniform. Observations near x will receive weight 2.65 whereas an observation which is $2h$ away will be given weights 0.35.

Special attention must be paid to the boundary points 0 and 1 of the observation interval. Estimation points x that are close to the boundary

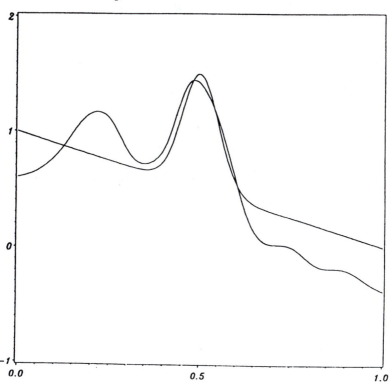

Figure 3.21.   A kernel smooth of the simulated data set. The solid line (label 1) denotes the underlying regression curve $m(x) = 1 - x + e^{-200\,(x-1/2)^2}$. The dashed line (label 2) is the kernel smooth $\hat{m}_h(x)$, $h = 0.05$, Gaussian kernel $K(u) = \exp(-u^2/2)/(\sqrt{2\pi})$ from the simulated data given in Table 2 in Appendix 2.

have only a one-sided neighborhood over which to average the Y-values. The kernel smoother must therefore be less accurate at the boundary (see Section 4.4 for a mathematical formulation of this problem). This inaccuracy can be seen from Figure 3.21 near the left boundary: Most of the observations there lie below the true regression curve; the asymmetric average therefore considerably underestimates the true $m(x)$ near $x \approx 0$.

The bandwidth $h = 0.05$ was chosen completely subjectively. I asked several colleagues and they felt that a higher amount of smoothing would "wash out" too much structure and a smaller bandwidth would give too rough a curve. Had another kernel been used, for instance a kernel with compact support, the picture would have been different for this specific

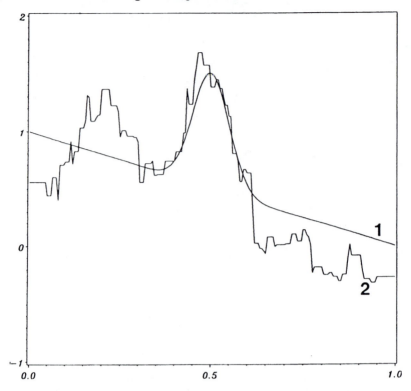

Figure 3.22.   A k-NN smooth of the simulated data set (Table 3.6.1). The solid line (label 1) denotes the underlying regression curve $m(x) = 1 - x + e^{-200\,(x-1/2)^2}$. The dashed line (label 2) is the k-NN smooth $\hat{m}_k(x), k = 11$.

bandwidth of $h = 0.05$. The reason is that different kernels are in general differently scaled. A way of adjusting the bandwidths and kernels to the same scale is discussed in Section 5.4.

The k-NN estimate produced a slightly rougher curve. In Figure 3.22 the graph of the k-NN smoother, as defined in (3.2.2), is displayed for $k = 11$. The reason for the "wiggliness" is the so-called uniform weight sequence that is used in (3.2.2). Theoretically speaking, the k-NN smooth is a discontinuous function.

In practice, this means that as the window of weights moves over the observation interval, new observations enter at the boundary of the "uniform window" according to the nearest neighbor rule. Any entering observation that has a value different from the current average will cause an abrupt change of the k-NN smoother. Such an effect would be diminished if a smoother k-NN weight sequence, like the one defined in (3.2.3), were used.

Here also boundary effects need special discussion. As the estimation point x moves to the boundary, the interval of observations entering the determination of the smoother becomes asymmetric. This was also the case for the kernel smoothers. Note, however, that, in contrast to kernel smoothing, the asymmetric region left or right of x always has the same number of points. The averaging procedure near the boundary thus involves a lot more points which, in general, have different mean values. This is not so drastic in our example since the regression curve is relatively flat at the boundaries. In cases where the regression function is steeper at the boundary the k-NN smoother is expected to be more biased than the kernel smoother.

The smoothing parameter k was also chosen subjectively here. A bigger k seemed to me to yield too smooth a curve compared to the raw observations. A smaller k produced too rough a curve, and amplified local spiky structures such as the one at $X \approx 0.85$.

The spline smoother $\hat{m}_\lambda(x)$ is shown in Figure 3.23. The algorithm of Reinsch (1967) was used to generate the smooth $\hat{m}_\lambda$. The smoothing parameter was chosen to be $\Lambda = 75$; that is, $\hat{m}_\Lambda$ is the solution to the minimization problem

$$\int [g''(x)]^2 dx = \min$$

under the constraint

$$\sum_{i=1}^{n}(Y_i - g(X_i))^2 \leq \Lambda.$$

The relation of Λ to the smoothing parameter λ was presented in Section 3.4.

In Table 3.6.3 the relation between Λ and $G(\Lambda) = \int(\hat{m}_\Lambda''(x))^2 dx$ is shown. As Λ increases the spline curve becomes flatter and flatter. In the limit it is equivalent to fitting a least squares line.

Table 3.6.4 presents the equivalent parameter Λ for various values of λ. The λ equivalent to $\Lambda = 75$ is therefore $\lambda = 0.6 \times 10^{-5}$.

By construction, the spline fit looks very smooth since it is a function that is glued together from pieces of cubic polynomials. The overall shape of the spline function is the same as that for the kernel and k-NN smooth. The peak in the middle of the observation interval is relatively well approximated (Figure 3.24), but to the left of it all smoothers ex-

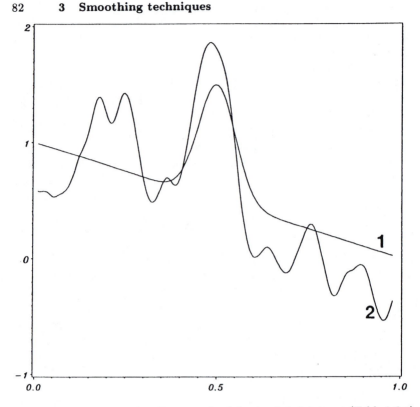

Figure 3.23.   A spline smooth of the simulated data set (Table 3.6.1). The solid line (label 1) denotes the underlying regression curve $m(x) = 1 - x + e^{-200\ (x-1/2)^2}$. The dashed line (label 2) is the spline smooth $\hat{m}_\Lambda(x)$, $\Lambda = 75$, computed with the IMSL routine ICSSCU.

hibit a somewhat smaller bump that is really only a random function of the data pattern.

Note that the spline smoother may produce a partially negative smooth even when all the response variables are positive. This can be understood from the asymptotic kernel representation (3.4.3) of $\hat{m}_\lambda$. Since the kernel K_s has negative side lobes (Figure 3.10) it may happen that for a sparse data pattern the resulting spline smooth is negative although one averages over purely positive observations.

A comparison of the behavior of all three smoothers can be obtained from Figure 3.24, the residual curves ("fit" minus "true") for the three approximation methods. All three smoothers have the artificial bump at

Table 3.6.3   *The function* $G(\Lambda) = \int (\hat{m}''_\Lambda(x))^2 dx$ *as a function of* Λ

Λ	$G(\Lambda) = \displaystyle\int (\hat{m}''_\Lambda(x))^2 dx$
45	0.18×10^9
50	0.72×10^8
55	0.29×10^8
60	0.11×10^8
65	0.36×10^7
70	0.10×10^7
75	0.21×10^6
80	0.24×10^5
85	0.35×10^4
90	0.38×10^3
95	0.23×10^2
100	0.23×10^1
105	0.68×10^{-26}

Table 3.6.4   *The parameter* λ *as a function of* Λ

Λ	$-1/G'(\Lambda)$
50	0.47×10^{-7}
55	0.12×10^{-6}
60	0.28×10^{-6}
65	0.70×10^{-6}
70	0.20×10^{-5}
75	0.61×10^{-5}
80	0.27×10^{-4}
85	0.24×10^{-3}
90	0.16×10^{-2}
95	0.14×10^{-1}
100	0.24
105	0.22×10^1

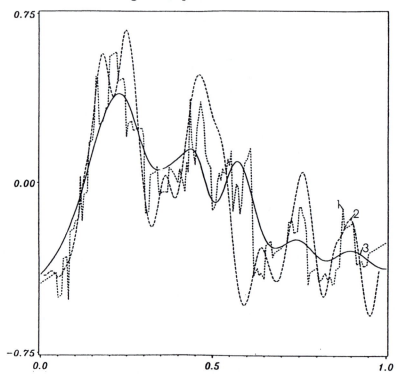

Figure 3.24.   Residual plot of k-NN, kernel and spline smoother for the simulated data set (Table 3.6.1). The fine dashed line (label 1) denotes the k-NN residual, $\hat{m}_k(x) - m(x), k = 11$. The dashed line (label 2) is the spline residual with $\hat{m}_\Lambda(x) - m(x), \Lambda = 75$. The solid line (label 3) is the kernel residual $\hat{m}_h(x) - m(x)$ with Gaussian kernel and bandwidth $h = 0.15$.

$x \approx 0.2$, introduced by the data pattern, but show essentially the same behavior in the residual curves.

Exercises

3.6.1 Try the kernel, k-NN and spline smoothings on the simulated data set with different smoothing parameters. Describe how you found a "good" smoothing parameter.

3.6.2 Quantify the behavior of the above smoothers at the boundary of the observation interval. Suppose $|m'(x)|$ is relatively large at the boundary. What do you expect from a local averaging method in this situation?

Complements

In the simulated data set from Table 2 no repeated observations (in the X-variable) have been observed. For the case of repeated observations the spline smoothing algorithm of Reinsch (1967) needs some preparatory steps. If one observes multiple responses for a fixed $X = x$ one pools the corresponding Y-values into one observation by averaging them. Suppose that there are $N_i \geq 1$ observations at each X_i. Then the spline algorithm solves the weighted minimization problem

$$\sum_{i=1}^{n} (Y_i - g(X_i))^2 / N_i + \lambda \int [g''(x)]^2 dx.$$

PART II

The kernel method

CHAPTER 4

How close is the smooth to the true curve?

It was, of course, fully recognized that the estimate might differ from the parameter in any particular case, and hence that there was a margin of uncertainty. The extent of this uncertainty was expressed in terms of the sampling variance of the estimator.

Sir M. Kendall and A. Stuart (1979, p. 109)

If the smoothing parameter is chosen as a suitable function of the sample size n, all of the above smoothers converge to the true curve if the number of observations increases. Of course, the convergence of an estimator is not enough, as Kendall and Stuart in the above citation say. One is always interested in the extent of the uncertainty or at what speed the convergence actually happens. Kendall and Stuart (1979) aptly describe the procedure of assessing measures of accuracy for classical parametric statistics: The extent of the uncertainty is expressed in terms of the sampling variance of the estimator which usually tends to zero at the speed of the square root of the sample size n.

In contrast to this is the nonparametric smoothing situation: The variance alone does not fully quantify the convergence of curve estimators. There is also a bias present which is a typical situation in the context of smoothing techniques. This is the deeper reason why up to this chapter the precision has been measured in terms of pointwise mean squared error (MSE), the sum of variance and squared bias. The variance alone doesn't tell us the whole story if the estimator is biased.

We have seen, for instance, in Section 3.2, that the pointwise MSE

$$E[\hat{m}(x) - m(x)]^2,$$

tends to zero for the k-NN smoother $\hat{m}_k$, if $k \to \infty$ and $k/n \to 0$. There are some natural questions concerning this convergence. How fast does the MSE tend to zero? Why should the measure of accuracy only be computed at one single point? Why not investigate a more "global" measure like the mean integrated squared error (MISE)? It is the purpose of this chapter to present several of such distance measures for functions and to investigate the accuracy of $\hat{m}(\cdot)$ as an estimate of

$m(\cdot)$ in a uniform and pointwise sense. In this chapter the response variable can also be a multidimensional variable in $\mathbb{R}^d$.

A variety of "global" distance measures can be defined. For instance, the integrated absolute deviation (weighted by the marginal density f)

$$d_{L_1}(\hat{m}, m) = \int |\hat{m}(x) - m(x)|\, f(x) dx$$

has been shown by Devroye and Wagner (1980a, 1980b) to converge almost surely to zero for kernel estimators $\hat{m}(x)$. Devroye and Györfi (1985) demonstrate an analogous result for the regressogram.

Another distance is defined through the maximal absolute deviation,

$$d_{L_\infty}(\hat{m}, m) = \sup_{x \in \mathcal{X}} |\hat{m}(x) - m(x)|,$$

where the $\sup_x$ ranges over a set $\mathcal{X} \in \mathbb{R}^d$ of interest. Devroye (1978a,b), Mack and Silverman (1982) and Härdle and Luckhaus (1984) investigated the speed at which this distance tends to zero for kernel estimators.

Quadratic measures of accuracy have received the most attention. A typical representative is the Integrated Squared Error (ISE)

$$d_I(\hat{m}, m) = \int (\hat{m}(x) - m(x))^2 f(x) w(x) dx,$$

where w denotes a weight function. A discrete approximation to d_I is the Averaged Squared Error (ASE)

$$d_A(\hat{m}, m) = n^{-1} \sum_{i=1}^{n} (\hat{m}(X_i) - m(X_i))^2 w(X_i).$$

In practice this distance is somewhat easier to compute than the distance measure d_I since it avoids numerical integration. A conditional version of d_A

$$d_C(\hat{m}, m) = E\{d_A(\hat{m}, m) \mid X_1, \ldots, X_n\}$$

has also been studied. The distance d_C is a random distance through the distribution of the Xs. Taking the expectation of d_I with respect to X yields the MISE

$$d_M(\hat{m}, m) = E\{d_I(\hat{m}, m)\}.$$

In order to simplify the presentation I will henceforth consider only kernel estimators. Most of the error calculations done for kernel smoothers in Section 3.1 can be extended in a straightforward way to show that kernel smoothers converge in the above global measure of accuracy to the true curve. But apart from such desirable convergence properties, it is important from both a practical and a theoretical point of view to exactly quantify the speed of convergence over a class of functions. This is the subject of the next section. In Section 4.2 pointwise confidence intervals are constructed. Global variability bands and error bars are presented in Section 4.3. The boundary problem, for example, the fact that the smoother behaves qualitatively differently at the boundary, is discussed in Section 4.4. The selection of kernel functions is presented in Section 4.5. Bias reduction techniques by the jackknife method are investigated in Section 4.6.

4.1   The speed at which the smooth curve converges

This section is rather theoretical in spirit. The reader more interested in practical consequences of the theoretical results should go directly to the Exercises and Complements.

In parametric problems the speed at which estimated parameters tend to the true value is typically $n^{-1/2}$ (Bickel and Doksum 1977, chapter 4.4). By contrast, in the nonparametric curve estimation setting, the rate of convergence, if quantified, for instance, by the square root of the quadratic deviation, is usually of slower order $n^{-r}, 0 < r < 1/2$. The subject of this section is to shed some light on the dependence of this rate r on four important qualitative features of regression smoothing,

(S) the *Smoothness* of m;

(D) the *Dimension* d of X;

(O) the *Object* $m^{(k)}$, the kth derivative of m, that is to be estimated;

(T) the *Type* of estimator that is used.

Other distance measures, for example, the uniform deviation $d_{L_\infty}(\hat{m}, m)$, depend also on these four characteristics of regression smoothing but might have a slightly different rate. Consider for the moment just the mean integrated squared error $d_M(\hat{m}, m)$ for which we would like to analyze the speed of convergence. Let b_n be a sequence of positive constants. It is called a *lower rate of convergence* if for some $c > 0$ and $n \geq n_0$

$$\inf_{\hat{m}} \sup_{m \in \mathcal{M}} d_M(\hat{m}, m) \geq c b_n^2.$$

Here the $\inf_{\hat{m}}$ denotes the infimum over all possible estimators $\hat{m}$ of m and the $\sup_{m \in \mathcal{M}}$ denotes the supremum over a class of functions $\mathcal{M}$ with certain smoothness properties. A *lower* rate of convergence b_n is thus a sequence of constants that tends to zero *faster* than any smoother

$\hat{m}$ converges to m in a uniform sense. The sequence is said to be an *achievable rate of convergence* if there is an estimator $\hat{m}$ and a $C > 0$ such that for $n \geq n_0$

$$\sup_{m \in \mathcal{M}} d_M(\hat{m}, m) \leq C b_n^2.$$

An *achievable* rate of convergence is thus a sequence that tends to zero *slower* than a specific smoother converges to the true regression function. An *optimal rate of convergence* is a rate that is both a *lower* and an *achievable* rate of convergence. A consequence of these definitions is that if b_n is a lower rate of convergence and b_n' is an achievable rate of convergence, the sequence b_n must tend to zero faster than b_n' in the sense that $b_n' \geq c_1 b_n$ for some $c_1 > 0$ and $n \geq n_0$. The notion of optimal rate of convergence is not unique since, with an optimal rate b_n, $b_n(1 + o(1))$ also is optimal. Asymptotically, optimal rates of convergence differ by only a constant, so it makes sense to call *any* optimal rate of convergence *the* optimal rate of convergence. A smoother $\hat{m}$ that achieves the optimal rate is called *asymptotically optimal.*

So far the concept of optimal rates of convergence has been defined through the mean integrated squared error (MISE) d_M. It turns out that for kernel estimators one could equally well have stated the concept of optimal rates with the integrated squared error d_I or some other distance measure, such as d_A; see Härdle (1986b). Asymptotically they define distance measures of equal sharpness, as is shown in the following theorem by Marron and Härdle (1986, theorem 3.4).

Theorem 4.1.1   Assume that
(A1) $E(Y^k|X = x) \leq C_k < \infty$, $k = 1, 2, \ldots$;
(A2) $f(x)$ is Hölder continuous and is positive on the support of w;
(A3) K is Hölder continuous.
   Then for kernel estimators

$$\sup_{h \in H_n} |d_A(h) - d_M(h)| / d_M(h) \to 0 \quad a.s.,$$

$$\sup_{h \in H_n} |d_I(h) - d_M(h)| / d_M(h) \to 0 \quad a.s.,$$

where $H_n = [n^{\delta - 1/d}, n^{-\delta}]$, $0 < \delta < 1/(2d)$ and $d_\bullet(h)$ is short for $d_\bullet(\hat{m}_h, m)$.

   The optimal global rates of convergence for nonparametric regression were derived for the case $d = 1$ by Ibragimov and Hasminskii (1980) and for the multidimensional case by Stone (1982), Nussbaum (1985) and Nemirovskii, Polyak and Tsybakov (1985). Nemirovskii et al. (1985) gave very general results on the optimal rates of convergence including the setup with an L_p loss function. Stone (1982) derived optimal global rates of convergence using d_I among other distance measures. The following theorem is the immediate consequence of Stone's (1982) theorem 1. To formulate it I need some notation. Let $\mathcal{M} = \mathcal{M}_{p,\beta}$ be the smoothness class of all p-times differentiable functions m on the real line such that the pth derivative is Hölder continuous with exponent β

$$|m^{(p)}(u) - m^{(p)}(v)| \leq L_\beta |u - v|^\beta,$$

where $0 < \beta \leq 1$.

Theorem 4.1.2   Suppose that

(A1) $w(x)$ is the indicator function of the compact set $\mathcal{X}$;

(A2)   the conditional distribution of Y given $X = x$ is normal with variance $\sigma^2(x)$;

(A3)   the conditional variance $\sigma^2(x)$ is bounded from above as well as bounded from zero on some compact set $\mathcal{X}' \subset \mathcal{X}$;

(A4)   the marginal density $f(x)$ is bounded away from zero on $\mathcal{X}'$;

(S) $m(x)$ is in smoothness class $\mathcal{M}_{p,\beta}$;

(D) X is one-dimensional;

(O) $m^{(k)}$, $k \leq p$, is to be estimated.

Then the lower rate of convergence is n^{-r} with

$$r = \frac{p + \beta - k}{2(p + \beta) + 1}. \tag{4.1.1}$$

Stone (1982) proved that under the assumptions of this theorem the rate n^{-r} with r as in (4.1.1) is also achievable in some weaker sense than defined earlier. He also showed that for a suitable generalization of $\mathcal{M}_{p,\beta}$ the optimal rate in this weaker sense is n^{-r} with

$$r = \frac{p + \beta - k}{2(p + \beta) + d}, \tag{4.1.2}$$

with d denoting the dimension of X. Ibgragimov and Hasminskii (1980), Nussbaum (1985) and Nemirovskii et al. (1985) proved that this rate is achievable under the equispaced design (or nearly equispaced design). The achievability for the one-dimensional case will become evident from the calculations given in this section and in Section 4.5. Pointwise convergence rates are analogous and were derived by Stone (1980).

Note that the optimal rate tends to zero faster if the regression curve has more derivatives existing. The optimal rate tends to zero slower if the X-variable is of higher dimension or if higher order derivatives $m^{(k)}$ of m are to be estimated.

Kernel estimators are asymptotically optimal if the bandwidth sequence and the kernel function are suitably chosen. Consider the fixed design model in which the data are taken at $X_i = i/n$ and $Y_i = m(X_i) + \varepsilon_i$, where ε_i is normal with variance σ^2. Suppose that m is four-times differentiable and it is desired to estimate the second derivative $m^{(2)}(x)$.

Theorem 4.1.2 says that for this estimation problem ($p = 4, k = 2, d = 1$) the best rate of convergence can only be $n^{-4/9}$. If this rate is also achievable it is optimal. In particular, $n^{-4/9}$ is a lower rate of convergence. (Recall the definition of optimal rate of convergence.) I shall show that the rate $n^{-4/9}$ is achievable over $\mathcal{M}_{4,0}$ for a certain kernel.

Take the Priestley–Chao kernel estimate with weight sequence $\{W_{hi}^{(2)}\}$:

$$m_h^{(2)}(x) = n^{-1}h^{-3} \sum_{i=1}^{n} K^{(2)}\left(\frac{x - X_i}{h}\right) Y_i, \qquad (4.1.3)$$

where $K^{(2)}$ denotes the second derivative of a symmetric kernel function. It is not hard to derive that (see the Complements of this section and of Section 3.1),

$$\text{var}\{m_h^{(2)}(x)\} = O(n^{-1}h^{-5})$$

$$\text{bias}^2\{m_h^{(2)}(x)\} = O\left(\int (m^{(4)}(x))^2 w(x)dx \; h^4\right), \qquad (4.1.4)$$

as $h \to 0, nh^5 \to \infty$. So if the bandwidth is set at $h \sim n^{-1/9}$,

$$\sup_{m \in \mathcal{M}_{4,0}} d_M(\hat{m}_h^{(2)}, m^{(2)}) \le Cn^{-4/9}$$

for some $C > 0$ and for $n \ge n_0$. Thus $n^{-4/9}$ is by definition an achievable rate of convergence.

Note that if h is chosen different from $n^{-1/9}$, in this example the kernel estimator will not achieve the optimal rate. To illustrate this, consider a bandwidth sequence $h = n^{-1/9+\delta}$ with δ positive or negative. If $\delta > 0$ then the squared bias component of $d_M(\hat{m}_h^{(2)}, m^{(2)})$ dominates and $d_M \approx n^{-4/9}(n^{4\delta})$. If $\delta < 0$ then the variance component of $d_M(\hat{m}_h^{(2)}, m^{(2)})$ dominates and $d_M \approx n^{-4/9}(n^{-5\delta})$. In any case, the rate of convergence is slower than the optimal rate $n^{-4/9}$.

This example shows that it is very important to tune the smoothing parameter h to the right speed to balance bias^2 and variance. In Section 5.1 it will be seen how data-driven bandwidths can be constructed which automatically achieve the correct rate of convergence, giving asymptotically optimal estimates. This might seem to be somewhat at odds with the merits of the nonparametric smoothing approach. One motivates nonparametric regression estimation by a desire to assume less about the structure of m than in a parametric framework, but in order to construct optimal estimators one seems to need the very specific assumption that higher derivatives up to certain order exist. A way out of this dilemma is presented in Section 5.1 where it is seen that the smoothing parameter can, in fact, be adapted to the degree of smoothness of m without prior knowledge of the degree of differentiability of m.

On the other hand, the aim to achieve the optimal rate over a specific smoothness class should not be taken too literally, since in a practical situation the number $n^{-r_1}, r_1 = p_1/(2p_1 + 1)$, will not be much different from $n^{-r_2}, r_2 = p_2/(2p_2 + 1)$. Suppose that $p_1 = 16$. Even if we double the degree of differentiability to achieve a better rate of convergence, the relative improvement, n^{-r_2}/n^{-r_1}, for a sample size of $n = 100$ is only 3.5 percent.

Note that there are kernel smoothers of the form (4.1.3) which do not achieve the optimal rate of $n^{-4/9}$. This addresses the fourth characteristic (T) of regression smoothing: The type of estimator has to be selected in a reasonable way in order to achieve the optimal rate. Suppose that we had taken an asymmetric kernel in (4.1.3) which did not fulfill the orthogonality condition $\int u\,K(u)du = 0$. A little calculus and integration by parts yields

$$\text{bias}\{\hat{m}_h^{(2)}(x)\} = \int K_h\,(x - u)\,[m^{(2)}(x) - m^{(2)}(u)]\,du$$

$$+ O(n^{-1}h^{-1}) + o(h) \qquad (4.1.5)$$

$$\approx hm^{(3)}(x) \int uK(u)du, \ h \to 0, \ nh \to \infty,$$

which converges more slowly than h^2, the order of bias for symmetric kernels.

Rates of convergence for nonquadratic distance measures

More general distance measures of the form

$$d_{L_\nu}\,(\hat{m}, m) = \left[\int |\hat{m}(x) - m(x)|^\nu\,w(x)dx\right]^{1/\nu}, \quad \nu \geq 1,$$

have also been considered in the literature (Prakasa Rao 1983, p. 244). The distance for $\nu = \infty$ is defined, as usual, as the uniform maximal deviation

$$\sup_{x \in \mathcal{X}} |\hat{m}(x) - m(x)|.$$

As with quadratic distance measures one can define an optimal rate of convergence. Stone proved that, with r as in Theorem 4.1.2, n^{-r} is the optimal rate of convergence for d_{L_ν}, if $1 \leq \nu < \infty$. If $\nu = \infty$, the optimal rate is $n^{-r}(\log n)^r$. The uniform maximal deviation thus converges slightly slower to zero. In the Complements of this section I show that under some weak conditions

$$\sup_{x \in \mathcal{X}} |\hat{m}(x) - m(x)| = O_p(\max\{(nh/(\log n))^{-1/2}, h\}). \qquad (4.1.6)$$

This result was also obtained by Mack and Silverman (1982, section 3). If the bandwidth sequence is chosen as $h = h_n = O((n/\log n)^{-1/3})$ one has the rate $O_p((n/\log n)^{-1/3})$ in (4.1.5) which is the optimal rate (4.1.2) for $p = 1, k = 0, d = 1$ and $\nu = \infty$. In Härdle, Janssen and Serfling (1988) this was shown to be an achievable rate of convergence not only for estimation of m but also for other smooth functionals of the conditional distribution function. Such functionals include the nonparametric scale curve (see also Section 6.2) and trimmed L-smoothers or M-smoothers (Section 6.1).

Exercises

4.1.1 From the discussion after Theorem 4.1.2 we have seen that the type of estimator has to be adapted as well to achieve the optimal rate of convergence. Consider now the fixed design setting and $m \in C^4$ and a positive kernel weight sequence. Such a kernel smoother cannot achieve the optimal rate which is

$$n^{-((2\cdot 4)/(2\cdot 4+1))}.$$

Why? Which rate is achieved instead?
[*Hint:* Compute the bias as in Section 3.1.]

4.1.2 Conduct a small Monte Carlo study in which you compare the distances d_{L_∞} and d_M for the same bandwidth. Do you observe the slower rate of convergence for d_{L_∞}?

4.1.3 Describe the qualitative differences of the accuracy measures d_{L_∞} and d_M.
[*Hint:* Consider a situation where the smooth curve contains a wild single spike or wiggles around the true curve with a small variation.]

4.1.4 Give exact arguments for (4.1.4) in the fixed design setting.
[*Hint*: Look up the paper by Gasser and Müller (1984).]

4.1.5 Compute the optimal bandwidth that minimizes the first two dominant terms of MISE. Interpret the constants occurring in this asymptotically optimal bandwidth. When will h tend to be large? When would you expect h to be small?

4.1.6 Compute the bandwidth that balances the stochastic and the bias term for the supremum distance. Is it going faster or slower to zero than the MSE optimal bandwidth?
[*Hint*: The stochastic term is of order $O_p((nh)^{-1/2}(\log n)^{1/2})$ as is shown in the complements. The systematic bias term is as seen above of the order $O(h^2)$ for $m \in C^2$.]

Complements

To have some insight into why the d_{L_∞} rate has this additional log term consider the one-dimensional case $d = 1$. We have to estimate the following probability.

$$P\{\sup_{x\in\mathcal{X}} |\hat{m}(x) - m(x)| > \delta\, b_n\}$$

$$= P\{\sup_{l=1,\dots,M_n} \sup_{|x-x_l|\leq\eta_n} |\hat{m}(x) - m(x)| > \delta\, b_n\}$$

$$\leq P\left\{\sup_{l=1,\dots,M_n} |\hat{m}(x_l) - m(x_l)| > \frac{\delta}{2}\, b_n\right\}$$

$$+ \sup_{l=1,\dots,M_n} P\left\{\left|\sup_{|x-x_l|\leq\eta_n} |\hat{m}(x) - m(x) - (\hat{m}(x_l) - m(x_l))\right| > \frac{\delta}{2}\, b_n\right\},$$

where the M_n intervals $\{x : |x - x_l| \leq \eta_n\}$ cover the compact set of interest $\mathcal{X}$. If η_n is chosen small enough, then the second term is negligible compared to the first one. The first term can be estimated via the Bonferroni inequality, so it remains to bound the following

$$\sum_{l=1}^{M_n} P\left\{|\hat{m}(x_l) - m(x_l)| > \frac{\delta}{2}b_n\right\}$$

$$\leq M_n \sup_{l=1,\dots,M_n} P\left\{|\hat{m}(x_l) - m(x_l)| > \frac{\delta}{2}b_n\right\}.$$

Suppose now that $\hat{m}$ is the kernel estimator, $d = 1, X_i = i/n$ and m is Lipschitz continuous, that is, $p = 1$. Then

$$|\hat{m}(x_l) - m(x_l)| \leq |E(\hat{m}(x_l)) - m(x_l)|$$
$$+ |\hat{m}(x_l) - E(\hat{m}(x_l))|$$
$$= O(h) + \left| n^{-1} \sum_{i=1}^{n} K_h(x_l - X_i)\varepsilon_i \right|.$$

Choosing $h = Cb_n$, where $C > 0$ is some small constant, we get

$$P\left\{ |\hat{m}(x_l) - m(x_l)| > \frac{\delta}{2} b_n \right\},$$

$$\leq P\left\{ \left| n^{-1} \sum_{i=1}^{n} K_h(x_l - X_i)\varepsilon_i \right| > \frac{\delta}{4} b_n \right\}.$$

If we assume that the errors are bounded and $|K(u)| \leq 1$ then we can estimate the last probability using Bernstein's inequality (Uspensky 1937).

$$P\left\{ \left| n^{-1} \sum_{i=1}^{n} K_h(x_l - X_i)\varepsilon_i \right| > \frac{\delta}{4} b_n \right\}$$

$$\leq 2 \exp\left(\frac{-n(\frac{\delta b_n}{4})^2}{2\sigma_n^2 + \frac{2}{3h}(\frac{\delta b_n}{4})} \right),$$

where

$$\sigma_n = E[h^{-2} K^2(x_l - X_i)] = O(h^{-1}).$$

It is easily seen now that if

$$b_n \sim n^{-1/3} \log n^{1/3}$$

then for $M_n = O(n)$ the term

$$M_n \cdot \sup_{l=1,\ldots,M_n} P\left\{ |\hat{m}(x_l) - m(x_l)| > \frac{\delta}{2} b_n \right\}$$

tends to zero as $\delta \to \infty$. This means that $b_n \sup_{x \in \mathcal{X}} |\hat{m}(x_l) - m(x_l)|$ is bounded in probability, that is,

$$\sup_{x \in \mathcal{X}} |\hat{m}(x_l) - m(x_l)| = O_p(n^{-1/3} \log n^{1/3}).$$

4.2   Pointwise confidence intervals

The aim of this section is to develop the construction of pointwise confidence intervals for kernel estimators and to prepare the ground for the uniform confidence bands which are treated in the next section. The basic idea is to derive the asymptotic distribution of the kernel smoothers and then to use either asymptotic quantiles or bootstrap approximations for these quantiles for the confidence intervals. The shrinkage rate of the confidence intervals is proportional to n^{-r}, the optimal rate of convergence if the bandwidth is chosen so that the optimal rate is achieved. It is certainly desirable to use smoothers that are asymptotically optimal since they give the narrowest confidence intervals obtainable and keep the squared bias and variance at the same order.

The reader more interested in practical aspects should not be discouraged by the rather theoretical beginning of this section, but instead should jump to Algorithm 4.2.1, which describes the construction of confidence intervals at k different points.

The asymptotic distribution is normal. The center of this distribution is shifted by the asymptotic bias which depends on derivatives of the regression curve and the marginal density of X. The asymptotic variance is a function of

the conditional variance $\sigma^2(x)$;

the kernel K; and

the marginal density $f(x)$.

The asymptotic bias is a function of

the kernel K; and

derivatives of m and f.

Before I come to the theoretical statement of the asymptotic distribution of kernel smoothers let me point out some simplifications. The kernel smoother $\hat{m}_h(x)$ is a ratio of random variables; direct central limit theorems therefore cannot be applied and the smoother has to be linearized. The kernel estimator has the same limit distribution as the right-hand side of the following linearization,

$$\hat{m}_h(x) - m(x) \approx \frac{\hat{r}_h(x) - m(x)\hat{f}(x)}{f(x)},$$

where

$$\hat{r}_h = n^{-1} \sum_{i=1}^{n} K_h(x - X_i) Y_i$$

denotes, as in Section 3.1, the numerator of the Nadaraya–Watson kernel smoother. The following theorem states the asymptotic distribution of the Nadaraya–Watson kernel estimator for one-dimensional predictor variables.

Theorem 4.2.1 Suppose that

(A1) $\int |K(u)|^{2+\eta} \, du < \infty$ for some $\eta > 0$;

(A2) $h \sim n^{-1/5}$;

(A3) m and f are twice differentiable;

(A4)   the distinct points $x_1, x_2, \ldots, x_k$ are continuity points of $\sigma^2(x)$ and $E\{|Y|^{2+\eta} \mid X = x\}$ and $f(x_j) > 0$, $j = 1, 2, \ldots, k$.

Then the suitably normalized Nadaraya–Watson kernel smoother $\hat{m}_h(x_j)$ at the k different locations $x_1, \ldots, x_k$ converges in distribution to a multivariate normal random vector with mean vector B and identity covariance matrix,

$$\left((nh)^{1/2} \left\{ \frac{(\hat{m}_h(x_j) - m(x_j))}{(\sigma^2(x_j) c_K / f(x_j))^{1/2}} \right\} \right)_{j=1}^{k} \xrightarrow{\mathcal{L}} N(B, I), \qquad (4.2.1)$$

where

$$B = \left(d_K \{ m''(x_j) + 2m'(x_j)(f'(x_j)/f(x_j)) \} \right)_{j=1}^{k}. \qquad (4.2.2)$$

The proof is given in the Complements extending results of Johnston (1979) and of Schuster (1972). The proof is based on the linearization given above.

The asymptotic bias (4.2.2) is proportional to the second moment of the kernel and a measure of local curvature of m. This measure of local curvature is not a function of m alone but also of the marginal density. At maxima or minima, the bias is a multiple of $m''(x)$ alone; at deflection points it is just a multiple of only $m'(x)(f'(x)/f(x))$.

This theorem can be used to define confidence intervals. Suppose that the bias is of negligible magnitude compared to the variance; then the following algorithm yields approximate confidence intervals.

Algorithm 4.2.1

STEP 1.

Compute the kernel smoother $\hat{m}_h$ and the density estimate $\hat{f}_h$ at distinct points $x_1, \ldots, x_k$.

STEP 2.

Construct an estimate of $\sigma^2(x)$,

$$\hat{\sigma}^2(x) = n^{-1} \sum_{i=1}^{n} W_{hi}(x)(Y_i - \hat{m}_h(x))^2,$$

$$W_{hi} = K_h(x - X_i)/\hat{f}_h(x).$$

STEP 3.

Take c_α, the $(100 - \alpha)$-quantile of the normal distribution, and let

$$CLO = \hat{m}_h(x) - c_\alpha c_K^{1/2} \hat{\sigma}(x)/(nh\hat{f}_h(x))^{1/2},$$
$$CUP = \hat{m}_h(x) + c_\alpha c_K^{1/2} \hat{\sigma}(x)/(nh\hat{f}_h(x))^{1/2}.$$

STEP 4.

Draw the interval $[CLO, CUP]$ around $\hat{m}_h(x)$ at the k distinct points $x_1, \ldots, x_k$.

This algorithm does not take the bias of $\hat{m}_h(x)$ into account, since the bias is a complicated function of m and f. Bias estimates could be built in by using estimates of the derivatives of m and f but would considerably complicate the algorithm. So if the bandwidth $h \sim n^{-1/5}$ then the above steps do not lead asymptotically to an exact confidence interval. However, if h is chosen proportional to $n^{-1/5}$ times a sequence that tends slowly to zero, then the bias vanishes asymptotically.

If the variation in m and f is moderate, little difference is to be expected between such two sequences of bandwidths, so one could use the unshifted confidence intervals as well. However, at small peaks (high bias!) it may be desirable to shift the $[CLO, CUP]$ interval by a bias estimate. The decision of the occurrence of such peaks has to be made by the statistician. The analysis of expenditure data is a field where we do not expect sudden and abrupt changes of $m(x)$. In Figure 4.1 an estimate of the regression curve for the potato versus net income example (Figure 1.1) is shown together with ten pointwise confidence intervals.

It is apparent from this picture that the confidence interval lengths increase as they move to the right boundary of the observation interval. Since the kernel is a fixed function, this must be due to the other factors controlling the variance of the kernel smoother. First, it is the conditional variance $\sigma^2(x)$ which increases as x goes to the right boundary (compare with Figure 1.1). Second, the inverse of the marginal X-distribution enters as a proportionality factor. Since the data are more sparse near the right boundary (compare with Figure 1.5), the variance estimate also gets inflated for this reason. A plot of $\hat{\sigma}(x)$, an estimate of the conditional standard deviation curve $\sigma(x)$, is presented in Figure 4.2.

As a possible way of visualizing both effects in one plot, I propose plotting confidence intervals at points x_j such that the number of observations between x_j and x_{j+1} is constant. As the marginal density

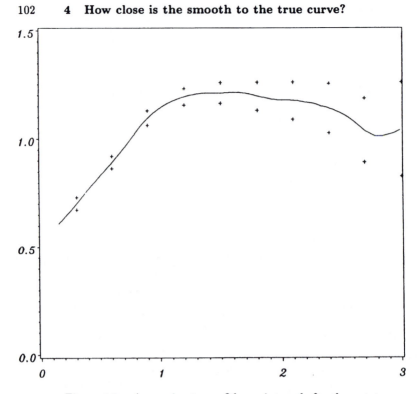

Figure 4.1.   Approximate confidence intervals for the potato versus net income data. 95 percent confidence intervals are shown for the kernel smoother $\hat{m}_h(x)$, $h = 0.6$, $n = 7125$, Epanechnikov kernel. The vertical axis is normalized by the mean expenditure. The horizontal axis is normalized by the mean net income for that year. Family Expenditure Survey (1973).

decreases, the Euclidean distance between neighboring points x_j will become bigger. This can be seen from Figure 4.3, which shows a kernel smooth ($h = 0.6$, Epanechnikov kernel) of the potato versus net income data together with confidence intervals. These intervals are placed such that in between successive intervals there are a fixed number of 700 data points.

There are always 700 observations between neighboring gridpoints x_j. In this plot, one not only sees an increase of the variance but also a decrease of the marginal density $f(x)$. This becomes apparent at the right boundary: The peak to the right of the approximate confidence interval at $x \approx 1.9$ is produced by less than fifty observations.

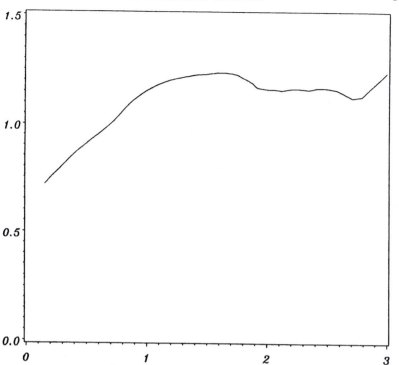

Figure 4.2. Conditional standard deviation curve for the potato versus net income data. The curve shown is

$$\hat{\sigma}(x) = (n^{-1} \sum_{i=1}^{n} W_{hi}(x)(Y_i - \hat{m}_h(x))^2)^{1/2},$$

$n = 7125$, $h = 0.6$ an estimate of $\sigma(x)$. Family Expenditure Survey (1968–1981).

Another method of constructing confidence bands is based on the bootstrap. The bootstrap is a resampling technique that prescribes taking "bootstrap samples" using the same random mechanism that generated the data. This prescription makes it necessary to handle the case of stochastic Xs differently from the case of deterministic X-values. To be precise, in the fixed design model the stochastic part of the data is contained only in the observation errors, so resampling should take place from residuals. If both X and Y are random, resampling can be done from the data pairs $\{(X_i, Y_i)\}_{i=1}^{n}$ according to the following algorithm.

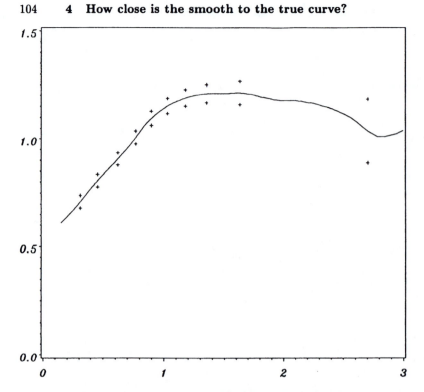

Figure 4.3.   Approximate confidence intervals for the potato versus net income data. 95 percent confidence intervals are shown for the kernel smoother $\hat{m}_h(x)$, $h = 0.6$, $n = 7125$, Epanechnikov kernel. The confidence intervals are placed such that the number of observations between successive intervals equals 700. The vertical axis is normalized by the mean expenditure. The horizontal axis is normalized by the mean net income for that year. Family expenditure Survey (1973).

Algorithm 4.2.2

b=0

REPEAT

b=b+1

STEP 1.

Sample $\{(X_i^*, Y_i^*)\}_{i=1}^n$ from the empirical distribution function of the data.

STEP 2.

Construct the kernel smoother $\hat{m}_h^*(x)$ from the bootstrap sample $\{(X_i^*, Y_i^*)\}_{i=1}^n$.

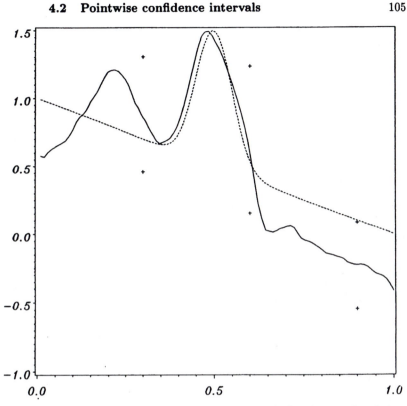

Figure 4.4.   Bootstrap confidence intervals for the simulated data set, Table 3.6.1.   The kernel smoother $\hat{m}_h(x)$, $h = 0.1$, $n = 100$, $B = 100$ with Epanechnikov kernel has been applied.

UNTIL b=B=number of bootstrap samples.
STEP 3.
Define CLO^* as the $\alpha/2$ empirical quantile of the B bootstrap estimates $\hat{m}_h^*(x)$. Define CUP^* analogously.
STEP 4.
Draw the interval $[CLO^*, CUP^*]$ around $\hat{m}_h(x)$ at the k-distinct points $x_1, \ldots, x_k$.

This bootstrap algorithm was proposed by McDonald (1982) in his Orion workstation film. Theoretical properties of this so-called *naive bootstrap* have been considered by Dikta (1988), again by disregarding bias terms. The above bootstrap procedure was applied with $B = 100$ to the simulated data set of Table 3.6.1. The result is depicted in Figure 4.4.

The kernel smooth for Figure 4.4 was computed with the Epanechnikov kernel $(K(u) = (3/4)(1 - u^2)I(|u| \leq 1))$ and bandwidth $h = 0.1$. Note that this bandwidth is bigger than the one chosen to produce the kernel smooth of Figure 3.21 but the curve from Figure 4.2 is smoother than that of Figure 3.21. The reason for this is the use of different kernels. A possible means of comparing these bandwidths is presented in Section 5.4.

In the case of the fixed design models with homoscedastic error structure one may use only the estimated residuals

$$\hat{\varepsilon}_i = Y_i - \hat{m}_h(X_i).$$

Resampling them as $\{\varepsilon_i^*\}_{i=1}^n$ gives bootstrap observations $Y_i^* = \hat{m}_h(x_i) + \varepsilon_i^*$. Of course, this makes sense only if the error distribution does not depend on x. If this is the case one constructs bootstrap smoothers $\hat{m}_h^*(x)$ and studies the distribution of $\hat{m}_h^*(x)$ suitably centered around $\hat{m}_h(x)$. Details of this procedure are given in Section 5.3.

This bootstrap from residuals can also be applied in the stochastic design setting. It is then able also to incorporate the bias term and is called *wild bootstrap* by Härdle and Mammen (1988). It is called *wild*, since at each observation point X_i (in the fixed or stochastic design setting) a bootstrap observation is drawn from *one* single estimated residual. This is done to better retain the conditional distributional characteristics of the estimate. It is not resampled from the entire set of residuals, as in Härdle and Bowman (1988).

A different possibility would be to resample from a set of residuals determined by a window function, but this has the disadvantage of requiring choice of the window width. To avoid this I propose wild bootstrapping, where each bootstrap residual is drawn from the two-point distribution which has mean zero, variance equal to the square of the residual, and third moment equal to the cube of the residual.

In particular, let

$$\hat{\varepsilon}_i = Y_i - \hat{m}_h(X_i)$$

be the observed residual at point X_i. Now define a new random variable ε_i^* having a two-point distribution $\hat{G}_i$, where

$$\hat{G}_i = \gamma \delta_a + (1 - \gamma)\delta_b \tag{4.2.3}$$

is defined through the three parameters a, b, γ, and where δ_a, δ_b denote point measures at a, b, respectively. Some algebra reveals that the parameters a, b, γ at each location X_i are given by

$$a = \hat{\varepsilon}_i(1 - \sqrt{5})/2,$$

$$b = \hat{\varepsilon}_i(1 + \sqrt{5})/2, \tag{4.2.4}$$
$$\gamma = (5 + \sqrt{5})/10.$$

These parameters ensure that $E\varepsilon^* = 0$, $E\varepsilon^{*2} = \hat{\varepsilon}_i^2$ and $E\varepsilon^{*3} = \hat{\varepsilon}_i^3$. A geometrical interpretation of these parameters is related to the Golden Section method by Euclid (–300, Second book, prop. 11), see Exercise 4.2.5. In a certain sense the resampling distribution $\hat{G}_i$ can be thought of as attempting to reconstruct the distribution of each residual through the use of one single observation. Therefore, it is called the wild bootstrap. It is actually the cumulative effect of all these residuals though that make this bootstrap work. After resampling, new observations

$$Y_i^* = \hat{m}_g(X_i) + \varepsilon_i^*$$

are defined, where $\hat{m}_g(x)$ is a kernel estimator with bandwidth g taken to be larger than h (a heuristic explanation of why it is essential to oversmooth g is given below).

Then the kernel smoother is applied to the bootstrapped data $\{(X_i, Y_i^*)\}_{i=1}^n$ using bandwidth h. Let $\hat{m}_h^*(x)$ denote this kernel smooth. A number of replications of $\hat{m}_h^*(x)$ can be used as the basis for a confidence interval because the distribution of $\hat{m}_h(x) - m(x)$ is approximated by the distribution of $\hat{m}_h^*(x) - \hat{m}_g(x)$, as Theorem 4.2.2 shows. Here the symbol $Y \mid X$ is used to denote the conditional distribution of $Y_1, \ldots, Y_n \mid X_1, \ldots, X_n$, and the symbol $*$ is used to denote the bootstrap distribution of $Y_1^*, \ldots, Y_n^* \mid (X_1, Y_1), \ldots, (X_n, Y_n)$.

Theorem 4.2.2   Given the assumptions of Theorem 4.2.1, along almost all sample sequences and for all $z \in \mathbb{R}$

$$|P^{Y|X}\{\sqrt{nh^d}[\hat{m}_h(x) - m(x)] < z\}$$
$$- P^*\{\sqrt{nh^d}[\hat{m}_h^*(x) - \hat{m}_g(x)] < z\}| \to 0.$$

For an intuitive understanding of why the bandwidth g used in the construction of the bootstrap residuals should be oversmoothed, consider the means of $\hat{m}_h(x) - m(x)$ under the $Y|X$-distribution and $\hat{m}_h^*(x) - \hat{m}_g(x)$ under the $*$-distribution in the simple situation when the marginal density $f(x)$ is constant in a neighborhood of x. Asymptotic analysis as in Rosenblatt (1969) shows that

$$E^{Y|X}(\hat{m}_h(x) - m(x)) \approx h^2 d_K m''(x)/2,$$
$$E^*(\hat{m}_h^*(x) - \hat{m}_g(x)) \approx h^2 d_K \hat{m}_g''(x)/2.$$

Hence for these two distributions to have the same bias one needs $\hat{m}_g''(x) \to m''(x)$. This requires choosing g tending to zero at a rate slower than the *optimal bandwidth* h (see Section 4.1) for estimating $m(x)$.

The advantage of the bootstrapping technique is that one does not have to compute various complicated constants, such as the bias described in Theorem 4.2.1. Algorithm 4.2.3 is thus easy to program but requires quite a bit of computer intensive resampling. This computational burden can be made easier by employing a discretization technique (WARPing) or an FFT-based approach as described in Section 3.1.

Algorithm 4.2.3

> b=0
> REPEAT
> b=b+1
> STEP 1.
> Sample ε_i^* from the two-point distribution $\hat{G}_i$ (4.2.3), where
>
> $$\hat{G}_i = \gamma \delta_a + (1-\gamma)\delta_b$$
>
> and as in (4.2.4)
>
> $a = \hat{\varepsilon}_i(1-\sqrt{5})/2,$
> $b = \hat{\varepsilon}_i(1+\sqrt{5})/2,$
> $\gamma = (5+\sqrt{5})/10.$
>
> STEP 2.
> Construct new observations
>
> $$Y_i^* = \hat{m}_g(X_i) + \varepsilon_i^*,$$
>
> where $\hat{m}_g(x)$ is a slightly oversmoothed kernel estimator with bandwidth g. Compute $\hat{m}_h^*(x)$ from the bootstrap sample $\{(X_i, Y_i^*)\}_{i=1}^n$.
> UNTIL b=B=number of bootstrap samples.
> STEP 3.
> Define CLO^* as the $\alpha/2$ empirical quantile of the B bootstrap estimates $\hat{m}_h^*(x)$. Define CUP^* analogously.
> STEP 4.
> Draw the interval $[CLO^*, CUP^*]$ around $\hat{m}_h(x)$ at the k-distinct points $x_1, \ldots, x_k$.

Exercises

4.2.1 Show that the difference between

$$\hat{m}_h(x) - m(x)$$

and its linearization

$$\frac{\hat{r}_h(x) - m(x)\hat{f}(x)}{f(x)}$$

is of order $o_p((nh)^{-1/2})$ under the assumptions of Theorem 4.2.1.
[*Hint*: Write the difference as

$$\left(\frac{\hat{r} - m\hat{f}}{f} \right)\left(\frac{f}{\hat{f}} - 1 \right)$$

and combine terms.]

4.2.2 Prove formula (4.2.2), that is, show that

$$nh \operatorname{var}\{H_n(x)\} \to (f(x))^{-1}\sigma^2(x) \int K^2(u)du;$$

$$n \operatorname{cov}\{H_n(x)\,H_n(y)\} \to 0, \quad \text{as } n \to \infty.$$

4.2.3 Write an efficient program for wild bootstrapping using the WARPing technique as described in Section 3.1.

4.2.4 Use the wild bootstrap confidence intervals in a real example. Compare them with the asymptotic confidence intervals from Theorem 4.2.1.

4.2.5 Ricardo Cao has found that the wild bootstrap is related to the Golden Section method of Euclid (−300). Show that the two-point distribution of the wild bootstrap can be found by using the outer Golden Section of the interval $E = [0, |\hat{\varepsilon}_i|]$.
[*Hint*: The outer Golden Section E' is that interval containing E such that the ratio of the length of E' to the length of E is the same as the ratio of the length of E to that of $E' - E$.]

Complements

Define $\hat{r}_h(x) = \hat{m}_h(x)\hat{f}_h(x) = n^{-1}\sum_{i=1}^{n} K_h(x - X_i)Y_i$. The difference between

$$\hat{m}_h(x) - m(x)$$

and its linearization

$$\frac{\hat{r}_h - m\hat{f}}{f}(x)$$

is of lower order, that is, of order $o_p((nh)^{-1/2})$, see Exercise 4.2.1.
The bias can then be written as

$$\frac{E\hat{r}_h - mE\hat{f}}{f}(x).$$

This term equals

$$\left(\frac{E\hat{f}}{f}(x)\right)\left(\frac{E\hat{r}_h}{E\hat{f}} - m\right)(x),$$

which is approximately equal to

$$m_n(x) - m(x),$$

where $m_n(x) = E\hat{r}_h(x)/E\hat{f}_h(x)$. Observe that

$$m_n(x) - m(x)$$

$$= (E\{K_h(x - X)\})^{-1}\left\{\int K_h(x - u)m(u)f(u)du - m(x)f(x)\right.$$

$$\left. + m(x)f(x) - m(x)\int K_h(x - u)f(u)du\right\} \qquad (4.2.5)$$

$$\approx \frac{h^2}{2}\int u^2 K(u)du(f(x))^{-1}((mf)''(x) - m(x)f''(x))$$

$$= \frac{h^2}{2}\int u^2 K(u)du\{m''(x) + 2m'(x)(f'(x)/f(x))\}.$$

Note that

$$\hat{m}_h - m_n = [\hat{r}_h/f - (\hat{f}_h/f)m_n](f/\hat{f}_h)$$

and $f(x)/\hat{f}_h(x) \xrightarrow{P} 1$, so that $\hat{m}_h(x) - m_n(x)$ will have the same asymptotic distribution as the term within square brackets above. Call this term $H_n(x)$. It can be shown in a straightforward but tedious way that if $x \neq y$

$$nh\,\text{var}\{H_n(x)\} \to (f(x))^{-1}\sigma^2(x)\int K^2(u)du;$$

$$n\,\text{cov}\{H_n(x)\,H_n(y)\} \to 0, \quad \text{as } n \to \infty. \qquad (4.2.6)$$

An application of the Cramer–Wold device (Serfling 1980, p. 18) then yields the asymptotic normality of the random vector

$$\left((nh)^{1/2}\left\{\frac{(\hat{m}_h(x_j) - m(x_j))}{(\sigma^2(x_j)c_K/f(x_j))^{1/2}}\right\}\right)_{j=1}^k.$$

4.3   Variability bands for functions

Variability bands for functions are intervals $[CLO(x), CUP(x)]$ (based on the sample $\{(X_i, Y_i)\}_{i=1}^n$) such that with probability $1 - \alpha$ the true curve is covered by the band $[CLO(x), CUP(x)]$, that is,

$$P\{CLO(x) \leq m(x) \leq CUP(x) \text{ for all } x \in \mathcal{X}\} = 1 - \alpha,$$

(4.3.1)

where x ranges over some (compact) set $\mathcal{X}$ of interest. Even in parametric models such bands are hard to compute; see Working and Hotelling (1929) or Wynn (1984) for bounds in polynomial regression. In the more complicated nonparametric situation useful bands $[CLO(\cdot), CUP(\cdot)]$ have been computed, which are conservative, that is, with equality replaced by "$\geq$" in (4.3.1). The bands are usually of the form

$$\begin{aligned} CLO(x) &= \hat{m}_h(x) - \hat{b}_n(x) - c_\alpha \hat{D}_n(x), \\ CUP(x) &= \hat{m}_h(x) + \hat{b}_n(x) + c_\alpha \hat{D}_n(x), \end{aligned}$$

(4.3.2)

where $\hat{b}_n(x)$ denotes an estimate of bias (mostly zero in parametric models) and $\hat{D}_n(x)$ is a measure of dispersion and c_α is the quantile to achieve level α confidence bands.

There are several approaches to computing upper and lower bands, $CUP(\cdot)$ and $CLO(\cdot)$. One approach is to use pointwise confidence intervals on a very fine grid of the observation interval. The level of these confidence intervals can be adjusted by the Bonferroni method in order to obtain uniform confidence bands. The gaps between the grid points can be bridged via smoothness conditions on the regression curve.

Another approach is to consider $\hat{m}_h(x) - m(x)$ as a stochastic process (in x) and then to derive asymptotic Gaussian approximations to that process. The extreme value theory of Gaussian processes yields the level of these confidence bands.

A third approach is based on the bootstrap. By resampling one attempts to approximate the distribution of

$$Z_n = \sup_{x \in \mathcal{X}} |\hat{m}_h(x) - m(x)|,$$

which yields $CLO(\cdot)$ and $CUP(\cdot)$ as bands computed from the $(\alpha/2)$- and $(1 - \alpha/2)$-quantiles of Z_n, respectively. Another bootstrap method is based on approximating the distribution of $\hat{m}_h(x) - m(x)$ at distinct points x and then to simultaneously correct the pointwise confidence intervals in order to obtain the joint coverage probability $1 - \alpha$.

Connected error bars

The approach by Hall and Titterington (1986b) is based on the discretization method, that is, constructing simultaneous error bars at different locations. They considered a fixed design regression model on the unit interval, that is,

$$Y_i = m(X_i) + \varepsilon_i,$$

where $X_i = i/n$ and the observation errors are normal with mean zero and variance σ^2. Take the Priestley–Chao-type kernel estimator with weight sequence

$$W_{hi}^{(2)}(x) = K_h(x - X_i),$$

and uniform kernel K. Their construction works as follows.

Divide the region of interest into M cells, the jth cell containing those observations (X_i, Y_i) such that

$$(j-1)q \le i \le jq, \ 1 \le j \le M.$$

The kernel estimator with uniform kernel for the M cells can be written as

$$\hat{m}_h(x_j) = (nh)^{-1} \sum_{i=(j-1)nh}^{jnh-1} Y_i, \tag{4.3.3}$$

where x_j is in block j and the bandwidth is chosen so that $q = nh$. The expected value of $\hat{m}_h(x_j)$ is

$$\mu_j = q^{-1}(m(q(j-1)/n) + m(q(j-1)/n + 1/n)$$
$$+ \cdots + m(q(j-1)/n + (q-1)/n))$$

and the variance is σ^2/q. The variability bands are computed from simultaneous intervals for the μ_js, with

$$P\{\hat{\mu}_j^L \le \mu_j \le \hat{\mu}_j^U, 1 \le j \le M\} = \alpha. \tag{4.3.4}$$

The gap between adjacent cells is handled through the smoothness of m. Assume that the first derivative of the regression function in adjacent cells is bounded by constants c_j, that is,

$$\sup_{(j-1)h \le u \le (j+1)h} |m'(u)| \le c_j, \ 1 \le j \le M. \tag{4.3.5}$$

For x in the jth cell the difference between $m(x)$ and μ_j can then be bounded by

$$V_j(\eta) = (1/2)((2\eta + 1)h + 1/n)c_j, \ 0 < \eta < 1.$$

This motivates defining the upper and lower confidence bands in a fixed cell j by

$$CUP((j + \eta)h) = \hat{\mu}_j^U + V_j(\eta), \ 0 < \eta < 1;$$
$$CLO((j + \eta)h) = \hat{\mu}_j^L - V_j(\eta), \ 0 < \eta < 1.$$

It remains to construct the simultaneous confidence intervals $\hat{\mu}_j^L$ and $\hat{\mu}_j^U$. Suppose first that the error variance σ^2 is known. Let Φ denote the standard normal distribution function, and c_γ denote the solution of $2\Phi(c_\gamma) - 1 = \gamma$. Define

$$\hat{\mu}_j^U = \hat{m}_h(x) + (nh)^{-1/2}\sigma c_\gamma,$$
$$\hat{\mu}_j^L = \hat{m}_h(x) - (nh)^{-1/2}\sigma c_\gamma$$

for x in the jth cell. Note that $\hat{m}_h(x)$ is normal with variance $(nh)^{-1}\sigma^2$ and mean μ_j. Then

$$P\{\hat{\mu}_j^L \leq \mu_j \leq \hat{\mu}_j^U, 1 \leq j \leq M\} = \gamma^M. \tag{4.3.6}$$

Taking $\gamma = \alpha^{1/M}$ will give simultaneous coverage probability α.

If the error variance is not known, Hall and Titterington (1986b) recommend constructing an estimate of σ^2 using differences of observations, that is

$$\hat{\sigma}^2 = (2n)^{-1} \sum_{i=2}^{n} (Y_i - Y_{i-1})^2.$$

Algorithm 4.3.1

Define the M cells and compute the kernel estimator as in (4.3.3).

STEP 1.

Define

$$\hat{\mu}_l^L = \hat{m}_h(x_l) - (nh)^{-1/2}\hat{\sigma}c_\gamma$$

and

$$\hat{\mu}_l^U = \hat{m}_h(x_l) + (nh)^{-1/2}\hat{\sigma}c_\gamma,$$

where $2\Phi(c_\gamma) - 1 = \gamma$, $\gamma^M = \alpha$.

STEP 2.

Let the bound of variation be

$$V_l(\eta) = (1/2)((2\eta + 1)h + 1/n)c_l, \quad 0 < \eta < 1,$$

where c_l the upper bound on $m'(x)$ as in (4.3.5).

STEP 3.

Define as in (4.3.6)

$$CUP((l + \eta)h) = \hat{\mu}_l^U + V_l(\eta), \quad 0 < \eta < 1;$$
$$CLO((l + \eta)h) = \hat{\mu}_l^L - V_l(\eta), \quad 0 < \eta < 1.$$

STEP 4.

Draw $CLO(\cdot)$ and $CUP(\cdot)$ around $\hat{m}_h(x_i)$.

The band $[CLO(x), CUP(x)]$ is a level α uniform confidence band for m as was shown by Hall and Titterington (1986b). The discretization method was also employed by Knafl, Sacks and Ylvisaker (1985) and Knafl et al. (1984).

Figure 4.5 gives an example of a uniform confidence band for the radiocarbon data set (Suess 1980). The variables are those of radiocarbon age and tree-ring age, both measured in years before 1950 A.D. and preprocessed so as to achieve equal spacing of the tree-ring ages. For more background on this calibration problem see Scott, Baxter and Aitchison (1984). Altogether, 180 points were included. Hall and Titterington have chosen $M = 30$ so that $q = 6$. The bands are constructed with $\alpha = 0.05$ and under the assumption of a single derivative with uniform bound $c = 1$ on $m'(x)$.

A different approach to handling the fluctuation of $m(x)$ in between the grid points could be based on the arc length of $m(x)$ between two successive knot points. Adrian Bowman suggested that instead of bounding derivatives of m, one could assume an upper bound on the arc length,

$$\int_{X_i}^{X_{i+1}} \sqrt{1 + (m'(x))^2} dx,$$

between two grid points X_i, X_{i+1}. In this case the gaps between mesh points are bridged by *a chain of ellipse shells* with the two foci in the endpoints of neighboring confidence intervals.

Smooth confidence bands

It was shown in Theorem 4.2.1 that the suitably scaled kernel smoother $\hat{m}_h(x)$ has an asymptotic normal distribution,

$$\sqrt{nh}(\hat{m}_h(x) - m(x)) \overset{\mathcal{L}}{\to} N(B(x), V(x)), \tag{4.3.7}$$

where $B(x)$ denotes the bias term and $V(x)$ is the asymptotic variance (depending on the kernel K and the bandwidth). More generally, consider now the left-hand side of (4.3.7) as a stochastic process in x. If this process converges in a suitable way to a Gaussian process $G(x)$ with known covariance structure, then a uniform confidence band can be constructed from the distribution of $\sup_x |G(x)|$. This latter distribution is well studied in extreme value theory of Gaussian processes.

In the setting of nonparametric regression use of this approach was made by Johnston (1982) for the kernel weights (with known marginal density f)

$$W_{hi}^{(1)}(x) = K_h(x - X_i)/f(X_i).$$

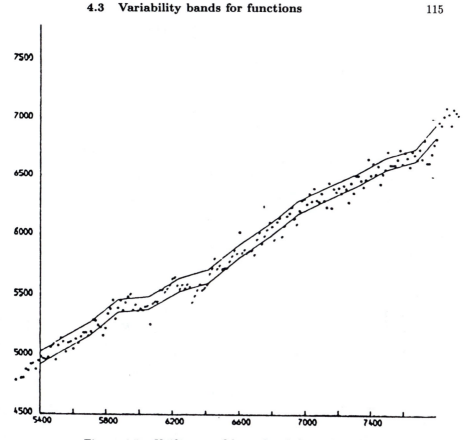

Figure 4.5. Uniform confidence band for radiocarbon band data (Suess 1980). The uniform confidence band is constructed with bandwidth $h = 15$. From Hall and Titterington (1986b).

Major (1973) used this method to find variability bands for the regressogram. Liero (1982) and Härdle (1987b) extended Johnston's results by allowing $W_{hi}(x)$ to be of the Nadaraya–Watson form.

The basic idea of the approach taken by these authors is to standardize the process $\sqrt{nh}[\hat{m}_h(x) - m(x)]$ and to approximate it by a suitable Gaussian process. More precisely, Johnston (1982) has shown that a suitably rescaled version of

$$\sqrt{nh}[\hat{m}_h(x) - m(x)]$$

has approximately the same distribution as the stationary Gaussian process

$$G(x) = \int K(x - u)dW(u), \tag{4.3.8}$$

with covariance function $\int K(x)K(u - x)dx$ and standard Wiener process $W(x)$. For a definition of a Wiener process see, for instance, Serfling (1980 p. 41). Bickel and Rosenblatt (1973) derived the asymptotic distribution of the supremum $\sup_x |G(x)|$ of the process (4.3.8). This result permits construction of approximate confidence bands.

Theorem 4.3.1   Define

$$\hat{\sigma}_h^2(x) = n^{-1} \sum_{i=1}^{n} K_h(x - X_i)Y_i^2/\hat{f}_h(x) - \hat{m}_h^2(x).$$

Suppose that $\mathcal{X} = [0,1]$ and
(A1) $m(x), f(x)$ and $\sigma^2(x)$ are twice differentiable;
(A2) K is a differentiable kernel with bounded support $[-A, A]$;
(A3) $E(|Y|^k |X = x) < C_k$, $k = 1, 2, \ldots$;
(A4) $f(\cdot)$ is strictly positive on $\mathcal{X}$;
(A5) $h = n^{-\delta}$, $1/5 < \delta < 1/3$.
*   Then the maximal deviation between $\hat{m}_h(x)$ and $m(x)$ over $\mathcal{X}$ has the limiting distribution*

$$P\left\{ (2\delta \log n)^{1/2} \left(\left(\frac{nh}{c_K}\right)^{1/2} \sup_{x \in \mathcal{X}} \left(\frac{\hat{f}_h(x)}{\hat{\sigma}_h^2(x)}\right)^{1/2} \right.\right.$$

$$\left.\left. \times |\hat{m}_h(x) - m(x)| - d_n \right) < z \right\} \to \exp(-2\exp(-z)), \ n \to \infty.$$

Here

$$d_n = (2\delta \log n)^{1/2} + \frac{1}{(2\delta \log n)^{1/2}} \{\log C_1 \pi^{-1/2}$$

$$+ (1/2) \log(\log n^\delta)\},$$

where

$$C_1 = \frac{K^2(A) + K^2(-A)}{2c_K}$$

if $C_1 > 0$, and otherwise

$$d_n = (2\delta \log n)^{1/2} + \frac{1}{(2\delta \log n)^{1/2}} \left\{ \log \left(\frac{C_2}{2\pi^2} \right)^{1/2} \right\},$$

where

$$C_2 = \frac{\int (K'(x))^2 dx}{2c_K}.$$

From this theorem one can obtain approximate confidence bands for m. Take the quartic kernel $K(u) = (15/16)(1 - u^2)^2 I(|u| \le 1)$, for instance. For this kernel $c_K = 5/7$ and it vanishes at the boundary of its support $[-1, 1]$, so $C_1 = 0$ in the Theorem 4.3.1. The following algorithm is designed for the quartic kernel.

Algorithm 4.3.2

    STEP 1.

    Define from $c_K = 5/7$ and $C_2 = (15/7)/(2c_K)$

$$d_n = (2 \log 1/h)^{1/2} + (2 \log 1/h)^{-1/2} \log \left(\frac{C_2}{2\pi^2} \right)^{1/2},$$

$$CLO(x) = \hat{m}_h(x) - [c_\alpha/(2 \log(1/h))^{1/2} + d_n]$$
$$\times [\hat{\sigma}_h^2(x)/(\hat{f}_h(x)nh)]^{1/2}/c_K$$

    and $CUP(x)$ analogously, where c_α is such that

    $\exp(-2 \exp(-c_\alpha)) = 1 - \alpha$.

    STEP 2.

    Plot the asymptotic confidence bands $CUP(x)$ and $CLO(x)$ around $\hat{m}_h(x)$.

Note that this theorem does not involve a bias correction as in Algorithm 4.3.1. The bias term is suppressed by assuming that the bandwidth h tends to zero slightly faster than the optimal rate $n^{-1/5}$. A bias term could be included, but it has the rather complicated form (4.2.2); see Theorem 4.2.1. A means of automatically correcting for the bias is presented subsequently in the wild bootstrapping algorithm.

Figure 4.6 shows an application of Algorithm 4.3.2, a uniform confidence band for the expenditure Engel curve for food with $1 - \alpha = 0.95$.

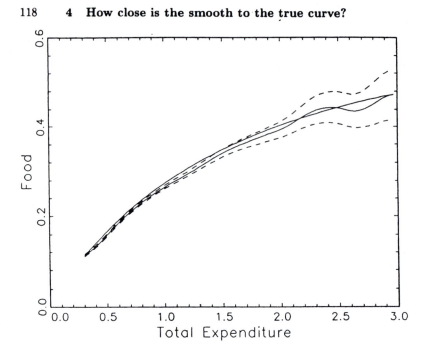

Figure 4.6.   Uniform confidence band for the food expenditure Engel curve for 1973. Shown is the kernel smooth $m_h(x)$, $h = 0.35$ (quartic kernel), and a parametric fit, a third-order polynomial through zero. Family Expenditure Survey (1968–1981).

Bootstrap bands

The idea of bootstrap bands is to approximate the distribution of

$$\sup_{x \in \mathcal{X}} |\hat{m}_h(x) - m(x)|$$

by the bootstrap technique. The following procedure proposed by Mc-Donald (1982) is based on the naive bootstrap. For this algorithm, unfortunately, no theoretical result is available.

Algorithm 4.3.3
>   b=0
>   REPEAT
>   b=b+1
>   STEP 1.
>   Sample $\{(X_i^*, Y_i^*)\}_{i=1}^n$ from the data $\{(X_i, Y_i)\}_{i=1}^n$.

STEP 2.

Construct a kernel smooth $\hat{m}_h^*(\cdot)$ from the bootstrap sample $\{(X_i^*, Y_i^*)\}_{i=1}^n$ and define $Z_b = \sup_{x \in \mathcal{X}} |\hat{m}_h^*(x) - \hat{m}_h(x)|$.

UNTIL b=B (=number of bootstrap samples).

STEP 3.

Define CLO^* as the $\alpha/2$ quantile of the B bootstrap deviations Z_b. By analogy, define CUP^* as the $1 - \alpha/2$ quantile.

STEP 4.

Draw the interval $[CLO^*, CUP^*]$ around every point x of the observation interval.

The above algorithm is extremely computer intensive since on a fine grid of points the statistic Z_b has to be computed B times. A computationally less intensive procedure is to consider not a band but rather a collection of error bars based on bootstrapping. This method is based on a pointwise bootstrap approximation to the distribution of $\hat{m}_h(x) - m(x)$. In the following I describe the approach taken by Härdle and Marron (1990), which uses the wild bootstrap technique to construct pointwise confidence intervals. How can these pointwise confidence intervals be modified in order to cover the true curve $m(x)$ with simultaneous coverage probability $1 - \alpha$?

A straightforward way of extending bootstrap pointwise intervals to M simultaneous confidence intervals is by applying the Bonferroni method. A drawback to the Bonferroni approach is that the resulting intervals will quite often be too long. The reason is that this method does not make use of the substantial positive correlation of the curve estimates at nearby points.

A more direct approach to finding simultaneous error bars is to consider the simultaneous coverage on pointwise error bars, and then adjust the pointwise level to give a simultaneous coverage probability of $1 - \alpha$. Fisher (1987, p. 394) called this a "confidence ribbon" since the pointwise confidence intervals are extended until they have the desired simultaneous coverage probability of $1 - \alpha$. A general framework, which includes both the Bonferroni and direct methods, can be formulated by thinking in terms of groups of grid points.

First, partition into M groups as in the Hall and Titterington approach, the set of locations where error bars are to be computed. Suppose the groups are indexed by $j = 1, \ldots, M$ and the locations within each group are denoted by $x_{j,k}, k = 1, \ldots, N_j$. The groups should be chosen so that for each j the $x_{j,k}$ values in each group are within $2h$ of each other. In the one-dimensional case this is easily accomplished by dividing the x-axis into intervals of length roughly $2h$.

In order to define a bootstrap procedure that takes advantage of this positive correlation consider a set of grid points $x_{j,k}$, $k = 1, \ldots, N_j$ that have the same asymptotic location c_k (not depending on n) relative to some reference point $x_{j,0}$ in each group j. Define

$$x_{j,k} = c_k h + x_{j,0}, \quad k = 1, \ldots, N_j.$$

In the multidimensional case, the simplest formulation is to have each group lying in a hypercube with length $2h$.

Now, within each group j use the wild bootstrap replications to approximate the joint distribution of

$$\{\hat{m}_h(x_{j,k}) - m(x_{j,k}) : k = 1, \ldots, N_j\}.$$

Recall Theorem 4.2.2 for the wild bootstrap approximation to this distribution. There it was shown that

$$\sqrt{nh}[\hat{m}_h(x) - m(x)]$$

and

$$\sqrt{nh}[\hat{m}_h^*(x) - \hat{m}_g(x)]$$

have the same limiting normal distribution. For each group j this joint distribution is used to obtain simultaneous $1 - \alpha/M$ error bars that are simultaneous over $k = 1, \ldots, N_j$ as follows. Let $\beta > 0$ denote a generic size for individual confidence intervals. The goal is to choose β so that the resulting simultaneous size is $1 - \alpha/M$.

For each $x_{j,k}$, $k = 1, \ldots, N_j$, define the interval $I_{j,k}(\beta)$ to have endpoints which are the $\beta/2$ and the $1 - \beta/2$ quantiles of the $(\hat{m}_g^*(x_{j,k}) - \hat{m}_g(x_{j,k}))$ distribution. Then define α_β to be the empirical *simultaneous* size of the β confidence intervals, that is, the proportion of curves which lie outside at least one of the intervals in the group j. Next find the value of β, denoted by β_j, which makes $\alpha_{\beta_j} = \alpha/M$. The resulting β_j intervals within each group j will then have confidence coefficient $1 - \alpha/M$. Hence, by the Bonferroni bound the entire collection of intervals $I_{j,k}(\beta_j)$, $k = 1, \ldots, N_j$, $j = 1, \ldots, M$, will simultaneously contain at least $1 - \alpha$ of the distribution of $\hat{m}_k^*(x_{j,k})$ about $\hat{m}_g(x_{j,k})$. Thus the intervals $I_{j,k}(\beta_j) - \hat{m}_g(x_{j,k}) + \hat{m}_h(x_{j,k})$ will be simultaneous confidence intervals with confidence coefficient at least $1 - \alpha$. The result of this process is summarized as the following theorem.

Theorem 4.3.2   Define M groups of locations $x_{j,k}$, $k = 1, \ldots, N_j$, $j = 1, \ldots, M$, where simultaneous error bars are to be established. Compute

*uniform confidence intervals for each group. Correct the significance
level across groups by the Bonferroni method. Then the bootstrap error
bars establish asymptotic simultaneous confidence intervals, that is,*

$$\lim_{n \to \infty} P\{m(x_{j,k}) \in I_{j,k}(\beta_j) - \hat{m}_g(x_{j,k}) + \hat{m}_h(x_{j,k}),$$

$$k = 1, \ldots, N_j, j = 1, \ldots, M, \} \geq 1 - \alpha.$$

As a practical method for finding β_j for each group j we suggest the
following "halving" approach. In particular, first try $\beta = \alpha/2M$, and
calculate α_β. If the result is more than α/M, then try $\beta = \alpha/4M$;
otherwise next try $\beta = 3\alpha/4M$. Continue this halving approach until
neighboring (since only finitely many bootstrap replications are made,
there is only a finite grid of possible βs available) values β_* and β^* are
found so that $\alpha_{\beta_*} < \alpha/M < \alpha_{\beta^*}$. Finally, take a weighted average of the
β_* and the β^* intervals where the weights are $(\alpha_{\beta^*} - \alpha/M)/(\alpha_{\beta^*} - \alpha_{\beta_*})$
and $(\alpha/M - \alpha_{\beta_*})/(\alpha_{\beta^*} - \alpha_{\beta_*})$, respectively.

Note that Theorem 4.3.2 contains, as a special case, the asymptotic
validity of both the Bonferroni and the direct simultaneous error bars.
Bonferroni is the special case $N_1 = \cdots = N_M = 1$, and the direct
method is where $M = 1$.

The wild bootstrap simultaneous error bars are constructed according
to the following algorithm.

Algorithm 4.3.4
        b=0
        REPEAT
        b=b+1
        STEP 1.
        Sample ε_i^* from the two-point distribution $\hat{G}_i$ (4.2.3), where

$\hat{G}_i = \gamma \delta_a + (1 - \gamma)\delta_b$

        STEP 2.
        Construct wild bootstrap observations

$Y_i^* = \hat{m}_g(X_i) + \varepsilon_i^*,$

        where $\hat{m}_g(x)$ is a slightly oversmoothed kernel estimator with
        bandwidth g. Compute $\hat{m}_h^*(x)$ at M different locations from the
        bootstrap sample $\{(X_i, Y_i^*)\}_{i=1}^n$.
        UNTIL b=B=number of bootstrap samples.
        STEP 3.
        Calculate $I_{j,k}(\beta_j)$ as follows.
        First try $\beta = \alpha/2M$, and calculate α_β.

If the result is more than α/M, then try $\beta = \alpha/4M$; otherwise next try $\beta = 3\alpha/4M$.

Continue this halving approach until neighboring values β_* and β^* are found so that $\alpha_{\beta_*} < \alpha/M < \alpha_{\beta^*}$.

Finally, take a weighted average of the β_* and the β^* intervals where the weights are

$$(\alpha_{\beta^*} - \alpha/M)/(\alpha_{\beta^*} - \alpha_{\beta_*})$$

and

$$(\alpha/M - \alpha_{\beta_*})/(\alpha_{\beta^*} - \alpha_{\beta_*}),$$

respectively.

Define

$$[CLO^*(x_{j,k}), CUP^*(x_{j,k})] = \hat{m}_h(x_{j,k}) - \hat{m}_g(x_{j,k}) + I_{j,k}(\beta_j).$$

STEP 4.

Draw the interval $[CLO^*, CUP^*]$ around $\hat{m}_h(x)$ at the M distinct points $x_1, \ldots, x_M$.

This wild bootstrap technique was applied to the potato versus net income example. Figure 4.7 displays the error bars for this data.

To study the practical difference between the various types of error bars, Härdle and Marron (1990) considered the distribution of $\hat{m}_h(x) - m(x)$ at a grid of x values for some specific examples. They chose the underlying curve to be of linear form, with an added bell shaped hump,

$$m(x) = x + 4e^{-2x^2}/\sqrt{2\pi}.$$

To see what this looks like, consider Figure 4.8. The solid curve in each part of Figure 4.8 is this $m(x)$.

The marginal distribution of X is $N(0,1)$, and the conditional distribution of $Y|X$ is $N(m(X), \sigma^2)$, for $\sigma = .3, .6, 1, 1.5$. For each of these four distributions 200 observations were generated. Figure 4.8 shows one realization from each of the four settings. Figure 4.8 also shows $\hat{m}_{h_0}(x)$, as calculated from the crosses, for each setting, together with a plot of the kernel function at the bottom, which shows the effective amount of local averaging being done in each case. The bandwidth for these is h_0, the optimal bandwidth as in Härdle and Marron (1985b), where the weight function $w(x)$ in that paper was taken to be the indicator function of $[-2, 2]$. As expected, more smoothing is required when the error variance is larger.

To study the differences among the various error bars, for each setting, 500 pseudo data sets were generated. Then kernel estimates were

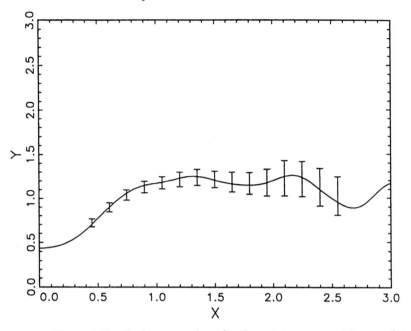

Figure 4.7.   Uniform error bars for the potato versus net income data
set for 1973. The solid line is the kernel smooth $m_h(x)$, $h = 0.35$
(quartic kernel). Family Expenditure Survey (1968–1981).

calculated, at the points $x = -2, -1.8, -1.6, \ldots, 1.8, 2$ using a standard
normal density as kernel. The bandwidth was chosen to be h_0. Figure 4.9
shows, for the $\sigma = 1$ distribution, $m(x)$ overlayed with error bars whose
endpoints are various types of quantiles of the distribution of $\hat{m}_h(x)$.
The centers of the error bars are at the means of these distributions,
and show clearly the bias that is inherent in nonparametric regression
estimation. Note, in particular, how substantial bias is caused by both
the curvature of $m(x)$ near the hump, and by the curvature of $f(x)$
near $x = -2, 2$. The bars in Figure 4.9a are 80% pointwise error bars.
In Figure 4.9b they are 80% simultaneous bars. In Figure 4.9c, the x
values were split up into the neighborhoods $\{-2, \ldots, -1\}$, $\{-.8, \ldots, 0\}$,
$\{.2, \ldots, 1\}$, $\{1.2, \ldots, 2\}$ and the neighborhood method of Theorem 4.3.2
was used. Figure 4.9d shows the completely Bonferroni 80% error bars.

For easy comparison of the lengths of these intervals, consider Figure
4.10. This shows, for the same x values, the lengths of the various bars
in Figure 4.9. Of course, these bars are shorter near the center, which
reflects the fact that there is more data there, so the estimates are more

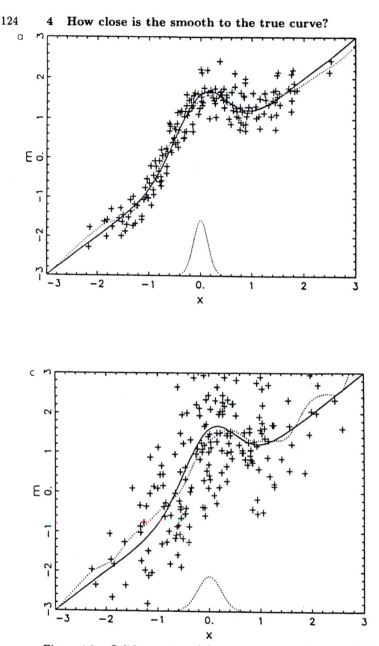

Figure 4.8. Solid curve is $m(x)$, crosses are a realization of $Y_1, \ldots,$ Y_{200} for (a) $\sigma = .3$, (b) $\sigma = .6$, (c) $\sigma = 1$, (d) $\sigma = 1.5$. Dotted curve is $\hat{m}_{h_0}(x)$; curve at bottom shows effective window width used by $\hat{m}_{h_0}(x)$. From Härdle and Marron (1990).

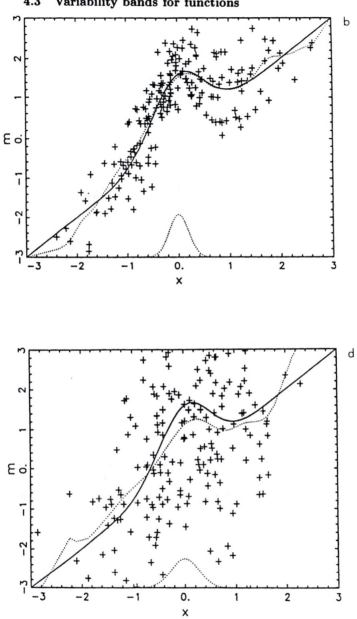

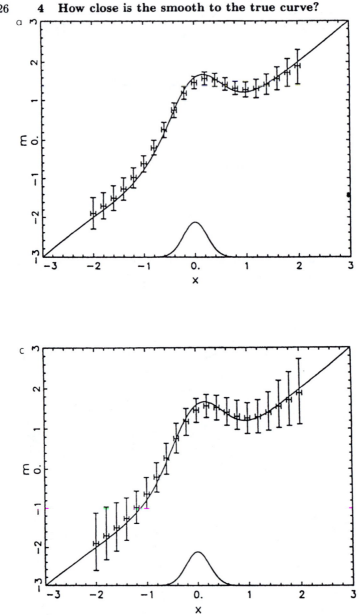

Figure 4.9.   Overlay of $m(x)$ with empirical (from 500 simulation runs) quantiles of $\hat{m}_{h_0}(x)$ distribution. Centers of bars are means of distributions. Error bars are (a) 80% pointwise, (b) 80% simultaneous, (c) 80% neighborhood, (d) 80% Bonferroni. From Härdle and Marron (1990).

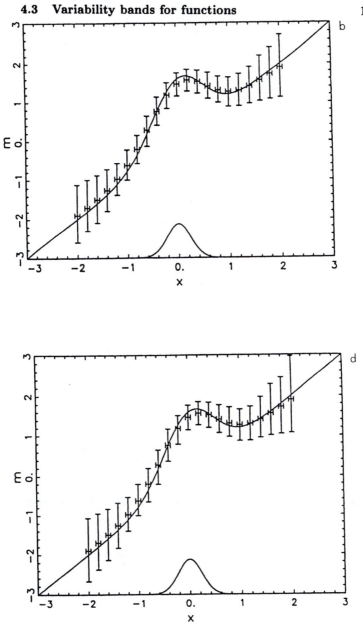

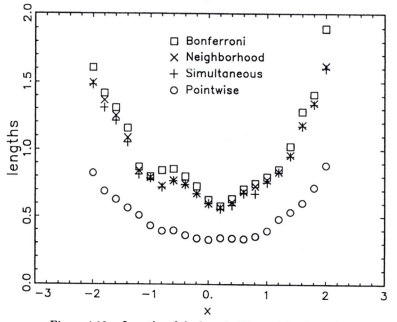

Figure 4.10.   Lengths of the bars in Figure 4.9, where the x locations are the same. From Härdle and Marron (1990).

accurate. As expected, the lengths increase from pointwise, to actual simultaneous, to neighborhood, to Bonferroni bars. Also note that, as stated above, the difference between the actual simultaneous bars and the neighborhood simultaneous bars is really quite small, whereas the pointwise bars are a lot narrower.

Exercises

4.3.1 Refine Algorithm 4.3.2 to allow a kernel with $K(A) > 0$.

4.3.2 Use the WARPing algorithm of Exercise 4.2.3 on the wild bootstrap smoothing to program Algorithm 4.3.4 for simultaneous error bars.

4.3.3 Compare the naive bootstrap bands with the wild bootstrap error bars. Where do you see the essential difference?
[*Hint*: Consider the bias of $\hat{m}_h(x)$.]

4.3.4 Use Algorithm 4.3.2 to find a smooth uniform confidence band for the motorcycle data set.

4.3.5 Could you translate Theorem 4.3.1 into the language of k-NN smoothing using the equivalence statements of Section 3.6?

Complements

An important issue is how to fine tune the choice of the pilot bandwidth g. Though it is true that the bootstrap works (in the sense of giving asymptotically correct coverage probabilities) with a rather crude choice of g, it is intuitively clear that specification of g will play a role in how well it works for finite samples. Since the main role of the pilot smooth is to provide a correct adjustment for the bias, we use the goal of bias estimation as a criterion. We think theoretical analysis of the above type will be more straightforward than allowing the N_j to increase, which provides further motivation for considering this general grouping framework.

In particular, recall that the bias in the estimation of $m(x)$ by $\hat{m}_h(x)$ is given by

$$b_h(x) = E^{Y|X}[\hat{m}_h(x)] - m(x).$$

The bootstrap bias of the estimator constructed from the resampled data is

$$\hat{b}_{h,g}(x) = E^*[\hat{m}_h^*(x)] - \hat{m}_g(x)$$

$$= n^{-1} \sum_{i=1}^{n} K_h(x - X_i)\hat{m}_g(X_i)/\hat{f}_h(x) - \hat{m}_g(x).$$

The following theorem gives an asymptotic representation of the mean square error for the problem of estimating $b_h(x)$ by $\hat{b}_{h,g}(x)$. It is then straightforward to find a g that minimizes this representation. Such a choice of g will make the means of the $Y|X$- and $*$-distributions close to each other.

Theorem 4.3.3   Under the conditions of Theorem 4.2.2, along almost all sample sequences,

$$E[(\hat{b}_{h,g}(x) - b_h(x))^2|X_1,\ldots,X_n] \sim h^4[C_1 n^{-1}g^{-5} + C_2 g^4],$$

in the sense that the ratio tends in probability to one, where

$$C_1 = \int (K'')^2 \frac{1}{2} d_K \sigma^2(x)/f(x),$$

$$C_2 = (\frac{1}{2} d_K)^4 [(mf)^{(4)} - (mf'')'']^2 (x)/f(x)^2.$$

An immediate consequence of Theorem 4.3.3 is that the rate of convergence of g for $d = 1$ should be $n^{-1/9}$. This makes precise the above intuition which indicated that g should be slightly oversmoothed. In addition, under these assumptions reasonable choices of h will be of the order $n^{-1/5}$. Hence, Theorem 4.3.3 shows once again that g should tend to zero more slowly than h. A proof of Theorem 4.3.3 is contained in Härdle and Marron (1990).

4.4   Behavior at the boundary

Near the boundary of the observation interval any smoothing method will become less accurate. At the boundary fewer observations can be averaged and thus variance or bias can be affected. Consider kernel weights; they become asymmetric as x approaches the boundary points. This "boundary effect" is not present for x in the interior of the observation interval, but for a small to moderate sample size, a significant proportion of the observation interval can be affected by the boundary behavior. Consider, for instance, the kernel smooth in Figure 3.2. The Gaussian kernel that has been used there is always truncated through boundary points. The whole observation interval is thus in a (strict) sense influenced by boundary effects. Note, however, that this kernel is effectively zero outside the range of three standard deviations, so a smaller proportion of the observations on each side are due to boundary effects.

In this section I describe the boundary effects and present a simple and effective solution to the boundary problem. This solution is due to Rice (1984b) and uses the (generalized) jackknifing technique. Boundary phenomena have also been discussed by Gasser and Müller (1979) and Müller (1984b) who proposed "boundary kernels" for use near the boundary. In the setting of spline smoothing Rice and Rosenblatt (1983) computed the boundary bias.

Consider the fixed design error model with kernels having support $[-1, 1]$. Take the kernel estimator

$$\hat{m}_h(x) = n^{-1} \sum_{i=1}^{n} K_h(x - X_i)\, Y_i,$$

which has expectation equal to (see Exercise 4.4.1)

$$\int_{(x-1)/h}^{x/h} K(u)\, m(x - uh)\, du + O(n^{-1}h^{-1}) \qquad (4.4.1)$$

as $nh \to \infty$. In the middle of the observation interval there is no problem since for h small, $x/h \geq 1$ and $(x-1)/h \leq -1$.

Now let $x = \rho h \leq 1-h$; then by a Taylor series expansion the expected value of $\hat{m}_h(x)$ can be approximated by

$$m(x) \int_{-1}^{\rho} K(u)\, du - hm'(x) \int_{-1}^{\rho} uK(u)\, du$$
$$+ \frac{1}{2} h^2 m''(x) \int_{-1}^{\rho} u^2 K(u)\, du$$
$$= m(x)\omega_K(0,\rho) - hm'(x)\omega_K(1,\rho)$$
$$+ \frac{1}{2} h^2 m''(x)\omega_K(2,\rho). \qquad (4.4.2)$$

Of course, if $\rho \geq 1$,

$$\omega_K(0,\rho) = 1,$$
$$\omega_K(1,\rho) = 0,$$
$$\omega_K(2,\rho) = d_K,$$

and we have the well-known bias expansion for the Priestley–Chao estimator. The idea of John Rice is to define a kernel depending on the relative location of x expressed through the parameter ρ.

Asymptotic unbiasedness is achieved for a kernel

$$K_\rho(\cdot) = K(\cdot)/\omega_K(0,\rho).$$

If x is away from the left boundary, that is, $\rho \geq 1$, then the approximate bias is given by the third term. If $\rho < 1$, the second term is of dominant order $O(h)$ and thus the bias is of lower order at the boundary than in the center of the interval.

The generalized jackknife technique (Gray and Schucany 1972) allows one to eliminate this lower order bias term. Let $\hat{m}_{h,\rho}(\cdot)$ be the kernel estimator with kernel K_ρ and let

$$\hat{m}_h^J(x) = (1 - R)\hat{m}_{h,\rho}(x) + R\hat{m}_{\alpha h,\rho}(x)$$

be the *jackknife estimator* of $m(x)$, a linear combination of kernel smoothers with bandwidth h and αh. From the bias expansion (4.4.2), the leading bias term of $\hat{m}_h^J(x)$ can be eliminated if

$$R = -\frac{\omega_K(1,\rho)/\omega_K(0,\rho)}{\alpha\omega_K(1,\rho/\alpha)/\omega_K(0,\rho/\alpha) - \omega_K(1,\rho)/\omega_K(0,\rho)}. \qquad (4.4.3)$$

This technique was also used by Bierens (1987) to reduce the bias inside the observation interval. In effect, the jackknife estimator is using the

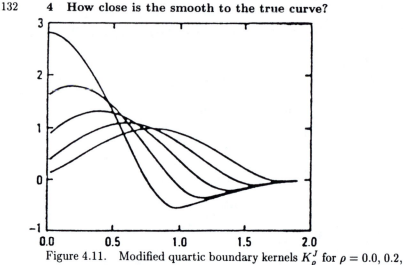

Figure 4.11. Modified quartic boundary kernels K_ρ^J for $\rho = 0.0, 0.2,$ 0.4, 0.6, 0.8. The symmetric kernel is the kernel K_1^J. From Rice (1984b) with permission of Marcel Dekker, Inc., New York.

kernel function

$$K_\rho^J(u) = (1 - R)K(u) - (R/\alpha)K(u/\alpha), \tag{4.4.4}$$

where R and α and thus K_ρ^J depend on ρ. In this sense, K_ρ^J can be interpreted as a "boundary kernel." Rice (1984b) has recommended the following for the choice of α:

$$\alpha = 2 - \rho.$$

As an example, take as the initial kernel the *quartic kernel*

$$K(u) = (15/16)(1 - u^2)^2 \, I(|u| \le 1). \tag{4.4.5}$$

The numbers $\omega_K(0, \rho)$, $\omega_K(1, \rho)$ can be computed explicitly. Figure 4.11 shows the sequence of boundary kernels K_ρ^J for $\rho = 0.1, 0.2, 0.4, 0.6, 0.8$. Note that the kernels have negative side lobes. Figure 4.12 shows the nonparametric estimate of the function $m(x) = x^2$ from $n = 15$ observations (Gaussian noise, $\sigma = 0.05$). The bandwidth h is 0.4; thus 60 percent of the observation interval is due to boundary effects.

Exercises

4.4.1 Compute the constants $\omega_K(0, \rho), \omega_K(1, \rho), \omega_K(2, \rho)$ from (4.4.2) for the quartic kernel. Construct an algorithm with bias correction at the boundary.

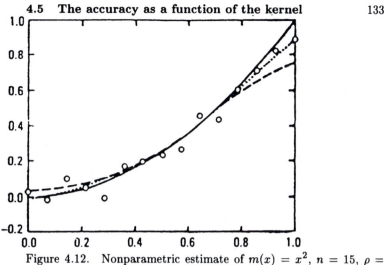

Figure 4.12.   Nonparametric estimate of $m(x) = x^2$, $n = 15$, $\rho = 0.05$, $h = 0.4$, quartic kernel. The solid line is the true function, the dotted line is the unmodified kernel estimate. From Rice (1984b) with permission of Marcel Dekker, Inc., New York.

[*Hint*: The system XploRe (1989) contains this algorithm for the triweight kernel.]

4.4.2 Prove formula (4.4.1) by comparing

$$E\hat{m}_h(x) = n^{-1} \sum_{i=1}^{n} K_h(x - X_i) m(X_i)$$

with

$$n^{-1} \sum_{i=1}^{n} \int_{\Delta_i} K_h(x - u) m(u) du,$$

where $\Delta_i = [X_{(i-1)}, X_{(i)}), X_0 = 0$.

4.5   The accuracy as a function of the kernel

The effective weight function $\{W_{hi}(x)\}$ of kernel smoothers is determined by the kernel K and the bandwidth sequence $h = h_n$. The accuracy of the estimated curve $\hat{m}_h(x)$ is not only a function of the bandwidth alone, but, more precisely, it is dependent upon the pair (K, h). In this section the behavior of quadratic distance measures is studied as a function of the kernel K. The variation of these distance measures as a function of the kernel can be uncoupled from the problem of finding a good smoothing parameter, as is shown in what follows. The bottom line of this section is that for practical problems the choice of the kernel is not so critical. The precision of $\hat{m}_h$ is more a question of the choice of bandwidth. Recall the asymptotic equivalence of the squared error distances as described in Theorem 4.1.1. Given this equivalence I concentrate on the behavior of MISE as a function of K.

In Section 3.1 we have seen that the MSE of $\hat{m}_h(x)$ can be written as

$$C_V c_K n^{-1} h^{-1} + C_B^2 d_K^2 h^4, \qquad (4.5.1)$$

where C_V, C_B are constants depending on the joint distribution of (X, Y). The bandwidth minimizing (4.5.1) is

$$h_0 = \left(\frac{C_V}{4C_B^2}\right)^{1/5} \left(\frac{c_K}{d_K^2}\right)^{1/5} n^{-1/5}. \qquad (4.5.2)$$

This smoothing parameter results in the following MSE

$$
\begin{aligned}
MSE_{\text{opt}} &= n^{-4/5} (4C_B^2)^{1/5} C_V^{4/5} c_K^{4/5} d_K^{2/5} \\
&\quad + n^{-4/5} (C_V/4)^{4/5} C_b^{2/5} c_K^{4/5} d_K^{2/5} \\
&= n^{-4/5} (C_V)^{4/5} C_B^{2/5} (4^{1/5} + 4^{-4/5}) c_K^{4/5} d_K^{2/5}.
\end{aligned}
$$

This minimal MSE depends on the kernel through the factor

$$V(K)B(K) = c_K^2 d_K = \left(\int K^2(u)du\right)^2 \int u^2 K(u)du. \qquad (4.5.3)$$

More generally, we can consider the case of estimating the kth derivative, $m^{(k)}$, of a p-times differentiable m. If we use derivative kernels, $K^{(k)}$, this functional then takes the form

$$V(K)B(K) = \left[\int_{-1}^{1} (K^{(k)}(u)^2 du\right]^{p-k} \left|\int_{-1}^{1} K^{(k)}(u)u^p du\right|^{2k+1}$$

How can this complicated expression be minimized as a function of K?

To answer this question note first that we have to standardize the kernel somehow since this functional of K is invariant under scale transformations

$$K^{(k)}(u) \rightarrow s^{-(k+1)} K^{(k)}(u/s). \qquad (4.5.4)$$

There are several approaches to this standardization question. Here I present the approach by Gasser, Müller and Mammitzsch (1985), who propose to set the support of K equal to $[-1, 1]$. A possible drawback of this standardization is that one can lose the feeling of what the bandwidth is really doing to the data. Consider, for instance, the kernel function

$$K(u) = C_\alpha (1 - u^2)^\alpha \, I(|u| \le 1),$$

Table 4.5.1   *Kernel functions minimizing $V(K)B(K)$*

k	p	kernel $K(u)$	
0	2	$(3/4)(-u^2 + 1)$	$I(|u| \le 1)$
0	4	$(15/32)(7u^4 - 10u^2 + 3)$	$I(|u| \le 1)$
1	3	$(15/4)(u^3 - u)$	$I(|u| \le 1)$
1	5	$(105/32)(-9u^5 + 14u^3 - 5u)$	$I(|u| \le 1)$
2	4	$(105/16)(-5u^4 + 6u^2 - 1)$	$I(|u| \le 1)$
2	6	$(315/64)(77u^6 - 135u^4 + 63u^2 - 5)$	$I(|u| \le 1)$

Source: Gasser, Müller and Mammitzsch (1985).

which has for all α support $[-1, 1]$. For large α the kernels become steeper and steeper and it becomes difficult to interpret the bandwidths as multiples of the support. In Section 5.4, when I discuss the canonical kernels of Marron and Nolan (1988), I come back to this standardization question.

Gasser, Müller and Mammitzsch (1985) used variational methods to minimize $V(K)B(K)$ with respect to K. The answers are polynomials of degree p. Some of these "optimal" kernels are presented in Table 4.5.1.

It is said that a kernel is *of order* (k, p) if it satisfies the following moment conditions:

$$\int_{-1}^{1} K(u)u^j \, du = 0, \quad j = 1, \ldots, p - k - 1;$$

$$= C_K(-1)^k \frac{(p - k)!}{k!}, \quad j = p - k.$$

Then $K^{(k)}$ satisfies

$$\int_{-1}^{1} K^{(k)}(u)u^j \, du = 0, \qquad j = 0, \ldots, k - 1, k + 1, \ldots, p - 1;$$

$$= (-1)^k k!, \quad j = k;$$

$$= C_K, \quad j = p.$$

The optimal kernels given in Table 4.5.1 are of order (k, p). Another important issue can be seen from Table 4.5.1: Derivatives of "optimal" kernels do not yield "optimal" kernels for estimation of derivatives, for example, the kernel for $(k, p) = (1, 3)$ is not the derivative of the one with $(k, p) = (0, 4)$. But note that the derivative of the latter kernel satisfies (4.5.3) with $(k, p) = (1, 3)$.

Figure 4.13 depicts two optimal kernels for $p = 2, 4$ and $k = 0$.

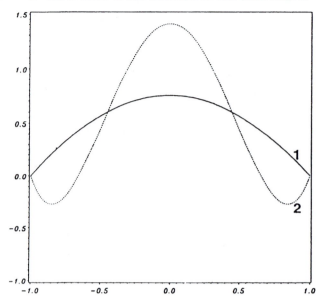

Figure 4.13. Two optimal kernels for estimating m (from Table 4.5.1). Label 1 (solid line): $(k, p) = (0, 2)$. Label 2 (dashed line): $(k, p) = (0, 4)$.

Note that the kernel with $p = 4$ has negative side lobes. The Epanechnikov kernel is "optimal" for estimating m when $p = 2$. The kernel functions estimating the first derivative must be odd functions by construction. A plot of two kernels for estimating the first derivative of m is given in Figure 4.14. The kernels for estimating second derivatives are even functions, as can be seen from Figure 4.15. A negative effect of using higher order kernels is that by construction they have negative side lobes. So a kernel smooth (computed with a higher order kernel) can be partly negative even though it is computed from purely positive response variables. Such an effect is particularly undesirable in demand theory, where kernel smooths are used to approximate statistical Engel curves; see Bierens (1987).

A natural question to ask is, how "suboptimal" are nonoptimal kernels, that is, by how much is the expression $V(K)B(K)$ increased for nonoptimal kernels? Table 4.5.2 lists some commonly used kernels (for $k = 0, p = 2$) and Figure 4.16 gives a graphical impression of these kernel. Their deficiencies with respect to the Epanechnikov kernel are defined as

$$D(K_{opt}, K) = [V(K_{opt})B(K_{opt})]^{-1}[V(K)B(K)].$$

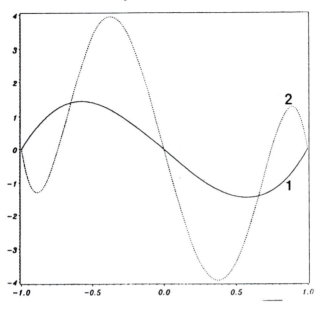

Figure 4.14.   Two optimal kernels for estimating m', the first derivative of m (from Table 4.5.1).   Label 1 (solid line): $(k, p) = (1, 3)$. Label 2 (dashed line): $(k, p) = (1, 5)$.

A picture of these kernels is given in Figure 4.16. The kernels really look different, but Table 4.5.2 tells us that their MISE behavior is almost the same.

The bottom line of Table 4.5.2 is that the choice between the various kernels on the basis of the mean squared error is not very important. If one misses the optimal bandwidth minimizing MISE (or some other measure of accuracy) by 10 percent there is a more drastic effect on the precision of the smoother than if one selects one of the "suboptimal" kernels. It is therefore perfectly legitimate to select a kernel function on the basis of other considerations, such as the computational efficiency (Silverman 1982; Härdle, 1987a).

Exercises

4.5.1 Verify the "small effect of choosing the wrong kernel" by a Monte Carlo study.   Choose

$$m(x) = \exp(-x^2/2), \varepsilon \sim N(0, 1), X \sim U(-1, 1), n = 100.$$

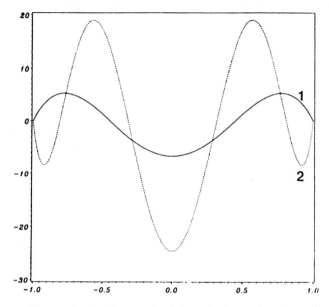

Figure 4.15. Two optimal kernels for estimating m'', the second derivative of m (from Table 4.5.1). Label 1 (solid line): $(k,p) = (2,4)$. Label 2 (dashed line): $(k,p) = (2,6)$.

Select as h the MSE optimal bandwidth for estimating $m(0)$. Compute the MSE at $x = 0$ for the different kernels over 10000 Monte Carlo experiments.

4.5.2 Compute $V(K)B(K)$ for the triweight kernel

$$K(u) = C_3(1 - u^2)^3 \, I(|u| \le 1).$$

Table 4.5.2   *Some kernels and their efficiencies*

Kernel	$K(u)$	$D(K_{\text{opt}}, K)$
Epanechnikov	$(3/4)(-u^2 + 1) \, I(|u| \le 1)$	1
Quartic	$(15/16)(1 - u^2)^2 \, I(|u| \le 1)$	1.005
Triangular	$(1 - |u|) \, I(|u| \le 1)$	1.011
Gauss	$(2\pi)^{-1/2} \exp(-u^2/2)$	1.041
Uniform	$(1/2) \, I(|u| \le 1)$	1.060

Note: The efficiency is computed as $\{V(K_{\text{opt}})B(K_{\text{opt}})/[V(K)B(K)]\}^{-1/2}$ for $k = 0$, $p = 2$.

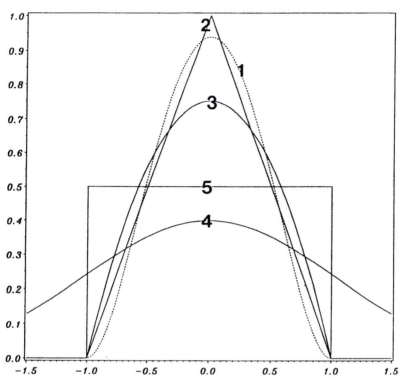

Figure 4.16.   Positive kernels for estimating m (from Table 4.5.2). Label 1: quartic; label 2: triangular; label 3: Epanechnikov; label 4: Gauss; label 5: uniform.

Insert the obtained efficiency loss into Table 4.5.2.

4.5.3 Prove that $V(K)B(K)$ as defined in (4.5.3) is invariant under the scale transformations (4.5.4).

4.5.4 A colleague has done the Monte Carlo study from Exercise 4.5.1 in the field of density smoothing. His setting was

$$f = \varphi, n = 100, x = 0$$

with a MSE optimal bandwidth h. From the 10,000 Monte Carlo runs he obtained the following table.

Do these numbers correspond to the values $D(K_{\text{opt}}, K)$ from Table 4.5.2?

Table 4.5.3   *Some kernels and their efficiencies*

Kernel	estimated MSE	95% confidence interval
Epanechnikov	0.002214	±0.000051
Quartic	0.002227	±0.000051
Triangular	0.002244	±0.000052
Gauss	0.002310	±0.000054
Uniform	0.002391	±0.000055

Note: The efficiency is computed as $\{[V(K_{opt})B(K_{opt})]/[V(K)B(K)]\}^{-1/2}$ for $k = 0$, $p = 2$.

Complements

I give a sketch of a proof for the optimality of the Epanechnikov kernel. First, we have to standardize the kernel since $V(K)B(K)$ is invariant under scale transformations. For reasons that become clear in Section 5.4, I use the standardization $V(K) = B(K)$. The task for optimizing $V(K)B(K)$ is then to minimize

$$\int K^2(u)du$$

under the constraints

(i) $\int K(u) = 1$,

(ii) $K(u) = K(-u)$,

(iii) $d_K = 1$.

If ΔK denotes a small variation for an extremum subject to the constraints (i)–(iii), the variation of

$$\int K^2(u)du + \lambda_1 \left[\int K(u)du - 1\right] + \lambda_2 \left[\int u^2 K(u)du - 1\right]$$

should be zero. This leads to

$$2\int K(u)\Delta K(u)du + \lambda_1 \left[\int \Delta K(u)du\right]$$
$$+ \lambda_2 \left[\int \Delta K(u)u^2\right] = 0.$$

Therefore,

$$2K(u) + \lambda_1 + \lambda_2 u^2 = 0.$$

The kernel $K(u)$ is zero at $u = \pm(-\lambda_1/\lambda_2)^{1/2}$. The answer is thus the Epanechnikov kernel if we determine λ_1, λ_2 from the constraints (i)–(iii). The above standardization of $c_K^2 = d_K$ gives then the rescaled version

$$K(u) = 3/(4 \cdot 15^{1/2})(1 - (u/15^{1/2})^2 I(|u/15^{1/2}| \leq 1)).$$

4.6   Bias reduction techniques

In this section we will see that the use of "higher order kernels" has the nice effect of reducing the bias. The kernels of Figure 4.13 are of higher order. The spline smoothing kernel (Figures 3.10, 3.11), for instance, is of order $(0, 4)$. (The order of a kernel was defined in the previous section.) Another technique for bias reduction is *jack-knifing*. I shall explain subsequently how jackknifing is related to higher order kernels and investigate the variance of higher order kernel smoothers.

Consider the fixed design model of equispaced and fixed $\{X_i = i/n\}$ on the unit interval. Suppose that it is desired to estimate the kth derivative $m^{(k)}$ of m. The kernel smoother for this problem is

$$\hat{m}_h^{(k)}(x) = n^{-1} h^{-(k+1)} \sum_{i=1}^{n} K^{(k)}\left(\frac{x - X_i}{h}\right) Y_i, \quad 0 < x < 1,$$

where $K^{(k)}$ is the kth derivative of a k-times differentiable kernel K for which it is required that

$$\text{support}(K) = [-1, 1];$$
$$K^{(j)}(1) = K^{(j)}(-1) = 0 \quad j = 0, \ldots, (k - 1).$$

Let m be p-times $(p \geq k + 2)$ differentiable and suppose that the kernel K is such that for some constant C_K

$$\int_{-1}^{1} K(u) u^j \, du = 0, \quad j = 1, \ldots, p - k - 1;$$

$$= C_K (-1)^k \frac{(p - k)!}{k!}, \quad j = p - k. \qquad (4.6.1)$$

Then $K^{(k)}$ satisfies

$$\int_{-1}^{1} K^{(k)}(u) u^j \, du = 0, \qquad j = 0, \ldots, k - 1, k + 1, \ldots, p - 1;$$

$$= (-1)^k k!, \qquad j = k;$$
$$= C_K, \qquad j = p.$$

$$(4.6.2)$$

The expectation of $\hat{m}_h^{(k)}(x)$ can be approximated as in (3.1.17) or (4.1.1) by

$$\int_{-1}^{1} K(u)m^{(k)}(x - uh)du \quad 0 < x < 1. \tag{4.6.3}$$

Expanding $m^{(k)}(x-uh)$ in a Taylor series around x one sees from (4.6.3) and (4.6.2) that with a kernel function satisfying (4.6.1) the bias of $\hat{m}_h^{(k)}(x)$ is, to first order, equal to

$$\frac{h^{(p-k)}}{p!} \left[\int_{-1}^{1} K^{(k)}(u)u^p \, du \right] m^{(p)}(x). \tag{4.6.4}$$

By increasing p, the degree of differentiability and the order of the kernel, one can make this quantity arbitrarily small. This technique is commonly called bias reduction through "higher order kernels."

Higher order kernel functions $K^{(k)}$ satisfy (4.6.3) with a large value of p (Müller 1984a; Sacks and Ylvisaker 1981). This means that $K^{(k)}$ has the first $(k-1)$ moments and then the $(k+1)$th up to the $(p-1)$th moment vanishing.

Since higher order kernels take on negative values the resulting estimates inherit this property. For instance, in the related field of density estimation, kernel smoothing with higher order kernels can result in negative density estimates. Also, in the setting of regression smoothing one should proceed cautiously when using higher order kernels. For example, in the expenditure data situation of Figure 2.3 the estimated expenditure Engel curve could take on negative values for a higher order kernel. For this reason, it is highly recommended to use a positive kernel even though one has to pay a price in bias increase.

It seems appropriate to remind the reader that "higher order" kernels reduce the bias in an asymptotic sense. Recall that when estimating m, the optimal rate of convergence (Section 4.1) for kernels with $p = 2$ is $n^{-2/5}$. If a kernel with $p = 4$ is used, then the optimal rate is $n^{-4/9}$. So using a "higher order" kernel results in a relatively small improvement $(2/45)$ in the order of magnitude of the best achievable squared error distance. For all except astronomical sample sizes this difference will become visible. Higher order kernels have other undesirable side effects as can be seen from the following discussion of the jackknifing approach.

Schucany and Sommers (1977) construct a jackknife kernel density estimator that yields a bias reducing kernel of higher order. The jackknife technique is also applicable for bias reduction in regression smoothing.

Consider the *jackknife estimate* (Härdle 1986a)

$$G(\hat{m}_{h_1}, \hat{m}_{h_2})(x) = (1 - R)^{-1}[\hat{m}_{h_1}(x) - R\hat{m}_{h_2}(x)],$$

where $R \neq 1$ is a constant. Here $\hat{m}_{h_l}(x)$ is a kernel smoother with bandwidth $h_l, l = 1, 2$. Suppose that the kernel K is of order 2, that is, satisfies (4.6.2) with $p = 2$ and the regression function is four-times differentiable. Then the bias term of the jackknife estimate $G(\hat{m}_{h_1}, \hat{m}_{h_2})$ can be expressed as:

$$(1 - R)^{-1} \sum_{j=1}^{2} [h_1^{2j} - Rh_2^{2j}]C_j(K)m^{(2j)}(x). \tag{4.6.5}$$

A good choice of R reduces this bias an order of magnitude. Define

$$R = h_1^2/h_2^2,$$

making the coefficient of $m^{(2)}(x)$ in (4.6.5) zero. Indeed, the bias of $G(\hat{m}_{h_1}, \hat{m}_{h_2})$ has been reduced compared with the bias of each single kernel smoother. Moreover, the jackknife estimator with this R, being a linear combination of kernel smoothers, can itself be defined by a kernel

$$K_{(c)}(u) = \frac{K(u) - c^3 K(cu)}{(1 - c^2)}$$

with

$$c = h_1/h_2 = \sqrt{R}.$$

Note that $K_{(c)}$ depends on n through c. The bias reduction by $K_{(c)}$ can also be seen by calculations as in Section 4.6: $K_{(c)}$ is indeed a "higher order" kernel satisfying (4.6.2) with $p = 4$ but is not optimal in the sense of minimizing $V(K)B(K)$. By l'Hospital's rule the limit of $K_{(c)}$ as $c \to 1$ is

$$K_{(1)}(u) = \frac{3}{2}K(u) + \frac{1}{2}uK'(u)$$

at points where K is differentiable.

At first sight the use of the jackknife technique seems to be a good strategy. If at the first step only a small amount of smoothness is ascribed to m, then in a further step the jackknife estimate will indeed reduce the bias, provided that m is four-times differentiable. However, a sharper analysis of this strategy reveals that the variance (for fixed n) may be inflated.

Consider the Epanechnikov kernel

$$K(u) = (3/4)(1 - u^2)I(|u| \leq 1).$$

Table 4.6.1   *The variance component*
$\int K^2_{(c)}(u)du$ *of the effective kernel as a*
function of c, and the relative deficiency
$\int K^2_{(c)}(u)du / \int K^2(u)du$ *with respect to*
the Epanechnikov kernel

c	$\int K^2_{(c)}(u)du$	$\dfrac{\int K^2_{(c)}(u)du}{\int K^2(u)du}$
0.10	0.610	1.017
0.20	0.638	1.063
0.30	0.678	1.130
0.40	0.727	1.212
0.50	0.783	1.305
0.60	0.844	1.407
0.70	0.900	1.517
0.80	0.979	1.632
0.90	1.050	1.751
0.91	1.058	1.764
0.92	1.065	1.776
0.93	1.073	1.788
0.94	1.080	1.800
0.95	1.087	1.812
0.96	1.095	1.825
0.97	1.102	1.837
0.98	1.110	1.850
0.99	1.117	1.862

Straightforward computations show that

$$c_K = \int K^2(u)du = 3/5,$$

$$\int K^2_{(c)}(u)du = \frac{\frac{9}{10}[c^3 + 2c^2 + 4/3c + 2/3]}{[c+1]^2}.$$

Table 4.6.1 shows the dependence of this number on c together with the increase in variance compared to K.

It is apparent from these figures that some caution must be exercised in selecting c (and R), since the variance increases rapidly as c tends to one. In order to compare the mean squared error of $\hat{m}_h$ with that of $G(\hat{m}_{h_1}, \hat{m}_{h_2})$ one could equalize the variances by setting

$$h_1 = \left[\int K^2_{(c)}(u)du / \int K^2(u)du \right] h.$$

Table 4.6.2   *The efficiency of the jackknifed kernel smoother*
$G[\hat{m}_{h_1}, \hat{m}_{h_2}]$ *with respect to the ordinary kernel estimator*

h \\ h_1	$c=0.1$			$c=0.2$			$c=0.3$			$c=0.4$			$c=0.5$		
	0.2	0.3	0.4	0.2	0.3	0.4	0.2	0.3	0.4	0.2	0.3	0.4	0.2	0.3	0.4
0.2	1.017	0.67	0.51	1.063	0.709	0.532	1.13	0.753	0.565	1.212	0.808	0.606	1.305	0.87	0.652
0.3	1.52	1.017	0.765	1.59	1.063	0.798	1.695	1.13	0.847	1.818	1.212	0.909	1.958	1.305	0.979
0.4	2.035	1.357	1.020	2.127	1.418	1.064	2.26	1.507	1.13	2.424	1.616	1.212	2.611	1.74	1.305

h \\ h_1	$c=0.6$			$c=0.7$			$c=0.8$			$c=0.9$		
	0.2	0.3	0.4	0.2	0.3	0.4	0.2	0.3	0.4	0.2	0.3	0.4
0.2	1.407	0.938	0.703	1.517	1.011	0.758	1.632	1.088	0.816	1.751	1.167	0.875
0.3	2.111	1.407	1.055	2.275	1.517	1.137	2.448	1.632	1.224	2.627	1.751	1.313
0.4	2.815	1.877	1.407	3.034	2.022	1.517	3.264	2.176	1.632	3.503	2.335	1.751

Note: Shown is the ratio: mean squared error $\{G[\hat{m}_{h_1}, \hat{m}_{h_2}]\}$/mean squared error $\{\hat{m}_h\}$ (for $n = 100$, $m(x) = \sin(x)$, $\sigma^2 = 1$, and $x = \pi/4$) as a function of c, h and h_1.
Source: Härdle (1986a), © 1986 IEEE.

Without loss of generality one can assume that $m^{(2)}(x)/10 = m^{(4)}(x)/280 = 1$. The leading bias term of $\hat{m}_h$ is then $h^2 + h^4$, whereas that of $G(\hat{m}_{h_1}, \hat{m}_{h_2})$ for $c = 0.99$ is equal to $\sqrt{152.76}h^4$. So, if $h^2 > 1/(\sqrt{152.76} - 1)$ the jackknifed estimator is less accurate than the ordinary kernel smoother.

Since the choice of R (and c) seems to be delicate in a practical example, it is interesting to evaluate the jackknifed estimator in a simulated example. Suppose that $m(x) = \sin(x), n = 100, \sigma^2 = 1$ and it is desired to evaluate the mean squared error at $x = \pi/4$. A bandwidth h, being roughly equal to 0.3, would minimize the mean squared error of $\hat{m}_h(x)$ (with the Epanechnikov kernel). Table 4.6.2 shows the ratio of the mean squared error of $G(\hat{m}_{h_1}, \hat{m}_{h_2})$ to that of $\hat{m}_h$ as c and h are varied.

The use of the higher order kernel technique, as is done by the jackknife technique, may thus result in a mean squared error nearly twice as large as the corresponding error of the ordinary Epanechnikov kernel smoother, as can be seen from the entry $(h, h_1, c) = (0.3, 0.3, 0.9)$ in Table 4.6.2.

Exercises

> **4.6.1** Why is it impossible to find a positive symmetric kernel of order $(0,4)$?
>
> **4.6.2** Compute the c_K for higher order kernels of order $(0,p)$ as a function of p. Do you observe an increasing value of c_K as p increases?

CHAPTER 5

Choosing the smoothing parameter

Tous les résultats asymptotiques que nous venons de considérer ne permettent pas de répondre à l'importante question que posent les praticiens de la Statistique: pour n fixé, comment choisir h_n?

Collomb (1981, p. 82)

The problem of deciding how much to smooth is of great importance in nonparametric regression. Before embarking on technical solutions of the problem it is worth noting that a selection of the smoothing parameter is always related to a certain interpretation of the smooth. If the purpose of smoothing is to increase the "signal to noise ratio" for presentation, or to suggest a simple (parametric) models, then a slightly "oversmoothed" curve with a subjectively chosen smoothing parameter might be desirable. On the other hand, when the interest is purely in estimating the regression curve itself with an emphasis on local structures then a slightly "undersmoothed" curve may be appropriate.

However, a good automatically selected parameter is always a useful starting (view)point. An advantage of automatic selection of the bandwidth for kernel smoothers is that comparison between laboratories can be made on the basis of a standardized method. A further advantage of an automatic method lies in the application of additive models for investigation of high-dimensional regression data. For complex iterative procedures such as projection pursuit regression (Friedman and Stuetzle 1981) or ACE (Breiman and Friedman 1985) it is vital to have a good choice of smoothing parameter for one-dimensional smoothers that are elementary building blocks for these procedures.

In the following sections various methods for choosing the smoothing parameters are presented. The choice is made so that some global error criterion is minimized. Section 5.2 discusses how far away the automatically chosen smoothing parameters are from their optimum. It will be seen that there is indeed room for subjective choice of the bandwidth within a slowly narrowing confidence interval of the optimum. Several possibilities for adapting the smoothing parameter to local curvature of the regression curve are presented in Section 5.3. In particular, I propose a method based on bootstrapping from estimated residuals. The *supersmoother*, proposed by Friedman (1984), is also presented there. The important practical question of how to compare automatically chosen bandwidths between laboratories is discussed in Section 5.4.

5.1   Cross-validation, penalizing functions and the plug-in method

The accuracy of kernel smoothers as estimators of m or of derivatives of m is a function of the kernel K and the bandwidth h. I have argued that the accuracy depends mainly on the smoothing parameter h (Section 4.5). In this section, several bandwidth selection procedures will be presented that optimize quadratic error measures for the regression curve and its derivatives. In particular, I consider the distances

$$d_A(h) = n^{-1} \sum_{j=1}^{n} [\hat{m}_h(X_j) - m(X_j)]^2 w(X_j),$$

$$d_I(h) = \int [\hat{m}_h(x) - m(x)]^2 w(x) f(x) dx,$$

$$d_C(h) = E[d_A(h)|X_1, \ldots, X_n],$$

where $w(x)$ is a nonnegative weight function. The form of the above distances is determined by a variance component (decreasing in h) and a bias^2 component (increasing in h). Consider, for instance, $d_C(h)$; here the bias$^2(h)$ is

$$b^2(h) = n^{-1} \sum_{j=1}^{n} \left[n^{-1} \sum_{i=1}^{n} W_{hi}(X_j) m(X_i) - m(X_j) \right]^2 w(X_j)$$

and the variance component is

$$v(h) = n^{-1} \sum_{j=1}^{n} \left[n^{-2} \sum_{i=1}^{n} W_{hi}(X_j) \sigma^2(X_j) \right] w(X_j),$$

where $W_{hi}(x) = K_h(x - X_i)/\hat{f}_h(x)$ are the Nadaraya–Watson weights. The fact that $b^2(h)$ increases as h increases can be seen in Figure 5.1, where for the the simulated data set (Table 2, Appendix 2) the function $d_C(\cdot)$ is presented as a function of h. The power of h at which $b^2(h)$ increases is a function of the selected kernel and the degree of differentiability of the regression function; see Section 4.6.

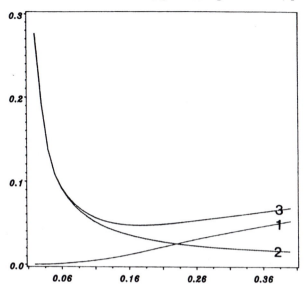

Figure 5.1. The conditional squared error $d_C(h)$ as the sum of the bias^2 component $b^2(h)$ and the variance $v(h)$ for the simulated data set (Table 2, Appendix 2). The weight function $w(x) = I(|x - 1/2| < 0.4)$ has been used. The function $b^2(h)$ is indicated as an increasing solid line (label 1). The variance is decreasing (fine dashed line, label 2) and d_C is the sum of both (long dashed line, label 3).

The decreasing curve in Figure 5.1 shows $v(h)$ roughly proportional to h^{-1}. The sum of both components is the conditional squared error $d_C(h)$, which is shown in Figure 5.1 as the curve above $b^2(h)$ and $v(h)$.

Theorem 4.1.1 about the asymptotic equivalence of d_I, d_A and d_C states that all three distances should have roughly the same minimum. The approximate identity of the three distances can be seen from Figure 5.2. It is highly desirable to choose a smoothing parameter that balances the systematic bias^2 effects versus the stochastic uncertainty expressed by the magnitude of the variance. For such a choice of smoothing parameter the squared bias and the variance are of the same order.

How can we find such a smoothing parameter? We have already seen a theoretical analysis of the MSE properties of kernel smoothers in Section 3.1. We know the asymptotic preferable choice of $h_0 \sim n^{-1/5}$, but the MSE and thus h_0 involved complicated unknowns that had to be estimated from the data as well.

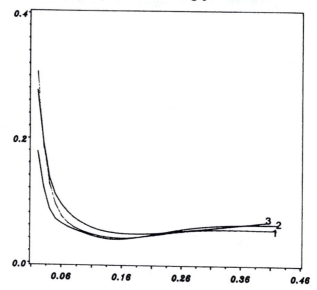

Figure 5.2.   Three measures of accuracy: d_I, d_A, d_C for the weight function $w(x) = I(|x - 1/2| \leq 0.4)$.   The integrated squared error (computed from 300 grid points) is shown as a solid line labeled 1. The averaged squared error is indicated as a fine dashed line (label 2) and the error measure d_C is displayed with label 3 as a long dashed line. Computed from the simulated data set (Table 2, Appendix 2).

The basic idea behind all smoothing parameter selection algorithms is to estimate the ASE or equivalent measures (up to some constant). The hope is then that the smoothing parameter minimizing this estimate is also a good estimate for the ASE itself. Expand the ASE as

$$d_A(h) = n^{-1} \sum_{j=1}^{n} m^2(X_j)w(X_j) + n^{-1} \sum_{j=1}^{n} \hat{m}_h^2(X_j)w(X_j)$$

$$- 2n^{-1} \sum_{j=1}^{n} m(X_j)\hat{m}_h(X_j)w(X_j).$$

Can we estimate this expression (up to a constant)? At first sight it seems possible. The first term is independent of the smoothing parameter. The second term can be computed entirely from the data. If the third term could be estimated and if it vanished faster than d_A itself

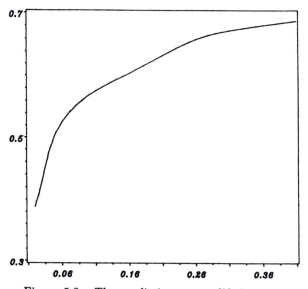

Figure 5.3. The prediction error $p(h)$ for the simulated data set (Table 2, Appendix 2). The weight function w was set to the indicator function on $[0.1, 0.9]$.

tends to zero, then indeed a device for selecting the bandwidth could be established quite easily.

A naive estimate of the third term would be

$$n^{-1} \sum_{j=1}^{n} Y_j \hat{m}_h(X_j) w(X_j),$$

where the unknown mean $m(X_j)$ is replaced by the observation Y_j at X_j. This is equivalent to considering the so-called *resubstitution estimate* of the prediction error

$$p(h) = n^{-1} \sum_{j=1}^{n} [Y_j - \hat{m}_h(X_j)]^2 w(X_j)$$

as a device for selecting h. Unfortunately, the prediction error is a biased estimate of d_A. Figure 5.3 shows $p(h)$ as an increasing function in h; the best bandwidth would thus be the smallest bandwidth!

The intuitive reason for the bias in $p(h)$ is that the observation Y_j is used (in $\hat{m}_h(X_j)$) to predict itself. To see this in more detail, consider the expansion

$$p(h) = n^{-1} \sum_{j-1}^{n} \varepsilon_j^2 w(X_j) + d_A(h)$$

$$- 2n^{-1} \sum_{j=1}^{n} \varepsilon_j (\hat{m}_h(X_j) - m(X_j))w(X_j).$$

The last term can be rewritten as

$$C_{1n}(h) = -2n^{-1} \sum_{j=1}^{n} \varepsilon_j \left[n^{-1} \sum_{i=1}^{n} W_{hi}(X_j)Y_i - m(X_j) \right] w(X_j),$$

(5.1.1)

which has expectation (given $\{X_1, \ldots, X_n\}$)

$$-2n^{-1} \sum_{j=1}^{n} [n^{-1} W_{hj}(X_j)\sigma^2(X_j)]w(X_j).$$

This quantity tends to zero at the same rate as the variance component of d_A, which explains the bias of $p(h)$ as an estimate of $d_A(h)$. There are at least three possible ways to find an unbiased estimate of d_A:

1.   a leave-out-technique to obtain zero expectation for (5.1.1);
2.   a modification of $p(h)$ such that bias terms like that of (5.1.1) cancel asymptotically;
3.   a "plug-in" method, using asymptotics of "optimal bandwidth" sequences.

Leave-one-out method, cross-validation

The *leave-out method* is based on regression smoothers in which *one*, say the jth, observation is left out:

$$\hat{m}_{h,j}(X_j) = n^{-1} \sum_{i \neq j} W_{hi}(X_j)Y_i. \tag{5.1.2}$$

With these modified smoothers, the function

$$CV(h) = n^{-1} \sum_{j=1}^{n} [Y_j - \hat{m}_{h,j}(X_j)]^2 w(X_j) \tag{5.1.3}$$

is formed.

The function CV is commonly called a *cross-validation function* since it validates the ability to predict $\{Y_j\}_{j=1}^{n}$ across the subsamples $\{(X_i, Y_i)\}_{i \neq j}$ (Stone 1974). In the context of kernel smoothing

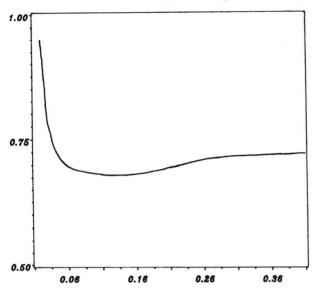

Figure 5.4.   The cross-validation function $CV(h)$ for the simulated data set (Table 2, Appendix 2).   The weight function $w(x) = I(|x - 1/2| \leq 0.4)$ was used.

this score function for finding h was proposed by Clark (1975). The idea is related to variables selection in linear regression. Allen (1974) proposed the related quantity PRESS (prediction sum of squares). Wahba and Wold (1975) proposed a similar technique in the context of spline smoothing. The general structure of smoothing methods in linear regression models is discussed in Hall and Titterington (1986a).

The reason why cross-validation works is simple: The cross-product term from the CV function, similar to (5.1.1), is

$$C_{2n}(h) = -2n^{-1} \sum_{j=1}^{n} \varepsilon_j \left[n^{-1} \sum_{\substack{i \neq j \\ i=1}}^{n} W_{hi}(X_j) Y_i - m(X_j) \right] w(X_j)$$

(5.1.4)

and has expectation zero. The CV-function for the simulated data set is shown in Figure 5.4.

Note that by itself the fact that (5.1.4) has expectation zero does not guarantee that $\hat{h} = \arg\min[CV(h)]$ minimizes d_A (or any other of the equivalent error measures). For this procedure it must be required that $C_{2n}(h)$ converges uniformly over h to zero. Note also that the bandwidth suggested here by cross-validation (for the quartic kernel, $h = 0.1$) is not exactly equal to the subjectively chosen bandwidth from Section 3.6. The reason may be twofold. First, the two bandwidths could be really different, even on the "correct scale." Second, they could be different since Figure 3.21 was produced with a Gaussian kernel and the above cross-validation function was computed using a quartic kernel. A "common scale" for comparing bandwidths from different kernels is derived in Section 5.4.

Penalizing functions

The second proposal, based on adjusting $p(h)$ in a suitable way, aims at an asymptotic cancellation of the bias (5.1.1). For this purpose introduce the penalizing function $\Xi(u)$ with first-order Taylor expansion

$$\Xi(u) = 1 + 2u + O(u^2), \quad u \to 0.$$

This form of the penalizing function will work out well as will be seen in what follows. The prediction error $p(h)$ is adjusted by $\Xi(n^{-1}W_{hj}(X_j))$, that is, modified to

$$G(h) = n^{-1} \sum_{j=1}^{n} (Y_j - \hat{m}_h(X_j))^2 \Xi(n^{-1}W_{hj}(X_j))w(X_j).$$

$$(5.1.5)$$

The reason for this adjustment is that the correction function

$$\Xi(n^{-1}W_{hj}(X_j)) = \Xi(n^{-1}h^{-1}K(0)/\hat{f}_h(X_j))$$

penalizes values of h too low. Recall that the naive approach to finding $h = \arg\min[p(h)]$ leads to too small an h. By penalizing $p(h)$ as in (5.1.5) one corrects for this too small h. Indeed, using the above Taylor expansion for Ξ, the score $G(h)$ is to first order

$$n^{-1} \sum_{j=1}^{n} \{[\varepsilon_j^2 + (m(X_j) - \hat{m}_h(X_j))^2 \qquad (5.1.6)$$
$$+ 2\varepsilon_j(m(X_j) - \hat{m}_h(X_j))]$$
$$\times [1 + 2n^{-1}W_{hj}(X_j)]\}w(X_j).$$

Multiplying out and disregarding lower order terms leads to

$$n^{-1} \sum_{j=1}^{n} \varepsilon_j^2 w(X_j) + d_A(h)$$

$$+ 2n^{-1} \sum_{j=1}^{n} \varepsilon_j (m(X_j) - \hat{m}_h(X_j)) w(X_j)$$

$$+ 2n^{-1} \sum_{j=1}^{n} \varepsilon_j^2 n^{-1} W_{hj}(X_j) w(X_j).$$

Note that the first term is independent of h and that the expectation (given $\{X_1, \ldots, X_n\}$) of the third term equals

$$-2n^{-1} \sum_{j=1}^{n} n^{-1} W_{hj}(X_j) \sigma^2(X_j) w(X_j),$$

which is the negative expected value of the last term. The last two terms cancel asymptotically so that $G(h)$ is (up to a shift by $n^{-1} \sum_{j=1}^{n} \varepsilon_j^2 w(X_j)$) roughly equal to $d_A(h)$. A number of penalizing functions Ξ have been proposed in the literature, the simplest of which is due to Shibata (1981):

$$\Xi(u) = 1 + 2u.$$

Some of the established correction functions are discussed and compared in their performance in the next section. Figure 5.10 gives an impression of some correction functions Ξ.

The plug-in method

The third method, the "plug-in" procedure, is based on the asymptotic expansion of the squared error for kernel smoothers:

$$MSE = n^{-1} h^{-1} \sigma^2(x) c_K / f(x)$$
$$+ h^4 [d_K(m''(x) + 2m'(x)(f'/f)(x))/2]^2.$$

An "optimal" bandwidth minimizing this expression would be (as pointed out in Section 4.1) proportional to $n^{-1/5}$ with constants depending on the unknowns $\sigma^2(x), m''(x)$ and so on. In practice, these quantities have to be estimated on the basis of some preliminary smoothing process which raises a second-order bandwidth selection problem. Although the "plug-in" method achieves the same efficiency as the two other methods (Section 5.2), it is due to considerable uncertainty about how to choose the bandwidth in that first step. Another disadvantage,

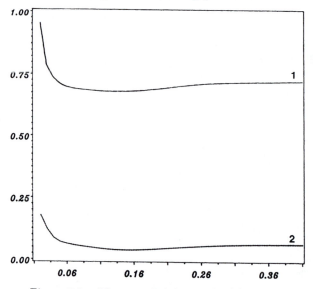

Figure 5.5. The cross-validation $CV(h)$ (label 1) and the averaged squared error $d_A(h)$ (label 2) for the simulated set (Table 2, Appendix 2). The weight function was $w(x) = I(|x - 1/2| \le 0.4)$.

from a theoretical point of view, is that one is always restricted to a certain smoothness class (in the above expansion, to twice differentiable regression functions).

The first two methods, the leave-out and the penalty technique, lead to estimates of d_A (up to a shift of h) and hence to estimates of d_I, d_C. The random constant by which the CV function or the G function differ from d_A is roughly $n^{-1} \sum_{j=1}^{n} \varepsilon_j^2 w(X_j)$, which tends to $\int \sigma^2(x) f(x) w(x) dx$. In Figure 5.5, the upper curve is the CV-function and the lower curve, with a similar shape, is the averaged squared error d_A for the simulation example (Table 2, Appendix 2).

The two curves in Figure 5.5 differ by a constant in the range $[0.7, 0.9]$, which is a remarkably accurate estimate of

$$0.8 = \int \sigma^2(x) f(x) w(x) dx = \int_{0.1}^{0.9} 1 dx.$$

Consider the example of finding the Engel curve of potatoes as a function of net income. Figure 1.1 shows the data in the form of a sunflower plot. The cross-validation curve $CV(h)$ of this data set is displayed in Figure 5.6.

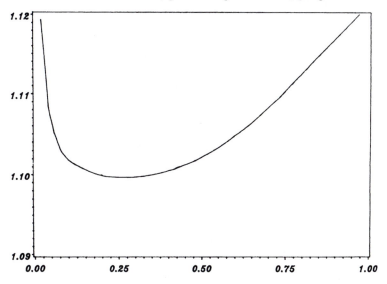

Figure 5.6.   The cross-validation function $CV(h)$ for the potato versus net income data set (see Figure 1.1). The quartic kernel leave-one-out smoother was computed on the inner 90 percent of the net income range (year 1973). Family Expenditure Survey (1968–1983).

The cross-validation function has a clear minimum at $h \approx 0.35$. The corresponding kernel smooth is shown in Figure 5.7.

The estimated curve shows the same nonlinearity as Figure 1.2 but is slightly rougher.

In order to make cross-validation or the penalty method a mathematically justifiable device for selecting the smoothing parameter, it must be shown that the score (CV or G) approximates (up to a constant) the accuracy measure $d_A(h)$ uniformly over h. If this is the case, then the relative loss for a selected bandwidth $\hat{h}$,

$$\frac{d_\bullet(\hat{h})}{\inf_{h \in H_n} d_\bullet(h)} \overset{a.s.}{\longrightarrow} 1. \tag{5.1.7}$$

Here H_n is a set of reasonable bandwidths and $d_\bullet(\cdot)$ is any of the discussed squared deviation measures. A *data-driven* bandwidth h that satisfies (5.1.7) is said to be *asymptotically optimal*. The following Theorem by Härdle and Marron (1985a, 1985b) says that CV and G yield optimal bandwidth selections.

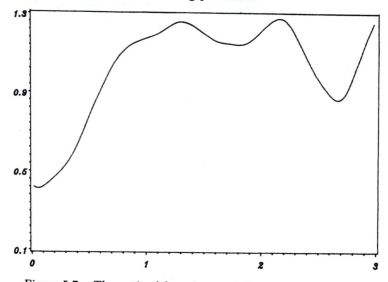

Figure 5.7.   The optimal kernel smooth for the potato versus net income data set with quartic kernel, $h = 0.35$, $n = 7125$. Family Expenditure Survey (1968–1981).

Theorem 5.1.1   *Suppose that*

(A1)   *for $n = 1, 2, \ldots$, $H_n = [\underline{h}, \overline{h}]$, where*

$$\underline{h} \geq C^{-1} n^{\delta - 1/d}, \quad \overline{h} \leq C n^{-\delta}$$

for some constants $C, \delta \in (0, 1/(2d))$;

(A2)   *K is Hölder continuous, that is, for some $L > 0$, $\xi \in (0, 1)$*

$$|K(u) - K(v)| \leq L \,\|u - v\|^\xi,$$

where $\|\cdot\|$ denotes Euclidean norm on $\mathbf{R}^d$ and also

$$\int \|u\|^\xi \,|K(u)| \, du < \infty;$$

(A3)   *the regression function m and the marginal density f are Hölder continuous;*

(A4)   *the conditional moments of Y given $X = x$ are bounded in the sense that there are positive constants $C_1, C_2, \ldots$ such that for $k = 1, 2, \ldots$, $E(Y^k | X = x) \leq C_k$ for all x;*

(A5)   *the marginal density $f(x)$ of X is bounded from below on the support of w;*

(A6)   *the marginal density $f(x)$ of X is compactly supported.*

Then the bandwidth selection rule, "Choose $\hat{h}$ to minimize $CV(h)$ (or $G(h))$" is asymptotically optimal.

Asymptotic optimality of the kernel smoother with weights $W_{hi}(x) = K_h(x - X_i)/f(x)$ was shown by Härdle and Kelly (1987) for a slightly larger range of bandwidths. Rice (1984a) proved a related theorem using penalizing functions in the fixed design setting. These penalizing functions do not yield asymptotically optimal smoothing parameters in the stochastic design setting, as was shown by Härdle and Marron (1985a).

It is remarkable that the above devices yield optimal smoothing parameters without reference to a specific smoothness class to which either m or f belongs. Minimization of h is performed over a wide range H_n of possible bandwidths. The method is not just restricted to a specific range, for example, $[an^{-1/5}, bn^{-1/5}]$, $0 < a < b$, containing, for example, the optimal smoothing parameters for twice differentiable regression functions. In this sense, the cross-validation and the penalty method yield optimal smoothing parameters uniformly over smoothness classes (see the remarks of Section 4.1). This, in turn, has the effect that the data-driven kernel smoothers achieve "their" optimal rate, independently of the smoothness of the underlying regression model (Härdle and Marron 1985b, section 3). From a practical point of view, this last theoretical property of cross-validated bandwidth sequences is welcome. The user of the cross-validation method need not worry about the roughness of the *underlying* curve. The cross-validated bandwidth will automatically give him the right amount of smoothing, independently of how smooth (in terms of degree of differentiability) the true regression curve is. This feature is not accomplished by the "plug-in" method.

The cross-validation procedure is formally described in the following algorithm.

Algorithm 5.1.1.

DO OVER (a dense grid H_n of h values)
STEP 1.
Compute the leave-out estimate

$$\hat{m}_{h,j}(X_j)$$

at the observation points.
STEP 2.
Construct the cross validation function

$$CV(h) = n^{-1} \sum_{j=1}^{n} (Y_j - \hat{m}_{h,j}(X_j))^2 w(X_j).$$

where w denotes a weight function.

END OVER.

STEP 3.

Define the automatic bandwidth as

$$\hat{h} = \arg\min_{h \in H_n} [CV(h)]$$

Bandwidth choice for derivative estimation

The principal idea for smoothing parameter selection in the setting of derivative estimation is similar to that of finding a bandwidth for estimating m itself. As in Rice (1985), consider the setting of fixed, equidistant predictor variables. The leave-out estimators for estimating m' are defined by leaving out the observations (X_j, Y_j) and (X_{j-1}, Y_{j-1}),

$$\hat{m}_{h,j}^{(1)}(x) = n^{-1} \sum_{\substack{i=1 \\ i \neq j, j-1}}^{n} W_{hi}^{(1)}(x) Y_i,$$

where $\{W_{hi}^{(1)}(x)\}$ are kernel derivative weights (see Section 3.1). Instead of comparing the leave-out estimators with the original response variables (at n points) one evaluates the prediction error (at $n_2 = n/2$ points)

$$CV^{(1)}(h) = n_2^{-1} \sum_{j=1}^{n_2} [Y_{(2j)}^{(1)} - \hat{m}_{h,(2j)}^{(1)}(X_{(2j)})]^2 w(X_{(2j)}),$$

where $\{(X_{(j)}, Y_{(j)})\}$ denote the input data, sorted by X, and $Y_{(j)}^{(1)} = \frac{Y_{(j)} - Y_{(j-1)}}{X_{(j)} - X_{(j-1)}}$ is the first difference of the Y-variables (sorted by X). Note that

$$E\{Y_{(j)}^{(1)} | X_1, \ldots, X_n\} = \frac{m(X_{(j)}) - m(X_{(j-1)})}{X_{(j)} - X_{(j-1)}} = m'(\xi_{(j)})$$

with $\xi_{(j)} \in [X_{(j-1)}, X_{(j)}]$. Squaring $CV^{(1)}(h)$ leads to

$$n_2^{-1} \sum_{j=1}^{n_2} [Y_{(j)}^{(1)} - m'(\xi_{(j)})]^2 w(X_{(j)})$$

$$+ n_2^{-1} \sum_{j=1}^{n_2} [m'(\xi_{(j)}) - \hat{m}_{h,(j)}^{(1)}(X_{(j)})]^2 w(X_{(j)})$$

$$+ 2n_2^{-1} \sum_{j=1}^{n_2} [Y_{(j)}^{(1)} - m'(\xi_{(j)})][m'(\xi_{(j)}) - \hat{m}_{h,(j)}^{(1)}(X_{(j)})] w(X_{(j)}).$$

As in ordinary cross-validation (for estimating m) the cross-product term asymptotically vanishes, so that the function $CV^{(1)}(h)$ behaves (up to a constant) like

$$n_2^{-1} \sum_{j=1}^{n_2} [m'(\xi_{(j)}) - \hat{m}_{h,(j)}^{(1)}(X_{(j)})]^2 w(X_{(j)})$$

$$\approx d_A^{(1)}(h)$$

$$= n_2^{-1} \sum_{j=1}^{n_2} [m'(X_{(j)}) - \hat{m}_h^{(1)}(X_{(j)})]^2 w(X_{(j)})$$

plus a constant (independent of h). This approach was considered in the random design setting by Härdle and Carroll (1989). Müller, Stadtmüller and Schmidt (1987) propose a so-called *factor method*, which is also based on the plug-in approach. The factor method is based on comparing bandwidths h_0 for estimating m with $h_0^{(k)}$ for estimating $m^{(k)}$. These bandwidths are the same up to a scale factor depending on k, p and the kernel function. More precisely, for a p-times differentiable function m the MSE for estimating $m^{(k)}(x)$ is, as seen before,

$$MSE \approx n^{-1} h^{-(2k+1)} \sigma^2 \int K^{(k)^2}(u) du$$

$$+ \left[h^{p-k} m^{(k)}(x)(-1)^p \int u^p K^{(k)}(u) du/p! \right]^2 .$$

The bandwidth that minimizes MISE is, as described in Section 4.1,

$$h_0^{(k)} = \left[\frac{2k+1}{2(p-k)} \right.$$

$$\left. \times \frac{\sigma^2 \int K^{(k)^2}(u) du}{[(-1)^p \int u^p K^{(k)}(u) du/p!]^2 \int m^{(k)^2}(x) dx} \right]^{1/(2p+1)} n^{-1/(2p+1)}.$$

If we compare the optimum h_0 with $h_0^{(k)}$ then we see that they differ by the factor

$$C_{0,k} = \left[\frac{(2k+1)p}{p-k} \right.$$

$$\left. \times \frac{\int K^{(k)^2}(u) du[(-1)^p \int u^p K(u) du/p!]^2}{\int K^2(u) du[(-1)^p \int u^p K^{(k)}(u) du/p!]^2} \right]^{1/(2p+1)} .$$

Thus the MISE optimal bandwidth $h_0^{(k)}$ is given by

$$h_0^{(k)} = C_{0,k} h_0.$$

The dependence of the smoothing parameter on the weight function

The weight function w was introduced to reduce boundary effects. If one had not introduced the weight function and just formed the bandwidth selection scores over the whole data range one would have obtained a bandwidth sequence optimized with respect to the "boundary behavior" of the kernel smoother. As pointed out in Section 4.4, the convergence rate is slightly slower at the boundary points. Since the cross-validation method, for example, is still asymptotically optimal (in the sense of Theorem 5.5.1) one would artificially select a slower rate of convergence in the center of the data range, where the majority of the data lie.

However, cutting the range of interest down to, say, 90 percent, doesn't solve the problem since typically the kernel weights cover more than 10 percent of the data range (see Figure 5.6). This raises the question of how variable the CV-function is as the weight function w is varied. Figure 5.8 shows an optimal kernel smooth estimating liver weights as a function of age. The CV-function was computed disregarding the outer 5 percent data on each side. What happens if the weight function w is varied?

Figure 5.9 shows cross-validation curves as the weights cut off 2, 4, 6, 8 and 10 percent of the data at each end of the data interval. The location of the minimum, the selected optimal bandwidth, is remarkably stable except for the case where only 80 percent of the data interval is cross-validated. I did similar comparisons for the simulated data set (Table 2, Appendix 2) and found qualitatively the same behavior: The weight function does not influence the selected bandwidth to a large extent.

Exercises

5.1.1 Try cross-validation and some of the penalizing functions to find a smoothing parameter for the simulated data set given in the appendix.

5.1.2 Recall the asymptotic equivalence of k-NN and kernel smoothing. How would you choose a good k with the cross-validation method?

5.1.3 How would you modify the penalizing functions in the setting of k-NN smoothing?

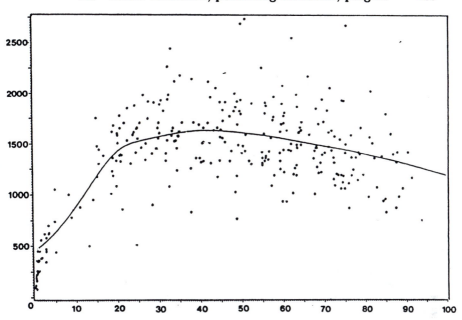

Figure 5.8.   Liver weights versus age of 300 female corpses (smoothed with cross-validated bandwidth $h = 22$ years). From Härdle and Marron (1985b) with permission of the Institute of Mathematical Statistics.

5.1.4 Write an efficient algorithm for computing the cross-validation function.

[*Hint*: Use the WARPing technique or the FFT method.]

5.1.5 One could argue that an asymptotically optimal smoothing parameter for m is also good for estimating m'. A good estimate for m should give a good estimate for m'! Can you find an argument against this?

5.1.6 Find $\hat{h} = \arg\min[CV(h)]$ and $\hat{h}^{(1)} = \arg\min[CV^{(1)}(h)]$. Compare $\hat{h}$ with $\hat{h}^{(1)}$. Do you find that $\hat{h} < \hat{h}^{(1)}$? [*Hint*: Study the factor method.]

Complements

Proof of Theorem 5.1.1

The proof of this theorem is based on the uniform approximation (over H_n) of the distances d_A, d_I, and so on; see Theorem 4.1.1. If suffices to prove the asymptotic optimality for $d_A(\cdot)$. The Hölder continuity

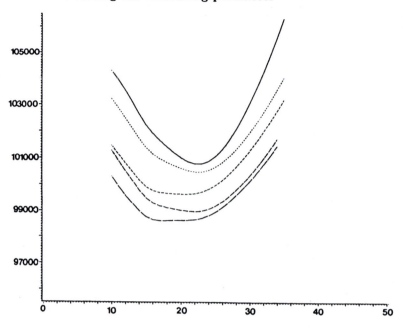

Figure 5.9.   Cross-validation curves as the weight function w is varied. The uppermost CV curve was computed leaving 2 percent of observations at each end. The curves below leave out 4, 6, 8, 10 percent at each end. From Härdle and Marron (1985b) with permission of the Institute of Mathematical Statistics.

of K, m, f ensures that it suffices to consider a discrete subset H'_n of H_n. The existence of all conditional moments of order k gives, over this sufficiently dense subset H'_n of H_n:

$$\sup_{h, h' \in H'_n} \left| \frac{d_A(h) - d_A(h') - (CV(h) - CV(h'))}{d_M(h) + d_M(h')} \right| \overset{a.s.}{\to} 0. \qquad (5.1.8)$$

A key step in proving (5.1.8) is Whittle's inequality (Whittle 1960) on bounding higher moments of quadratic forms of independent random variables. Using the Hölder continuity of K, m and f and Theorem 4.1.1 gives

$$\sup_{h, h' \in H_n} \left| \frac{d_A(h) - d_A(h') - (CV(h) - CV(h'))}{d_A(h) + d_A(h')} \right| \overset{a.s.}{\to} 0. \qquad (5.1.9)$$

Now let $\varepsilon > 0$ be given and let

$$\hat{h}_0 = \underset{h \in H_n}{\arg\min}[d_A(h)],$$

$$\hat{h} = \arg\min_{h \in H_n}[CV(h)].$$

From (5.1.9) we have with probability 1,

$$\frac{d_A(\hat{h}) - d_A(\hat{h}_0) - (CV(\hat{h}) - CV(\hat{h}_0))}{d_A(\hat{h}) + d_A(\hat{h}_0)} \le \varepsilon.$$

This implies

$$0 \ge CV(\hat{h}) - CV(\hat{h}_0) \ge (1 - \varepsilon)d_A(\hat{h}) - (1 + \varepsilon)d_A(\hat{h}_0),$$

which entails

$$1 \le \frac{d_A(\hat{h})}{d_A(\hat{h}_0)} \le \frac{1 + \varepsilon}{1 - \varepsilon}.$$

Since ε was arbitrary,

$$P\left\{\lim_{n \to \infty}\left|\frac{d_A(\hat{h})}{d_A(\hat{h}_0)} - 1\right| < \delta\right\} = 1 \; \forall \delta > 0,$$

which means that $\hat{h}$ is asymptotically optimal.

5.2 Which selector should be used?

There are a number of different automatic selectors that produce asymptotically optimal kernel smoothers. Certainly, any such bandwidth selector is desirable but there may be data sets where a specific selector may outperform other candidates. This raises the question of which selector to use and how far a specific automatic bandwidth is from its optimum. A further interesting question is how close the deviations $d_\bullet(\cdot)$, evaluated at the asymptotically optimal bandwidth, are from the smallest possible deviations. The answers to these questions are surprising. All presented selectors are equivalent in an asymptotic sense. The speed at which an estimated bandwidth tends to the best possible bandwidth is extremely slow. In addition, theoretical studies show that the optimally data-driven bandwidth is negatively correlated with the best possible theoretical bandwidth.

Unfortunately, the mathematics necessary to investigate this issue are rather complicated so I prefer to work in the fixed design model with equispaced design variables on the unit interval, that is, $\{X_i = i/n\}_{i=1}^n$. Assume further that the ε_i have common variance, σ^2, say. The kernel estimator proposed by Priestley and Chao (1972) is considered,

$$\hat{m}_h(x) = n^{-1} \sum_{i=1}^n K_h(x - X_i)\, Y_i.$$

Extensions to random X-values and the case of a multivariate X-variate are possible but require substantially more work. The *optimal bandwidth* is taken here in this section to be $\hat{h}_0$, the minimizer of the average square error (ASE),

$$d_A(h) = n^{-1} \sum_{i=1}^{n} (\hat{m}_h(X_i) - m(X_i))^2 \, w(X_i).$$

Of course, this is just one way to define an optimal bandwidth. An asymptotically equivalent measure of accuracy is the mean average square error (see Theorem 4.1.1)

$$MASE = d_{MA}(h) = E d_A(h).$$

Another good candidate for a selected bandwidth could therefore be h_0, the minimizer of d_{MA}. The optimal bandwidth $\hat{h}_0$ makes $\hat{m}_h$ as close as possible to the regression curve m for the data set at hand, whereas h_0 tries to optimize an average distance over all possible data sets.

How fast do $\hat{h}_0$ and h_0 tend to zero? We have seen that $\hat{h}_0$ and h_0 are each roughly equal to

$$h_0^* = C_0 \, n^{-1/5},$$

where

$$C_0 = \left\{ \frac{\sigma^2 \left(\int w(u) du \right) c_K}{d_K \int (m''(u))^2 w(u) du} \right\}^{1/5}. \tag{5.2.1}$$

Of course, we can try to estimate C_0 by the plug-in method, but there may be a difference when using cross-validation or the penalizing function approach. In this setting of equidistant X_i on the unit interval, the penalizing functions that are presented in Section 5.1 can be written as

$$G(h) = p(h) \, \Xi \, (n^{-1} h^{-1}),$$

where

$$p(h) = n^{-1} \sum_{i=1}^{n} (Y_i - \hat{m}_h(X_i))^2 \, w(X_i)$$

denotes the prediction error and where Ξ denotes the penalizing function that corrects the biasedness of $p(h)$ as an estimator for $d_A(h)$.

Simple examples are:

(i)   *Generalized Cross-validation* (Craven and Whaba 1979; Li 1985),

$$\Xi_{GCV} \, (n^{-1} h^{-1}) = (1 - n^{-1} h^{-1} K(0))^{-2};$$

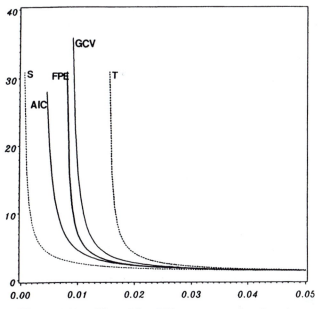

Figure 5.10.   Plot of five different correction functions
$\Xi(n^{-1}h^{-1}K(0))$ as a function of h. The sample size was assumed to
be $n = 75$ and the Epanechnikov kernel with $K(0) = 0.75$ was used.

(ii)   *Akaike's Information Criterion* (Akaike 1970)

$$\Xi_{AIC}(n^{-1}h^{-1}) = \exp\,(2n^{-1}h^{-1}K(0));$$

(iii)   *Finite Prediction Error* (Akaike 1974),

$$\Xi_{FPE}(n^{-1}h^{-1}) = (1 + n^{-1}h^{-1}K(0))/(1 - n^{-1}h^{-1}K(0));$$

(iv)   *Shibata's (1981) model selector,*

$$\Xi_S(n^{-1}h^{-1}) = 1 + 2n^{-1}h^{-1}K(0);$$

(v)   *Rice's (1984a) bandwidth selector,*

$$\Xi_T(n^{-1}h^{-1}) = (1 - 2n^{-1}h^{-1}K(0))^{-1}.$$

To gain some insight into how these selection functions differ from
each other, consider Figure 5.10.

Each of the displayed penalizing functions has the same Taylor expansion, more precisely, as $nh \to \infty$,

$$\Xi\,(n^{-1}h^{-1}) = 1 + 2n^{-1}h^{-1}K(0) + O(n^{-2}h^{-2}).$$

The main difference among the Ξ-functions occurs at the left tail, where small bandwidths are differently penalized. Note also that the cross-validation method can be seen as penalizing the prediction error $p(h)$, since

$$CV(h)/p(h) = 1 + 2n^{-1}h^{-1}K(0) + O_p(n^{-2}h^{-2}). \qquad (5.2.2)$$

This last statement can be shown to hold also for bandwidth selectors based on unbiased risk estimation,

$$\tilde{R}(h) = n^{-1} \sum_{i=1}^{n} \{(Y_i - \hat{m}_h(X_i))^2 $$
$$ + n^{-1}h^{-1}K(0)\,(Y_i - Y_{i-1})^2\}\,w(X_i);$$

see Rice (1984a).

All the above bandwidth selectors are asymptotically optimal, that is, the ratio of estimated loss to minimum loss tends to one,

$$\frac{d_A(\hat{h})}{d_A(\hat{h}_0)} \xrightarrow{p} 1, \qquad (5.2.3)$$

and the ratio of bandwidths tends to one,

$$\frac{\hat{h}}{\hat{h}_0} \xrightarrow{p} 1. \qquad (5.2.4)$$

The question of how fast this convergence in (5.2.3) and (5.2.4) occurs is answered by computing the asymptotic distributions of the difference.

Theorem 5.2.1   Suppose that
   (A1)   the errors $\{\varepsilon_i\}$ are independent and identically distributed with mean zero, variance σ^2, and all other moments finite;
   (A2)   the kernel K is compactly supported with a Hölder continuous second derivative;
   (A3)   the regression function m has a uniformly continuous integrable second derivative.
   Then, as $n \to \infty$,

$$n^{3/10}(\hat{h} - \hat{h}_0) \xrightarrow{\mathcal{L}} N(0, \sigma_1^2), \qquad (5.2.5)$$
$$n(d_A(\hat{h}) - d_A(\hat{h}_0)) \xrightarrow{\mathcal{L}} C_1\chi_1^2,$$

where σ_1 and C_1 are constants depending on the kernel, the regression function and the observation error, but not on the specific Ξ-function that has been selected.

Precise formulas for σ_1 and C_1 are given subsequently. A proof of this theorem may be found in Härdle, Hall and Marron (1988).

Between $\hat{h}$ and $\hat{h}_0$, the above convergence speeds (5.2.5) are saying that the relative difference

$$\frac{\hat{h} - \hat{h}_0}{\hat{h}_0},$$

decreases at the (slow) rate $n^{-1/10}$. Also

$$\frac{d_A(\hat{h}) - d_A(\hat{h}_0)}{d_A(\hat{h}_0)}$$

has the (slow) rate $n^{1/5}$. Of course, in practical research the speed of $\hat{h}$ is not of interest per se. The researcher cares more about the precision of the curve measured in $d_A(\hat{h})$. However, both these rates seem at first glance to be extremely disappointing, but they are of the same order as the differences between $\hat{h}_0$ and h_0 and $d_A(h_0) - d_A(\hat{h}_0)$.

Theorem 5.2.2   Suppose that $(A1) - (A3)$ in Theorem 5.2.1 hold, then

$$n^{3/10}(h_0 - \hat{h}_0) \xrightarrow{\mathcal{L}} N(0, \sigma_2^2),$$

$$n[d_A(h_0) - d_A(\hat{h}_0)] \xrightarrow{\mathcal{L}} C_2 \chi_1^2, \qquad (5.2.6)$$

where σ_2^2 and C_2 are defined in what follows.

The constants $\sigma_1, \sigma_2, C_1, C_2$ from the above two Theorems are

$$\sigma_1^2 = \sigma_4^2/C_3^2,$$
$$\sigma_2^2 = \sigma_3^2/C_3^2,$$
$$C_1 = C_3\sigma_1^2/2,$$
$$C_2 = C_3\sigma_2^2/2,$$

where (letting $*$ denote convolution)

$$\sigma_4^2 = \frac{8}{C_0^3}\sigma^4\left[\int w^2\right]\left[\int (K-L)^2\right] + 4C_0^2\sigma^2 d_K^2\left[\int (m'')^2 w^2\right],$$

$$L(u) = -uK'(u),$$

$$\sigma_3^2 = \frac{8}{C_0^3}\sigma^4\left[\int w^2\right]\left[\int (K*K - K*L)^2\right]$$
$$+ 4C_0\sigma^2 d_K^2\left[\int (m'')^2 w^2\right],$$

$$C_3 = \frac{2}{C_0^3}\sigma^2 c_K^2\left[\int w\right] + 3C_0^2 d_K^2\left[\int (m'')^2 w^2\right].$$

An important consequence of these two limit theorems describing the behavior of automatically selected bandwidths is that they imply that the "plug-in" method of choosing h (in which one substitutes estimates of the unknown parts of d_{MA}), even if one knew the unknowns σ^2 and $\int (m'')^2 w$, has an algebraic rate of convergence no better than that of the $\hat{h}$s given in Algorithm 5.1.1. Hence the additional noise involved in estimating these unknown parts in practice, especially the second derivative part in the case where m is not very smooth, casts some doubt on the applicability of the plug-in estimator.

By comparing σ_1^2 and σ_2^2, the asymptotic variances of the previous two theorems, one sees that $\sigma_2^2 \leq \sigma_1^2$, so h_0 is closer to $\hat{h}_0$ than $\hat{h}$ is in terms of asymptotic variances. It is important to note that the asymptotic variance σ_1^2 is *independent* of the particular correction function $\Xi(n^{-1}h^{-1})$, although simulation studies to be mentioned subsequently seem to indicate a different performance for different Ξs. In the related field of density estimation Hall and Marron (1987) showed that the relative rate of convergence of

$$\frac{\hat{h} - \hat{h}_0}{\hat{h}_0}$$

cannot be improved upon $n^{-1/10}$. This suggests that also in the present setting there is no better estimator $\hat{h}$ for $\hat{h}_0$. This issue is further pursued in the Complements to this section.

Several extensions of the above limit theorems are possible. For instance, the assumption that the errors are identically distributed can be relaxed to assuming that ε_i has variance $\sigma^2(X_i)$, where the variance function $\sigma^2(x)$ is a smooth function. Also the design points need not be univariate. In the multivariate case with the X_i having dimension d, the exponents of the first parts of (5.2.5) and (5.2.6) change from $3/10$ to $(d+2)/(2(d+4))$.

The kernel K can also be allowed to take on negative values to exploit possible higher rates of convergence (Section 4.1). In particular, if K is of order $(0, p)$ (see Section 4.5) and if m has a uniformly continuous pth derivative, then the exponents of convergence change from $3/10$ to $3/(2(2p + 1))$. This says that the relative speed of convergence for estimated bandwidths is slower for functions m with higher derivatives than it is for functions with lower derivatives. One should look not only at the bandwidth limit theorems but also at the limit result for d_A. In the case in which m has higher derivatives, d_A converges faster to zero, specifically, at the rate $n^{-2p/(2p+1)}$. However, this issue seems to be counterintuitive. Why is the relative speed for $\hat{h}$ for higher order kernels

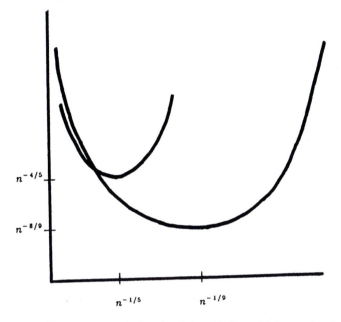

Figure 5.11. A sketch of $d_{MA}(\cdot)$ for a higher order $(p = 4)$ and a lower order $(p = 2)$ kernel for $d = 1$.

slower than that for lower order kernels? To get some insight into this consider Fig. 5.11 showing $d_{MA}(\cdot)$ for higher and lower order kernels.

One can see that $d_{MA}(\cdot)$ for the higher order kernel has a flatter minimum than that for the lower order kernel. Therefore, it is harder to approximate the true bandwidth. But since the minimum value $n^{-8/9}$ is smaller than the minimum value $n^{-4/5}$ for the lower order kernel it does not matter so much to miss the minimum $\hat{h}_0$!

Rice (1984a) and Härdle, Hall and Marron (1988) performed a simulation study in order to shed some light on the finite sample performance of the different selectors. One hundred samples of $n = 75$ pseudo-random normal variables, ε_i, with mean zero and standard deviation $\sigma = 0.0015$ were generated. These were added to the curve $m(x) = x^3(1 - x)^3$, which allows "wrap-around-estimation" to eliminate boundary effects. The kernel function was taken to be a rescaled quartic kernel

$$K(u) = (15/8)(1 - 4u^2)^2 I(|u| \le 1/2).$$

The result of these simulation studies can be qualitativly described as follows. The selectors have been compared using the number of times out of 100 Monte Carlo repetitions that either the ratio of MASE

$$d_{MA}(\hat{h})/d_{MA}(h_0)$$

or the ratio of ASE

$$d_A(\hat{h})/d_A(\hat{h}_0)$$

exceeded $1.05, 1.1, \ldots$ and so on. The T selector turned out to be the best in these simulations. To understand this better, consider the form of the selectors more closely. All these selectors have a trivial minimum at $h = n^{-1}K(0) = 0.025$, the "no smoothing" point where $\hat{m}_h(X_i) = Y_i$. The prediction error $p(h)$ has a second-order zero at the "no smoothing" point. GCV counters this by using a correction factor which has a double pole there, as does T. On the other hand, FPE has only a single pole, while AIC and S have no poles at the "no smoothing" point.

The ordering of performance that was observed in both studies can be qualitatively described through the number of poles that a selector had at the "no smoothing" point. The more poles the penalizing function had the better it was in these studies.

Figure 5.12 gives an indication of what the limit theorems actually mean in terms of the actual curves, for one of the actual curves and for one of the 100 data sets (with $\sigma = 0.011$ and $n = 75$). The solid curve in each plot is $m(x)$. The dashed curves are the estimates $\hat{m}_h(x)$.

In Figure 5.12a the dashed curve is computed with $\hat{h} = .26$, the minimizer of S for that data set. In Figure 5.12b, $\hat{m}_h$ is computed with $h = .39$, the minimizer of ASE. Finally, in Figure 5.12c the curve suggested by all the other selectors ($h = .66$) is shown. This example of how different the selectors can be for a specific data set was chosen to demonstrate again the slow rate of convergence in the above limit theorems. More details about this study, for example, the question of how close to normality the distribution of $n^{3/10}(\hat{h} - \hat{h}_0)$ is, for this small sample size, can be found in Härdle, Hall and Marron (1988).

Table 5.2.1 shows the sample mean and standard deviation of the bandwidth minimizing the quantity listed at the left. It is interesting that the selector whose mean matches best with $\hat{h}_0$ is the rather poorly performing FPE, which is not surprising given the comments on the poles above. The selector T biases slightly toward $\hat{h}$, while FPE biases more downwards. The last two columns show the sample correlation coefficients for the selected bandwidth with $\hat{h}_0$ and $\hat{h}_{GCV}$, the minimizer of GCV, respectively.

The simulations shown in Table 5.2.1. indicated that, despite the equivalence of all selectors, Rice's T had a slightly better performance. This stemmed, as explained, from the fact that the selector T has a

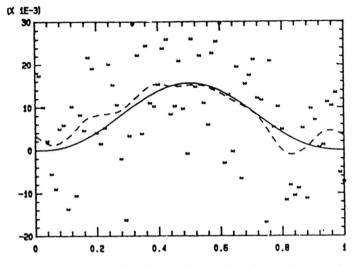

Figure 5.12a.   Plot of $n = 75$ regression observations simulated from solid curve $m(x) = x^3(1-x)^3$ and kernel smooth (quartic kernel) with $h = 0.26$. From Härdle, Hall and Marron (1988) with permission of the American Statistical Association.

slight bias toward oversmoothing (pole of T at twice the "no smoothing" point). The performance of T should get worse if the simulation setting is changed in such a way that "reduction of bias is more important than reduction of variance." In other words the right branch of the $d_A(h)$ curve becomes steeper than the left.

A simulation study in this direction was carried out by Härdle (1986e). The sample was constructed from $n = 75$ observations with normal errors, $\sigma = 0.05$, and a sinusoidal regression curve $m(x) = \sin(\lambda 2\pi x)$. The quartic kernel was chosen. The number of exceedances (formulated as above) for $\lambda = 1, 2, 3$ was studied.

As expected, the performance of T got worse as λ increased, which supports the hypothesis that the relatively good performance of T was due to the specific simulation setting. The best overall performance, though, showed GCV (generalized cross-validation).

Exercises

5.2.1 Prove that in the setting of this section the cross-validation function approach is also based on a penalizing idea, that is, prove

(X 1E-3)

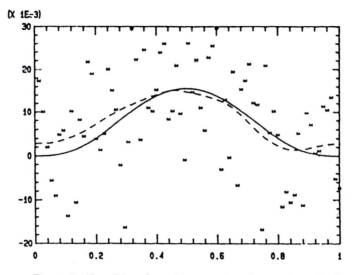

Figure 5.12b.   Plot of $n = 75$ regression observations simulated from solid curve $m(x) = x^3(1-x)^3$ and kernel smooth (quartic kernel) with $h = 0.39$. From Härdle, Hall and Marron (1988) with permission of the American Statistical Association.

formula (5.2.2)

$$CV(h)/p(h) = 1 + 2n^{-1}h^{-1}K(0) + O_p(n^{-2}h^{-2}).$$

5.2.2 Show that $\tilde{R}(h)$, the unbiased risk estimation selection function, satisfies

$$\tilde{R}(h)/p(h) = 1 + 2n^{-1}h^{-1}K(0) + o_p(n^{-1}h^{-1}).$$

5.2.3 Interpret the penalizing term for a uniform kernel using the fact that $N = 2nh$ points fall into a kernel neighborhood. What does "penalizing" now mean in terms of N?

5.2.4 Prove that from the relative convergence (5.2.3)

$$\frac{d_A(\hat{h})}{d_A(\hat{h}_0)} \xrightarrow{p} 1$$

it follows that the ratio of bandwidths tends to one, that is,

$$\frac{\hat{h}}{\hat{h}_0} \xrightarrow{p} 1.$$

[*Hint* : Use Theorem 4.1.1 and Taylor expansion.]

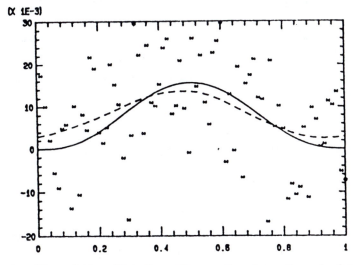

Figure 5.12c.   Plot of $n = 75$ regression observations simulated from solid curve $m(x) = x^3(1-x)^3$ and kernel smooth (quartic kernel) with $h = 0.66$. From Härdle, Hall and Marron (1988) with permission of the American Statistical Association.

5.2.5 Recall the variances of Theorem 5.2.1 and 5.2.2. Show that

$$\sigma_2^2 \le \sigma_1^2.$$

[*Hint* : Use the Cauchy–Schwarz inequality.]

5.2.6 Can you construct a confidence interval for the bandwidths $\hat{h}_0$?

5.2.7 Can you construct a confidence interval for the distance $d_A(\hat{h}_0)$?

5.2.8 (hard) How would you extend Theorem 5.2.1 and 5.2.2 to the random design setting?

[*Hint* : Look at Härdle, Hall and Marron (1990) and use the linearization of the kernel smoother as in Section 4.2.]

Complements

I have mentioned that in the related field of density estimation there is a lower-bound result by Hall and Marron (1987) which shows that

$$\frac{\hat{h} - \hat{h}_0}{\hat{h}_0}$$

cannot be smaller than $n^{-1/10}$. A natural question to ask is whether this relative difference can be made smaller when $\hat{h}_0$ is replaced by h_0, the

Table 5.2.1   *Summary statistics for automatically chosen and optimal bandwidths from 100 data sets*

$\hat{h}$	$\mu_n(\hat{h})$	$\sigma_n(\hat{h})$	$\rho_n(\hat{h}, h_0)$	$\rho_n(\hat{h}, \hat{h}_{GCV})$
		$n = 75$		
ASE	.51000	.10507	1.00000	−.46002
T	.56035	.13845	−.50654	.85076
CV	.57287	.15411	−.47494	.87105
GCV	.52929	.16510	−.46602	1.00000
R	.52482	.17852	−.40540	.83565
FPE	.49790	.17846	−.45879	.76829
AIC	.49379	.18169	−.46472	.76597
S	.39435	.21350	−.21965	.52915
		$n = 500$		
ASE	.36010	.07198	1.00000	−.31463
T	.32740	.08558	−.32243	.99869
GCV	.32580	.08864	−.31463	1.00000
AIC	.32200	.08865	−.30113	.97373
S	.31840	.08886	−.29687	.97308

Source: From Härdle, Hall and Marron (1988) with permission of the American Statistical Association.

minimizer of MISE. In the paper by Hall and Marron (1988) it is argued that this relative difference can be made as small as $n^{-1/2}$. This looks like a drastic improvement, but as Mammen (1988) shows, the search for such bandwidths is *not* justified. In particular, he shows

Theorem 5.2.3   *Suppose that there exists a data-based bandwidth $\hat{h}$ with*

$$\frac{\hat{h} - h_0}{h_0} = o_p(n^{-1/10}).$$

Then there exists another data-based bandwidth $\tilde{h}$ such that

$$n(d_I(\tilde{h}) - d_I(\hat{h}_0)) \xrightarrow{\mathcal{L}} \gamma_1 \chi_1^2,$$
$$n(d_I(\hat{h}) - d_I(\hat{h}_0)) \xrightarrow{\mathcal{L}} \gamma_2 \chi_1^2,$$

with $0 < \gamma_1 < \gamma_2$.

This theorem suggests that

$$\frac{E(d_I(\tilde{h})) - E(d_I(\hat{h}_0))}{E(d_I(\hat{h})) - E(d_I(\hat{h}_0))}$$

converges to a constant, which is strictly smaller than one. Clearly $d_I(\tilde{h}) \geq d_I(\hat{h}_0)$ and $d_I(\hat{h}) \geq d_I(\hat{h}_0)$. Therefore, this would imply that using the bandwidth $\tilde{h}$ leads to a smaller risk than using $\hat{h}$. For more details see Mammen (1988).

5.3   Local adaptation of the smoothing parameter

A smoothing parameter that is selected by one of the previously described methods optimizes a global error criterion. Such a "global" choice need not necessarily be optimal for the estimation of the regression curve at one particular point, as the trivial inequality

$$\inf_h \int E(\hat{m}_h - m)^2 \geq \int \inf_h E(\hat{m}_h - m)^2$$

shows. In this section I present two methods for locally adapting the choice of the smoothing parameter. The first one is based on the idea of approximating the distribution of $\sqrt{nh}(\hat{m}_h - m)$ by bootstrapping. The second one, the *supersmoother* developed by Friedman (1984), is constructed via a "local cross-validation" method for k-NN smoothers.

Improving the smooth locally by bootstrapping

We have already seen that the so-called wild bootstrap method (Section 4.2) allows us to approximate the distribution of $\sqrt{nh}(\hat{m}_h - m)$. In the following, though, I would like to present a slightly different bootstrap method in the simpler setting of i.i.d. error terms. This simpler setting has the advantage that resampling can be done from the whole set of observed residuals. Let $X_i = i/n$ and $\mathrm{var}(\varepsilon_i) = \sigma^2$. The stochastics of the observations are completely determined by the observation error. Resampling should therefore be performed with the estimated residuals,

$$\hat{\varepsilon}_i = Y_i - \hat{m}_g(X_i)$$
$$= Y_i - n^{-1} \sum_{j=1}^n K_g(X_i - X_j)Y_j, \quad i = 1,\ldots,n,$$

where g denotes a pilot bandwidth. Since the estimate is more biased near the boundary it is advisable to use only residuals from an interior subinterval $[\eta, 1-\eta], 0 < \eta < 1/2$. In order to let the resampled residuals reflect the behavior of the true regression curve they are recentered by their mean:

$$\tilde{\varepsilon}_i = \hat{\varepsilon}_i - \mathrm{mean}\{\hat{\varepsilon}_i\}.$$

Bootstrap residuals $\{\varepsilon_i^*\}$ are then created by sampling with replacement from $\{\tilde{\varepsilon}_i\}$, producing *bootstrap response variables*

$$Y_i^* = \hat{m}_g(X_i) + \varepsilon_i^*.$$

A bootstrap estimator $\hat{m}^*$ of m is obtained by smoothing $\{(X_i, Y_i^*)\}$ rather than $\{(X_i, Y_i)\}$. It is commonly said that the *bootstrap principle* holds if the distributions of $\hat{m}^*(x)$ and $\hat{m}(x)$, when suitably normalized, become close as the sample size n increases. If convergence of these distributions is examined in the Mallows metric (Bickel and Freedman 1981), then the second moments of these distributions also become close. Since at a fixed point x the MSE,

$$E(\hat{m}_h(x) - m(x))^2,$$

is the quantity we are interested in, the bootstrap approximation in terms of the Mallows metric will give us a method for estimating the local mean squared error. To simplify the following calculations assume that the kernel is standardized to have $d_K = 1$.

In the bootstrap, any occurrence of ε_i is replaced by ε_i^*, and therefore

$$\hat{m}_{h,g}^*(x) = n^{-1} \sum_{i=1}^n K_h(x - X_i)(\hat{m}_g(X_i) + \varepsilon_i^*)$$

is the bootstrap smoother. It is the aim of the bootstrap to approximate the distribution of $\sqrt{nh}(\hat{m}_h(x) - m(x))$, where

$$\hat{m}_h(x) - m(x) = n^{-1} \sum_{i=1}^n K_h(x - X_i)\varepsilon_i$$
$$+ (h^2/2)m''(x) + o(n^{-1/2}h^{-1/2} + h^2)$$
$$\approx n^{-1} \sum_{i=1}^n K_h(x - X_i)\varepsilon_i$$
$$+ (h^2/2)m''(x), \quad h \to 0, \quad nh \to \infty.$$

If this expansion is mirrored by the bootstrap estimator $\hat{m}_{h,g}^*$, one should center first around the expectation under the bootstrap distribution, which is approximately

$$\hat{m}_{C,h,g}(x) = n^{-1} \sum_i K_1(x - X_i; h, g)Y_i, \qquad (5.3.1)$$

where

$$K_1(v; h, g) = K_h * K_g = \int K_h(u)K_g(v - u)du$$

is the convolution kernel of K_h and K_g. The bias component $(h^2/2)m''(x)$ may be estimated by employing a consistent estimator of $m''(x)$. (In Section 3.1 I defined kernel estimators of derivatives.) This results in the bootstrap approximation

$$\sqrt{nh}(\hat{m}^*_{h,g}(x) - \hat{m}_{C,h,g}(x) + (h^2/2)\hat{m}''(x)),$$

where $\hat{m}''(x)$ denotes any consistent estimate of the second derivative $m''(x)$. Härdle and Bowman (1988) proved that the bootstrap principle holds.

Theorem 5.3.1 *If h and g tend to zero at the rate $n^{-1/5}$, the kernel function K is Lipschitz continuous and m is twice differentiable, then the bootstrap principle holds, that is,*

$$d_2(\sqrt{nh}(\hat{m}_h(x) - m(x)),$$
$$\sqrt{nh}(\hat{m}_{h,g}(x) - \hat{m}_{C,h,g}(x) + (h^2/2)\hat{m}''(x)))\overset{p}{\to} 0,$$

where

$$d_2(F,G) = \inf_{\substack{X \sim F \\ Y \sim G}} [E_{(X,Y)}(X - Y)^2]^{1/2}$$

denotes the Mallows metric.

The MSE $d_M(x,h) = E(\hat{m}_h(x) - m(x))^2$ can then be estimated by

$$\hat{d}_M(x;h) = \int (\hat{m}^*_{h,g}(x) - \hat{m}_{C,h,g}(x) + (h^2/2)\hat{m}''(x))^2 dF^*_n,$$

where F^*_n denotes the empirical distribution function of $\{\tilde{\varepsilon}_i\}$. Denote by $\hat{h}(x)$ the bandwidth that minimizes $\hat{d}_M(x;h)$ over a set of smoothing parameters H_n.

This choice of *local adaptive bandwidth* is asymptotically optimal in the sense of Theorem 5.1.1 as Härdle and Bowman (1988) show; that is,

$$\frac{d_M(x;\hat{h}(x))}{\inf_{h \in H_n} d_M(x,h)} \overset{p}{\to} 1. \tag{5.3.2}$$

This adaptive choice of $h = h(x)$ is illustrated in Figure 5.13, which displays some data simulated by adding a normally distributed error, with standard deviation 0.1, to the curve $m(x) = \sin(4\pi x)$ evaluated at $X = \frac{(i-1/2)}{100}$, $i = 1,\ldots,n = 100$. Cross-validation was used to select a good global smoothing parameter ($g = 0.03$) and the resulting estimate of the regression function shows the problems caused by bias at the peaks and troughs, where $|m''(x)|$ is high.

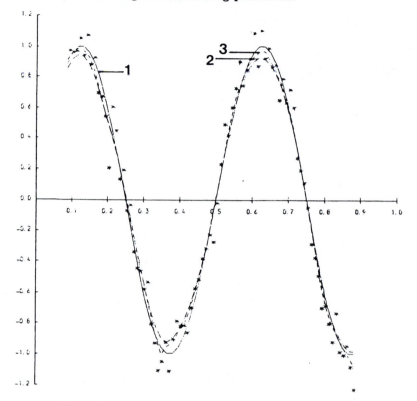

Figure 5.13.   Data simulated from the curve $m(x) = \sin(4\pi x)$, with $N(0, (0.1)^2)$ error distribution. True curve (solid line, label 1); global smoothing (dashed line, label 2); local adaptive smoothing (fine dashed line, label 3). From Härdle and Bowman (1988) with permission of the American Statistical Association .

To see what local smoothing parameters have been actually used consider Figure 5.14. This figure plots the local smoothing parameters obtained by minimizing the bootstrap estimate $\hat{d}_M(x, h)$ as a function of x.

For comparison, the asymptotically optimal local smoothing parameters

$$h_0^*(x) = C_0(x)\, n^{-1/5},$$

with

$$C_0(x) = \left[\frac{\sigma^2\, c_K}{d_K\, m''(x))^2} \right]^{1/5},$$

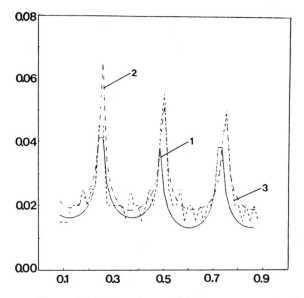

Figure 5.14. Local smoothing parameters for the simulated data of Figure 5.13. Asymptotically optimal (solid line, label 1); direct estimation (dashed line, label 2); bootstrap (fine dashed line, label 3). From Härdle and Bowman (1988) with permission of the American Statistical Association .

are also plotted. It can be seen that an appropriate pattern of local smoothing has been achieved. Comparison with the "plug-in" local smoothing parameters (based on estimating C_0) revealed for this example little difference. The advantage of the above bootstrap method though lies in the fact that it is insensitive to irregularites introduced by estimation of $m''(x)$; see Härdle and Bowman (1988). Also, the plug-in method requires an estimate of bias; see Müller and Stadtmüller (1987). The above idea of bootstrapping from estimated residuals has been applied to spectral density estimation by Franke and Härdle (1988).

The supersmoother

The so-called *supersmoother* proposed by Friedman (1984) is based on local linear k-NN fits in a variable neighborhood of the estimation point x. "Local cross-validation" is applied to estimate the optimal span as a function of the predictor variable. The algorithm is based on the k-NN updating formulas as described in Section 3.2. It is therefore highly computationally efficient.

The name "supersmoother" stems from the fact that it uses optimizing resampling techniques at a minimum of computational effort. The basic idea of the supersmoother is the same as that for the bootstrap smoother. Both methods attempt to minimize the local mean squared error. The supersmoother is constructed from three initial smooths, the *tweeter*, *midrange* and *woofer*. They are intended to reproduce the three main parts of the frequency spectrum of $m(x)$ and are defined by k-NN smooths with $k = 0.05n$, $0.2n$ and $0.5n$, respectively. Next, the cross-validated residuals

$$r_{(i)}(k) = [Y_i - \hat{m}_k(X_i)] \left(1 - 1/k - \frac{(X_i - \overline{\mu}_{X_i})^2}{V_{X_i}}\right) \qquad (5.3.3)$$

are computed, where $\overline{\mu}_{X_i}$ and V_{X_i} denote the local mean and variance from the k nearest neighbors of X_i as in Section 3.2. Then the best span values $\hat{k}(X_i)$ are determined by minimizing $r_{(i)}(k)$ at each X_i over the tweeter, midrange and woofer value of k.

Since a smooth based on this span sequence would, in practice, have an unnecessarily high variance, smoothing the values $\left|r_{(i)}(k)\right|$ against X_i is recommended using the resulting smooth to select the best span values, $\hat{k}(X_i)$. In a further step the span values $\hat{k}(X_i)$ are smoothed against X_i (with a midrange smoother). The result is an estimated span for each observation with a value between the tweeter and the woofer values.

The resulting curve estimate, the supersmoother, is obtained by interpolating between the two (out of the three) smoothers with closest span values. Figure 5.15 shows $n = 200$ pairs $\{(X_i, Y_i)\}_{i=1}^n$ with $\{X_i\}$ uniform on $[0, 1]$,

$$Y_i = \sin(2\pi(1 - X_i)^2) + X_i\varepsilon_i,$$

where the $\{\varepsilon_i\}$ are i.i.d. standard normal variates. The resulting supersmoother is shown as a solid line.

Figure 5.16 shows the estimated optimal span $\hat{k}(X_i)$ as a function of X_i. In the "low-noise high-curvature" region $(x < 0.2)$ the tweeter span is proposed. In the remaining regions a span value about the midrange is suggested.

When $m(x)$ is very smooth, more accurate curve estimates can be obtained by biasing the smoothing parameter toward larger span values. One way of doing this would be to use a smoothing parameter selection criterion that penalizes more than the "no smoothing" point $k = 1$. For example, Rice's T (Figure 5.10) would bias the estimator toward smoother curves. Friedman (1984) proposed parameterizing this "selection bias" for enhancing the bass component of the smoother output.

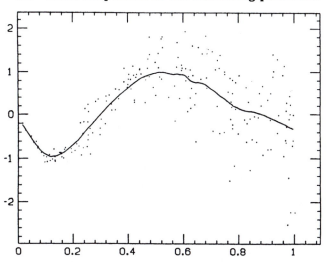

Figure 5.15.   A scatter plot of $n = 200$ data points $\{(X_i, Y_i)\}_{i=1}^{n}$. X_i is uniformly distributed over $[0,1]$, $Y_i = \sin(2\pi(1 - X_i)^2 + X_i\varepsilon_i, \varepsilon_i \sim N(0,1)$. The solid line indicates the supersmoother. From Friedman (1984) with permission of the author.

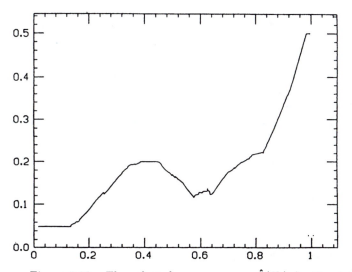

Figure 5.16.   The selected span sequence $\hat{k}(X_i)$ for the data from Figure 5.15. From Friedman (1984) with permission of the author.

For this purpose, introduce the span

$$\tilde{k}(X_i) = \hat{k}(X_i) + (k_W - \hat{k}(X_i))R_i^{10-\alpha}$$

with

$$R_i = \left[\frac{\hat{e}(X_i, \hat{k}(X_i))}{\hat{e}(X_i, k_W)} \right],$$

where $\hat{e}(x, k)$ denotes the estimated residual at x with smoothing parameter k, and $k_W = 0.5n$ is the woofer span. The parameter $0 \le \alpha \le 10$ is called the *tone control*. The value $\alpha = 0$ corresponds to very little bass enhancement, whereas $\alpha = 10$ corresponds to the woofer (maximum bass). A choice of *alpha* between these two extremes biases the selection procedure toward larger span values.

Exercises

5.3.1 Prove that the term $\hat{m}_{C,h,g}(x)$ is an approximation of lower order than $\sqrt{nh}$ to $E_{F_n^*}\hat{m}^*_{h,g}(x)$,

$$\hat{m}_{C,h,g}(x) = E_{F_n^*}\hat{m}^*_{h,g}(x) + o_p(n^{1/2}h^{1/2}).$$

5.3.2 What is the difference between the method here in Section 5.3 and the wild bootstrap? Can you prove Theorem 5.3.1 without the bias estimate?
[*Hint*: Use an oversmooth resampling mean $\hat{m}_g(x)$ to construct the boostrap observations, $Y_i^* = \hat{m}_g(X_i) + \varepsilon_i^*$. The difference

$$E_{F_n^*}\hat{m}_{g,h}(x) - \hat{m}_g(x)$$

will reflect, as in the wild bootstrap, the bias of $\hat{m}_h(x)$.]
5.3.3 Show that the cross-validated residuals (5.3.3) stem from the leave-out technique applied to k-NN smoothing.
5.3.4 Try the woofer, midrange and tweeter on the simulated data set from Table 2, Appendix 2. Compare it with the super-smoother. Can you comment on where and why the super-smoother changed the smoothing parameter?
[*Hint*: Use XploRe (1989) or a similar interactive package.]

5.4   Comparing bandwidths between laboratories (canonical kernels)

Observe that if one used a kernel of the form

$$K_s(u) = s^{-1}K(u/s)$$

and rescaled the bandwidth by the factor s one would obtain the same estimate as with the original kernel smoother. A kernel can therefore be seen as an equivalence class of functions K with possible rescalings by s. A consequence of this scale dependence is that the bandwidth selection problem is not identifiable if the kernel K is determined only up to scale. Which member of this equivalence class is "most representative"?

More generally, consider the situation in which two statisticians analyze the same data set but use different kernels for their smoothers. They come up with some bandwidths that they like. Their smoothing parameters have been determined subjectively or automatically, but they have been computed for different kernels and therefore cannot be compared directly. In order to allow some comparison one needs a common scale for both bandwidths. How can we find such a "common scale"?

A desirable property of such a scale should be that two kernel smoothers with the same bandwidth should ascribe the same amount of smoothing to the data. An approach to finding a representative member of each equivalence class of kernels has already been presented in Section 4.5. Epanechnikov (1969) has selected kernels with kernel constant $d_K = 1$. Another approach taken by Gasser, Müller and Mammitzsch (1985) insists that the support of the kernel be $[-1, 1]$. A drawback to both methods is that they are rather arbitrary and are not making the attempt to give the same amount of smoothing for different kernels.

An attempt for such a joint scale is given by so-called *canonical kernels* in the class of kernels K_s (Marron and Nolan 1988). It is based on the well-known expansion of the MSE for $d = 1, p = 2$ and $K = K_s$,

$$d_M(h) \approx n^{-1}h^{-1}c_{K_s}C_1 + h^4 d^2_{K_s}C_2, \quad h \to 0, \ nh \to \infty,$$

where C_1, C_2 denote constants depending on the unknown distribution of the data. A little algebra shows that this is equal to

$$n^{-1}h^{-1}C_1(s^{-1}c_K) + h^4 C_2(s^2 d_K)^2. \tag{5.4.1}$$

Observe that the problems of selecting K and h are "uncoupled" if

$$s^{-1}c_K = (s^2 d_K)^2.$$

This uncoupling can be achieved by simply defining

$$s = s^* = \left[\frac{c_K}{d_K^2}\right]^{1/5}$$

Hence, define the *canonical kernel* K^* as that kernel of the class K_s with $s = s^*$. For this canonical kernel one has

$$\left(\int u^2 K^*(u)du\right)^2 = \int (K^*(u))^2 du$$

$$= (s^*)^{-1} c_K = \frac{d_K^{2/5}}{c_K^{1/5}} c_K$$

$$= d_K^{2/5} c_K^{4/5}.$$

Hence, for the canonical kernel,

$$d_M(h) \approx (d_K)^{2/5} (c_K)^{4/5} [n^{-1}h^{-1}C_1 + h^4 C_2],$$

which shows again that the canonical kernel K^* uncouples the problems of kernel and bandwidth selection. Note that K^* does not depend on the starting choice of K: One could replace K by any K_s and K^* would still be the same.

The advantage of canonical kernels is that they allow simple comparison between different kernel classes. Suppose that $K_{(1)}$ and $K_{(2)}$ are the canonical kernels from each class and that one wants the two estimated curves to represent the same amount of smoothing, that is, the variance and bias^2 trade-off should be the same for both smoothers. This is simply achieved by using the *same bandwidth for both estimators*. If canonical kernels are used, the $d_M(h)$ functions will look different for the two kernels, as one is a multiple of the other, but each will have its minimum at the same place. The kernel class that has the lowest minimum is given by the "optimal kernel" of order 2, the so-called Epanechnikov kernel.

One interesting family of kernels, which contains many of the kernels used in practice, is

$$K^\alpha(u) = C_\alpha (1 - x^2)^\alpha I(|u| \leq 1),$$

where C_α makes K^α a probability density:

$$C_\alpha = \Gamma(2\alpha + 2)\Gamma(\alpha + 1)^{-2} 2^{-2\alpha - 1}.$$

The first three columns of Table 5.4.1 show the values of α and C_α for the most common cases. The normal case is included as $\alpha = \infty$. It is simple to check that the rescaling factor s^* for each K^α is

$$s^* = 2^{-1/5}\Gamma(\alpha + 1)^{-4/5}(2\alpha + 3)^{2/5}\Gamma(2\alpha + 2)^{2/5}$$
$$\times \Gamma(2\alpha + 1)^{2/5}\Gamma(4\alpha + 2)^{-1/5}.$$

In practice, one uses kernels that are not necessarily canonical, since one is used to thinking in terms of a certain scale of the kernel, for

Table 5.4.1   *Canonical kernels from the family*
K^α

Kernel	α	C_α	s^*
Uniform	0	1/2	$(9/2)^{1/5} \approx 1.3510$
Epanechnikov	1	3/4	$15^{1/5} \approx 1.7188$
Quartic	2	15/16	$35^{1/5} \approx 2.0362$
Triweight	3	35/32	$(9450/143)^{1/5} \approx 2.3122$
Gaussian	∞	—	$(1/(4\pi))^{1/10} \approx 0.7764$

example, multiples of the standard deviation for the normal kernel. How does one then compare the smoothing parameters h_1, h_2 between laboratories? The following procedure is based on canonical kernels. First transform the scale of both kernel classes to the canonical kernel $K^*(u) = (s^*)^{-1}K(u/s^*)$. Then compare the bandwidths for the respective canonical kernels. More formally, this procedure is described in Algorithm 5.4.1.

Algorithm 5.4.1

Suppose that lab j used kernel K_j and bandwidth h_j, $j = 1, 2$.
STEP 1.
Transform h_j to canonical scale:

$$h_j^* = h_j/s_j^*, \ j = 1, 2.$$

STEP 2.
Decide from the relation of h_1^* to h_2^* whether both labs have produced the same smooth or whether one or the other has over- or undersmooothed.

Suppose, for example, that laboratory 1 used the Gaussian kernel and came up with a bandwidth of, say, $h_1 = 0.05$ (see Figure 3.21). Another statistician in laboratory 2 used a quartic kernel and computed from cross-validation a bandwidth of $h_2 = 0.15$ (see Figure 5.4). A typical situation is depicted in Figure 5.17, showing the average squared error $d_A(h)$ for the Gaussian and the quartic kernel smoothers as applied to the simulated data set from Table 2 in Appendix 2. Obviously, the bandwidth minimizing each of these functions gives the same amount of trade-off between bias^2 and variance.

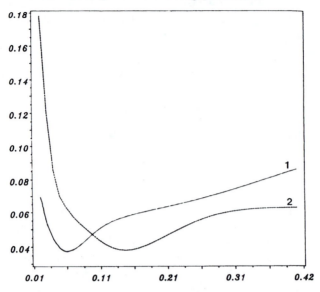

Figure 5.17.   The averaged squared error $d_A(h)$ averaged from the simulated data set (Table 3.6.1) for Gaussian (solid line, label 1) and quartic (dashed line, label 2) kernel smoothers with weight function $w(u) = I(|u - 0.5| \leq 0.4)$.

Let me compute s^* explicitly for this example. The factor s_1^* for the Gaussian kernel is

$$s_1^* = \left(\int \left(\frac{1}{2\pi} \right) e^{-u^2} du \right)^{1/5} = (2\sqrt{\pi})^{-1/5} \approx 0.776.$$

The bandwidth for the canonical normal kernel is therefore $h_1^* = h_1/0.776 = 0.0644$. The quartic kernel $K(u) = (15/16)(1 - u^2)^2 I(|u| \leq 1)$ has $d_K = 1/7$ and $c_K = 15/21$; the "canonical quartic kernel" is therefore determined by

$$s_2^* = \left(\frac{15 \cdot 49}{21} \right)^{1/5} = 35^{1/5} = 2.036,$$

which means that $h_2^* = h_2/2.036 = 0.0736$.

In summary, the optimal bandwidth $\hat{h}_0 = \arg\min[d_A(h)]$ is 0.0736 (on the canonical kernel scale), which means that my subjective choice (Figure 3.21) for this simulated example of $h_2^* = 0.0644$ resulted in slight undersmoothing.

Exercises

5.4.1 Compute the canonical kernel from the triangular kernel.

5.4.2 Derive the canonical kernels for the derivative kernels from Section 4.5.

5.4.3 Try kernel smoothing in practice and transform your bandwidth by the procedure of Algorithm 5.4.1. Compare with another kernel smooth and compute the bandwidth that gives the same amount of smoothing for both situations.

CHAPTER 6

Data sets with outliers

> In exploratory data analysis one might wish instead to dis-
> cover patterns while making few assumptions about data struc-
> ture, using techniques with properties that change only gradu-
> ally across a wide range of noise distributions. Nonlinear data
> smoothers provide a practical method of finding general smooth
> patterns for sequenced data confounded with long-tailed noise.
>
> P. Velleman (1980, p. 609)

Suppose that one observes data such as those in Figure 6.1: the main
body of the data lies in a strip around zero and a few observations,
governing the scaling of the scatter plot, lie apart from this region. These
few data points are obviously *outliers*. This terminology does not mean
that outliers are not part of the joint distribution of the data or that
they contain no information for estimating the regression curve. It means
rather that outliers look as if they are too small a fraction of the data
to be allowed to dominate the small-sample behavior of the statistics to
be calculated. Any smoother (based on local averages) applied to data
like that in Figure 6.1 will exhibit a tendency to "follow the outlying
observations." Methods for handling data sets with outliers are called
robust or *resistant*.

From a data-analytic viewpoint, a nonrobust behavior of the smoother
is sometimes undesirable. Suppose that, a posteriori, a parametric model
for the response curve is to be postulated. Any erratic behavior of the
nonparametric pilot estimate will cause biased parametric formulations.
Imagine, for example, a situation in which an outlier has not been identified and the nonparametric smoothing method has produced a slight
peak in the neighborhood of that outlier. A parametric model which
fitted that "nonexisting" peak would be too high-dimensional.

In this case, a robust estimator, insensitive to a single wild spike
outlier, would be advisable. Carroll and Ruppert (1988, p. 175) aptly
describe this as follows:

*Robust estimators can handle both data and model inadequacies. They
will downweight and, in some cases, completely reject grossly erroneous*

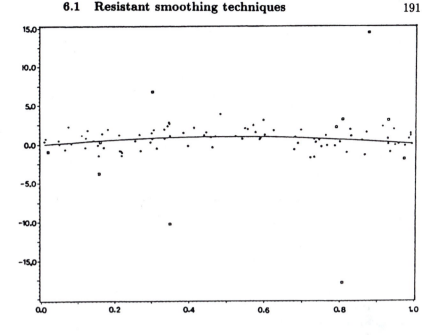

Figure 6.1.   A simulated data set with outliers. The joint probability density function of $\{(X_i, Y_i)\}_{i=1}^n$, $n = 100$, was $f(x, y) =$
$g(y - m(x))I(x \in [0, 1])$ with $m(x) = \sin(\pi x)$ and the mixture density $g(x) = (9/10)\varphi(x) + (1/10)(1/9)\varphi(x/9)$, where φ denotes the
standard normal density. The data points coming from the long tail
mixture part $(1/9)\varphi(x/9)$ are indicated by squares. The regression
line $m(x)$ is shown as a solid line. From Härdle (1989).

*data. In many situations, a simple model will adequately fit all but a
few unusual observations.*

In this chapter, several resistant smoothing techniques are presented.
It is seen how basic ideas from robust estimation of location can be used
for nonparametric resistant smoothing. From the discussion also evolves
an asymptotically efficient smoothing parameter selection rule.

6.1   Resistant smoothing techniques

A linear local average of the response variable is, per se, not robust
against outliers. Moving a response observation to infinity would drag
the smooth to infinity as well. In this sense, local averaging smoothing has unbounded capacity to be influenced by "far out" observations.
Resistance or "bounded influence" against outliers can be achieved

by downweighting large residuals which would otherwise influence the smoother.

We have already encountered a straightforward resistant technique: median smoothing. It is highly robust since the extreme response observations (stemming from predictor variables in a neighborhood around x) do not have any effect on the (local) median of the response variables. A slight disadvantage of median smoothing, though, is that it produces a rough and wiggly curve. *Resmoothing* and *twicing* are data-analytic techniques to ameliorate median smoothing in this respect; see Velleman (1980) and Mallows (1980).

LOcally WEighted Scatter plot Smoothing (LOWESS)

Cleveland (1979) proposed the following algorithm, LOWESS, a resistant method based on local polynomial fits. The basic idea is to start with a local polynomial least squares fit and then to "robustify" it. "Local" means here a k-NN type neighborhood. The procedure starts from a k-NN pilot estimate and iteratively defines robustness weights and resmoothes several times.

Algorithm 6.1.1

LOWESS

STEP 1.

Fit a polynomial regression in a neighborhood of x, that is, find coefficients $\{\beta_j\}_{j=0}^p$ which minimize

$$n^{-1} \sum_{i=1}^n W_{ki}(x) \left(Y_i - \sum_{j=0}^p \beta_j x^j \right)^2 ,$$

where $\{W_{ki}(x)\}$ denote k-NN weights.

FOR $i = 1$ TO *maxiter* DO BEGIN

STEP 2.

Compute from the estimated residuals $\{\hat{\varepsilon}_i\}$ the scale estimate $\hat{\sigma}$ =med $\{|\hat{\varepsilon}_i|\}$ and define robustness weights $\delta_i = K(\hat{\varepsilon}_i/(6\hat{\sigma}))$, where K denotes the quartic kernel, $K(u) = (15/16)(1 - u^2)^2 I(|u| \leq 1)$.

STEP 3.

Fit a polynomial regression as in STEP 1 but with weights

$\{\delta_i W_{ki}(x)\}$.

END (* i *).

ORDINATES

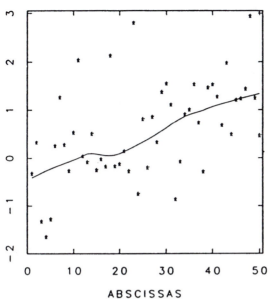

ABSCISSAS

Figure 6.2. Scatter plot of artificially generated data ($n = 50$, $Y_i = 0.02X_i + \varepsilon_i$, $X_i = i$, $\varepsilon_i \sim N(0,1)$) and robust smoothed values with $p = 1$, *maxiter* $= 2$, $k = [n/2]$. From Cleveland (1979) with permission of the American Statistical Association.

Cleveland recommends the choice $p = 1$ (as for the *supersmoother*) as striking a good balance between computational ease and the need for flexibility to reproduce patterns in the data. The smoothing parameter can be determined by cross-validation as in Section 5.1. Figure 6.2 shows an application of Cleveland's algorithm to a simulated data set. It is quite obvious that the LOWESS smooth is resistant to the "far out" response variables at the upper borderline of the plot.

L-smoothing

Another class of resistant smoothers is given by local *trimmed averages* of the response variables. If $Z_{(1)}, Z_{(2)}, \ldots, Z_{(N)}$ denotes the order statistic from N observations $\{Z_j\}_{j=1}^{N}$, a trimmed average (mean) is defined by

$$\overline{Z}_\alpha = (N - 2[\alpha N])^{-1} \sum_{j=[\alpha N]}^{N-[\alpha N]} Z_{(j)}, 0 < \alpha < 1/2,$$

the mean of the "inner $100(1-2\alpha)$ percent of the data." A local trimmed average at the point x from regression data $\{(X_i, Y_i)\}_{i=1}^n$ is defined as a trimmed mean of the response variables Y_i such that X_i is "in a neighborhood of x." (The neighborhood could be parameterized, for instance, by a bandwidth sequence $h = h_n$.) Adopting terminology from robust theory of estimation, this type of smoothing is called *L-smoothing* .

L-smoothing is a resistant technique: the "far out extremes" at a point x do not enter the local averaging procedure. More generally, one considers a conditional L-functional

$$l(x) = \int_0^1 J(v) F^{-1}(v|x) dv, \qquad (6.1.1)$$

where $F^{-1}(v|x) = \inf\{y : F(y|x) \geq v\}, 0 < v < 1$, denotes the conditional quantile function associated with $F(\cdot|x)$, the conditional distribution function of Y given $X = x$. For $J(v) \equiv 1, l(x)$ reduces to the regression function $m(x)$, since by substituting $y = F^{-1}(v|x)$,

$$\int_0^1 F^{-1}(v|x) dv = \int_{F^{-1}(0|x)}^{F^{-1}(1|x)} y dF(y|x) = m(x).$$

The same occurs in the case $J(v) = I(\alpha \leq v \leq 1 - \alpha)/(1 - 2\alpha)$, where $0 < \alpha < 1/2$, with symmetric conditional distribution function. Median smoothing is a special case of L-smoothing with $\alpha = 1/2$.

In practice, we do not know $F(\cdot|x)$ and we have to estimate it. If $F_n(\cdot|x)$ denotes an estimator of $F(\cdot|x)$, one obtains from formula (6.1.1) the L-smoothers. Estimates of $F(t|x)$ can be constructed, for example, by the kernel technique,

$$F_h(t|x) = \frac{n^{-1} \sum_{i=1}^n K_h(x - X_i) I(Y_i \leq t)}{\hat{f}_h(x)},$$

to obtain

$$\hat{m}_h^L(x) = \int_0^1 J(v) F_h^{-1}(v|x) dv.$$

Stute (1984) and Owen (1987) show asymptotic normality of such conditional functionals. Härdle, Janssen and Serfling (1988) derive (optimal) uniform consistency rates for L-smoothers.

R-smoothing

Yet another class of smoothers are the *R-smoothers* derived from *R*-estimates of location. Assume that $F(\cdot|x)$ is symmetric around $m(x)$ and that J is a nondecreasing function defined on $(0,1)$ such that $J(1 - s) =$

$-J(s)$. Then the score

$$T(\theta, F(\cdot|x)) = \int_{-\infty}^{\infty} J\left(\frac{1}{2}(F(v|x) + 1 - F(2\theta - v|x))\right) dF(v|x)$$

is zero for $\theta = m(x)$. The idea now is to replace $F(\cdot|x)$ by an estimate $F_n(\cdot|x)$. If $F_n(\cdot|x)$ denotes such an estimate of the conditional distribution function $F(\cdot|x)$, then this score should be roughly zero for a good estimate of $m(x)$. The motivation for this R-smoothing technique stems from rank tests.

Consider a two-sample rank test for shift based on the sample $\{Z_i\}_{i=1}^n$ and $\{2\theta - Z_i\}_{i=1}^n$, that is, a mirror image of the first sample serves as a stand-in for the second sample. Now try to adjust θ in such a way that the test statistic $T_n = n^{-1}\sum_{i=1}^n a(R_i)$ based on the scores

$$a(i) = \left(2n \int_{(i-1)/2n}^{i/2n} J(s) ds\right)$$

of the ranks R_i of $\{Z_i\}$ in the combined sample $\{Z_i\} + \{2\theta - Z_i\}$ is roughly zero (see Huber 1981, chapter 3.4). This would make the two samples $\{Z_i\}$ and $\{2\theta - Z_i\}$ almost indistinguishable or, in other words, would make θ a good estimate of location. If this T_n is translated into the setting of smoothing then the above form of $T(\theta, F(\cdot|x))$ is obtained.

A solution of $T(\theta, F_n(\cdot|x)) = 0$ is, in general, not unique or may have irregular behavior. Cheng and Cheng (1986) therefore suggested

$$\hat{m}_h^R = \frac{1}{2}[\sup\{\theta : T(\theta, F_n(\cdot|x)) > 0\} + \inf\{\theta : T(\theta, F_n(\cdot|x)) < 0\}]$$

$$(6.1.2)$$

as an estimate for the regression curve $m(x)$. Consistency and asymptotic normality of this smoothing technique are derived in Cheng and Cheng (1987).

M-smoothing

Resistant smoothing techniques based on M-estimates of location are called M-smoothers. Recall that all smoothers of the form

$$\hat{m}(x) = n^{-1} \sum_{i=1}^n W_{ni}(x) Y_i$$

can be viewed as solutions to (local) least squares problems; see (3.1.8). The basic idea of M-smoothers is to reduce the influence of outlying observations by the use of a nonquadratic loss function in (3.1.8). A well-known example (see Huber 1981) of such a loss function with "lighter tails" is

$$\rho(u) = \begin{cases} (1/2)u^2, & \text{if } |u| \leq c; \\ c|u| - (1/2)c^2, & \text{if } |u| > c. \end{cases} \qquad (6.1.3)$$

The constant c regulates the degree of resistance. For large values of c one obtains the ordinary quadratic loss function. For small values ($c \approx$ one or two times the standard deviation of the observation errors) one achieves more robustness.

In the setting of spline smoothing, an M-type spline was defined by Cox (1983)

$$\arg \min_{g} \left\{ n^{-1} \sum_{i=1}^{n} \rho(Y_i - g(t_i)) + \lambda \int [g''(x)]^2 dx \right\} \qquad (6.1.4)$$

where, again, ρ is a loss function with "lighter" tails than the quadratic. Related types of M-smoothers were considered by Huber (1979), Nemirovskii, Polyak and Tsybakov (1983, 1985) and Silverman (1985).

Kernel smoothers can be made resistant by similar means. Assume that the conditional distribution $F(\cdot|x)$ is symmetric. This assumption ensures that we are still estimating $m(x)$, the conditional mean curve. Define a robust kernel M-smoother $\hat{m}_h^M(x)$ as

$$\arg \min_{\theta} \left\{ n^{-1} \sum_{i=1}^{n} W_{hi}(x)\rho(Y_i - \theta) \right\} \qquad (6.1.5)$$

where $\{W_{hi}(x)\}_{i=1}^n$ denotes a positive kernel weight sequence. Differentiating (6.1.5) with respect to θ yields, with $\psi = \rho'$,

$$n^{-1} \sum_{i=1}^{n} W_{hi}(x)\psi(Y_i - \theta) = 0. \qquad (6.1.6)$$

Since the kernel M-smoother is implicitly defined, it requires iterative numerical methods. A fast algorithm based on the Fast Fourier Transform and a "one-step" approximation to $\hat{m}_h^M$ are given in Härdle (1987a). A wide variety of possible ψ-functions yield consistent estimators $\hat{m}_h^R(x)$. (Consistency follows by arguments given in Huber (1981, chapter 3).) Note that the special case with linear $\psi(u) = u$ reproduces the ordinary kernel smoother $\hat{m}_h(x)$. To understand what resistant M-smoothers are actually doing to the data, define unobservable *pseudo-observations*

$$\tilde{Y}_i = m(X_i) + \frac{\psi(\varepsilon_i)}{q(X_i)}$$

with

$$q(X_i) = E(\psi'(\varepsilon_i)|X_i).$$

The following theorem can be derived using methods given in Tsybakov (1982b) and Härdle (1984b).

Theorem 6.1.1   Let $\hat{m}_h^M(x)$ be the kernel M-smoother computed from $\{(X_i, Y_i)\}_{i=1}^n$ and let $\hat{m}_h(x)$ be the ordinary kernel smoother applied to the pseudo-data $\{(X_i, \tilde{Y}_i)\}_{i=1}^n$; then $\sqrt{nh}(\hat{m}_h(x) - m(x))$ and $\sqrt{nh}(\hat{m}_h^M(x) - m(x))$ have the same asymptotic normal distribution with mean as in (4.2.1) and asymptotic variance

$$V_x(\psi, K) = \frac{c_K}{f(x)} \frac{E(\psi^2(\varepsilon)|X = x)}{q^2(x)}.$$

This result deserves some discussion. First, it shows that kernel M-smoothers can be interpreted as ordinary kernel smoothers applied to nonobservable pseudo-data with transformed errors $\psi(\varepsilon_i)/q(X_i)$. This sheds some light on how the resistance of M-smoothers is achieved: The "extreme" observation errors ε_i are "downweighted" by the nonlinear, bounded function $\psi(\varepsilon_i)/q(X_i)$. Second, Theorem 6.1.1. reveals that the bias of the ordinary kernel smoother is the same as that for the kernel M-smoother. The nonlinear definition of $\hat{m}_h^M(x)$ does not affect the (asymptotic) bias properties. Third, the product form of the asymptotic variance $V_x(\psi, K)$ as a product of $c_K/f(x)$ and $E(\psi^2(\varepsilon)|X = x)/q^2(x)$ allows optimization of $V_x(\psi, K)$ simply by considering ψ and K separately.

The first of these two separate problems was solved in Section 4.5. By utilizing classical theory for M-estimates of location, the second problem can be treated as in Huber (1981, chapter 4). The details of this optimization technique are rather delicate; the reader is referred to the standard literature on robust estimation. Optimization of the smoothing parameter is discussed in Härdle (1984c) and more recently by Leung (1988). Both authors consider the direct analogue of cross-validation, namely, constructing robust leave-one-out smoothers and then proceeding as in Section 5.1.

A natural question to ask is, how much is gained or lost in asymptotic accuracy when using an M-smoother? The bias is the same as for the kernel smoother. A way of comparing the nonresistant and the resistant technique is therefore to study the ratio of asymptotic variances,

$$\frac{\sigma^2(x)}{E(\psi^2(\varepsilon)|X = x)/q^2(x)}, \tag{6.1.7}$$

of the Nadaraya–Watson kernel smoother to the kernel M-smoother (based on the same kernel weights). But this relative efficiency (6.1.7)

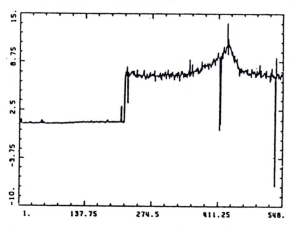

Figure 6.3.   A Raman spectrum with two single spike outliers. From Härdle and Gasser (1984) with permission of the Royal Statistical Society.

is the same as for the estimation of location. The reader is therefore referred to the literature on robust estimation (see e.g. Huber 1981).

As an example, I would like to present a smoothing problem in physical chemistry. Raman spectra are an important diagnostic tool in that field. One would like to identify the location and size of peaks and troughs of spectral bands; see Hillig and Morris (1982) and Bussian and Härdle (1984). Unfortunately, small-scale instrumental noise and a certain proportion of observation error which is caused by random external events blur the observations. The latter type of error causes high frequency signals or bubbles in the sample and produces single spikes like those in Figure 6.3.

Estimating with $\hat{m}_h(x)$, the ordinary Nadaraya–Watson kernel smoother, results in the curve depicted in Figure 6.4.

The single spike outliers obviously produced two spurious neighboring peaks. The resistant smoothing technique, on the other hand, leads to Figure 6.5.

The influence of the outliers is obviously reduced. Uniform confidence bands – based on asymptotic extreme value theory – may be constructed using the methods presented in Section 4.3; see Härdle (1987b). Figure 6.6 depicts a kernel M-smoother $\hat{m}_h^M$ together with uniform confidence bands, and $\hat{m}_h$, the Nadaraya–Watson kernel smoother, for the data presented in Figure 6.1.

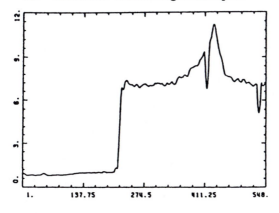

Figure 6.4.   The kernel smoother $\hat{m}_h(x)$ applied to the spectrum shown in Figure 6.3, $h = 9$, $K(u) = (3/4)(1 - u^2)I(|u| \leq 1)$. From Härdle and Gasser (1984) with permission of the Royal Statistical Society.

Optimal uniform convergence rates (see Section 4.1) for kernel M-smoothers have been derived in Härdle and Luckhaus (1984). In the context of time series, robust estimation and prediction has been discussed by Velleman (1977, 1980), Mallows (1980) and Härdle and Tuan (1986). Robust nonparametric prediction of time series by M-smoothers

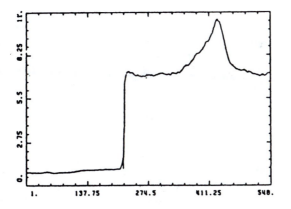

Figure 6.5.   The resistant kernel M-smoother $\hat{m}_h^M(x)$ applied to the spectrum shown in Figure 6.3, $h = 9$, $c = 0.9$, $K(u) = (3/4)(1 - u^2)I(|u| \leq 1)$. From Härdle and Gasser (1984) with permission of the Royal Statistical Society.

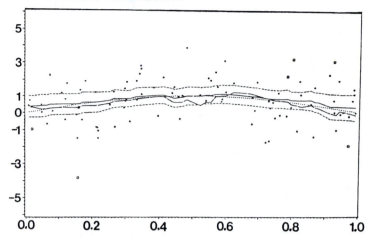

Figure 6.6.   The kernel M-smoother with uniform confidence bands and the kernel smoother $\hat{m}_h(x)$. The original data are those of Figure 6.1. From Härdle (1989).

has been investigated by Robinson (1984, 1987b), Collomb and Härdle (1986) and Härdle (1986c). Robust kernel smoothers for estimation of derivatives have been investigated in Härdle and Gasser (1985) and Tsybakov (1986).

Exercises

6.1.1 Find conditions such that L-smoothers, as defined in (6.1.1), are consistent estimators for the regression curve.

6.1.2 Find conditions such that R-smoothers, as defined in (6.1.2), asymptotically converge to the true regression curve.

6.1.3 Do you expect the general L-smoothers (6.1.1) to produce smoother curves than the running median?

6.1.4 Construct a fast algorithm for L-smoothers (6.1.1). Based on the ideas of efficient running median smoothing (Section 3.5) you should be able to find a code that runs in $O(n \log k)$ steps (k is the number of neighbors).

6.1.5 Prove consistency for the M-smoother (6.1.4) for monotone ψ functions.
[*Hint*: Follow the proof of Huber (1981, chapter 3).]

6.1.6 Can you extend the proof of Exercise 6.1.5 to nonmonotone ψ functions such as Hampel's "three-part redescender"?

Complements

In order to make an M-type kernel estimate scale invariant, it must be coupled with an estimate of scale. This coupling can be done by simultaneously estimating the regression and the scale curve. To fix ideas, assume that

$$f(y|x) = (1/\sigma(x))f_0((y - m(x))/\sigma(x)), x \in \mathbb{R}^d,$$

with an unknown f_0 and regression curve $m(x)$ and scale curve $\sigma(x)$. Define, for the moment,

$$\psi(u) = -(d/du)\log f(u|x)$$

and

$$\chi(u) = (\psi(u)u - 1).$$

Also define for $v \in \mathbb{R}, w \in \mathbb{R}^+$ and fixed $x \in \mathbb{R}^d$,

$$T_1(v, w) = \int \psi\left(\frac{y - v}{w}\right) dF(y|x) \tag{6.1.8}$$

$$T_2(v, w) = \int \chi\left(\frac{y - v}{w}\right) dF(y|x). \tag{6.1.9}$$

The curves $(m(x), \sigma(x))$ satisfy by definition

$$T_1(m(x), \sigma(x)) = T_2(m(x), \sigma(x)) = 0.$$

In practice, one does not know $F(\cdot|x)$ and hence cannot compute T_1 or T_2. The approach taken is to replace $F(\cdot|x)$ by $F_n(\cdot|x)$, a kernel estimate of the conditional distribution function, and to assume that ψ and χ are bounded functions to achieve desirable robustness properties. Huber (1981, chapter 6.4) gives examples of functions ψ and χ. One of them is

$$\psi(u) = \min(c, \max(-c, u)), \ c > 0,$$
$$\chi(u) = \psi^2(u) - \beta,$$

with $\beta = E_\Phi \psi^2(u)$, where Φ denotes the standard normal distribution. Consistency for the scale estimate may be obtained for the normal model: Under the assumption that the error is standard normally distributed, the functions $\psi(u) = u$ and $\chi(u) = \psi^2(u) - \beta = u^2 - 1$ give the conditional mean as regression curve $m(x)$ and the conditional standard deviation as scale curve $\sigma(x)$. In fact, the parameter β plays the role of a normalizing constant: If one wishes to "interpret" the scale curve with respect to some other distribution G different from the normal Φ, one can set $\beta = E_G \psi^2(u)$.

The functions T_1 and T_2 can be estimated by Nadaraya–Watson kernel weights $\{W_{hi}(x)\}_{i=1}^n$ (as in (3.1.1))

$$\hat{T}_{1h}(v, w) = n^{-1} \sum_{i=1}^n W_{hi}(x)\psi\left(\frac{Y_i - v}{w}\right),\qquad(6.1.10)$$

$$\hat{T}_{2h}(v, w) = n^{-1} \sum_{i=1}^n W_{hi}(x)\chi\left(\frac{Y_i - v}{w}\right).\qquad(6.1.11)$$

Call a joint solution of $T_{1h}(v, w) = T_{2h}(v, w) = 0$ a *resistant regression and scale curve smoother* $(\hat{m}_h^M(x), \hat{\sigma}_h^M(x))$. Consistency and asymptotic normality of this smoother were shown under regularity conditions on the kernel and the functions $(m(x), \sigma(x))$ in Härdle and Tsybakov (1988). Optimization of the smoothing parameter for this procedure was considered by Tsybakov (1987).

CHAPTER 7

Nonparametric regression techniques for correlated data

> It is well known that the best predictor for y_{n+l} is the conditional expectation of y_{n+l} given the entire past $z_n, z_{n-1}, \ldots$. Moreover, if (z_t) is stationary and Gaussian this conditional expectation takes the form of an infinite moving average. If the process (z_t) is not Gaussian the question arises how the conditional expectation $E(y_{n+l}|z_n, z_{n-1}, \ldots)$ looks like [sic].
>
> H. Bierens (1988)

The statistical properties of regression smoothers have been mainly analyzed in the framework of an "i.i.d observation structure." The assumption that the pairs $\{(X_i, Y_i)\}_{i=1}^{n}$ are an independent sample from an unknown distribution can often be justified in practice and simplifies technical matters. Certainly in the expenditure data example in which the observations have been gathered from a quite realistic cross-section of the population, the assumptions of independence and identical distributions seem to be justifiable.

However, there are practical situations in which it is not appropriate to assume that the observations $(X_1, Y_1), (X_2, Y_2), \ldots$ are independent. In particular, if the data have been recorded over time from one object under study, it is very likely that the object's response will depend on its previous response. Such a structure of dependency can be modeled in various contexts. I concentrate on the following three mathematical concepts, for which there exists a large body of literature.

Model (S) A Stationary sequence $\{(X_i, Y_i), i \geq 1\}$, which may be stochastically dependent, is observed and it is desired to estimate $m(x) = E(Y|X = x)$.

Model (T) A Time series $\{Z_i, i \geq 1\}$ is observed, and one is interested in predicting Z_{n+1} by $m(x) = E(Z_{n+1}|Z_n = x)$.

Model (C) The observation errors $\{\varepsilon_{in}\}$ in the fixed design regression model

$$Y_{in} = m(i/n) + \varepsilon_{in}$$

form a sequence of Correlated random variables.

In Section 7.1 the first model (S) and a framework for mapping the second model (T) into the first are presented. Results on optimal non-parametric prediction are given. These prediction methods are applied to a time series of gold prices. Section 7.2 deals with the third model (C), in which only the observation errors are assumed to form a correlated sequence.

7.1   Nonparametric prediction of time series

The nonparametric smoothing problem has been studied under various mixing conditions on the observation process (see e.g. Collomb 1985a, 1985b). One such assumption in the framework of model (S) is that $\{(X_i, Y_i)\}_{i=1}^{n}$ form a φ-mixing process. A process $\{(X_i, Y_i), i \geq 1\}$ is called φ-mixing (uniformly mixing) (Billingsley 1968) if for a sequence $\{\varphi_k\}$ tending to zero,

$$|P(A \cap B) - P(A)P(B)| \leq \varphi_k P(A),$$

for all $n \geq 1, k \geq 1$ and any set A in

$$\mathcal{F}_1^n = \sigma((X_1, Y_1), \ldots, (X_n, Y_n))$$

and B in

$$\mathcal{F}_{n+k}^{\infty} = \sigma((X_{n+k}, Y_{n+k}), \ldots).$$

Another mixing condition is the α-mixing or strong mixing condition which is weaker than the φ-mixing condition. A sequence is called α-mixing if for a sequence $\{\alpha_k\}$ tending to zero,

$$\sup_{A \in \mathcal{F}_1^n, B \in \mathcal{F}_{n+k}^{\infty}} |P(A \cap B) - P(A)P(B)| \leq \alpha_k,$$

for all $n \geq 1, k \geq 1$.

The one-step prediction problem (T) of a one-dimensional time series can be mapped into the first model class. Define for a stationary time series

$$\{Z_i; i \geq 1\}$$

the lagged value Z_{i-1} as X_i and the present value Z_i as Y_i. Then the problem of predicting Z_{n+1} from $\{Z_i\}_{i=1}^n$ can be considered as a regression smoothing problem for $\{(X_i, Y_i)\}_{i=2}^n = \{(Z_{i-1}, Z_i)\}_{i=2}^n$. Clearly if $\{Z_i; i \geq 1\}$ is φ-mixing then $\{(X_i, Y_i)\}$ is also φ-mixing.

Doukhan and Ghindes (1980) have investigated, for example, the nonlinear autoregressive process $Z_i = m(Z_{i-1}) + \varepsilon_i$. They showed that if m is a bounded continuous function and the random errors $\{\varepsilon_i\}$ are independent, identically distributed and have bounded support, then the sequence $(X_i, Y_i) = (Z_i, Z_{i+1})$ is φ-mixing. The prediction problem for the time series $\{Z_i\}$ is thus the same as to estimate $m(x) = E(Y|X = x)$ for the two-dimensional time series $\{(X_i, Y_i)\}_{i=1}^n$. For more details concerning this nonlinear autoregressive process, see Györfi et al. (1989).

Yakowitz (1987) has considered the k-NN prediction (with uniform weights) of a stationary Markov sequence and compared the nonparametric predictors with parametric ARMA models. He showed under assumptions very similar to those for Theorem 4.2.1 that the k-NN estimator in this prediction context satisfies for $k \sim n^{4/5}$

$$E(\hat{m}_k(x) - m(x))^2 = O\left(n^{-4/5}\right).$$

This parallels the results for the i.i.d. case, in particular, the rates given in Table 3.2.1. It also shows that the k-NN estimator achieves the optimal rate of convergence (Section 4.1) in this setting.

Yakowitz (1985a, 1985b) applies the k-NN predictor to the flood warning problem for rivers. Figure 7.1 shows the predicted runoff Z_{n+1} compared to the actual runoff for two parametric models (Sacramento and ARMAX) and the nonparametric predictor. Yakowitz reports that the nonparametric method produces roughly the same overall prediction curve as the two parametric approaches but seems to model the peak flow levels slightly better. A detailed discussion of this flood warning problem can be found in the Yakowitz reference.

A different predictor of future values of Y is based upon the mode function (assuming that it is uniquely defined),

$$m(x) = \arg\max_y [f(y|x)],$$

where $f(y|x)$ denotes the conditional density of Y given X. Collomb, Härdle and Hassani (1987) estimated $f(y|x)$ from a sequence of φ-mixing observations. They used a kernel estimate for $f_n(y|x)$, defined the *empirical mode predictor* as the maximum of $f_n(y|x)$ over $y \in \mathrm{IR}$ and showed uniform convergence (over x) of this estimator to the mode function.

Truong and Stone (1987b) considered prediction based on local median smoothing and kernel smoothing in the α-mixing context. Robin-

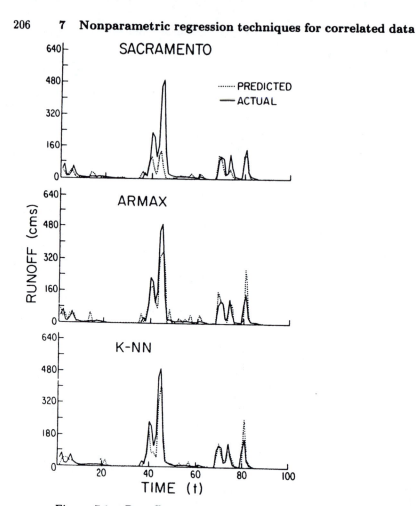

Figure 7.1. Runoff measurements of the bird creek data. From Yakowitz (1987) with permission of Basil Blackwell Ltd.

son (1983) and Singh and Ullah (1985) showed strong consistency and asymptotic normality for α-mixing observations.

Bierens (1983, 1987) and Collomb and Härdle (1986) considered in the φ-mixing case the Nadaraya–Watson kernel predictor,

$$\hat{m}_h(x) = \frac{n^{-1} \sum\limits_{i=1}^{n} K_h(x - X_i)Y_i}{n^{-1} \sum\limits_{i=1}^{n} K_h(x - X_i)}, \tag{7.1.1}$$

and derived uniform consistency of this predictor and robust relatives of it. For the uniform convergence result an extension of Bernstein's inequality for φ-mixing observations as given in Collomb (1984) was used.

How can we find a smoothing parameter in (7.1.1) that asymptotically minimizes the ASE

$$d_A(h) = n^{-1} \sum_{i=1}^{n} (m(X_i) - \hat{m}_h(X_i))^2 \, w(X_i).$$

Härdle and Vieu (1987) showed that the leave-out technique works also for φ-mixing observations. Define as in Section 5.1 the *leave-out estimator*

$$\hat{m}_{h,i}(x) = \frac{n^{-1} \sum_{i \neq j} K_h(x - X_j) Y_j}{n^{-1} \sum_{i \neq j} K_h(x - X_j)}$$

and define the cross-validation function

$$CV(h) = n^{-1} \sum_{i=1}^{n} (Y_i - \hat{m}_{h,i}(X_i))^2 \, w(X_i).$$

Theorem 7.1.1 In addition to the assumptions of Theorem 5.1.1 assume that the process (X_i, Y_i) is exponentially φ-mixing, that is, $\varphi_k = \alpha \lambda^k, \lambda < 1$. Then $\hat{h}$, selected so as to minimize $CV(h)$ over a discrete set of bandwidths $h \sim n^{-1/5}$, asymptotically minimizes ASE, that is,

$$\frac{d_A(\hat{h})}{\inf_h d_A(h)} \xrightarrow{p} 1.$$

Note that Theorem 7.1.1. contains a slightly weaker notion of asymptotic optimality. The cross-validation curve for a simulated process is shown in Figure 7.2. The time series for this example was generated from model (T) and defined as

$$Z_{i+1} = 2Z_i/(1 + Z_i^2) + \varepsilon_i, \quad i = 1, \ldots, n-1,$$

with independent $\{\varepsilon_i\}_{i=1}^{n}$, $n = 100$, uniformly distributed over $[-1, 1]$. The starting Z_1 was generated by pre-running the process from Z_{-100} to Z_1.

The bandwidth which minimizes this function is $h = 0.55$ and leads to the prediction curve depicted in Figure 7.3.

An application of model (T) is the nonparametric prediction of gold prices. Let me illustrate this prediction technique for a series of gold prices which were kindly provided by D. Sondermann. In Figure 7.4, the time series $\{Z_i\}$ of gold prices (in DM) from 1978 to 1985 is plotted as

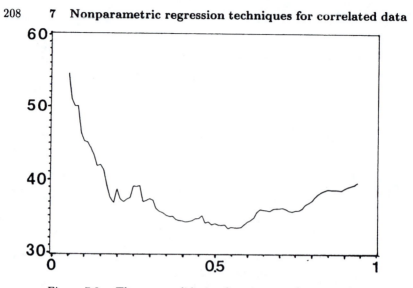

Figure 7.2.   The cross-validation function as a function of the bandwidth.

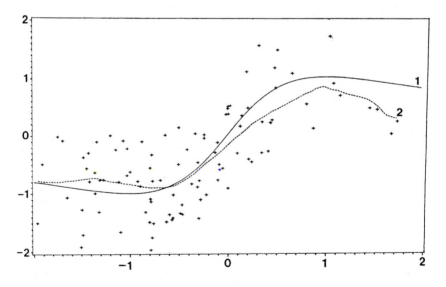

Figure 7.3.   The true autoregression curve (solid line, label 1) and its estimate (dashed curve, label 2) with the bandwidth minimizing the CV function (Figure 7.2) and the raw data.

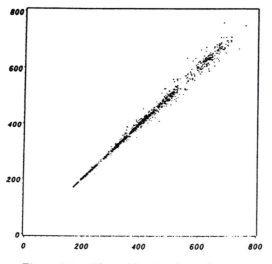

Figure 7.4.   The gold price data. Scatter plot of $Y = Z_{i+1} = $ gold price tomorrow versus $X = Z_i = $ gold price today (both reported in DM). From Härdle and Vieu (1989).

$(X_i, Y_i) = (Z_{i-1}, Z_i)$. Since the data look quite heteroscedastic it makes sense to take logarithms on both axes in order to stabilize variance. The cross-validation function for the log-data shows a clear minimum at $h = 0.03$ for the Epanechnikov kernel. For details see Härdle and Vieu (1989). The cross-validated bandwidth led to Figure 7.5, which suggests a quite nonlinear prediction curve rather than a global linear predictor.

7.2   Smoothing with dependent errors

In this section we deal with model (C), that is, we consider the fixed design model

$$Y_{in} = m(i/n) + \varepsilon_{in},$$

with correlated errors $\{\varepsilon_{in}\}$. To give an impression of how methods designed for the i.i.d. case fail in the setting of smoothing with dependent errors consider Figure 7.6. It shows the raw data connected by lines together with the regression curve for two different kinds of error structure for the $\{\varepsilon_{in}\}$. The plot to the left is for the i.i.d. case and the plot to the right shows autoregressive errors.

Both data sets were smoothed with a kernel smoother using cross-validation. The result is shown in Figure 7.7. It is obvious that cross-validation has selected too small a bandwidth, the reason being that

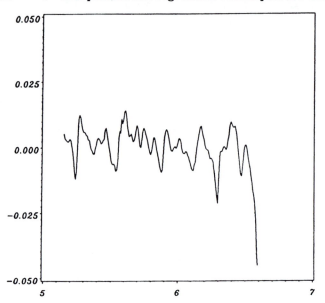

Figure 7.5.   The gold price curve. Plot of the predicted price tomorrow minus the price today, $\hat{m}_{\hat{h}}(x) - x$, $\hat{h} = 0.03$, for the gold
price data set with optimized bandwidth determined by minimizing
the CV score. Kernel $K(u) = 0.75(1 - u^2)I(|u| \leq 1)$. From Härdle
and Vieu (1989).

this method interpreted the existing correlation in the errors as part of
the regression curve. (If we try to smooth by eye we would probably
also undersmooth.)

In the asymptotic analysis of model (C) I follow Hart and Wehrly
(1986). They assume, as in Azzalini (1984), a collection of time series

$$Y_{ij} = m(X_i) + \varepsilon_{ij}, \quad i = 1, \ldots, n, \quad j = 1, \ldots, N.$$

The interpretation is that at each X_i we have N experimental units
available. Suppose that the data at the ith unit are serially correlated
but samples are independent across experimental units. More formally,
the errors ε_{ij}s are zero mean random variables satisfying

$$\operatorname{cov}(\varepsilon_{ij}, \varepsilon_{kl}) = \begin{cases} \sigma^2 \rho(X_i - X_k), & \text{if } j = l; \\ 0, & \text{if } j \neq l. \end{cases}$$

Assume also that the correlation function ρ is even with $\rho(0) = 1$ and
$|\rho(u)| \leq 1$ for all $u \in [-1, 1]$.

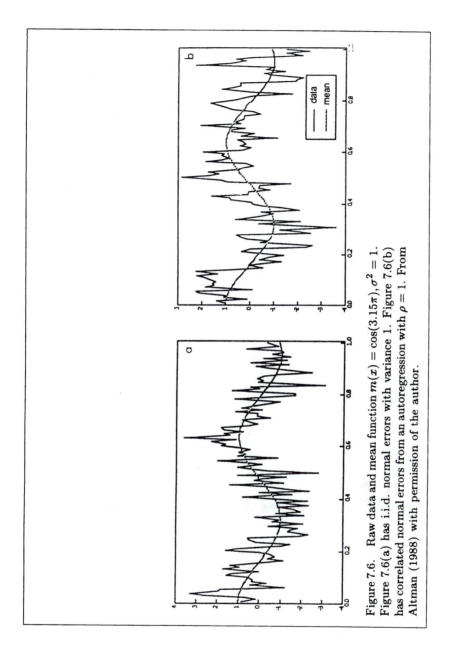

Figure 7.6. Raw data and mean function $m(x) = \cos(3.15\pi)$, $\sigma^2 = 1$. Figure 7.6(a) has i.i.d. normal errors with variance 1. Figure 7.6(b) has correlated normal errors from an autoregression with $\rho = 1$. From Altman (1988) with permission of the author.

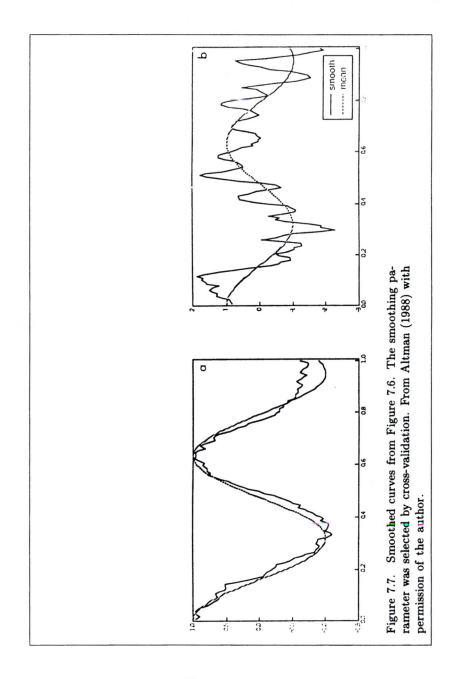

Figure 7.7. Smoothed curves from Figure 7.6. The smoothing parameter was selected by cross-validation. From Altman (1988) with permission of the author.

The estimation problem of m is based on averaged responses

$$Y_{i_\bullet} = N^{-1} \sum_{j=1}^{N} Y_{ij}.$$

Expressing the model now as

$$Y_{i_\bullet} = m(X_i) + \varepsilon_{i_\bullet}$$

links this setting in an obvious way to the analysis of independent random errors. In fact, the averaged random errors $\varepsilon_{i_\bullet}$ satisfy

$$\text{cov}(\varepsilon_{i_\bullet}, \varepsilon_{k_\bullet}) = (\sigma^2/N)\, \rho\, (X_i - X_k). \tag{7.2.1}$$

One can now see the problem of estimation of m as that of fitting a smooth curve through the sample means at each unit. The estimator that Hart and Wehrly (1986) used was a kernel estimator applied to $\{Y_{i_\bullet}\}_{i=1}^{n}$ with weights

$$W_{hi}^{(3)}(x) = n \int_{S_{i-1}}^{S_i} K_h(x - u)\,du,$$

where $S_0 = 0$, $S_i = (X_i + X_{i+1})/2$, $i = 1, \ldots, n-1$, $S_n = 1$.

The following proposition shows that, with correlated errors, a kernel estimator is not consistent for $m(x)$ unless the number N of experimental units at each X_i tends to infinity.

Proposition 7.2.1 If m is twice differentiable and ρ is a Lipschitz continuous function then the MSE of

$$\hat{m}_h(x) = n^{-1} \sum_{i=1}^{n} W_{hi}^{(3)}\, Y_{i_\bullet}$$

is

$$E(\hat{m}_h(x) - m(x))^2 \approx (\sigma^2/N) \int_{-1}^{1} \int_{-1}^{1} \rho(h(u - v)) K(u) K(v)\, du\, dv$$

$$+ \frac{h^4}{4} [m''(x)]^2 d_K^2, \tag{7.2.2}$$

$$n \to \infty,\ N \to \infty,\ h \to 0,\ nh \to \infty.$$

The result is immediate from (7.2.1) and the bias expansions given in Section 3.1. An important question is how the optimal choice of bandwidth changes if correlation of the $\{\varepsilon_{in}\}_{i=1}^{n}$ is allowed. This is made precise in theorem 4 of Hart and Wehrly (1986).

Theorem 7.2.2   Assume that ρ is twice differentiable and that $(N/n) = o(1)$, then the asymptotic expansion (7.2.2) of the MSE of $\hat{m}_h(x)$ is

$$E(\hat{m}_h(x) - m(x))^2 \approx (\sigma^2/N)(1 + h^2 \rho''(0) \, d_K)$$
$$+ \frac{h^4}{4} \, [m''(x)]^2 \, d_K^2. \qquad (7.2.3)$$

This theorem suggests choosing a bandwidth

$$h_N^{(1)} = \left\{ \frac{-2\sigma^2 \rho''(0)}{d_K^2 [m''(x)]^2} \right\}^{1/2} N^{-1/2}$$

which minimizes (7.2.3) as a function of N. This bandwidth can be compared with the "optimal" bandwidth in the case of independent observations

$$h_N^{(2)} = \left\{ \frac{\sigma^2 \, c_K}{d_K^2 \, [m''(x)]^2} \right\}^{1/5} (nN)^{-1/5}$$

(see Section 5.1). Comparing $h_N^{(1)}$ and $h_N^{(2)}$ shows that $h_N^{(1)} < h_N^{(2)}$ is impossible for n and N sufficiently large. However, if n is small and serial correlation is large (that is, ρ is "flat" near 0), the situation may be reversed. Figure 7.8 shows the kernel smoother $\hat{m}_h(x)$ for the plasma citrate data using bandwidths assuming uncorrelated and correlated observations, respectively.

The bandwidths have been determined by minimizing estimates of the mean averaged squared error d_M. Assuming independent errors, the accuracy measure d_M can be approximated as in Chapter 5. For the case of correlated observations the unknown correlation function ρ in (7.2.3) has to be estimated. One could use the canonical estimate

$$\hat{\rho}(k) = \hat{c}(k)/\hat{c}(0),$$

where

$$\hat{c}(k) = (nN)^{-1} \sum_{j=1}^{N} \sum_{i=1}^{n-k} (Y_{ij} - Y_{i\bullet})(Y_{i+k,j} - Y_{i+k,\bullet}).$$

The two estimated d_M curves are displayed in Figure 7.9.

The bandwidth to be picked for the case of dependent observations is slightly smaller than that for the case of independent errors. So, if there is a reason to believe that the data are correlated, it is recommended

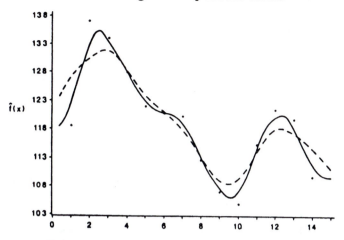

Figure 7.8. Two smooths for the plasma citrate data. The black squares denote Y_i, the mean response over experimental units. The dashed curve is the kernel smooth using the estimated optimum bandwidth assuming uncorrelated observations. The solid line is the kernel estimate using an estimated optimum bandwidth allowing serial correlation. From Hart and Wehrly (1986) with permission of the American Statistical Association.

that such two estimates of the accuracy be plotted in order to see how the picture changes with correlated errors.

Exercises

7.2.1 Derive formula (7.2.1).

7.2.2 Make precise the arguments needed to prove the MSE expansion (7.2.2).

7.2.3 Show formula (7.2.3). Why is $h_N^{(1)} > h_N^{(2)}$ as N, n tend to infinity?

Complements

Another approach to modeling dependence in nonparametric regression consists of assuming that the regression curve is in some sense asymptotically constant overlaid with a time series of *fixed* dependence structure. This concept can, in fact, be seen to parallel the model that the observation errors become less dependent as n tends to infinity. More precisely, if it is assumed that the $\{\varepsilon_{in}\}$ are sampled from a continuous

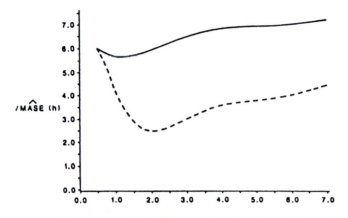

Figure 7.9.   Two CV scores for the plasma citrate data. The dashed line was computed under the assumption of uncorrelated observations. The solid line curve was obtained allowing for correlation among observations at different design points. From Hart and Wehrly (1986) with permission of the American Statistical Association.

process $V(t)$ with decreasing correlation function such that

$$\varepsilon_{in} = V(t_i/c_n)$$

with discretization points $\{t_i\}$ and a sequence c_n tending to zero, then the $\{\varepsilon_{in}\}$ become asymptotically less dependent.

In this framework it can be shown that kernel smoothers and robust relatives of them (kernel M-smoothers) converge to the true regression function and are asymptotically normal with identical bias term, as in the independent case. The asymptotic variance in this case depends also on the covariances of the noise process (Härdle and Tuan 1986).

CHAPTER 8

Looking for special features and qualitative smoothing

> Many economists uncritically accept the appropriateness of a functional form on the basis of convention or convenience; others try several forms for their relations but report only the one that in some sense "looks best" a posteriori.
>
> C. Hildreth (1954, p. 600)

One is often interested not only in the curve itself but also in special qualitative characteristics of the smooth. The regression function may be constrained to simple shape characteristics, for example, and the smooth should preferably have the same qualitative characteristics. A quite common shape characteristic is a monotonic or unimodal relationship between the predictor variable and the response variable. This a priori knowledge about the qualitative form of the curve should be built into the estimation technique. Such qualitative features do not necessarily lead to better rates of convergence but help the experimenter in interpretation of the obtained curves.

In economic applications involving demand, supply and price, functions with prescribed shape (monotonicity, convexity, etc.) are common. Lipsey, Sparks and Steiner (1976, chapter 5) present a number of convex decreasing demand curves and convex increasing supply curves (in both cases, price as a function of quality). They also give an example for quantity demanded as a function of household income. A more complex procedure could be applied to the potato Engel curve in Figure 1.2. The nonparametric fit shows a partially increasing and a decreasing segment. This curve could be estimated by a unimodal regression technique.

Another qualitative characteristic of a regression fit is location of zeros or extrema. They often yield a rough impression of the regression curve. Experience based on such features might tell us immediately something about the curve itself, and the information they contain may suffice to establish a reasonable parametric model.

In this chapter I discuss techniques for smoothing under the following qualitative constraints: monotonicity and unimodality (Section 8.1). The estimation of zeros and extrema is presented in Section 8.2. More

217

complicated shape constraining procedures, such as convex (concave) smoothing, for example, have been treated by Hanson and Pledger (1976) and Wright and Wegman (1980).

8.1   Monotonic and unimodal smoothing

The problem of monotonic smoothing on a set $\{(X_i, Y_i)\}_{i=1}^{n}$ of two-dimensional data can be formalized as follows.   Sort the data $\{(X_i, Y_i)\}_{i=1}^{n}$ by X into $\{(X_{(i)}, Y_{(i)})\}_{i=1}^{n}$. Find $\{\hat{m}(X_{(i)})\}_{i=1}^{n}$ to minimize $n^{-1} \sum_{i=1}^{n}(Y_{(i)} - \hat{m}(X_{(i)}))^2$ subject to the monotonicity restriction

$$\hat{m}(X_{(1)}) \le \hat{m}(X_{(2)}) \le \cdots \le \hat{m}(X_{(n)}).$$

Such a solution exists and can be obtained from the *pool adjacent violators* algorithm (Barlow et al. 1972, p. 13; Hanson, Pledger and Wright 1973). The pool-adjacent-violators algorithm (from the left) can be formalized as follows.

Pool-adjacent-violators (PAV) Algorithm 8.1.1

Algorithm 8.1.1

STEP 1.

Start with $Y_{(1)}$, move to the right and stop if the pair $(Y_{(i)}, Y_{(i+1)})$ violates the monotonicity constraint, that is, $Y_{(i)} > Y_{(i+1)}$. Pool $Y_{(i)}$ and the adjacent $Y_{(i+1)}$, by replacing them both by their average,

$$Y_{(i)}^* = Y_{(i+1)}^* = (Y_{(i)} + Y_{(i+1)})/2 \ .$$

STEP 2.

Next check that $Y_{(i-1)} \le Y_{(i)}^*$. If not, pool $\{Y_{(i-1)}, Y_{(i)}, Y_{(i+1)}\}$ into one average. Continue to the left until the monotonicity requirement is satisfied. Then proceed to the right. The final solutions are $\hat{m}(X_{(i)})$.

There are four remarkable facts about this solution. First, if the data are already monotone, then the PAV algorithm will reproduce the data. Second, since each $\hat{m}(X_{(i)})$ is an average of the observations near $X_{(i)}$ the solution is a step function as in Figure 8.1. Third, if there are outliers or aberrant observations the PAV algorithm will produce long, flat levels. Fourth, suppose the algorithm is started from the right with the aim of pooling to obtain a decreasing fit (looking from the right). The fits starting from left and right are different (Exercise 8.1.5). Especially the third fact about outlier dependence could be treated by first smoothing (with a robust technique) and then isotonizing the smooth. On the other

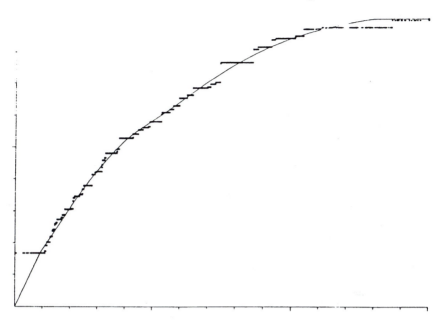

Figure 8.1.   A spline smooth through the midpoints of the PAV
step function. The isotonic regression curve was computed from the
food versus income data set (Family Expenditure Survey 1968–1983).
From Hildenbrand and Hildenbrand (1986) with permission of Elsevier Science Publishers.

hand, one could also first apply the PAV algorithm and then smooth the
solution. Hildenbrand and Hildenbrand (1986) applied the first strategy
in nonparametric estimation of Engel curves. Figure 8.1 shows a spline
smooth and a PAV smooth obtained from estimating the Engel curve of
food as a function of income.

On the contrary, Friedman and Tibshirani (1984) proposed smoothing
the data first and then searching for a monotone approximation of the
smooth. This second algorithm can be summarized as follows. First,
smooth Y on X, that is, produce an estimate $\hat{m}_1(X_{(i)})$ with a cross-
validated smoothing parameter. Second, find the monotone function
$\hat{m}(X_{(i)})$ closest to $\hat{m}_1(X_{(i)})$ by means of the PAV algorithm. Friedman and Tibshirani (1984) gave an example of this algorithm to find
an optimal transformation for a nonparametric version of the Box–Cox
procedure (1964).

Kelly and Rice (1988) used monotone smoothing in a similar model
for assessment of synergisms. The goal of the nonparametric Box–Cox
procedure is to identify the smooth monotone link function $\theta(\cdot)$ and the

parameter β in the model

$$\theta(Y) = \beta^T X + \varepsilon.$$

This can be achieved by finding a function $\hat{\theta}(\cdot)$ and an estimate $\hat{\beta}$ that minimize

$$n^{-1} \sum_{i=1}^{n} (\hat{\theta}(Y_i) - \hat{\beta}^T X_i)^2$$

subject to

$$n^{-1} \sum_{i=1}^{n} \left(\hat{\theta}(Y_i) - n^{-1} \sum_{j=1}^{n} \hat{\theta}(Y_j) \right)^2 = 1.$$

Note that this procedure is a special case of the ACE algorithm (Section 10.3), which consists of finding $\hat{\beta}$ for fixed $\hat{\theta}(\cdot)$ and vice versa.

The Box–Cox procedure and a method proposed by Kruskal (1965) are variants of this procedure. The Box–Cox procedure consists of using the *parametric* transformation family

$$g_\lambda(Y) = \begin{cases} (Y^\lambda - 1)/\lambda, & \text{if } \lambda > 0; \\ \log Y, & \text{if } \lambda = 0, \end{cases} \qquad (8.1.1)$$

to model the unknown function $\theta(\cdot)$. Kruskal used isotonic regression (by the PAV algorithm) to estimate $\theta(\cdot)$. Friedman and Tibshirani applied the nonparametric procedure to the same data and showed that the monotone smooth transformation $\hat{\theta}(\cdot)$ came remarkably close to the log-transformation selected by Box and Cox (1964); see Figure 8.2.

Figure 8.3 shows the result of Kruskal's algorithm together with the log-transformation. The transformation suggested by the Kruskal method by construction lacks smoothness, whereas the monotone smooth gives evidence for a log-transformation; see Figure 8.3.

It is, of course, interesting to ask which method is to be preferred in which situation. Should we smooth first and then isotonize the smooth via the PAV algorithm or should we apply the PAV algorithm first and then smooth? Mammen (1987) investigated this question in the fixed design model. His theoretical comparison is given in more detail in the Complements to this section. It is remarkable from Mammen's results that neither method outperforms the other. More precisely, isotonizing the observations first leads to a smaller variance and a larger bias. The Friedman–Tibshirani method can have a smaller MSE but conditions when this will happen are rather complicated and depend on the unknown regression function.

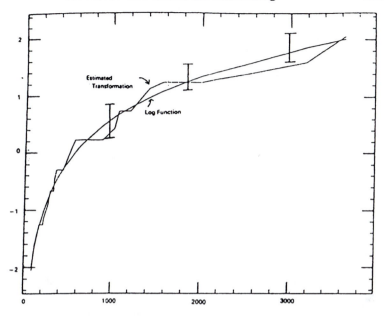

Figure 8.2. The monotone smooth selected by the Friedman–Tibshirani algorithm and the log-transformation. From Friedman and Tibshirani (1984) with permission of the American Statistical Association.

Variants of the above methods are monotone median and percentile regression. They have been investigated by Cryer et al. (1972) and Casady and Cryer (1976). Two-dimensional isotonic smoothing is given as algorithm AS 206 in Bril et al. (1984).

The problem of unimodal smoothing can be related to monotone smoothing. Suppose that $m(x)$ has a mode at $x = \alpha$. This means that

$$x_1 \leq x_2 \leq \alpha \;\Rightarrow\; m(x_1) \leq m(x_2)$$

and

$$\alpha \leq x_1 \leq x_2 \;\Rightarrow\; m(x_1) \geq m(x_2).$$

Then the function

$$g(x) = \begin{cases} 2m(\alpha) - m(x), & \text{if } x \geq \alpha; \\ m(x), & \text{if } x \leq \alpha, \end{cases}$$

is monotone.

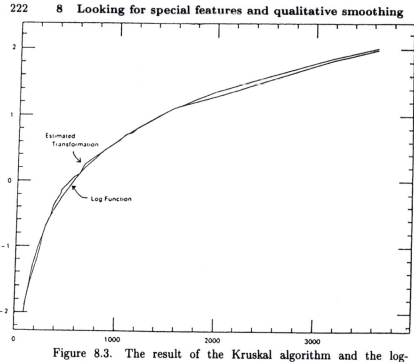

Figure 8.3.   The result of the Kruskal algorithm and the log-transformation. From Friedman and Tibshirani (1984) with permission of the American Statistical Association.

(The problem of "U–shaped regression" can be defined analogously by smoothing $-g(x)$.) A possible way of finding a unimodal smooth is to mirror the observations at possible mode points and then to find a monotone smooth of the partially mirrored data.

More formally, the unimodal regression problem is to find a smooth which minimizes $n^{-1} \sum_{i=1}^{n}(Y_{(i)} - \hat{m}(X_{(i)}))^2$ subject to the restrictions:

$$X_{(i)} \leq X_{(j)} \leq X_{(k)} \;\Rightarrow\; \hat{m}(X_{(i)}) \leq \hat{m}(X_{(j)})$$

and

$$X_{(k)} < X_{(i)} \leq X_{(j)} \;\Rightarrow\; \hat{m}(X_{(i)}) \geq \hat{m}(X_{(j)})$$

for some k.

Frisén and Goteborg (1980) proposed treating the index k as a parameter, and then, solving for each k, a monotone increasing smoothing problem for the data $\{(X_{(i)}, Y_{(i)})\}_{i=1}^{k}$ and a monotone decreasing smoothing problem for the data $\{(X_{(i)}, Y_{(i)})\}_{i=k+1}^{n}$. Then one chooses the empirical mode $X_{(k)}$ that leads to the lowest residual sum of squares.

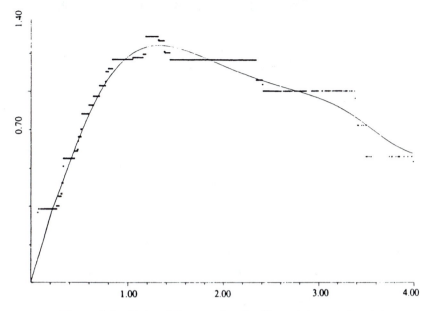

Figure 8.4.   Unimodal regression for the potato versus net income example. The points indicate the unimodal regression and the solid line a spline smooth of the unimodal regression step function. From Hildenbrand and Hildenbrand (1986) with permission of Elsevier Science Publishers.

Hildenbrand and Hildenbrand (1986) report that the above algorithm tends to produce a spike at $X_{(k)}$. For this reason it makes sense to first estimate the mode by $\hat{\alpha} = \arg\max[\hat{m}(x)]$ in a "presmoothing step." In a second step, one then considers unimodal regression with pre-estimated mode $\hat{\alpha}$ by mirroring the right half of the data at the empirical mode $\hat{\alpha}$. This algorithm has been applied to the potato versus net income example; see Figure 8.4.

Exercises

8.1.1 (by Kurt Hildenbrand)
Consider the following algorithm for PAV smoothing. The input is contained in Y[1...N], the isotonic output in R[1... N]. Explain the role of the vector NEXT(I)!
DO I= N TO 1 by -1;
    R(I) = Y(I); NEXT(I) = I+1;

DO WHILE (NEXT(I) <= N)   IF R(I)*(NEXT(NEXT(I))-
NEXT(I))
   < R(NEXT(I))*(NEXT(I)−I) THEN LEAVE; (this loop)
   R(I) = R(I) + R(NEXT(I));
   NEXT(I) = NEXT(NEXT(I));
   END;
END;
DO I = 1 REPEAT NEXT(I) UNTIL (NEXT(I) > N);
   IF NEXT(I)-I > 1 THEN DO;
   R(I) = R(I)/(NEXT(I)-I);
   DO I1 = I + 1 TO NEXT(I)−1; R(I1) = R(I); END;
   END;
END;

8.1.2 Explain qualitatively when you would like to prefer to smooth
first and then to isotonize.

8.1.3 Calculate the asymptotic MSE from Theorem 8.1.1 in the Complements to this section.

8.1.4 Use an asymptotic MSE optimal bandwidth h_0 in (8.1.5). How
does the condition then look?

8.1.5 Rewrite the PAV algorithm so that it starts from the right and
does pooling while descending. Why is the answer, in general,
different from the fit starting from the left?

Complements

Let me compare the two proposed methods
   SI   *Smooth* first then *Isotonize*,
   IS   *Isotonize* first then *Smooth*.
Consider the fixed design case. Let $\hat{m}_h(x)$ denote the Priestley–Chao
kernel estimator and $\hat{m}_h^{IS}(x), \hat{m}_h^{SI}(x)$ the variants of it according to the
above two methods. Mammen (1987) showed the following theorem.

Theorem 8.1.1   Assume that
(A1) $X_i = i/n$, $i = 0, \pm 1, \ldots, \pm n$,
(A2) $E(\exp(t\varepsilon_i)) < \infty$ for t small enough,
(A3) $m \in C^2$, $m' \geq 0$, $x \in [-1,1]$, $m'(0) > 0$.
Then

$$\hat{m}_h^{SI}(0) = \hat{m}_h(0) + o_p(1/n). \tag{8.1.2}$$

Furthermore, there exist independent random mean zero variables
U_{1n}, U_{2n} *such that for some universal constants* c_1, c_2, c_3 *the following*

expansions hold.

$$\hat{m}_h^{SI}(0) = \beta_n + U_{1n} + o_p(n^{-2/3}), \tag{8.1.3}$$

$$\hat{m}_h^{IS}(0) = \beta_n + \delta_n + (1 - \eta_n)U_{1n} + U_{2n} + o_p(n^{-2/3}), \tag{8.1.4}$$

where

$$\beta_n = (1/2)m''(0)d_K n^{-2/5},$$

$$\delta_n = c_3\sigma^{4/3}m''(0)[m'(0)]^{-4/3}n^{-2/3},$$

$$\eta_n = c_2\sigma^{4/3}[m'(0)]^{-4/3}c_K^{(1)}c_K^{-1}n^{-4/15},$$

$$c_K^{(1)} = \int [K'(u)]^2 du.$$

Furthermore, $n^{2/5}U_{1n}$ and $n^{8/15}U_{2n}$ are asymptotically normal with variances $\sigma^2 c_K$ and $c_1\sigma^{10/3}[m'(0)]^{-4/3}c_K^{(1)}$, respectively.

The theorem can be used to calculate the asymptotic MSE, see Exercise 8.1.3. Mammen reports that simulations show that $c_1 < 2c_2$. Therefore, the method IS leads to a variance reduction and a larger bias. Furthermore, it can be computed from (8.1.3, 8.1.4) that $\hat{m}_h^{IS}(0)$ has a smaller MSE than $\hat{m}_h^{SI}(0)$ if and only if

$$\frac{h^5 d_K[m''(0)]^2}{\sigma^2 c_K^{(1)}} < \frac{2c_2 - c_1}{2c_3}. \tag{8.1.5}$$

The universal constants come from the technique used by Mammen, the approximation of the empirical distribution function by a sequence of Brownian bridges. It is very interesting that the asymptotic variance of $\hat{m}_h^{IS}(0)$ has a second-order term of the order $O(n^{-16/15})$, where the constant in this rate is negative and proportional to $[m'(0)]^{-4/3}$. This seems to be quite intuitive: If the slope at a point is not very steep we expect the IS method to behave better than the SI method. Certainly, if $m'(0)$ is small we can allow for a broad (random) bandwidth from the PAV algorithm.

8.2   Estimation of zeros and extrema

It is often sufficient to report a few significant points of a curve in order to describe the nature of its form. Such significant points are, for example, locations of zeros, peaks, troughs or inflection points. These significant points usually have an interpretation in terms of the field of application and, moreover, can be used for comparing groups of similar data sets with respect to each other. There have been two different models and approaches for estimation of zeros or extrema. The first model is concerned with the situation that the statistician has already sampled the data and then wants to estimate these points. The second model deals with the case that data are observed sequentially (e.g. screening studies) and every new observation is used to improve the information about the current estimate of the zero or extremum.

Müller (1985) investigated the question of estimating zeros and the location and sizes of extrema in the first model. He assumed the standard fixed design model

$$Y_i = m(X_i) + \varepsilon_i, \quad i = 1, \ldots, n$$

with $X_i = i/n$. Such a model makes sense, for example, in growth curve analysis, where different (but similar) individuals are compared. A comparison across individuals can then be done on the basis of location and size of the maximal value of an individual growth curve, for instance.

Assume that $m^{(k)}(x)$, the kth derivative of the regression function, has a unique maximum at α_k, that is,

$$m^{(k)}(\alpha_k) = \max_{x \in (0,1)} m^{(k)}(x).$$

From a kernel smooth $\hat{m}_h^{(k)}(x)$ one constructs the empirical (most left) location

$$\hat{\alpha}_{k,h} = \inf\{x \colon \hat{m}_h^{(k)}(x) = \max\}$$

and the size $\hat{m}_h^{(k)}(\hat{\alpha}_{k,h})$ of a maximum. In the same way, an empirical zero of m is defined by

$$\hat{z}_{k,h} = \inf\{x \colon \hat{m}_h^{(k)}(x) = 0\}.$$

It is known from (4.1.6) in Section 4.1 that the maximal deviation between kernel smoothers and the true regression function converges to zero at the rate $\gamma_n \sim \max\{(nh/\log n)^{-1/2}, h\}$, provided m is Lipschitz continuous. If m is twice differentiable then the bias is, as we have seen many times, of the order $O(h^2)$. Balancing bias against the stochastic term of the kernel smoother, we obtain as in Section 4.1 for $h \sim (n/\log n)^{-1/5}$ the rate

$$\gamma_n = O((n \log n)^{-2/5})$$

for the supremum distance

$$\sup_x |\hat{m}_h(x) - m(x)| = O_p(\gamma_n).$$

From this rate emerges the speed of convergence for the location of the extremum as the following proposition by Müller (1985) shows.

Proposition 8.2.1 *If*

$$|m^{(k)}(u) - m^{(k)}(\alpha_k)| \geq c|u - \alpha_k|^\rho, \; \rho \geq 1,$$

in a neighborhood of α_k, *then*

$$|\hat{\alpha}_{k,h} - \alpha_k| = O_p([\gamma_n]^{1/\rho}) \quad and$$
$$|\hat{m}_h^{(k)}(\hat{\alpha}_{k,h}) - m^{(k)}(\alpha_k)| = O_p(\gamma_n).$$

An analogous result holds for the estimation of zeros z_k of $m^{(k)}$.

Proposition 8.2.2 *If*

$$|m^{(k)}(u)| \geq c|u - z_k|v^\tau, \; \tau \geq 1,$$

in a neighborhood of z_k, *then*

$$|\hat{z}_{k,h} - z_k| = O_p([\gamma_n]^{1/\tau}).$$

Müller (1985) also computed the asymptotic distribution of $\hat{\alpha}_{k,h}$ and $\hat{z}_{k,h}$. The method works remarkably well even on small data sets, as Figure 8.5 indicates. The points in this picture indicate $n = 15$ hormone levels. The solid line corresponds to a kernel with order $(k,p) = (0,2)$ (see (4.5.2)), whereas the dashed line was computed for $(k,p) = (0,4)$. Estimated coordinates of the peak and size are $\hat{\alpha}_{k,h} = 14.14$ and $\hat{m}_h^{(k)}(\hat{\alpha}_{k,h}) = 4.21$ for the first kernel smooth. Note that the higher order kernel models peak a little more sharply than the lower order kernel. Bandwidths were determined by Rice's T, as described in Section 5.2.

The second model for estimating zeros and extrema has only been recently investigated in the stochastic design case. Assume that $(X_1, Y_1), (X_2, Y_2), \ldots$ come in sequentially. With the above method used for the fixed sample case, the whole regression curve would have to be recomputed when a new observation enters, in order to define the peak location or the height of the maximum. This estimation technique can therefore be extremely time and space consuming.

When the statistician has complete control over the predictor variables X, less space- and time-consuming methods for finding zeros or the location of extremal values are available. In the fifties Robbins and Monro (1951) and Kiefer and Wolfowitz (1952) defined recursive stochastic approximation methods for estimating these points. The Robbins–Monro

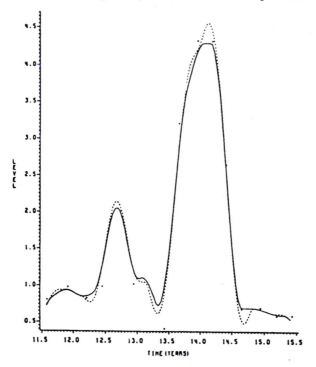

Figure 8.5.   A hormone level example. The points indicate $n = 15$ hormone levels. The solid line corresponds to a kernel with order $(k, p) = (0, 2)$ (see (4.5.2)), whereas the dashed line was computed for $(k, p) = (0, 4)$. Estimated coordinates of the peak and size are $\hat{a}_{k,h} = 14.14$ and $\hat{m}_h^{(k)}(\hat{a}_{k,h}) = 4.21$ for the first kernel smooth. From Müller (1985) with permission of the *Scandinavian Journal of Statistics*.

procedure, for instance, is defined through

$$X_{n+1} = X_n - a_n Y_n, \quad n \geq 1.$$

(New observations $Y_{n+1} = m(X_{n+1}) + \varepsilon_{n+1}$ can be drawn since the statistician can observe the curve (up to error) at any point x.) For suitable choice of $\{a_n\}$ this sequence converges to the (unique) zero of $m(x)$.

This algorithm can be extended to the stochastic design model. Motivated by the Robbins–Monro procedure define an estimator sequence

Z_n for the zero of $m(x)$

$$Z_{n+1} = Z_n - a_n K_h(Z_n - X_n)Y_n, \quad n \geq 1, \tag{8.2.1}$$

with an arbitrary starting random variable and $\{a_n\}$ a sequence of positive constants tending to zero. The basic idea of this algorithm is to stay *passive* if an observation enters that is outside some neighborhood of the zero. The neighborhood of the zero is defined as usual by a kernel sequence. For this reason it is called a *passive stochastic approximation (PSA)* method; see Tsybakov (1988).

In fact, the sequence $\{Z_n\}$ in (8.2.1) will eventually converge to the (unique) zero of

$$r(x) = m(x)f(x).$$

The arguments for estimating z_0, the unique zero of $m(x)$, can be extended to the problem of estimating the location of extrema. Note that $m = r/f$ and therefore

$$m' = \frac{r'f - rf'}{f^2}.$$

Under suitable assumptions the problem of finding an extremum of m is equivalent to finding a (unique) zero of $r'f - rf'$. It has been proposed in Härdle and Nixdorf (1987) that the estimation be performed recursively:

$$\begin{aligned}
Z'_{n+1} = Z'_n - a_n h^{-3} Y_n \{ & K((Z'_n - \overline{X}_n)/h)K'((Z'_n - X_n)/h) \\
& - K'((Z'_n - \overline{X}_n)/h)K((Z'_n - X_n)/h)\}, \quad n \geq 1 .
\end{aligned}$$
$$\tag{8.2.2}$$

Here $\{\overline{X}_n\}$ denotes an additional i.i.d. sequence with the same distribution as X. The asymptotic normality is shown in the following theorem.

Theorem 8.2.1   Assume that apart from minor technical conditions $a_n = n^{-1}$, $h = n^{-1/5}$ and

$$\inf_{\eta \leq |u - z_0| \leq \eta^{-1}} (u - z_0)r(u) > 0 \qquad \text{for all } \eta > 0 .$$

Then the recursively defined sequence $\{Z_n\}$ is asymptotically normal, that is,

$$n^{2/5}(Z_n - z_0) \xrightarrow{\mathcal{L}} N(B, V) ,$$

where

$$B = r''(z_0)d_K/(2r'(z_0) - 4/5),$$
$$V = c_K(\sigma^2(x) + m^2(x))f(z_0)/(2r'(z_0) - 4/5).$$

Note that the rate of convergence here is slightly better (by a log term) than that in Proposition 8.2.1 for $\rho = 1$. The reason is that Proposition 8.2.1 is proved by employing a uniform convergence rate, whereas the the proof of Theorem 8.2.3 uses local properties of r near z_0. Optimality of the passive stochastic approximation algorithm (8.2.1) was considered by Tsybakov (1988).

Exercises

8.2.1 Prove Proposition 8.2.1 by applying the uniform rate result as given in Section 4.1.

8.2.2 Recall the uniform rate for a function of higher degree of differentiability. How does the rate change from

$$\gamma_n = O((n/\log n)^{-2/5})$$

to a faster rate if $m \in C^4$?

8.2.3 Depict graphically the condition of Proposition 8.2.1 on the local behavior of $m(\cdot)$ near the zero.

Complements

In sequential estimation of zeros or extrema it is interesting to stop the procedure once a desired precision of the sequence $\{Z_n\}$ is achieved. For this purpose one defines a stopping rule

$$N(d) = \inf\{n \geq 1 | V_n + n^{-1} \leq n^{4/5}d^2/(q_{\alpha/2})^2\}, \qquad (8.2.3)$$

where d is the desired precision of the zero, V_n is an estimate of V, the asymptotic variance of Z_n from Theorem 8.2.1 and $q_{\alpha/2}$ is the $(1 - \alpha/2)$-quantile of the standard normal distribution. This stopping rule yields with an estimate B_n of B a fixed-width confidence interval

$$[Z_{N(d)} - n^{-2/5}B_n - d, Z_{N(d)} - n^{-2/5}B_n + d].$$

Using the randomly stopped sequence $Z_{N(d)}$ does not change the asymptotic distribution, as the following theorem shows.

Theorem 8.2.2   Let a_n and h be defined as in Theorem 8.2.1. Then if $N(d)$ is defined as in (8.2.3),

$$N(d)^{2/5}(Z_{N(d)} - z_0) \xrightarrow{\mathcal{L}} N(B, V),$$

where the bias B and the variance V are defined as in Theorem 8.2.1.

Analogous results can be obtained for the estimation of extrema via the sequence $\{Z'_n\}$. Härdle and Nixdorf (1987) applied this algorithm to determine age as a function of height from some forensic medicine data.

CHAPTER 9

Incorporating parametric components

We must confine ourselves to those forms that we know how to handle, or for which any tables which may be necessary have been constructed.

Sir R.A. Fisher (1922)

For a pragmatic scientist the conclusion of Fisher (1922), to "confine ourselves to those forms that we know how to handle, " must have an irresistible attractive power. Indeed, we know that the nonparametric smoothing task is hard, especially in high dimensions. So why not come back to parametrics, at least partially? A parametric together with a nonparametric component may handle the model building even better than just the nonparametric or the parametric approach! In this chapter I present approaches from both views. The discussed models incorporate both parametric and nonparametric components and are therefore called *semiparametric models.*

Three topics are addressed. First, the estimation of parameters in a partial linear model. Second, the comparison of individual curves in a shape-invariant context. Third, a method is proposed to check the appropriateness of parametric regression curves by comparison with a nonparametric smoothing estimator.

An example of a semiparametric model is

$$Y_i = \beta^T Z_i + m(X_i) + \varepsilon_i, \quad i = 1, \ldots, n \qquad (9.0.1)$$

where $\beta^T = (\beta_1, \ldots, \beta_p)$ is a p-vector of unknown regression coefficients and m: $\mathbb{R}^d \to \mathbb{R}$ is an unknown smooth regression function. Here the response Y depends on a pair of predictor variables (X, Z) such that the mean response is linear on $Z \in \mathbb{R}^p$ (parametric component) and possibly nonlinear on $X \in \mathbb{R}^d$ (nonparametric component). For the structure of its parametric component this model is called a *partial linear model.*

Another semiparametric model is motivated from growth curve analysis. In this setting one observes that individual curves differ but have the same general overall shape. More formally, suppose that at least two sets of regression data

$$Y_{ij} = m_j(X_{ij}) + \varepsilon_{ij}, \quad i = 1,\ldots,n, \; j = 1,\ldots,J, \; J \geq 2,$$
$$(9.0.2)$$

have been observed and that each "individual curve" $m_j(\cdot)$ is modeled
nonparametrically. The same "overall shape" of the curves m_j can be
expressed formally by the existence of transformations S_θ, T_θ such that

$$m_j(x) = S_{\theta_j}^{-1}[m_1(T_{\theta_j}^{-1}(x))], \; j \geq 2. \qquad (9.0.3)$$

The "individual curves" m_j are thus mapped into each other by means
of certain parametric transformations. Examples of possible transformations are shift/scale families, that is,

$$m_j(x) = \theta_{3j} + \theta_{4j} m_1((x - \theta_{1j})/\theta_{2j}), \quad j \geq 2, \qquad (9.0.4)$$

where both S_θ and T_θ are of the form $(x-u)/v, \quad v \neq 0$. Since with these
specific transformations S_θ, T_θ the shape of all individual curves $m_j(\cdot)$
is the same for all j, this model has also been called *shape invariant*.

As an example of a shape-invariant model consider the issue of constant demand Engel curves over time (Hildenbrand 1985). Figure 9.1
shows expenditure Engel curves for food as a function of income for five
different years (1969, 1971, 1973, 1975, 1977). All the curves look similar except that they have different lengths, which corresponds to the
presence of inflation and price changes over years.

Inserting such a scaling parameter into the shape-invariant model
makes it possible to test and to evaluate the evolution of Engel curves;
see Härdle and Jerison (1988).

Some additive models for multivariate data, for example, projection
pursuit, could – in a strict sense – be considered semiparametric as
well. The main feature of these models though is the additivity of their
components. This is the reason why these models are presented in a
separate chapter on additive models; see Chapter 10.

In Section 9.1 I present some recent results on partial linear models.
Section 9.2 of this chapter is devoted to shape-invariant modeling. Section 9.3 discusses the comparison of nonparametric versus parametric
regression fitting through evaluation of the squared deviation between
the two curves.

9.1   Partial linear models

A *partial linear model* is a semiparametric regression model of the form

$$Y_i = \beta^T Z_i + m(X_i) + \varepsilon_i, \quad i = 1,\ldots,n,$$

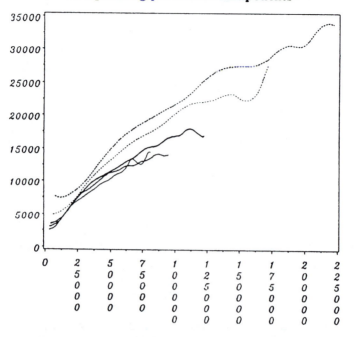

Figure 9.1.   Expenditure Engel curves for food as a function of total expenditure. The shortest line is the curve for year 1969, the next curve is that for year 1971 and the longest is computed from data for year 1977. Family Expenditure Survey, Annual Base Tapes (1968–1983).

where Z_i is a predictor in $\mathbb{R}^p$ and m is an unknown one-dimensional regression function. Such models have been investigated by Spiegelman (1976), Green, Jennison and Seheult (1985), Robinson (1987a), Speckman (1988) and Carroll and Härdle (1989).

Speckman (1988) motivated nonparametric smoothing together with parametric estimation in this context by considering first a parametric representation of m as $W\gamma$, where W is a $(n \times q)$-matrix of full rank and γ is an additional parameter. The partial linear model reads, then, in matrix notation

$$Y = Z\beta + W\gamma + \varepsilon.$$

The normal equations for determining β and γ are

$$Z^T Z \beta = Z^T (Y - W\gamma),$$
$$W\gamma = P_W (Y - Z\beta),$$

(9.1.1)

where $P_W = W(W^T W)^{-1} W^T$ denotes projection onto the column space of W and Z denotes the $(n \times p)$-matrix of the predictors of the parametric part. Green, Jennison and Seheult (1985) proposed replacing the projection operator in (9.1.1) by a smoother $\hat{m}$ and then defining

$$\hat{\beta}_{GJS} = (Z^T(I - W_h)Z)^{-1}Z^T(I - W_h)Y,$$
$$\hat{m}_{GJS} = W_h(Y - Z\hat{\beta}_{GJS}).$$

Estimators for the parametric component are motivated by the following observation. Since P_W is idempotent, the estimates for β and γ can be expressed as

$$\hat{\beta} = [Z^T(I - P_W)^T(I - P_W)Z]^{-1}Z^T(I - P_W)^T(I - P_W)Y,$$
$$W\hat{\gamma} = P_W(Y - Z\hat{\beta}). \tag{9.1.2}$$

Another way of looking at this solution is to say that we are estimating β by first adjusting Z and Y for the nonparametric component and then regressing the residual $(I - P_W)Y$ on the residual $(I - P_W)Z$. Replacing P_W by the kernel smoothing operator $W_h = \{W_{hi}\}_{i=1}^n$, $W_{hi}(X_j) = K_h(X_i - X_j)/\hat{f}_h(X_j)$, let

$$\tilde{Z} = (I - W_h)Z$$

and

$$\tilde{Y} = (I - W_h)Y.$$

The equations (9.1.2) then have the nonparametric analogue

$$\hat{\beta} = (\tilde{Z}^T\tilde{Z})^{-1}\tilde{Z}^T\tilde{Y},$$
$$\hat{m}_h = W_h(Y - Z\hat{\beta}). \tag{9.1.3}$$

Again these formulas may be interpreted as normal equations for a parametric regression model with partially adjusted residuals.

Assume now that Z is related to a one-dimensional X in the following way:

$$Z_{il} = g_l(X_i) + \eta_{li}, \ i = 1, \ldots, n, \ l = 1, \ldots, d,$$

with continuous functions $\{g_l\}_{l=1}^d$ and random errors $\eta = \{\eta_{li}\}_{l=1\ i=1}^{p\ \ n}$ such that $n^{-1}\eta^T\eta$ tends to a positive definite $(d \times d)$-matrix V. Speckman (1988) characterized the asymptotic behavior of the parametric estimator in the partial linear model as follows.

Theorem 9.1.1 Suppose that g and m are p-times differentiable and that the observation error has variance σ^2. Then for the estimation *technique defined in (9.1.3)*

$$\beta - E\hat{\beta} = h^{2p}V^{-1}\int g^{(p)}(u)m^{(p)}(u)du + o(h^p n^{-1/2}),$$

$$var(\hat{\beta}) = \sigma^2 n^{-1}V^{-1} + o(n^{-1}).$$

provided $h \sim n^{-1/(2p+1)}$.

Note that the variance converges at the "parametric rate" $n^{-1/2}$ whereas the bias has the usual "nonparametric rate" $o(h^{2p})$. By contrast, the bias of the above $\hat{\beta}_{GJS}$ is of order $O(h^p)$; see Exercise 9.1.3.

Engle et al. (1986), Rice (1986) and Heckman (1986) used spline smoothing in the partial linear model, that is, finding coefficients β and a function m such that

$$n^{-1}\sum_{i=1}^{n}(Y_i - \beta^T Z_i - m(X_i))^2 + \lambda \int [m''(u)]^2 du$$

is minimized. In the setting of spline smoothing Rice (1986) found a similar interplay between the parametric and the nonparametric part of the partially linear model as is described in Theorem 9.1.1. Heckman (1986) considered the case $g_l(x)$ = constant and derived asymptotic zero bias for $\hat{\beta}$. (Compare with Theorem 9.1.1.) Speckman (1988) gave an application of a partial linear model to a mouthwash experiment. A control group ($Z = 0$) used only a water rinse for mouthwash and an experimental treatment group ($Z = 1$) used a common brand of analgesic. Figure 9.2 shows the raw data and the partial kernel regression estimates for this data set.

The two estimated regression curves $\hat{m}_h(x)$ and $\hat{m}_h(x) + \hat{\beta}$ ($Z_i = 1$ for the treatment group) are superimposed on this scatter plot. One clearly sees the parametric shift of the nonparametric component of the regression model due to the treatment effect.

Exercises

9.1.1 Another method for finding estimators for β is to compute the *average derivative*

$$\delta = E_U[g'(U)],$$

where g denotes the sum $\beta^T Z + m(X)$ as a function of $U = (Z, X)$. Show that the first p components of the average derivative are equal to β. Average derivatives are considered more closely in Chapter 10.

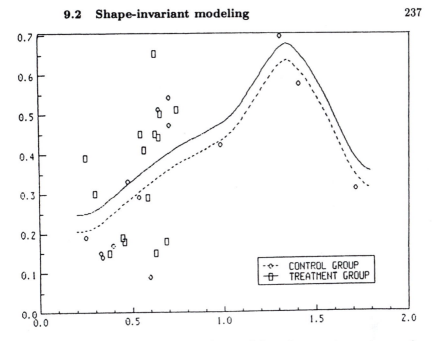

Figure 9.2.   Raw data and partial kernel regression estimates for mouthwash data. The predictor variable is X = baseline SBI, the response is $Y = SBI$ index after three weeks. The SBI index is a measurement indicating gum shrinkage. From Speckman (1988) with permission of the Royal Statistical Society.

9.1.2 Prove that (9.1.1) are the normal equations for the partial linear model

$$Y = Z\beta + W\gamma + \varepsilon.$$

9.1.3 Prove that the bias of $\hat{\beta}_{GJS}$ is of order $O(h^p)$.
[*Hint*: See Green, Jennison and Seheult (1985).]

9.2   Shape-invariant modeling

Lawton, Sylvestre and Maggio (1972) considered the volume of air expelled from the lungs as a function of time (spirometer curves). They found that these spirometer curves have the same shape but differed in location or scale. This motivated them to consider the following framework for comparison of similar curves. One observes data $\{(X_i, Y_i)\}_{i=1}^n$ and $\{(X_i', Y_i')\}_{i=1}^n$ with regression curve $m_1(x)$ and $m_2(x)$, respectively. The idea for formalizing the similarity between the two curves m_2 and

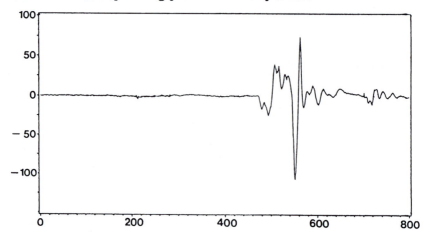

Figure 9.3a.   Acceleration curve of side impact data. The X-variable is time (in milliseconds), the Y-variable is acceleration (in g) after impact, test object $= TO4$.

m_1 is to introduce transformations S_θ, T_θ such that

$$m_2(x') = S_\theta^{-1} m_1(T_\theta^{-1} x'), \quad \theta \in \mathbb{R}^4. \tag{9.2.1}$$

Here S_θ, T_θ denote shift/scale transformations $S_\theta(u) = \theta_3 + \theta_4 u$ and $T_\theta(u) = \theta_1 + \theta_2 u$. Because of the nature of these transformations this model is called a *shape-invariant model*.

An example of such a relationship between the two curves is given in Figure 9.3 from a study on automobile side impacts (Kallieris and Mattern, 1984; Kallieris, Mattern and Härdle, 1986).

The curves give the impression that they are noisy versions of similar regression curves with the same shape. The main difference is that the X-axis is shifted and there is a vertical rescaling. This example is considered in more detail in what follows.

Another example stems from the analysis of human growth curves (Gasser et al. 1985; Stuetzle et al. 1980). Individual curves have been approximated by nonparametric estimation techniques but may have a simple (parametric) relationship between them. Kneip and Gasser (1988) consider an extension by defining a random-coefficient shape-invariant model to fit individual differences. They investigate a method for simultaneous estimation of m and θ by making use of prior information.

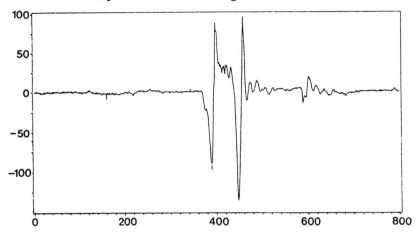

Figure 9.3b.   Acceleration curve of side impact data. The X-variable is time (in milliseconds), the Y-variable is acceleration (in g) after impact, test object $= TO3$.

In this section I consider the fixed design model of equispaced $\{X_i\}_{i=1}^n$ on the unit interval. I will assume throughout that

$$Y_i = m_1(X_i) + \varepsilon_i, \quad \text{var}(\varepsilon_i) = \sigma^2,$$
$$Y_i' = m_2(X_i') + \varepsilon_i', \quad \text{var}(\varepsilon_i') = \sigma'^2,$$

where ε_i, $1 \leq i \leq n$, are i.i.d. mean zero random errors with all moments existing and m_1, m_2 are Hölder continuous.

Suppose that in (9.2.1) there exists a true θ_0 mapping m_1 into m_2 and vice versa. A good estimate of θ_0 will be provided by a value of θ for which the curve $m_1(x)$ is closely approximated by

$$M(x, \theta) = S_\theta m_2(T_\theta x).$$

The effectiveness of an estimate of θ_0 is assessed here by the loss function

$$L(\theta) = \int [m_1(x) - M(x, \theta)]^2 w(x) dx,$$

where w is a nonnegative weight function. Note that $M(x, \theta_0) = m_1(x)$, so θ_0 minimizes $L(\theta)$.

The unknown regression functions are estimated by Priestley–Chao-type kernel smoothers

$$\hat{m}_{h1}(x) = n^{-1} \sum_{i=1}^{n} K_h(x - X_i)Y_i,$$

$$\hat{m}_{h'2}(x') = n^{-1} \sum_{i=1}^{n} K_{h'}(x' - X_i')Y_i'.$$

Since θ_0 minimizes $L(\theta)$ it is natural to define the estimate $\hat{\theta}$ of θ to be the argument which minimizes

$$\hat{L}(\theta) = \int [\hat{m}_{h1}(x) - \hat{M}_{h'}(x, \theta)]^2 w(x)dx,$$

where

$$\hat{M}_{h'}(x, \theta) = S_\theta \hat{m}_{h'2}(T_\theta x).$$

This estimate $\hat{\theta}$ of θ_0 is consistent, as the following theorem shows.

Theorem 9.2.1   Suppose that $L(\theta)$ is locally convex in the sense that given $\varepsilon > 0$, there is a $D(\varepsilon) > 0$ such that $|\theta - \theta_0| > \varepsilon$ implies

$$L(\theta) - L(\theta_0) > D(\varepsilon).$$

Furthermore, assume that S_θ and T_θ are smooth in the sense that

$$\sup_{\theta \in \Theta} \sup_{x \in [0,1]} |S_\theta'(x)| < \infty,$$

$$\sup_{\theta \in \Theta} \sup_{x \in [0,1]} |(T_\theta^{-1})'(x)| < \infty,$$

where

$$S_\theta'(u) = \frac{d}{du}S_\theta(u)$$

and

$$(T_\theta^{-1})'(u) = \frac{d}{du}(T_\theta^{-1})(u).$$

Then with h, h' in

$$H_n = [C^{-1}n^{-1+\delta}, Cn^{-\delta}],$$

$$\sup_{h,h' \in H_n} |\hat{\theta} - \theta_0| \overset{a.s.}{\to} 0, \quad n \to \infty.$$

Let me apply this method to the acceleration curve example. From looking at Figures 9.3a, 9.3b it makes sense to say that the main acceleration in the curve in Figure 9.3a is somewhat "later" and less "expanded"

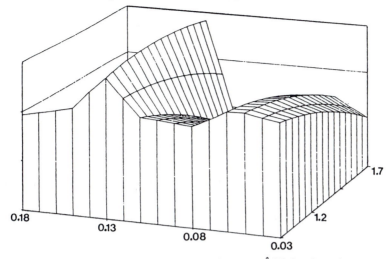

Figure 9.4. The negative loss function $\hat{L}(\theta)$ for the side impact data set. The weight function was the indicator function on the interval (0.1, 0.7). From Härdle and Marron (1989) with permission of the Institute of Mathematical Statistics.

than that of Figure 9.3b. The shift/scale model

$$T_\theta(u) = \theta_1 + u,$$
$$S_\theta(u) = \theta_4 u$$

is therefore applied to this data set. (This notation is consistent with the model (9.2.1).) A plot of the loss function $\hat{L}(\theta)$ for these transformations is given in Figure 9.4.

As expected from a comparison of Figure 9.3a and 9.3b, the choice of θ is more critical than that of θ_4. The "side ridges" in the negative loss correspond to values of $\theta^{(1)}$ where there is matching of "first peaks" to "second peaks." The loss function was minimized at $\hat{\theta} = (\hat{\theta}_1, \hat{\theta}_4) = (0.13, 1.45)$. Figure 9.5 shows how $\hat{m}_{h1}$ matches with $\hat{M}_{h'}(x, \theta)$.

To obtain the asymptotic normality of $\hat{\theta}$ in a straightforward way I shall assume that

$$T_\theta(u) = \theta_1 + \theta_2 u,$$

and that S_θ depends only on $\theta_3, \dots, \theta_d$, where d denotes the dimension of the parameter vector. Furthermore, assume that $h' = \theta_2 h$ and that $H(\theta_0)$ is positive definite, where $H(\theta)$ is the $d \times d$ Hessian matrix with

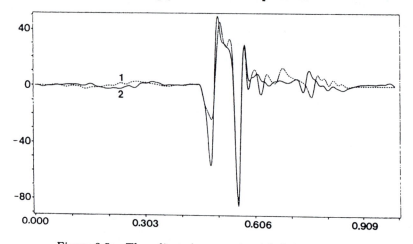

Figure 9.5.   The adjusted curves $\hat{m}_{h1}(x)$ (label 1, dashed line) and $\hat{M}_{h'}(x, \hat{\theta})$ (label 2, solid line), $\hat{\theta} = (0.13, 1.45)$ for the side impact data set. From Härdle and Marron (1989) with permission of the Institute of Mathematical Statistics.

l, l'th entry

$$\int M_l(x, \theta) M_{l'}(x, \theta) w(x) dx$$

using the notation

$$M_l(x, \theta) = \frac{\partial}{\partial \theta_l} M(x, \theta).$$

The asymptotic distribution of $\hat{\theta}$ is given in Härdle and Marron (1990).

Theorem 9.2.2   Under the previous assumptions,

$$\sqrt{n}(\hat{\theta} - \theta_0) \xrightarrow{\mathcal{L}} N(0, H^{-1}(\theta_0) \Sigma H^{-1}(\theta_0)),$$

where the l, l'th entry of Σ is

$$4 \int [\sigma^2 + \sigma'^2 (S'_{\theta_0}(m_2(T_{\theta_0} x)))^2] M_l(x, \theta_0) M_{l'}(x, \theta_0) w(x) dx.$$

The case $T_\theta(u) = \theta_1 + \theta_2 u$ and $S_\theta(u) = \theta_3 + \theta_4 u$ is considered in more detail in Exercise 9.2.1.

Exercises

9.2.1 To gain some insight into the assumptions of this section, consider the case $T_\theta(u) = \theta_1 + \theta_2 u$ and $S_\theta(u) = \theta_3 + \theta_4 u$, where

$$M_1(x,\theta) = \theta_4 m_2'(\theta_1 + \theta_2 x),$$
$$M_2(x,\theta) = \theta_4 x m_2'(\theta_1 + \theta_2 x),$$
$$M_3(x,\theta) = 1,$$
$$M_4(x,\theta) = m_2(\theta_1 + \theta_2 x).$$

What is the positive definiteness of $H(\theta_0)$ then essentially requiring?

9.2.2 What other loss functions may be possible to compare the goodness of fit?

9.2.3 Recall the mouthwash experiment at the end of Section 9.1. There, Z denoted the indicator variable for the treatment effect. This special partial linear model fits also in the present setting of shape-invariant modeling. What are the transformations T_θ and S_θ?

Complements

Proof of Theorem 9.2.1
To prove this theorem note that given $\varepsilon > 0$

$$P\left\{ \sup_h |\hat\theta - \theta_0| > \varepsilon \right\}$$

$$\leq P\left\{ \sup_h (L(\hat\theta) - L(\theta_0)) > D(\varepsilon) \right\}$$

$$\leq P\left\{ \sup_h (L(\hat\theta) - \hat L(\hat\theta) + \hat L(\theta_0) - L(\theta_0)) > D(\varepsilon) \right\}$$

$$\leq P\left\{ \sup_h (L(\hat\theta) - \hat L(\hat\theta)) > D(\varepsilon)/2 \right\}$$

$$+ P\left\{ \sup_h (\hat L(\theta_0) - L(\theta_0)) > D(\varepsilon)/2 \right\},$$

where $\sup_h$ means $\sup_{h,h' \in H_n}$. By rearranging terms and using the triangle inequality it suffices to show that

$$\sup_h \int (\hat m_1(x) - m(x))^2 w(x) dx,$$

$$\sup_\theta \sup_h \int (\hat M_h(x,\theta) - M(x,\theta))^2 w(x) dx$$

$$\tag{9.2.2}$$

tend almost surely to zero. Now apply Proposition 4.1.1 with uniform convergence also over θ to see that both terms in (9.2.2) tend to zero with probability one.

9.3   Comparing nonparametric and parametric curves

The appropriateness of parametric modeling of regression data may be judged by comparison with a nonparametric smoothing estimator. For this purpose one may use a squared deviation measure between the two fits. In this section the wild bootstrap will be used to evaluate the stochastic behavior of this deviation. It will be seen that this bootstrap works (in contrast to more classical forms of bootstrap).

The squared deviation measure can be used as a test statistic to test the parametric model, where the critical value is determined by the wild bootstrap. In particular, I apply this method of comparison to decide about the parametric form of Engel curves. Leser (1963, p. 694) stresses the point that emphasis in statistical estimation of Engel curves has been mainly on parametric models and thus flexible form methods have been neglected.

The problem of finding the most appropriate form of an Engel function is an old one in econometrics, but as yet no solution appears to have found general acceptance. Generally speaking, it is perhaps true to say that the specification of the form of relationships has attracted less attention than have methods of estimating parameters for specified equations.

Leser's observation motivates me to consider parametric and nonparametric curves jointly and to decide, probably by a graphical method, which one fits the data better. To formalize this, consider for the regression curve a given parametric model

$$\{m_\theta \colon \theta \in \Theta\}. \tag{9.3.1}$$

Possible parametric models for Engel curves include the Working curve

$$m_\theta(x) = \theta_1 x + \theta_2 x \log x$$

or the Leser curve. The parametric fit $m_{\hat{\theta}}$ shall be compared with the nonparametric $\hat{m}_h$.

Then the question arises, can visible differences between $m_{\hat{\theta}}$ and $\hat{m}_h$ be explained by stochastic fluctuations or do they suggest the use of nonparametric instead of parametric methods? One way to proceed is to measure the difference between $m_{\hat{\theta}}$ and $\hat{m}_h$ by a metric and to use this metric as a test statistic for testing the parametric model. A related approach for estimating parameters of a linear model based on a pilot nonparametric smooth was pursued by Cristóbal Cristóbal, Faraldo Roca and González Manteiga (1987).

To formalize this metric let $\mathcal{K}_{h,n}$ denote the (random) smoothing operator

$$\mathcal{K}_{h,n}g(x) = \frac{\sum_{i=1}^{n} K_h(x - X_i)g(X_i)}{\sum_{i=1}^{n} K_h(x - X_i)}.$$

Note that $E(\hat{m}_h(x)|X_1, ..., X_n) = \mathcal{K}_{h,n}m(x)$. So if we compare with an unbiased parametric model we should correct the parametric model for this bias (see Exercise 9.3.5 for an illustrative example). I therefore consider the following modification of the squared deviation between $\hat{m}_h$ and $m_{\hat{\theta}}$:

$$T_n = nh^{d/2} \int (\hat{m}_h(x) - \mathcal{K}_{h,n}m_{\hat{\theta}}(x))^2 w(x)dx.$$

T_n may serve as a test statistic to test the parametric hypothesis:

$$m(\cdot) \in \{m_\theta(\cdot): \theta \in \Theta\}.$$

For an approximate calculation of critical values, the asymptotic distribution of T_n for a parametric $m = m_{\theta_0}$ is determined by Theorem 9.3.1. Furthermore, for a comparison of T_n with other goodness-of-fit tests the asymptotic power of T_n may be calculated if m lies in the alternative: say, $m(x) = m_{\theta_0}(x) + c_n \Delta_n(x)$. Clearly, θ_0 and Δ_n are not uniquely defined by m. We will see later how to choose θ_0 and Δ_n dependent on m. It is most appropriate to choose c_n such that the asymptotic power of T_n is bounded away from one and from the level. It will turn out that for $\Delta_n(x) = \Delta(x)$ fixed $c_n = n^{-1/2}h^{-d/4}$ works.

The assumptions on the stochastic nature of the observations and the parametric estimator of the regression function are given in detail in the Complements to this section. About the parametric estimator, I assume that

(P1) $m_{\hat{\theta}}(x) - m_{\theta_0}(x) = \frac{1}{n}\sum_{i=1}^{n}\langle g(x), h(X_i)\rangle \varepsilon_i + o_p\left(\frac{1}{n\log n}\right)^{\frac{1}{2}}$ (uniformly in x), where g and h are bounded functions taking values in $\mathbb{R}^k$ for some k and $\langle\cdot\rangle$ denotes the inner product in $\mathbb{R}^k$.

For the kernel K and the bandwidth h we make the following standard assumptions.

(K1)   The kernel K is a symmetric bounded probability density function with compact support,

(K2)   The bandwidth h fulfills $h = h_n \sim n^{-1/(d+4)}$. Especially (K2) is fulfilled for every asymptotically optimal choice of the bandwidth h; see Section 5.1.

In the following theorem the distribution of T_n is approximated by a Gaussian distribution which may depend on n. The distance between these distributions is measured by the Mallows metric as in Section 4.3.

Theorem 9.3.1   Assume (A1)–(A5), (P1), (K1), (K2). Then

$$d_2 \left(\mathcal{L}(T_n), N \left(b_h + \int (\mathcal{K}_h \Delta_n)^2 w, V \right) \right) \to 0,$$

where

$$b_h = h^{-d/2} K^{(2)}(0) \int \frac{\sigma^2(x) w(x)}{f(x)} dx,$$

$$V = 2K^{(4)}(0) \int \frac{\sigma^4(x) w(x)^2}{f^2(x)} dx.$$

Here $\mathcal{K}_h$ denotes the smoothing operator

$$\mathcal{K}_h g(x) = \int K_h(x - t) g(t) dt$$

and $K_h^{(j)}$ denotes the j-times convolution product of K_h.

The theorem shows that for $d = 1$ the power of the goodness-of-fit test based on T_n is asymptotically constant on regions of the form

$$\left\{ m_{\theta_0} + n^{-9/20} \Delta \colon \int (\mathcal{K}_h \Delta)^2 w = \text{const.} \right\}.$$

This can be compared with the behavior of other goodness-of-fit tests. More classical tests of Cramer von Mises type or of Kolgomorov-Smirnov type have nontrivial power on points contiguous to the parametric model, that is, $m = m_{\theta_0} + n^{-1/2}\Delta$ – but they are of more parametric nature – in the sense that they prefer certain deviations $\Delta_{n,1}, \Delta_{n,2}, \dots$ (Durbin and Knott 1972).

The nonparametric behavior of T_n (nearly the same power for all deviations of fixed weighted L_2-norm) must be paid by the larger distance ($n^{-9/20}$ instead of $n^{-1/2}$) at which the test works. The theorem should thus be interpreted and applied very carefully and should be used only to give a rough idea of the stochastic behavior of T_n. For practical applications I recommend bootstrap methods.

The *naive bootstrap* consists of simple resampling of the original observations. That is, the bootstrap sample $\{(X_i^*, Y_i^*)\}_{i=1}^n$ is drawn (with replacement) out of the set $\{(X_i, Y_i)\}_{i=1}^n$. Then create $T^{*,N}$ like T_n by the squared deviance between the parametric fit and the nonparametric fit. From $\mathcal{L}(T^{*,N})$ define the $(1 - \alpha)$-quantile $\hat{t}_\alpha^N$ and reject the parametric hypothesis if $T_n > \hat{t}_\alpha^N$. Another procedure consists of correcting for the bias in the asymptotic distribution, that is, one determines the sample quantile from $\mathcal{L}^*(T^{*,N} - E^* T^{*,N})$ and checks whether the original $T_n - \hat{b}_h$ falls above this last bias corrected $(1 - \alpha)$-quantile, where $\hat{b}_h$ is an estimate of b_h, for instance, $\hat{b}_h = c_K n^{-1} \sum_{i=1}^n (Y_i - \hat{m}_h(X_i))^2 / (\sum_{j=1}^n K_h(X_i - X_j))^2$.

Härdle and Mammen (1988) show that these procedures do *not* work in the sense that the bootstrap distribution of $T^{*,N}$ does not approximate that of T_n.

At first sight this result seems to be surprising and against the intuition of the bootstrap. The deeper reason though lies in the fact that the regression function is *not* the conditional expectation of the observation under the bootstrap distribution. As an alternative I recommend the *wild bootstrap*, which is related to proposals of Wu (1986) (see Beran 1986). This approach does not mimic the i.i.d. structure of (X_i, Y_i). It is rather constructed so that

$$E^*(Y_i^* - m(X_i^*)|X_i^*) = 0.$$

For this purpose define as in Section 4.2

$$\tilde{\varepsilon}_i = Y_i - \hat{m}_h(X_i).$$

Since we are going to use this *single residual* $\tilde{\varepsilon}_i$ to estimate the distribution of $(Y_i - m(X_i)|X_i)$ by an $\hat{F}_i$ we are calling it the *wild bootstrap*. More precisely, define $\hat{F}_i$ by a two-point distribution such that $E_{\hat{F}_i} Z^2 = (\tilde{\varepsilon}_i)^2$ and $E_{\hat{F}_i} Z^3 = (\tilde{\varepsilon}_i)^3$. Now construct independent $\varepsilon_i^* \sim \hat{F}_i$ and use

$$(X_i, Y_i^* = m_{\hat{\theta}}(X_i) + \varepsilon_i^*)$$

as bootstrap observations. Then create $T^{*,W}$ like T_n by the squared deviance between the parametric fit and the nonparametric fit. From $\mathcal{L}(T^{*,W})$ define the $(1 - \alpha)$-quantile $\hat{t}_\alpha^W$ and reject the parametric hypothesis if $T_n > \hat{t}_\alpha^W$. The following theorem shows that this procedure works.

Theorem 9.3.2   *Assume (A1),...,(A4),(A5'),(P1),(K1),(K2). Assume for the parametric estimator $\hat{\theta}$ based on the bootstrap sample*

$$(P1'') \quad m_{\hat{\theta}^*}(x) - m_{\hat{\theta}}(x) = \frac{1}{n} \sum_{i=1}^n <g(x), h(X_i)> \varepsilon_i^*$$

$$+ o_{p^*}\left(\frac{1}{\sqrt{n \log n}}\right).$$

Then

$$d_2(\mathcal{L}^*(T^{*,W}), N(b_h, V)) \xrightarrow{p} 0,$$

where b_h and V are defined in Theorem 9.3.1.

Let us check the validity of the asymptotic results in a Monte Carlo experiment. In a first simulation I generated $\{X_i\}_{i=1}^n, n = 100$, uniformly in $[0, 1]$ and $Y_i = m(X_i) + \varepsilon_i, m(u) = 2u - u^2$ with $\varepsilon_i \sim \sigma = 0.1$, independent of X_i. For construction of the kernel smooth I have used the quartic kernel. The bootstrap resampling was performed $B = 100$ times and the whole procedure was carried out $M = 1000$ times.

I considered the parametric model of polynomials of degree 2. The true regression curve $m(\cdot)$ is in this model class. For the kernel estimator the bandwidth $h = 0.2$ has been chosen. In Figure 9.6 four curves for one Monte Carlo run are displayed.

The thin line (label 1) denotes the Monte Carlo kernel density estimate of the L_2-distance from the M runs. The medium thin line (label 2) is the kernel density of one bootstrap sample out of the M runs (taken at random). The thick line corresponds to the normal theory density as given in Theorem 9.3.1 based on the true b_h and V (label 3). The dashed line finally shows the normal theory density based on estimated b_h and V (label 4). In all four cases the bootstrap estimates the distribution of the distance quite well. The normal approximations are totally misleading.

To study the power of this bootstrap test I have chosen the parametric model

$$m_\theta(x) = \theta_1 + \theta_2 x + \theta_3 x^2 \tag{9.3.2}$$

and for different c the regression function

$$m(x) = 2x - x^2 + c\left(x - \frac{1}{4}\right)\left(x - \frac{1}{2}\right)\left(x - \frac{3}{4}\right). \tag{9.3.3}$$

Monte Carlo estimates of the power ($\alpha = 0.05$) are summarized in Table 9.3.1 for different values of c and bandwidth h. Clearly, the bootstrap test rejects the hypothesis for $c = 1$.

Figure 9.7 shows a linear fit and a Working curve and a nonparametric smoothing estimate for the Engel curve for food as a function of total expenditure. The data came from the Family Expenditure Survey (1968–1981). The bootstrap test rejected the linear regression model for any bandwidth. The Working curve has been rejected for some small bandwidths. Details of this study also applied to other commodities are presented in Härdle and Mammen (1988).

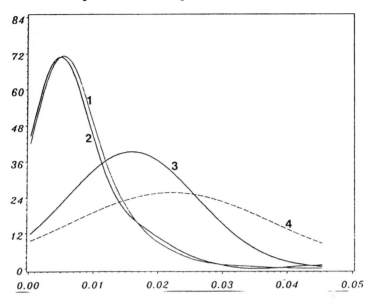

Figure 9.6.   Four densities of T_n. The line with label 1 denotes the (kernel) density of the distribution of T_n over *all* Monte Carlo runs ($M = 1000$). The line with label 2 is the (kernel) density of T_n from *one* Monte Carlo run using the wild bootstrap method from $B = 100$ bootstrap curves. The curve labeled 3 is the normal theory density from Theorem 9.3.1 with the *known* constants b_h and V. The curve labeled 4 is the normal theory density from Theorem 9.3.1 with *estimated* constants $\hat{b}_h$ and $\hat{V}$. From Härdle and Mammen (1988).

Exercises

9.3.1 Program the wild bootstrap goodness-of-fit test. Apply it to the simulated data set and test whether the regression curve is linear.

Table 9.3.1   *Monte Carlo estimates of power of the bootstrap test*

h, c	0.0	0.5	1.0	2.0
0.1	0.105	0.157	0.325	0.784
0.2	0.054	0.120	0.252	0.795
0.25	0.053	0.099	0.263	0.765
0.3	0.039	0.078	0.225	0.714

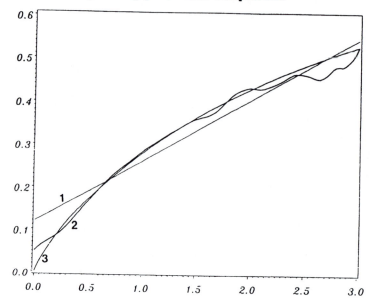

Figure 9.7.   Engel curves. The curve labeled 1 is a linear regression line for food (1973) of the Family Expenditure Survey. The curve labeled 2 is a nonparametric kernel smooth. The curve labeled 3 is a Working curve fit.

9.3.2 Consider the linear model

$$m_\theta(x) = \theta_1 g_1(x) + \cdots + \theta_k g_k(x) = \langle \theta, g(x) \rangle,$$

where g is a $\mathbb{R}^k$-valued function (for some k). With a smooth weight function W the weighted least squares estimator $\hat\theta_n = \hat\theta$ is defined by

$$\hat\theta = \arg\min_\theta \left[\sum_{i=1}^n W(X_i)(Y - m_\theta(X_i))^2 \right].$$

In the linear model, $\hat\theta$ can easily be calculated,

$$\hat\theta = \left(\sum_{i=1}^n W(X_i)g(X_i)g(X_i)^T \right)^{-1} \sum_{i=1}^n W(X_i)g(X_i)Y_i.$$

Consider, now, a fixed regression function m which may lie in the hypothesis or in the alternative. We want to write m as $m(x) = m_{\theta_0}(x) + c_n \Delta_n(x)$ for some θ_0 and Δ_n. θ_0 and $\Delta_n(x)$

may be chosen as follows

$$\theta_0 = \arg\min_{\theta} \left[\int W(x)(m(x) - m_\theta(x))^2 dx \right],$$

$$\Delta_n(x) = \frac{1}{c_n}(m(x) - m_{\theta_0}(x)).$$

With this choice of m_{θ_0} and Δ_n, in an appropriate scalar product Δ_n is orthogonal to $\{m_\theta(x): \theta \in \Theta\}$:

$$\int W(x)f(x)\Delta_n(x)g(x)dx = 0.$$

This will imply that the expectation of $\hat{\theta}$ is approximately θ_0. This can be seen by the following stochastic expansion of $\hat{\theta}$:

$$\hat{\theta} = \theta_0 + \left(\int W(x)f(x)g(x)g(x)^T dx \right)^{-1}$$

$$\left\{ \frac{1}{n} \sum_{i=1}^{n} W(X_i)g(X_i)\varepsilon_i \right.$$

$$\left. + c_n \int W(x)f(x)\Delta_n(x)g(x)dx \right\}$$

$$+ O_p\left(\frac{c_n}{\sqrt{n}} \right)$$

$$= \theta_0 + \frac{1}{n} \sum_{i=1}^{n} h(X_i)\varepsilon_i + O_p\left(\frac{c_n}{\sqrt{n}} \right),$$

where

$$h(x) = \left(\int W(x)f(x)g(x)g(x)^T dx \right)^{-1} W(x)g(x).$$

Can you now put the functions g, h into assumption (P1)? Is (P1) true for this linear model?

9.3.3 Show that (P1) holds also for weighted least squares estimators $\hat{\theta}$ in nonlinear models if $m(\cdot)$ and $W(\cdot)$ are "smooth" and Δ_n and θ_0 are chosen such that Δ_n is "orthogonal" to the parametric model. Note that

$$\int W(x)f(x)\Delta_n(x)\frac{\partial}{\partial\theta}m_{\theta_0}(x)dx = 0.$$

(Trivially this includes the parametric case: $\Delta_n \equiv 0$.) (P1) holds with

$$h(x) = \left(\int W(t) f(t) \left(\frac{\partial}{\partial \theta} m_{\theta_0}(t) \right) \left(\frac{\partial}{\partial \theta} m_{\theta_0}(t) \right)^T dt \right)^{-1}$$

$$W(x) \frac{\partial}{\partial \theta} m_{\theta_0}(x),$$

$$g(x) = \frac{\partial}{\partial \theta} m_{\theta_0}(x).$$

9.3.4 Perform the bootstrap test with the curves and models as in (9.3.2) and (9.3.3). Convince yourself that the "extra wiggle" for $c = 1$ is not very pronounced on a joint plot of the model and the true curve.

9.3.5 Suppose you have a regression curve $m(x) = (1/10)\varphi(x/10)$ which has a sharp peak. Of course, there is a parametric model for this curve. Assume now that you have smoothed nonparametrically and the peak is thus undersmoothed. You might now say that the parametric model differs very much from the nonparametric one and therefore you reject it. How can you correct this bias?

[*Hint*: See the definition of the distance T_n.]

Complements

Assumptions

(A1)   With probability 1, X_i lies in a compact set (without loss of generality $[0, 1]^d$). The marginal density $f(x)$ of X_i is bounded away from zero.

(A2) $m(\cdot)$ and $f(\cdot)$ are twice continuously differentiable. w is continuously differentiable.

(A3) $\Delta_n(x)$ is bounded (uniformly in x and n) and $c_n = n^{-1/2}h^{-d/4}$. In particular, this contains the parametric case because Δ_n may be chosen $\equiv 0$.

(A4) $\sigma^2(x) = \text{var}(Y_i|X_i = x)$ is bounded away from zero and from infinity.

(A5) $E\varepsilon_i^4 < \infty$. Instead of (A5) the following stronger assumption will also be used.

(A5') $E(\exp(t\varepsilon_i))$ is uniformly bounded in i and n for $|t|$ small enough.

Proof of Theorem 9.3.1

Without loss of generality, we will give the proofs only for $d = 1$ and $w(x) \equiv 1$. First note that

$$\hat{f}_h(x) = \frac{1}{n} \sum_{i=1}^{n} K_h(X_i - x),$$

$$= f(x) + O_p(n^{-2/5}\sqrt{\log n}) \quad \text{(uniformly in } x),$$

$$\hat{m}_h(x) = m(x) + O_p(n^{-2/5}\sqrt{\log n}) \quad \text{(uniformly in } x).$$

This gives

$$T_n = n\sqrt{h} \int_0^1 \left(\hat{m}_h(x) - \mathcal{K}_{h,n}m_{\hat{\theta}}(x)\right)^2 dx$$

$$n = \sqrt{h} \int_0^1 (\hat{m}_h(x) - \mathcal{K}_{h,n}m_{\hat{\theta}}(x))^2 \left(\frac{\hat{f}_h(x)}{f(x)}\right)^2 dx + o_p(1)$$

$$= n\sqrt{h} \int_0^1 \left(\frac{1}{n}\sum_{i=1}^{n} \frac{K_h(X_i - x)(m(X_i) + \varepsilon_i - m_{\hat{\theta}}(X_i))}{f^2(x)}\right)^2 dx$$

$$+ o_p(1).$$

Now apply (P1) and $m(\cdot) = m_{\theta_0}(\cdot) + n^{-9/20}\Delta_n(\cdot)$:

$$T_n = \frac{\sqrt{h}}{n} \int_0^1 f(x)^{-2} \sum_{i=1}^{n} K_h(X_i - x)$$

$$\times \left(n^{-9/20}\Delta_n(X_i) + \varepsilon_i - n^{-1}\sum_{j=1}^{n} g(X_j)^T h(X_j)\varepsilon_j\right)^2 dx + o_p(1).$$

By straightforward calculations, one gets

$$T_n = T_{n,1} + T_{n,2} + T_{n,3} + o_p(1)$$

with

$$T_{n,1} = \frac{\sqrt{h}}{n} \sum_{i=1}^{n} \frac{K_h^{(2)}(0)}{f^2(X_i)}\varepsilon_i^2,$$

$$T_{n,2} = \frac{\sqrt{h}}{n} \sum_{i \neq j} \frac{K_h^{(2)}(X_i - X_j)}{f(X_i)f(X_j)}\varepsilon_i\varepsilon_j,$$

$$T_{n,3} = \int_0^1 \left(\frac{n^{-1}\sum_{i=1}^{n} K_h(X_i - x)\Delta_n(X_i)}{f(x)}\right)^2 dx.$$

Now note that

$$T_{n,1} = b_h + o_p(1),$$

$$T_{n,3} = \int_0^1 \mathcal{K}_h \Delta_n(x)^2 dx + o_p(1).$$

So it remains to prove asymptotic normality of $T_{n,2}$. We will use an approach which also works in the proof of Theorem 9.3.2. According to theorem 2.1 in de Jong (1987) it suffices to prove:

$$\max_{1 \le i \le n} \sum_{j=1}^n \mathrm{var}(W_{ijn}) / \mathrm{var}(T_{n,2}) \to 0,$$

$$E(T_{n,2}^4 / (\mathrm{var}(T_{n,2}))^2) \to 3,$$

where

$$W_{ijn} = \frac{\sqrt{h}}{n} \frac{K_h^{(2)}(X_i - X_j)}{f(X_i) f(X_j)} \varepsilon_i \varepsilon_j, \quad \text{if } i \ne j;$$

$$= 0, \quad \text{else.}$$

The proof of the first statement is straightforward. For the proof of the second statement note that:

$$E(T_{n,2}^4) = 12 \sum^{\ne} EW_{ijn}^2 W_{kln}^2$$

$$+ 8 \sum^{\ne} EW_{ijn}^4 + 48 \sum_{i,j,k,l}^{\ne} EW_{ijn} W_{jkn} W_{kln} W_{lin}$$

$$+ 192 \sum^{\ne} EW_{ijn} W_{ikn}^2 W_{jkn}$$

$$= 3 \, \mathrm{var}(T_{n,2})^2 + o(1).$$

Here

$$\sum^{\ne}$$

denotes summation over only all pairwise different indexes.

PART III

Smoothing in high dimensions

CHAPTER 10

Investigating multiple regression by additive models

> While it is possible to encode several more dimensions into pictures by using time (motion), color, and various symbols (glyphs), the human perceptual system is not really prepared to deal with more than three continuous dimensions simultaneously.
>
> Huber, P.J. (1985, p. 437)

The basic idea of scatter plot smoothing can be extended to higher dimensions in a straightforward way. Theoretically, the regression smoothing for a d-dimensional predictor can be performed as in the case of a one-dimensional predictor. The local averaging procedure will still give asymptotically consistent approximations to the regression surface. However, there are two major problems with this approach to multiple regression smoothing. First, the regression function $m(x)$ is a high dimensional surface and since its form cannot be displayed for $d > 2$, it does not provide a geometrical description of the regression relationship between X and Y. Second, the basic element of nonparametric smoothing – averaging over neighborhoods – will often be applied to a relatively meager set of points since even samples of size $n \geq 1000$ are surprisingly sparsely distributed in the higher dimensional Euclidean space. The following two examples by Werner Stuetzle exhibit this "curse of dimensionality."

A possible procedure for estimating two-dimensional surfaces could be to find the smallest rectangle with axis-parallel sides containing all the predictor vectors and to lay down a regular grid on this rectangle. This gives a total of one hundred cells if one cuts each side of a two-dimensional rectangle into ten pieces. Each inner cell will have eight neighboring cells. If one carried out this procedure in ten dimensions there would be a total of $10^{10} = 10,000,000,000$ cells and each inner cell would have $3^{10} - 1 = 59048$ neighboring cells. In other words, it will be hard to find neighboring observations in ten dimensions! Suppose now one had $n = 1000$ points uniformly distributed over the ten dimensional unit cube $[0, 1]^{10}$. What is our chance of catching some points in a neighborhood of reasonable size? An average over a neighborhood of diameter 0.3 (in each coordinate) results in a volume of $0.3^{10} \approx 5.9 \cdot 10^{-6}$ for the corresponding ten-dimensional cube. Hence, the expected number of observations in this cube will be $5.9 \cdot 10^{-3}$ and not much averaging can be expected. If, on the other hand, one fixes the count $k = 10$ of observations over which to average, the diameter of the typical (marginal) neighborhood will be larger than 0.63, which means that the average is extended over at least two-thirds of the range along each coordinate.

A first view of the sparsity of high dimensional data could lead one to the conclusion that one is simply in a hopeless situation – there is just not enough clay to make the bricks! This first view, however, is, as many first views are, a little bit too rough. Assume, for example, that the ten-dimensional regression surface is only a function of x_1, the first coordinate of X, and constant in all other coordinates. In this case the ten-dimensional surface collapses down to a one-dimensional problem. A similar conclusion holds if the regression surface is a function only of certain linear combinations of the coordinates of the predictor variable. The basic idea of additive models is to take advantage of the fact that a regression surface may be of a simple, additive structure.

A *regression tree* is based on such a structure. The regression surface is approximated by a linear combination of step functions

$$m(x) = \sum_{i=1}^{p} c_i I \{x \in N_i\},$$

where the N_i are disjoint hyper-rectangles with sides parallel to the coordinate axes. The hyper-rectangles are constructed by succesive splits and can be represented as a tree. A recursive splitting algorithm (RPR) to construct such a tree is described in Section 10.1.

Another additive model is *projection pursuit regression (PPR)* (Friedman and Stuetzle 1981). This model is an extension of the regression tree model and is defined through projections $\beta_j^T x, \|\beta_j\| = 1, j = 1, \ldots, p$. It models the regression surface as

$$m(x) = \sum_{j=1}^{p} g_j(\beta_j^T x);$$

see Section 10.2.

PPR involves one-dimensional nonparametric functions on linear combinations of predictor variables, whereas the alternative ACE-model determines a linear combination of nonparametric one-dimensional func-

tions operating on the coordinates of the predictor variable with unknown possibly nonlinear transformations; see Section 10.3.

The last technique considered here is related to PPR,

$$Y = g(\delta^T X) + \varepsilon = m(X) + \varepsilon.$$

The coefficients δ are defined differently as $\delta = E[m'(X)]$, an average
derivative (ADE); see Section 10.4. This estimation technique is also
important in theoretical economics in particular in questions related to
the law of demand (see Härdle, Hildenbrand and Jerison 1989).

10.1   Regression trees

The structure of the regression surface estimates that is assumed for
regression trees is of the form (Gordon and Olshen 1980)

$$m(x) = \sum_{j=1}^{p} c_j \, I(x \in N_j), \qquad (10.1.1)$$

where the c_j are constants and the N_j are disjoint hyper-rectangles with
sides parallel to the coordinate axes such that

$$\bigcup_{j=1}^{p} N_j = \mathbb{R}^d \ .$$

Models of this form are sometimes called *piecewise constant regression models* and can be determined by *recursive partitioning regression
(RPR)*. If the regression surface $m(x)$ is itself a piecewise constant model
with known neighborhoods N_j, it is not hard to see that the best estimates for c_i (in a least squares sense) are

$$\hat{c}_j = \sum_{\{i:X_i \in N_j\}} Y_i / \#\{i: X_i \in N_j\} \ . \qquad (10.1.2)$$

Thus the estimate of $m(x)$ for predictor vectors X_i in N_j is simply the
average response of the Y-observations with predictor vectors in N_j.
Note, however, that RPR is different from the smoothing techniques
described before. The neighborhoods can be stretched out in directions
along which the response does not vary a lot, and can be skinny in
directions along which the response varies rapidly. RPR achieves this
goal by the technique of *recursive splitting*.

Consider first the special case $p = 2$. The task of determining the
neighborhoods N_j is solved by determining a *split coordinate l* and a
split point s. A split coordinate and a split point define the rectangles

N_j by

$$N_1(l, s) = \{x | x_l < s\},$$
$$N_2(l, s) = \{x | x_l \geq s\},$$

where x_l denotes the lth coordinate of the vector X. The corresponding partitioning of the sample is given by

$$S_1(l, s) = \{i | X_i \in N_1(l, s)\},$$
$$S_2(l, s) = \{i | X_i \in N_2(l, s)\}.$$

The least squares optimal constants are

$$\hat{c}_1(l, s) = \sum_i Y_i \, I\{i \in S_1(l, s)\}/\#S_1(l, s),$$

$$\hat{c}_2(l, s) = \sum_i Y_i \, I\{i \in S_2(l, s)\}/\#S_2(l, s).$$

It is not hard to see that the residual sum of squares (RSS) of the model defined by split coordinate l and split point s is given by

$$\text{RSS}(l, s) = \text{var}\{Y_i | i \in S_1(l, s)\} + \text{var}\{Y_i | i \in S_2(l, s)\}.$$

$$(10.1.3)$$

The goal is to find that pair (l, s) such that $\text{RSS}(l, s)$ is minimal. Note that this requires only $(n - 1)$ splits for each coordinate since the RSS changes only when s crosses an observation. If there are 3 neighborhoods $\{N_j\}$ we have $(n - 1)d$ possibilities for the first split and $(n - 2)d$ possibilities for the second split, if the first split is given. In total we have $(n - 1)(n - 2)d^2$ operations to find the best splits for $p = 3$ neighborhoods. For general p there are

$$(n - 1)(n - 2) \cdots (n - p + 1)d^{p-1}$$

possibilities. This number can be too big for a successful exhaustive search, so one will try the elementary operation for $p = 2$ recursively. This is the basic idea of recursive partitioning. One starts with the minimization problem for $p = 2$, as described above. This gives split coordinate and split point (l, s) and corresponding hyper-rectangles $N_1(l, s), N_2(l, s)$. The first split now stays fixed and the same splitting procedure is applied recursively to the two rectangles N_1, N_2. This procedure will, in general, not result in the best partitioning but it has the advantage that the computational effort grows only linearly in n and p.

The splitting procedure can be represented by a binary tree shown in Figure 10.1.

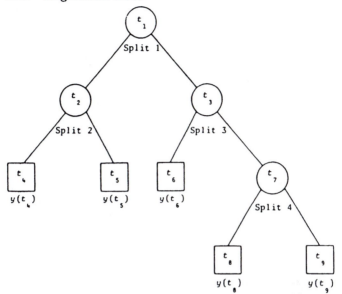

Figure 10.1. A regression tree with five terminal nodes, indicated by squares. (The predicted value is denoted here as $y(t)$.) From Breiman et al. (1984) with permission of Wadsworth Ltd.

In each terminal node t the fitted response value $\hat{m}(x)$ is constant. The tree can also be thought of as a multivariate regressogram estimate of the regression surface (see Figure 10.2).

Each node in the tree corresponds to

- a rectangular region of the predictor space;
- a subset of the observations lying in the regions determined by (l, s);
- a constant c which is the average response of the observations in $S(l, s)$.

Note that this tree (and every subtree) completely specifies a piecewise constant model. The tree representation has the advantage that the fitted model can be looked at very quickly. One can also get an idea about the geometry of the regression surface, which is not so easy for the local averaging procedures just described.

As an example consider the Boston housing data set. Harrison and Rubinfeld (1978) collected $n = 506$ observations for each census district of the Boston metropolitan area. The predictor variable was $d = 13$ dimensional.

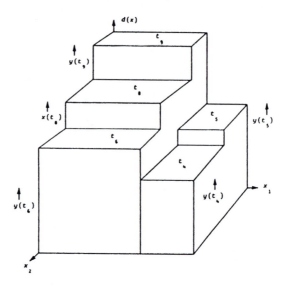

Figure 10.2.   The corresponding regression surface for the regression tree from Figure 10.1. From Breiman et al. (1984) with permission of Wadsworth Ltd.

response   median value of owner-occupied homes in
          thousands of dollars (MV)
predictors   crime rate $(CRIM)$
          percent land zoned for large lots (ZN)
          percent nonretail business $(INDUS)$
          Charles river indicator, 1 if on Charles River,
            0 otherwise $(CHAS)$
          nitrogen oxide concentration (NOX)
          average number of rooms (RM)
          percent built before 1980 (AGE)
          weighted distance to employment centers (DIS)
          accessibility to radial highways (RAD)
          tax rate (TAX)
          pupil–teacher ratio (PT)
          percent black (B)
          percent lower status $(LSTAT)$

The RPR as shown in Breiman et al. (1984) leads to the following regression tree.

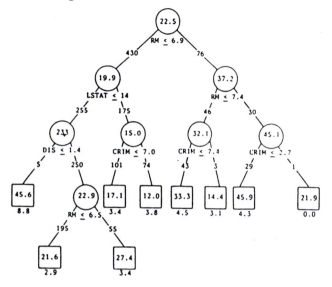

Figure 10.3.   The regression tree for the Boston housing data set. The numbers inside the circles are the piecewise constant estimates of the RPR model (10.1.1). (Note that the constant at the node $DIS \leq$ 1.4 is 23.3, not 233.) From Breiman et al. (1984) with permission of Wadsworth Ltd.

Note that the splitting process stops when no more observations are left over to split (minimal bucket size rule). This stopping rule could give trees which are too complex. An idea for reducing complexity is to stop splitting when the RSS is not sufficiently reduced. However, this is not a good approach, since the actual split might not help much but further splits might be more interesting. It is therefore suggested that the following procedure be performed:

- split down to a very complex tree;
- decide which nodes to recombine by a bottom-up recombination (pruning).

The recombination is done by introducing a cost function for each node t:

$$\text{cost of node } t = \begin{cases} RSS(t), & \text{if node terminal,} \\ c(l(t)) + c(r(t)) + \lambda, & \text{otherwise,} \end{cases}$$

where $l(t)$ denotes the node left of t and $r(t)$ the node right of t. Consider, then, a split as being worthwhile if the cost of making a node terminal is greater than the cost of making a node nonterminal. The parameter λ can be interpreted as a complexity parameter of the tree. If λ is large the splitting procedure will end up with a small tree. How can λ be selected?

Define $T(\lambda)$ as the minimum cost subtree of T (= tree with minimum bucket size) for complexity parameter λ. The tree $T(\lambda)$ has the following properties:

1. $T(0) = T$;
2. $T(\infty)$ is the tree consisting of a root node only, hence the model is the global average;
3. If $\lambda_1 > \lambda_2$, then $T(\lambda_1)$ is a subtree of $T(\lambda_2)$;
4. If T has k terminal nodes, there are at most k different subtrees that can be obtained by picking different λs.

The best choice for λ can be determined, for instance, by cross-validation.

Algorithm 10.1.1

> STEP 1.
> Divide the training sample into N subsamples.
> STEP 2.
> FOR $j = 1$ TO N DO BEGIN.
> STEP 3.
> Set subsample j aside.
> STEP 4.
> Build tree from remaining observations.
> STEP 5.
> Calculate all optimally terminated subtrees $T(\lambda)$ for different λ.
> STEP 6.
> Compute $CV_j(\lambda) = RSS$ when predicting j using the tree $T(\lambda)$
> END.
> STEP 7.
> Set $CV(\lambda) = \sum_{j=1}^{N} CV_j(\lambda)$.
> STEP 8.
> Find the best λ as $\lambda_{opt} = \arg\min_\lambda CV(\lambda)$.

Exercises

10.1.1 Prove that the coefficients $\hat{c}_j$ in (10.1.2) are the least squares estimates of c_j in model (10.1.1). Also prove (10.1.3).

10.1.2 Consider the case of one-dimensional X ($d = 1$). Describe the difference to the regressogram.

10.1.3 What would the RPR algorithm produce if the regression surface demands a split *not* along a coordinate axis but rather along a line not parallel to one of the axes?

10.2 Projection pursuit regression

The recursive partitioning regression (RPR) basically operates as follows: A certain split coordinate giving the best variance reduction determines two hyper-rectangles on which constant regression surfaces are fitted. This splitting procedure is then applied recursively to each of the regions obtained. An obvious limitation of this RPR is that splits only occur parallel to particular coordinate projections. Regression functions that are piecewise constant, but in a different, rotated coordinate system, would not be approximated well. A simple function such as $m(x) = m(x_1, x_2) = x_1 x_2$ would not be well represented by the RPR technique.

Note that this particular m can be written as $\frac{1}{4}(x_1 + x_2)^2 - \frac{1}{4}(x_1 - x_2)^2$, a sum of two functions operating on projections

$$\beta_1^T x = (1, 1) \begin{pmatrix} x_1 \\ x_2 \end{pmatrix}$$

and

$$\beta_2^T x = (1, -1) \begin{pmatrix} x_1 \\ x_2 \end{pmatrix}.$$

This motivates a generalization of RPR: Instead of using constant functions of projections along the coordinate axis, the regression surface is approximated by a sum of empirically determined univariate *ridge functions* $\{g_j\}$ of projections $\beta^T x$,

$$m(x) = \sum_{j=1}^{p} g_j(\beta_j^T x) . \tag{10.2.1}$$

This representation need not be unique; see Exercise 10.2.1 and Diaconis and Shahshahani (1984). The ridge functions $\{g_j\}$ can be thought of as generalizations of linear functions: They are also constant on hyperplanes.

The idea of approximating high dimensional functions by simpler functions that operate on projections goes back at least to Kruskal (1969). Friedman and Tukey (1974) applied this idea of searching for "interesting" projections in an analysis of a particle physics data set. (An interactive graphical analysis with PRIM-9 (Fisherkeller, Friedman and Tukey 1974) suggested that this data set consisted of a number of low dimensional "rods.") Theoretical aspects of PPR can be found in Hall (1988). A discussion of this technique with a variety of examples also from projection pursuit density estimation is presented in Jones and Sibson (1987).

The projections of the *additive model* (10.2.1) are constructed in an iterative manner by looping over β_js and g_js. Friedman and Stuetzle (1981) proposed the following algorithm.

Algorithm 10.2.1
  Projection Pursuit Regression (PPR)
  STEP 1.
  Center the response: $n^{-1} \sum_{i=1}^{n} Y_i = 0$.
  STEP 2.
  Initialize current residuals

  $$\hat{\varepsilon}_i^{(0)} = Y_i, \quad i = 1, \ldots, n,$$

  and set $p = 0$.
  STEP 3.
  Search for the next term in the model (10.2.1). For a given linear combination $Z_i = \beta^T X_i$ find a smooth $\{\hat{g}_{p+1}(Z_i)\}_{i=1}^{n}$. Evaluate the current smooth in terms of the fraction of unexplained variance

  $$q_{p+1}(\beta) = 1 - \sum_{i=1}^{n} [\hat{\varepsilon}_i^{(p)} - \hat{g}_{p+1}(\beta^T X_i)]^2 / \sum_{i=1}^{n} [\hat{\varepsilon}_i^{(p)}]^2.$$

  Find the projection vector β_{p+1} that maximizes $q_{p+1}(\beta)$ (*projection pursuit*) and the corresponding smooth $\hat{g}_{p+1}$.
  STEP 4.
  If the criterion of fit $q(\beta)$ is smaller than a user-specified threshold, STOP.
  Otherwise construct the next set of residuals

  $$\hat{\varepsilon}_i^{(p+1)} = \hat{\varepsilon}_i^{(p)} - \hat{g}_{p+1}(\beta_{p+1}^T X_i), \quad i = 1, \ldots, n,$$

  $$p = p + 1.$$

  and go to STEP 3.

For its highly iterative character the smoothing procedure in this algorithm should be computationally efficient. I would recommend using the symmetrized k-NN (Section 3.2) or the WARPed kernel smoother (Section 3.1). The projections β_{p+1} maximizing $q_{p+1}(\beta)$ can be found by the

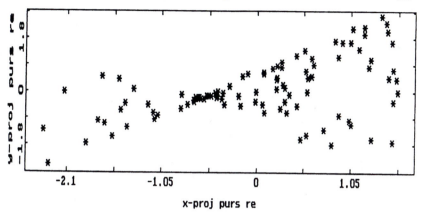

Figure 10.4.   The response Y versus the initial projection $\beta_1^T X, \beta_1^T = (1,0)$. Made with XploRe (1989).

Newton–Raphson method. Friedman and Stuetzle (1981) constructed an artificial example with $m(x) = x_1 x_2$. A sample of $n = 200$ observations was generated with (X_1, X_2) uniformly distributed in $(-1,1)^2$ and $\varepsilon \sim N(0, (0.2)^2)$. I present a session with this data using the above algorithm as implemented in XploRe (1989).

Figure 10.4 shows Y plotted against starting projection $\beta_1 = (1,0)^T$. The algorithm then uses the Newton–Raphson method to find another direction. An intermediate step in this search is shown in Figure 10.5. The first estimated ridge function $\hat{g}_1(\cdot)$ is shown in Figure 10.6. The fraction of explained variance and the value of β_1 is displayed in Figure 10.7. The projection $\hat{\beta}_1^T = (0.669, -0.74)$ was found by projection pursuit with the corresponding smooth $\hat{g}_1(\hat{\beta}_1^T x)$. The algorithm in XploRe (1989) then goes on by constructing the residuals and continues as described in the above algorithm.

Figure 10.8 shows the result after fitting the residuals with the PPR algorithm. The second estimated ridge function $\hat{g}_2(\cdot)$ is shown together with the data points. The fraction of explained variance is 0.80725 and the value of $\hat{\beta}_2$ is $\hat{\beta}_2^T = (0.668, 0.74)$. A third projection is not accepted by the algorithm because the criterion of fit is below the user-defined threshold of 0.1. The pure quadratic shapes of $\hat{g}_1$ and $\hat{g}_2$ together with the coefficient vectors $\hat{\beta}_1$ and $\hat{\beta}_2$ suggest that PPR has essentially found the additive form of $m(x)$,

$$m(x) = x_1 x_2 = \frac{1}{4}(x_1 + x_2)^2 - \frac{1}{4}(x_1 - x_2)^2 \ .$$

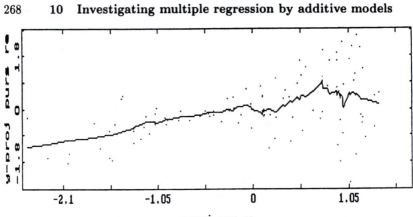

Figure 10.5.   The response Y and the smooth (midrange k-NN) in
an intermediate step. Made with XploRe (1989).

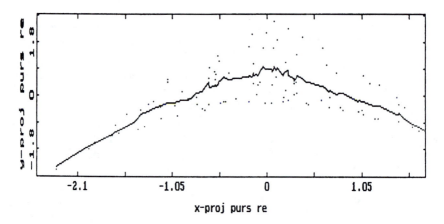

Figure 10.6.   The response Y and the first ridge function g_1. $\hat{\beta}_2^T =$
$(0.668, 0.74)$. Made with XploRe (1989).

Exercises

10.2.1 Find infinitely many representations of $m(x_1, x_2) = x_1 x_2$ as a
sum of two ridge functions.

10.2.2 Find a function that cannot be represented as a sum of *finitely*
many ridge functions.

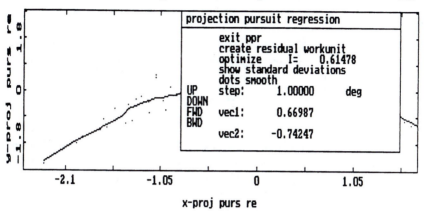

Figure 10.7.   The control menu of the PPR modul of XploRe (1989).

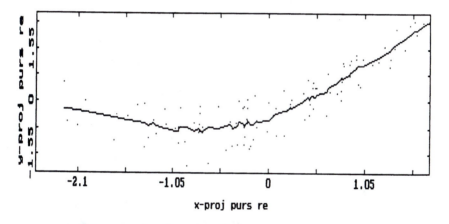

Figure 10.8.   The response Y and the second ridge function g_2. $\hat{\beta}_2^T = (0.668, 0.74)$. Made with XploRe (1989).

10.3   Alternating conditional expectations

Breaking down an intricate regression with many variables into a system of simpler relationships – each involving fewer variables – is a desirable goal when modeling high dimensional regression data. Leontief (1947a), for example, considers the process of steel production and points out that the various materials involved in the production of steel should be combined into additional, intermediate variables. Such a goal can be achieved, for instance, by an additive model in which the multivariate regression function $m(x)$ splits up into a sum of nonparametric functions.

More precisely, let $\Psi(Y), g_1(X_1), \ldots, g_d(X_d)$ be arbitrary measurable mean zero functions of the corresponding random variables. The fraction of variance not explained by a regression of $\Psi(Y)$ on $\sum_{j=1}^{d} g_j(X_j)$ is

$$
e^2(\Psi, g_1, \ldots, g_d) = \frac{E\{[\Psi(Y) - \sum_{j=1}^{d} g_j(X_j)]^2\}}{E\Psi^2(Y)}. \tag{10.3.1}
$$

Define the *optimal transformations* $\Psi^*, g_1^*, \ldots, g_d^*$ as minimizers of (10.3.1). Such optimal transformations exist and the ACE algorithm (Breiman and Friedman 1985) gives estimates of these transformations. Leontief (1947b) calls such a model *additive separable* and describes a method of checking this additive separability.

For the bivariate case $(d = 1)$ the optimal transformations Ψ^* and g^* satisfy

$$
\rho^*(X, Y) = \rho(\Psi^*, g^*) = \max_{\Psi, g} \rho(\Psi(Y), g(X)),
$$

where ρ is the correlation coefficient. The quantity ρ^* is also known as the *maximal correlation coefficient* between X and Y and is used as a general measure of dependence. For theoretical properties of maximal correlation I refer to Breiman and Friedman (1985). These authors also report that according to Kolmogorov if $(Y, X_1, \ldots, X_d)$ are jointly normally distributed then the transformations Ψ, g_j having maximal correlation are linear.

Suppose that the data are generated by the regression model

$$
\Psi(Y) = \sum_{j=1}^{d} g_j(X_j) + \varepsilon.
$$

Note that the optimal transformations do *not* correspond to the conditional mean function here. Looking for functions that maximize correlation is not the same as estimating the conditional mean function. However, if the $g_j(X_j)$ have a joint normal distribution and ε is an independent normal random variable then the optimal transformations are exactly the (linear) transformations Ψ and g_j. In general, though, for a regression model of this form with ε independent of X, the *optimal* transformations are different from the transformations used to construct the model. In practice, the transformations found by the ACE algorithm are sometimes *different*, as will be seen in the Exercises.

To illustrate the ACE algorithm consider first the bivariate case:

$$
e^2(\Psi, g) = E[\Psi(Y) - g(X)]^2 . \tag{10.3.2}
$$

The optimal $\Psi(Y)$ for a given $g(X)$, keeping $E\Psi^2(Y) = 1$, is

$$\Psi_1(Y) = E[g(X)|Y] / \|E[g(X)|Y]\|, \tag{10.3.3}$$

with $\| \cdot \| = [E(\cdot)^2]^{1/2}$. The minimization of (10.3.2) with respect to $g(X)$ for given $\Psi(Y)$ gives

$$g_1(X) = E[\Psi(Y)|X]. \tag{10.3.4}$$

The basis of the following iterative optimization algorithm is the *alternation* between the *conditional expectations* (10.3.3) and (10.3.4).

Basic ACE Algorithm 10.3.1

> SET $\Psi(Y) = Y/\|Y\|$;
> REPEAT $g_1(X) = E[\Psi(Y)|X]$;
> Replace $g(X)$ with $g_1(X)$;
> $\Psi_1(Y) = E[g(X)|Y]/\|E[g(X)|Y]\|$
> Replace $\Psi(Y)$ with $\Psi_1(Y)$
> UNTIL $e^2(\Psi, g)$ fails to decrease.

The more general case of multiple predictors can be treated in direct analogy with the basic ACE algorithm. For a given set of functions $\{g_j(X_j)\}_{j=1}^d$ minimization of (10.3.1), with respect to $\Psi(Y)$, holding $E\Psi^2(Y) = 1$, $E\Psi = Eg_1 = \cdots = Eg_d = 0$, yields

$$\Psi_1(Y) = E\left[\sum_{j=1}^d g_j(X_j)|Y\right] / \left\|E\left[\sum_{j=1}^d g_j(X_j)|Y\right]\right\|.$$

Next (10.3.1) is minimized with respect to a single function $g_k(X_k)$ for given $\Psi(Y)$ and given $g_1(X_1),\ldots,g_{k-1}(X_{k-1}),g_{k+1}(X_{k+1}),\ldots,g_d(X_d)$. This iterative procedure is described in the full ACE algorithm.

Full ACE Algorithm 10.3.2

> SET $\Psi(Y) = Y/\|Y\|$ and $g_j(X_j) = 0,\quad 1 \le j \le d$;
> REPEAT
> REPEAT
> FOR $k = 1$ TO d DO BEGIN
> $g_{k,1}(X_k) = E[\Psi(Y) - \sum_{j \ne k} g_j(X_j)|X_k]$;
> $g_k(X_k) = g_{k,1}(X_k)$;
> END;
> UNTIL $e^2(\Psi, g_1,\ldots,g_d)$ fails to decrease;
> $\Psi_1(Y) = E[\sum_{j=1}^d g_j(X_j)|Y]/\|E[\sum_{j=1}^d g_j(X_j)|Y]\|$;
> $\Psi(Y) = \Psi_1(Y)$;
> UNTIL $e^2(\Psi, g_1,\ldots,g_d)$ fails to decrease.

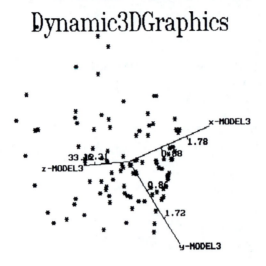

Figure 10.9.   A simulated data set. X_1, X_2, ε independent standard normal, $Y_i = (X_{i1} + X_{i2})^3 + \varepsilon_i, 1 \leq i \leq n = 100$. Made with XploRe (1989).

In practice, one has to use smoothers to estimate the involved conditional expectations. Use of a fully automatic smoothing procedure, such as the *supersmoother*, is recommended. Figure 10.9 shows a three-dimensional data set (X_1, X_2, Y) with X_1, X_2 independent standard normals and

$$Y = (X_1 + X_2)^3 + \varepsilon,$$

with standard normal errors ε. The ACE algorithm produced the transformation g_1 presented in Figure 10.10.

The estimated transformation is remarkably close to the transformation $g_1(x_1) = x_1$. Figure 10.11 displays the estimated transformation Ψ, which represents the function $\Psi(y) = y^{1/3}$ extremely well.

Breiman and Friedman (1985) applied the ACE methodology also to the Boston housing data set (Harrison and Rubinfeld 1978; and Section 10.1). The resulting final model involved four predictors and has an e^2 of 0.89. (An application of ACE to the full 13 variables resulted only in an increase for e^2 of 0.02.) Figure 10.12a shows a plot from their paper of the solution response surface transformation $\Psi(y)$. This function is seen to have a positive curvature for central values of y, connecting two straight line segments of different slope on either side. This suggests that the log-transformation used by Harrison and Rubinfeld (1978) may

Static 2DGraphics

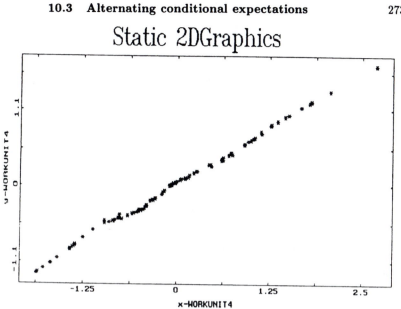

Figure 10.10.   The estimated ACE transformation $g_1(X_1)$. Made with XploRe (1989).

be too severe. Figure 10.12b shows the response transformation for the original untransformed census measurements. The remaining plot in Figure 10.12 displays the other transformation g_j; for details see Breiman and Friedman (1985).

Exercises

10.3.1 Prove that in the bivariate case the function given in (10.3.3) is indeed the optimal transformation Ψ^*.

10.3.2 Prove that in the bivariate case the function given in (10.3.4) is indeed the optimal transformation g^*.

10.3.3 Try the ACE algorithm with some real data. Which smoother would you use as an elementary building block?

10.3.4 In the discussion to the Breiman and Friedman article D. Pregibon and Y. Vardi generated data from

$$Y = X_1 X_2$$

with $X_1 \sim U(-1,1)$ and $X_2 \sim U(0,1)$. What are possible transformations Ψ, g?

Static 2DGraphics

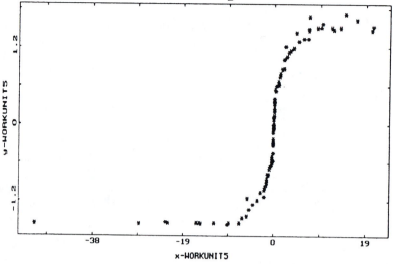

Figure 10.11. The estimated transformation $\psi(Y)$. Made with XploRe (1989).

10.3.5 Try the ACE algorithm with the data set from Exercise 10.3.4. What transformations do you get? Do they coincide with the transformations you computed in 10.3.4?

[*Hint*: See the discussion of Breiman and Friedman (1985).]

10.4   Average derivative estimation

The primary motivation for studying the *average derivative*

$$\delta = E[m'(X)]$$

with

$$m'(X) = \left(\frac{\partial m}{\partial x_1}, \ldots, \frac{\partial m}{\partial x_d}\right)(X),$$

comes from models where the mean response depends on X only through a linear combination $\beta^T x$. That is, similarly to projection pursuit regression,

$$m(x) = g(x^T \beta) \qquad (10.4.1)$$

for some nonparametric function g.

The average derivative δ is proportional to β since

$$\delta = E[m'(X)] = E[dg/d(x^T\beta)]\beta.$$

Thus the average derivative vector δ determines β up to scale. In this section a nonparametric estimator $\hat{\delta}$ of the average derivative is considered which achieves the rate $n^{-1/2}$ (typical for parametric problems). From this $\hat{\delta}$ the multivariate $\hat{m}(x) = \hat{g}(x^T\hat{\delta})$ is constructed which achieves the rate $n^{-4/5}$ (typical for one dimensional smoothing problems). A weighted average derivative estimator has been introduced by Powell, Stock and Stoker (1989).

Assume that the function $g(x^T\delta) = E(Y|X = x^T\delta)$ is normalized in such a way that $E[dg/d(x^T\delta)] = 1$. *Average derivative estimation*(ADE) yields a direct estimator for the weights β in (10.4.1). (Note that as in PPR the model (10.4.1) is not identifiable unless we make such a normalization assumption.)

Let $f(x)$ denote the marginal density,

$$f' = \partial f/\partial x$$

its vector of partial derivatives and

$$l = -\partial \log f/\partial x = -f'/f$$

the negative log-density derivative. Integration by parts gives

$$\delta = E[m'(X)] = E[lY]. \tag{10.4.2}$$

Consequently, if $\hat{f}_h$ denotes a kernel estimator of $f(x)$ and $\hat{l}(x) = -\hat{f}_h'(x)/\hat{f}_h(x)$, then δ can be estimated by the sample analogue

$$\hat{\delta}^* = n^{-1} \sum_{i=1}^{n} \hat{l}(X_i)Y_i .$$

Since this estimator involves dividing by $\hat{f}_h$, a more refined estimator $\hat{\delta}$ of δ is advisable in practice. For this reason the following estimator is proposed:

$$\hat{\delta} = n^{-1} \sum_{i=1}^{n} \hat{l}_h(X_i)Y_i\hat{I}_i, \tag{10.4.3}$$

with the indicator variables

$$\hat{I}_i = I\{\hat{f}_h(X_i) > b_n\}, \quad b_n \to 0,$$

and the density estimator

$$\hat{f}_h(x) = n^{-1} \sum_{j=1}^{n} h^{-d}K\left(\frac{x - X_j}{h}\right).$$

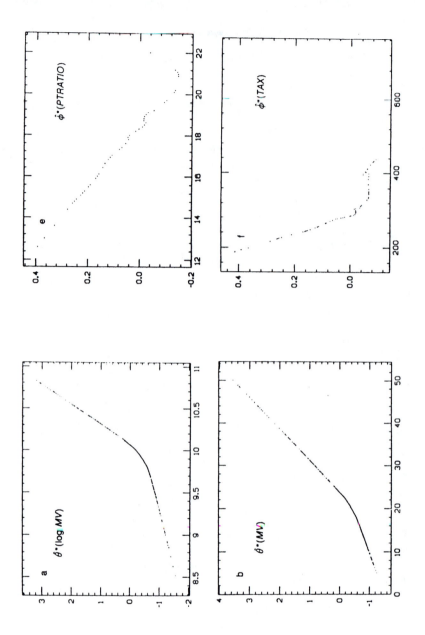

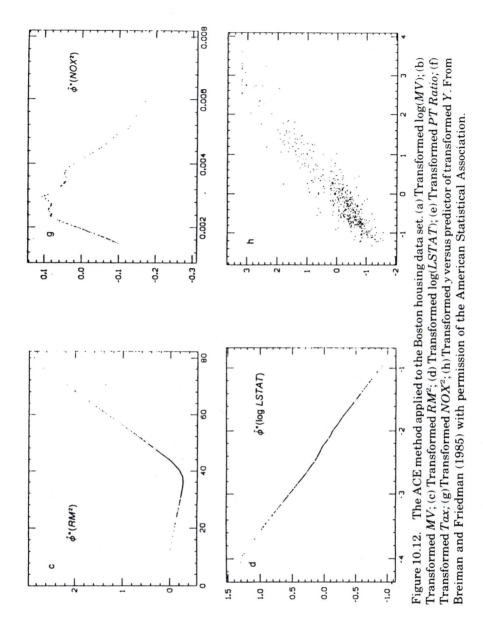

Figure 10.12. The ACE method applied to the Boston housing data set. (a) Transformed log(MV); (b) Transformed MV; (c) Transformed RM^2; (d) Transformed RM^2; (d) Transformed log($LSTAT$); (e) Transformed $PT\ Ratio$; (f) Transformed Tax; (g) Transformed NOX^2; (h) Transformed y versus predictor of transformed Y. From Breiman and Friedman (1985) with permission of the American Statistical Association.

Note that here the kernel function K is a function of d arguments. Such a kernel can be constructed, for example, as a product of one-dimensional kernels; see Section 3.1. The main result of Härdle and Stoker (1989) is Theorem 10.4.1.

Theorem 10.4.1   Assume that apart from very technical conditions, f is p-times differentiable, $\{b_n\}$ "slowly" converges to zero and $nh^{2p-2} \to 0$, where p denotes the number of derivatives of f. Then the average derivative estimator $\hat{\delta}$ has a limiting normal distribution,

$$\sqrt{n}(\hat{\delta} - \delta) \xrightarrow{\mathcal{L}} N(0, \Sigma),$$

where Σ is the covariance matrix of

$$l(X)Y + [m'(X) - l(X)m(X)] \ .$$

There are some remarkable features about this result. First, the condition on the bandwidth sequence excludes the optimal bandwidth sequence $h \sim n^{-1/(2p+d)}$; see Section 4.1. The bandwidth h has to tend to zero faster than the optimal rate in order to keep the bias of $\hat{\delta}$ below the desired $n^{-1/2}$ rate. A similar observation has been made in the context of semiparametric models; see Section 8.1. Second, the covariance matrix is constructed from two terms, $l(X)Y$ and $m'(X) - l(X)m(X)$. If one knew the marginal density then the first term $l(X)Y$ would determine the covariance. It is the estimation of $l(X)$ by $\hat{l}(X)$ that brings in this second term. Third, the bandwidth condition is of qualitative nature, that is, it says that h should tend to zero not "too fast" and not "too slow." A more refined analysis (Härdle, Hart, Marron and Tsybakov 1989) of second-order terms shows that for $d = 1$ the MSE of $\hat{\delta}$ can be expanded as

$$MSE(\hat{\delta}) \sim n^{-1} + n^{-1}h^{-3} + h^4. \tag{10.4.4}$$

A bandwidth minimizing this expression would therefore be proportional to $n^{-2/7}$. Fourth, the determination of the cutoff sequence b_n is somewhat complicated in practice; it is therefore recommended to just cut off the lower 5 percent of the $\hat{l}(X_i)$.

Let me come now to the estimation of g in (10.4.1). Assume that in a first step $\hat{\delta}$ has been estimated, yielding the one-dimensional projection $\hat{Z}_i = \hat{\delta}^T X_i$, $i = 1, \dots, n$. Let $\hat{g}_{h'}(z)$ denote a kernel estimator with one-dimensional kernel K^z of the regression of Y on $\hat{Z}$, that is,

$$\hat{g}_{h'}(z) = n^{-1} \sum_{i=1}^{n} K^z_{h'}(z - \hat{Z}_i)Y_i / n^{-1} \sum_{i=1}^{n} K^z_{h'}(z - \hat{Z}_i). \tag{10.4.5}$$

Suppose, for the moment, that $Z_i = \delta^T X_i$ instead of $\hat{Z}_i$ were used in 10.4.5. In this case, it is well known (Section 4.2) that the resulting regression estimator is asymptotically normal and converges at the optimal pointwise rate $n^{-2/5}$. Theorem 10.4.2 states that there is no cost in using the estimated projections $\{\hat{Z}_i\}$, that is, one achieves through additivity a dimension reduction, as considered by Stone (1985).

Theorem 10.4.2 *If the bandwidth $h' \sim n^{-1/5}$ then*

$$n^{2/5}[\hat{g}_{h'}(z) - g(z)]$$

has a limiting normal distribution with mean $B(z)$ and variance $V(z)$, where, with the density f_z of $\delta^T X$,

$$B(z) = \frac{1}{2}[g''(z) + g'(z)f_z'(z)/f_z(z)]d_{K^z},$$
$$V(z) = var[Y|\delta^T X = z]c_{K^z}.$$

More formally, the ADE procedure is described in

Algorithm 10.4.1
   STEP 1.
      Compute $\hat{\delta}$ by (10.4.3) with a cut off $\alpha = 5\%$.
   STEP 2.
      Compute $\hat{g}$ by (10.4.5) from $(\hat{\delta}^T X_i, Y_i)$ with a one-dimensional cross-validated bandwith.
   STEP 3.
      Compose both steps into the function
      $\hat{m}(x) = \hat{g}(\hat{\delta}x).$

An application of this technique is given in Appendix 2 where I consider a desirable computing environment for high dimensional smoothing techniques. Simulations from the ADE algorithm for different nonparametric models in more than four dimensions can be found in Härdle and Stoker (1989). One model in this article is

$$Y_i = \sin\left(\sum_{j=1}^{4} X_{ij}\right) + 0.1\varepsilon_i, \quad i = 1, \ldots, n,$$

where $\varepsilon_i, X_{i1}, \ldots, X_{i4}$ are independent standard normally distributed random variables.

Table 10.4.1   *ADE estimation of the Sine model*

	$h = 0.9$	$h = 0.7$	$h = 1.5$	known density
$\hat{\delta}_1$	0.1134	0.0428	0.1921	0.1329
	(0.0960)	(0.0772)	(0.1350)	(0.1228)
$\hat{\delta}_2$	0.1356	0.0449	0.1982	0.1340
	(0.1093)	(0.0640)	(0.1283)	(0.1192)
$\hat{\delta}_3$	0.1154	0.0529	0.1837	0.1330
	(0.1008)	(0.0841)	(0.1169)	(0.1145)
$\hat{\delta}_4$	0.1303	0.0591	0.2042	0.1324
	(0.0972)	(0.0957)	(0.1098)	(0.1251)
b	0.0117	0.0321	0.0017	

Note: In brackets are standard deviations over the Monte Carlo simulations. $n = 100$, $\alpha = 0.05$.

The average derivative takes the form

$$\delta = \delta_0 (1, 1, 1, 1)^T,$$

and some tedious algebra gives $\delta_0 = 0.135$. Table 10.4.1 reports the result over 100 Monte Carlo simulations with a cutoff rule of $\alpha = 0.05$. It is remarkable that even in the case of a known density (therefore, l is known) the standard deviations (given in brackets) are of similar magnitude to those in the case of unknown l. This once again demonstrates that there is no cost (parametric rate!) in not knowing l. An actual computation with $n = 200$ resulted in the values of $\delta = (0.230, 0.023, 0.214, 0.179)$. The correlation between $Z_i = \delta^T X_i$ and $\hat{Z}_i = \hat{\delta}^T X_i$ was 0.903. The estimated function $\hat{g}_{h'}(z)$ is shown in Figure 10.13 together with the points $\{\hat{Z}_i, Y_i\}_{i=1}^n$. A kernel smooth based on the true projections Z_i is depicted together with the smooth $\hat{g}_{h'}(z)$ in Figure 10.14. The estimated $\hat{g}_{h'}(z)$ is remarkably close to the true regression function as Figure 10.15 suggests.

Exercises

10.4.1 Prove formula (10.4.2).

10.4.2 Explain the bandwidth condition "that h has to tend to zero faster than the optimal rate" from formula (10.4.4).

10.4.3 Assume a partial linear model as in Chapter 8. How can you estimate the parametric part by ADE?

10.4.4 Assume X to be standard normal. What is l in this case?

10.4.5 In the case of a pure linear model $Y = \beta^T X$ what is δ?

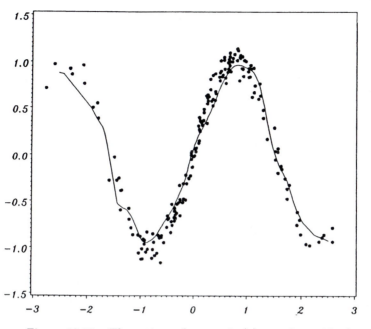

Figure 10.13. The estimated curve $\hat{g}_{h'}(z)$ together with the projected data $\{\hat{Z}_i, Y_i\}_{i=1}^{n}$.

10.5   Generalized additive models

Generalized linear models (GLIM) are regression models where a linear predictor

$$\eta = \beta^T X, \qquad X \in \mathbb{R}^d, \tag{10.5.1}$$

is connected with the discrete response variable $Y \in \{0,1\}$ through a *link* function $G(\cdot)$. A well-known model is the logistic *dose response* model where at each value of the covariate X, the probability of the binary response

$$p(x) = P(Y = 1|X = x)$$

is modeled by a logistic function,

$$p(x) = \frac{\exp(\eta)}{1 + \exp(\eta)}. \tag{10.5.2}$$

Here the *logit* link function is

$$G(p) = \log(p/(1-p)) = \eta. \tag{10.5.3}$$

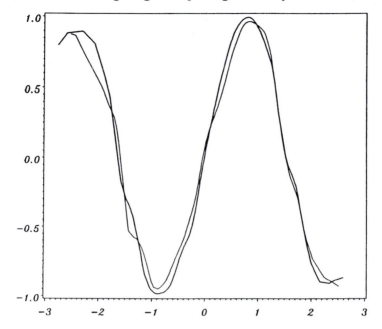

Figure 10.14.   Two kernel smooths based on $\{Z_i, Y_i\}_{i=1}^n$, $\{\hat{Z}_i, Y_i\}_{i=1}^n$, respectively. The thin line indicates the ADE smooth based on the estimated projections $\hat{Z}_i = \hat{\delta}^T X_i$. The thick line is the kernel smooth based on the true projections $Z_i = \delta^T X_i$.

In the economic literature such models are called *discrete choice models*. Many empirically important economic decisions involve choice among discrete alternatives. The indicator variable Y may denote a decision about travel mode (car or bus?), for example. Many more examples can be found in Manski and McFadden (1981). The basic idea of the discrete choice is to model the decision about a certain object of economic relevance by a binomial distribution dependent on $\beta^T X$. In the travel mode decision the predictor variable X might be the distance to the working place and an indicator of social status, for example. Basically, the model (10.5.2) is parametric in its nature and one might question why the predictor variables enter in a linear way into the probabilistic decision-making process.

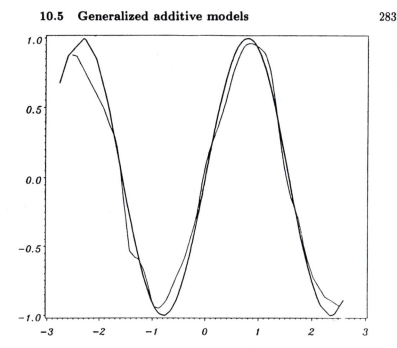

Figure 10.15.   The ADE smooth and the true curve. The thin line indicates the ADE smooth as in Figure 10.14 and Figure 10.13; the thick line is the true curve $g(\delta^T X_i)$.

Hastie and Tibshirani (1986) generalized the above additive model to the form

$$\eta = \sum_{j=1}^{d} g_j(X_j), \qquad\qquad (10.5.4)$$

where g_j are nonparametric regression functions. They called the model (10.5.4) with *known* link function $G(\cdot)$ a *generalized additive model (GAM)*.

In the framework of GLIM (McCullagh and Nelder 1983) the parameter β in (10.5.3) is found by a weighted least squares regression method. More precisely, given $\hat{\eta}$ (a current estimate of the linear predictor), with corresponding fitted value

$$\hat{\mu} = G^{-1}(\hat{\eta}),$$

one forms the adjusted dependent variable

$$Z = \hat{\eta} + (Y - \hat{\mu})(d\eta/d\mu). \qquad\qquad (10.5.5)$$

Then one defines weights W by

$$W^{-1} = (d\eta/d\mu)^2 V,$$

where V is the variance of Y at $\mu = \hat{\mu}$. (In the logit case $W_i = \hat{p}(X_i)(1 - \hat{p}(X_i))$.) The algorithm proceeds by regressing Z on X with weights W to obtain an estimate $\hat{\beta}$. Using $\hat{\beta}$, a new $\hat{\mu}$ and $\hat{\eta}$ are computed. A new Z is computed and the process is repeated until the change in the log-likelihood is sufficiently small.

This same idea underlies the *local scoring algorithm* for fitting GAMs by Hastie and Tibshirani (1987). The core of this local scoring algorithm is the backfitting algorithm for estimating additive regression functions

$$m(x) = \alpha + \sum_{j=1}^{d} g_j(x_j)$$

assuming that

$$Eg_j(X_j) = 0.$$

Backfitting Algorithm 10.5.1
    INITIALIZATION
        $\hat{g}_j(x) = 0$ for all x, j, $\hat{\alpha} = n^{-1} \sum_{i=1}^{n} Y_i = \bar{Y}$;
    REPEAT
        FOR $j = 1$ TO d DO BEGIN
        FOR $i = 1$ TO n DO BEGIN
        $\hat{\varepsilon}_i = Y_i - \hat{\alpha} - \sum_{k \neq j}^{d} \hat{g}_k(X_{ik})$.
        $\hat{g}_j(X_{ij}) = SMOOTH(\hat{\varepsilon}_i)$ AT X_{ij}.
        END
        END
    UNTIL $RSS = \sum_i (Y_i - \hat{\alpha} - \sum_j \hat{g}_j(X_{ij}))^2$ converges.

Smooth at X denotes here a fast and efficient smoother, for example, the FFT kernel smoother or the k-NN with symmetric weights (Sections 3.1, 3.2). As an easy to implement smoother I recommend the k-NN with a "midrange" k. More sophisticated users might want to install the supersmoother. The local scoring algorithm is based on the backfitting technique and is defined as follows.

Local Scoring Algorithm 10.5.2
    INITIALIZATION
        $\hat{g}_j^{(0)}(x) = 0$ for all x, j, $\hat{\alpha}^{(0)} = logit(\bar{Y})$.
    REPEAT OVER k

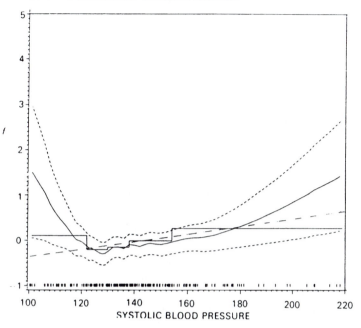

Figure 10.16.   The estimated contribution $\hat{g}_1$ of SBP to $logit(p(x))$ is the solid bold curve. The two dashed lines are $\hat{g}_1 \pm 2STD(\hat{g}_1)$. From Hastie and Tibshirani (1987) with permission of the Royal Statistical Society.

FOR $i = 1$ TO n DO BEGIN
$\hat{\eta}^{(k)}(X_i) = \hat{\alpha}^{(k)} + \sum_{j=1}^{d} \hat{g}_j^{(k)}(X_{ij})$.
$\hat{p}(X_i) = logit^{-1}(\hat{\eta}^{(k)}(X_i))$.
$Z_i = \hat{\eta}^{(k)}(X_i) + (Y_i - \hat{p}(X_i))/(\hat{p}(X_i)(1 - \hat{p}(X_i)))$.
$W_i = \hat{p}(X_i)(1 - \hat{p}(X_i))$.
END
OBTAIN
    $\hat{\alpha}^{(k+1)}, \hat{g}_j^{(k+1)}$
by backfitting Z_i on X_i with weigths W_i.
UNTIL the deviance
    $DEV = -2\sum_i (Y_i \log \hat{p}(X_i) + (1 - Y_i) \log(1 - \hat{p}(X_i)))$
converges.

An example in Hastie and Tibshirani (1987) is the analysis of a coronary heart disease study. The indicator variable Y denoted the presence

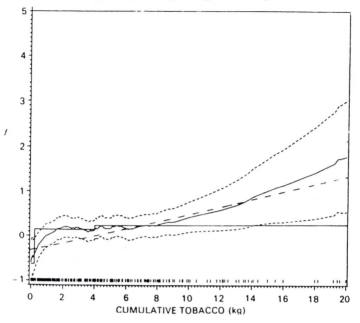

Figure 10.17.   The estimated contribution $\hat{g}_2$ of CTI to $logit(p(x))$ is the solid bold curve. The two dashed lines are $\hat{g}_2 \pm 2STD(\hat{g}_2)$. From Hastie and Tibshirani (1987) with permission of the Royal Statistical Society.

of heart disease. The predictor variable X was six-dimensional and included factors such as systolic blood pressure (SBP) and cumulative tobacco intake (CTI). An application of this local scoring algorithm to survival data is presented in Figure 10.16. In this figure the estimated contribution $\hat{g}_1$ of SBP to $logit(p(x))$ is shown and seen to be quite different from the linear classical logit model. See also Figure 10.17.

One clearly sees the nonlinear structure of the conditional probability curve in the logit scale. Theoretical properties of this algorithm are not known to date.

Exercises

10.5.1 What is the basic difference between the ACE model and the GAM?

10.5.2 Derive the weights and the adjusted residuals for the logit case

$$G(p) = \log(p/(1-p)).$$

10.5.3 Apply the GAM technique to the side impact data given in Table 3 of Appendix 2.

Appendixes

A desirable computing environment

> How we think about data analysis is strongly influenced by the computing environment in which the analysis is done.
>
> McDonald and Pederson (1986)

A statistican who investigates unknown relationships by smoothing procedures of exploratory or experimental character does in fact a special kind of programming work. McDonald and Pederson (1986) were among the first to realize that the computing environment strongly influences the data analysis. In other words, the computing environment determines the depth in which an analysis can be performed and it determines the outcome of a model-building process based upon nonparametric smoothing techniques.

For this purpose an interactive computing environment that is designed for the special needs of experimental programming in data smoothing is most appropriate. To see why this experimental smoothing cannot be performed with batch-oriented systems, consider the following typical analysis cycle.

First, a smoother is computed with a specific method and smoothing parameter. Second, the fit and residuals are examined for certain features (for example, does the smooth have the peaks at the expected locations or is there remaining structure in the residual pattern?). In a third step one might evaluate the effect and impact of detected features on the fitted curve. In a last step in this round, along an analysis cycle one might compare the current smooth with other fits, possibly stemming from alternative, parametric models. Of course, such turns along that cycle may be repeated many more times. It is impossible to effectively perform this analysis cycle in a batch-oriented computing environment since in such an environment only static sequences of analysis views are technically available.

Another scenario requiring interactive possibilities is the labeling of data points (for example, outliers). One might want to put aside some of the points and run a certain manipulation with the remaining data in order to study the effect of the left-out points. Batch-oriented systems most badly serve this need for interactive decision making since one would basically have to write an additional program for identifying the points which are to be left out. In an interactive computing environment such points would be marked by a mouse click, for instance.

The design of XploRe (1989) meets such desiderata for improvisational programming by extensive use of interactive graphical methods (mouse-oriented selection and identification; pull-down menus). Moreover, it supports the user with a set of utilities for masking, brushing, labeling and even rotation of data. Higher dimensional data clouds can be analyzed by means of additive models: Projection Pursuit Regression, Recursive Partioning Regression Trees, Alternating Conditional Expectations and Average Derivative Estimation.

Help files can be attached by the user through a stack of "help windows". The designer of the computing environment determines at which analysis stage which "help windows" should appear. The help information is simply obtained by pressing **F1**. Subsequent pressing of the help key guides through the stack of currently attached help windows.

XploRe is an open system which is written in TURBO PASCAL 5.0. It is basically a framework awaiting more "soft work" that enhances the capabilities. Its construction has been influenced by similar systems such as S (Becker and Chambers 1984) or DINDE (Oldford and Peters 1985). XploRe uses the object-oriented approach and makes use of the inheritance concept to be described subsequently. A detailed description of the functions and procedure to install user-written code is given in Broich, Härdle and Krause (1989). XploRe is written for IBM PC/AT, XT or compatibles (under MS-DOS). A SUN version (written in C) is available from David Scott, Rice University, Houston, Texas.

XploRing data

XploRe is an interactive, graphically oriented computing environment designed to analyze various kinds of relations among data and to apply and compare different smoothing methods. XploRe is suitable for investigating high dimensional data. It supports the user with sophisticated data management tools such as masking, brushing, labeling and rotation of data.

XploRe is an object-oriented system. An object can be of one of four types:

- VECTOR
- WORKUNIT
- PICTURE
- TEXT

A *vector* object is a data vector as a logical unit with which to work. This vector may contain strings or real numbers and can be of variable length. The simplest form of a *workunit* object is an ordered collection of data vectors. However, a workunit can also include display attributes and a mask vector. Display attributes concern the layout of scatter plots such as data marking symbols, line style, line pattern, line thickness and so forth. A *text* object is necessary to show information as text on the display. This can be data you are analyzing, documentation you want to pin down or system output. A *picture* object contains the view-port characteristics of certain views that you have on data, for example, the name of the picture and the axes and the scaling of the axes. For 3D-rotation the rotation angles, the initial distance from the point cloud, location of the origin and zooming increments are kept in this picture object.

Moreover, objects can inherit certain properties. Before I explain this inheritance principle in more detail I would like to cite Oldford and Peters (1985).

Inheritance avoids redundant specification of information and simplifies modification, since information that is common is defined in, and need be changed in, only one place.

I find that Oldford and Peters make it very clear why inheritance is a good concept to exploit in the setting of nonparametric smoothing. Recall the above analysis cycle. A standard operation in this cycle will be to trace certain information through several stages of an analysis. One important piece of information, especially in the analysis of high dimensional data, is a mask that has been defined to highlight certain interesting points. This mask can be inherited by a spring-off workunit, say, a smooth computed from the actual workunit. Workunits can also inherit display attributes, such as line style or symbols.

XploRe has a menu structure. Two menu bars will appear on your display. A third menu bar appears if you press and hold down the <**ALT**> key. You can choose an option by typing the capitalized letter of the corresponding menu entry. Whenever a pull-down menu appears at the next step, it is in most cases possible to get *quick help* by pressing <**ALT**>+**F1**. For example, if you are not familiar with the ACE algorithm, you press this key sequence and a help file explaining the algorithm pops up. The main keys are explained below.

OBJECTS (o,O) After clicking OBJECTS you can see an overview of the existing objects with their current names. In addition, the type of object (vector, workunit, ...) is indicated.

CREATE (c,C) You are asked which object you would like to create. Clicking WORKUNIT will show you a window "select a vector

number: 1 or ESC" containing all vectors of the active workunit. In this way you can create other workunits from existing vector objects. You can select as many vectors you want. Clicking *Vector* will allow you to make a new vector from an existing vector, for example, by taking logs. After clicking PICTURE, you are asked for a desired picture type. By choosing the option STATIC2DGRAPHICS you can create a picture object for two-dimensional static graphics, while the option DYNAMIC3DGRAPHICS defines an object for dynamic 3D graphics. The menu entry DRAFTMANSPLOT will create up to 25 two-dimensional scatter plots by plotting each of up to five selected vectors (which are kept in the same workunit) against each other. After clicking TEXT a window "create text" appears on the screen. This means that you have invoked the editor of XploRe and are able to write ASCII texts. It is now possible to write datasets or comments on data without leaving XploRe.
ACTIVATE (a,A) You are asked which object type you would like to activate. By clicking the object of a certain type (in a window "activation") you activate the object. This means that this object becomes the default data set or picture for following operations.
DISPLAY (d,D) This feature allows you to display any existing object of XploRe. Again you will be asked by a window to select an object type to display. Suppose you have created some workunits and you want to display one of them. First you will be asked to choose a corresponding picture object by showing a window. The picture object contains the characteristics of the view port (axes and origin) of the graphical display. There are three different kinds of display styles available. The option STATIC2DGRAPHICS will show you a two-dimensional picture display of two selected vectors of your dataset, whereas DYNAMIC3DGRAPHICS will show you a three-dimensional picture display of accordingly three vectors of the workunit. If you would like to display a data set with more than three dimensions, you have the possibility to display two-dimensional scatter plots of up to five vectors against each other. In this case you must choose the option DRAFTMANSPLOT. If you want to display a text object (the data vectors of a workunit or the corresponding explanations) you first have to read the workunit or the corresponding text file as a TEXT object. After this action you can display the vectors or the explanatory help file.
READ (r,R) You are asked what kind of object you want to read. If you want to display data as text it is necessary to choose the TEXT option. Next you have to select the subdirectory of your file . You can choose a standard DOS wildcard mask. After you click a file, XploRe creates and then reads the desired object.

WORKUNIT INFORMATION (i,I) By clicking the menu option INFO you first have to select a workunit. After it a window with the values of that specific workunit will be shown.

MANIPULATE (m,M) With this operation you invoke the manipulation part of XploRe. At first it is necessary to activate the corresponding object you would like to use by the MANIPULATE option (see ACTIVATE). Then you can select an operation under the menu entry MANIPULATE. At the next step you have to select an XploRe object which should be the "input" of the selected operation. The calculation time depends on the complexity of the procedure being used. The result of this operation is stored in a new workunit which will be the top most entry in the window if you click the menu option OBJECTS.

SESSION INFORMATION (s,S) This menu option shows a window containing all important information on the actual XploRe session. These are the active objects, time and the remaining memory (number of available bytes).

GRAPHICSTATUS (g,G) This option allows you to alter the graphics driver of your screen display. You have a choice of eight drivers. These are

- CGA
- MCGA
- EGA64
- EGAMONO
- HERCMONO
- ATT400
- VGA
- PC3270

BASIC STATISTICS (b,B) By this menu option you can select one of the following four basic statistics. The menu option BOX PLOT shows you a parallel box plot of all vectors which correspond to the workunit you have to select. In the box on the left side of your display you can see a scale (extends from minimum to maximum of all data) and a legend which contains the marker symbols of median, mean, inner fence and outer fence. The option STEM AND LEAF PLOT shows you the corresponding display of all vectors after selecting the desired workunit. The option DATA SUMMARY gives a summary of a selected workunit by showing minimum, maximium, range, mean, median, variance and upper and lower quantile of all vectors. Finally, the last option CORRELATION MATRIX shows a matrix containing the correlation between all vectors of the workunit.

TOOLS (t,T) You can EDIT WORKUNIT DISPLAY ATTRIBUTES and EDIT PICTURE DISPLAY ATTRIBUTES. If you have created many new objects during an XploRe session and you don't want to write all objects separately, it is useful to click the option SAVE ALL in order to write all existing objects held in memory at this moment. To read all objects of an XploRe session back into memory you have to click the option LOAD ALL.

HELP (h,H) This option informs you about some important keys to get help or to leave XploRe.

CLEARSCREEN (<ALT>+c,C) Clears the screen, but leaves the current objects active.

EXIT (<ALT>+x,X) With this option you can leave XploRe and return to DOS. Don't forget to save the XploRe objects which you want to keep on disk for later use.

OS SHELL (<ALT>+o,O) If you want to use the DOS shell during an XploRe session, type one of the above keys. To go back to XploRe type EXIT and the main menu appears again.

DELETE (<ALT>+d,D) You are asked which object type you would like to delete. By clicking the object type and the object name a deletion of the object is performed.

ENVIRONMENT (<ALT>+e,E) This option shows the content of the pascal source file typedef.pas and contains the declarations of the variable types used by the XploRe pascal modules.

INVERTSCREEN (<ALT>+i,I) Inverts the actual screen display.

I present an analysis using XploRe with the side impact data set given in Table 3 in Appendix 2. The data stem from Kallieris, Mattern and Härdle (1986). These data have been gained by simulating side impacts with post mortal test objects (PMTO). The response variable is $Y \in \{0,1\}$ a binary variable denoting fatal injury ($Y = 1$) or nonfatal injury ($Y = 0$). The predictor variables are $X_1 = AGE$, the age of the PMTO, and $X_2 = ROSYM$, the measured accelaration (in g) at the twelfth rib. The aim of the analysis is to devise a model from which the probability of fatal injury can be predicted given a certain x.

Figure A.1 shows a parallel box plot of the variables in this side impact data set. One can immediately see the range and the distribution of the variables. The variable AGE, for example, has half of the observations in the center box between 26 and 52 years.

Figure A.2 shows a draftman's plot, a system of all pairwise scatter plots. By using a brush (in the Y versus X_2 scatter) and by highlighting the values with $Y = 0$ we can see that those observations correspond to roughly a lower triangle of values in the X_1 versus X_2 scatter. We also see an interesting cluster of five data points having $Y = 0$, although

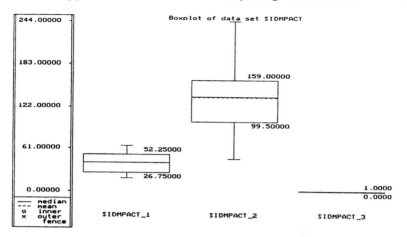

Figure A.1.   A parallel box plot of the variables in the data set.

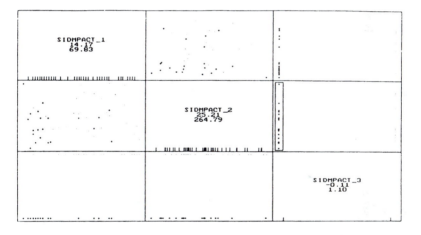

Figure A.2.   A draftman's plot with a brush at the scatterplot $Yvs.X_2$.

they are high on the AGE scale (scatter $SIDEMPACT1$ versus Y). By masking those points we can see that they correspond to observations with a low biomechanical input ($ROSYM$). Next we highlight with the same brush the observations with $Y = 1$ and see that they correspond to the upper triangle in the scatter of X_1 versus X_2. A hyperplane separating those triangles would, therefore, nicely separate the observations. Unfortunately, this cluster of five points (old PMTOs, high $ROSYM$)

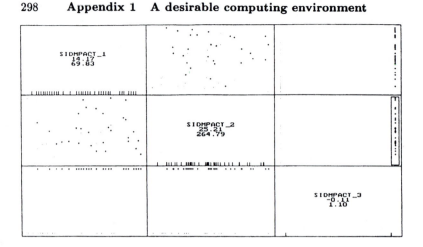

Figure A.3. A draftman's plot with a brush at the scatterplot $Yvs.X_2$.

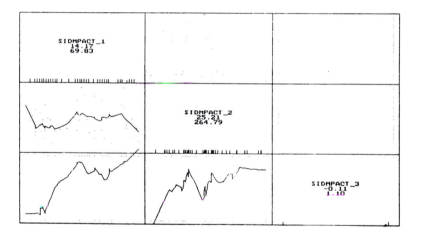

Figure A.4.   A draftman's plot with k-NN smooth.

does not fall into this scheme. However, a k-NN in each scatter plot reveals that we can still expect a monotonic relation between AGE, $ROSYM$ and Y (Figure A.4)

Next we apply the ADE method. We press "M", for manipulation and have a menu of a variety of smoothing techniques (Figure A.5). After pressing the ENTER key when the cursor is on the "ADE" line we have

Figure A.5.   The Manipulations of workunits for Smoothing.

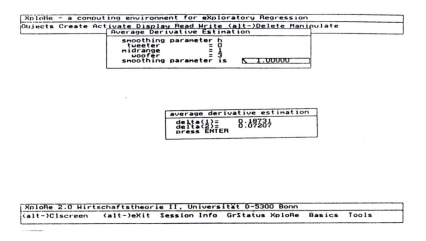

Figure A.6.   The request for bandwidth in the ADE procedure.

the request to enter the bandwidth h. Using a bandwidth of $h = 1$ we obtain a value of $\delta = (0.187, 0.072)$ (Figure A.6).

The corresponding projection $\hat{\delta}^T X$ versus. Y is shown in Figure A.7 together with an isotonic regression smooth and an iterated $k\text{-}NN$ smooth. One clearly sees the nonlinearity of the response function due to the cluster of the irregular five points.

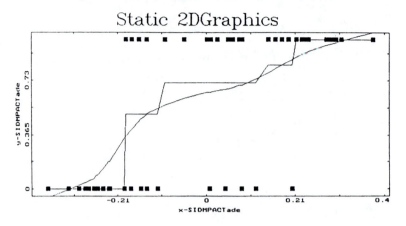

Figure A.7.   The projected data, a iterated k-NN smooth and an isotonic regression in a STATIC2DGRAPHICS Picture.

Tables

Appendix 2   Tables

Table 1   *The motorcycle data set*

x	y	x	y	x	y	x	y
2.4	0.0	65.6	−21.5	23.4	−128.5	34.8	75.0
2.6	−1.3	15.8	−21.5	24.0	−112.5	35.2	−16.0
3.2	−2.7	15.8	−50.8	24.2	−95.1	35.2	−54.9
3.6	0.0	16.0	−42.9	24.2	−81.8	35.4	69.6
4.0	−2.7	16.0	−26.8	24.6	−53.5	35.6	34.8
6.2	−2.7	16.2	−21.5	25.0	−64.4	35.6	32.1
6.6	−2.7	16.2	−50.8	25.0	−57.6	36.2	−37.5
6.8	−1.3	16.2	−61.7	25.4	−72.3	36.2	22.8
7.8	−2.7	16.4	−5.4	25.4	−44.3	38.0	46.9
8.2	−2.7	16.4	−80.4	25.6	−26.8	38.0	10.7
8.8	−1.3	16.6	−59.0	26.0	−5.4	39.2	5.4
8.8	−2.7	16.8	−71.0	26.2	−107.1	39.4	−1.3
9.6	−2.7	16.8	−91.1	26.2	−21.5	40.0	−21.5
10.0	−2.7	16.8	−77.7	26.4	−65.6	40.4	−13.3
10.2	−5.4	17.6	−37.5	27.0	−16.0	41.6	30.8
10.6	−2.7	17.6	−85.6	27.2	−45.6	41.6	−10.7
11.0	−5.4	17.6	−123.1	27.2	−24.2	42.4	29.4
11.4	0.0	17.6	−101.9	27.2	9.5	42.8	0.0
13.2	−2.7	17.8	−99.1	27.6	4.0	42.8	−10.7
13.6	−2.7	17.8	−104.4	28.2	12.0	43.0	14.7
13.8	0.0	18.6	−112.5	28.4	−21.5	44.0	−1.3
14.6	−13.3	18.6	−50.8	28.4	37.5	44.4	0.0
14.6	−5.4	19.2	−123.1	28.6	46.9	45.0	10.7
14.6	−5.4	19.4	−85.6	29.4	−17.4	46.6	10.7
14.6	−9.3	19.4	−72.3	30.2	36.2	47.8	−26.8
14.6	−16.0	19.6	−127.2	31.0	75.0	47.8	−14.7
14.6	−22.8	20.2	−123.1	31.2	8.1	48.8	−13.3
14.8	−2.7	20.4	−117.9	32.0	54.9	50.6	0.0
15.4	−22.8	21.2	−134.0	32.0	48.2	52.0	10.7
15.4	−32.1	21.4	−101.9	32.8	46.9	53.2	−14.7
15.4	−53.5	21.8	−108.4	33.4	16.0	55.0	−2.7
15.4	−54.9	22.0	−123.1	33.8	45.6	55.0	10.7
15.6	−40.2	23.2	−123.1	34.4	1.3	55.4	−2.7
						57.6	10.7

Note: The X-values denote time (in milliseconds) after a simulated impact with motorcycles. The response variable Y is the head acceleration [in g] of a PTMO (post mortem human test object).
Source: Schmidt, Mattern and Schüler (1981).

Table 2   *A simulated data set*

x	y	x	y	x	y
0.00452	1.83613	0.30060	0.64960	0.68085	−0.17996
0.00837	−0.97443	0.32759	−0.16932	0.69696	−0.42336
0.01229	0.53992	0.35690	1.12878	0.70432	−0.26322
0.03682	0.46113	0.35891	0.33772	0.71094	−0.52858
0.03688	2.00374	0.36202	1.05152	0.71561	0.50815
0.04753	−0.72132	0.36487	0.41197	0.71813	0.94339
0.07120	1.28708	0.36566	−0.41853	0.72874	−0.91171
0.08281	−1.26908	0.36627	3.03907	0.73008	0.27614
0.08511	2.63863	0.38073	0.64303	0.76162	0.98254
0.09017	−0.25029	0.38979	−0.54217	0.77494	0.63778
0.09331	0.73673	0.40219	0.71329	0.78354	−0.80649
0.11212	0.26705	0.42153	0.97109	0.79327	0.55979
0.11457	0.81824	0.45009	1.97278	0.81226	−0.69888
0.11467	0.05118	0.48200	2.04211	0.81868	−0.72442
0.11752	0.48483	0.50161	3.54774	0.82433	−0.14897
0.11922	2.22813	0.50202	0.98850	0.82645	−1.42030
0.11952	1.57051	0.50203	0.28272	0.82654	−0.02744
0.14354	0.57802	0.51123	1.71133	0.82768	−0.12909
0.14526	0.59176	0.52401	2.83595	0.84186	0.36166
0.15239	0.89032	0.52426	0.57377	0.85518	0.78004
0.17781	2.86420	0.52614	1.84754	0.86838	−1.11895
0.19420	0.92809	0.53805	−0.12198	0.89536	0.18627
0.19606	2.88992	0.54039	0.07410	0.89737	−0.14874
0.20214	0.07135	0.54042	2.70415	0.91137	−0.55851
0.20355	0.32582	0.54090	2.77430	0.91171	1.05371
0.21694	0.95779	0.56182	0.18000	0.91372	0.41848
0.21793	0.80795	0.57445	−0.32403	0.91578	0.70488
0.21796	0.85995	0.58101	0.74803	0.91668	−1.54878
0.23354	0.83378	0.59064	−0.46347	0.91789	−0.59214
0.24067	3.08766	0.61799	−0.10944	0.96018	−0.29103
0.27053	1.46206	0.62652	0.12693	0.96152	−1.99601
0.29464	0.41268	0.64060	0.90819	0.96505	−0.78273
0.29908	0.70020	0.65604	−0.21575	0.96909	0.51049
				0.98453	−0.10069

Note: The raw data $\{(X_i, Y_i)\}_{i=1}^{n}$, $n = 100$, were constructed from $Y_i = m(X_i) + \varepsilon_i$, $\varepsilon_i \sim N(0,1)$, $X_i \sim U(0,1)$ and $m(x) = 1 - x + e^{-200\,(x-1/2)^2}$

Appendix 2   Tables

Table 3   *The side impact data set*

AGE	ROSYM	Y	AGE	ROSYM	Y
33.0000	109.0000	1.0000	62.0000	141.0000	1.0000
53.0000	162.0000	0.0000	23.0000	89.0000	0.0000
29.0000	137.0000	0.0000	19.0000	243.0000	0.0000
39.0000	152.0000	1.0000	29.0000	62.0000	0.0000
28.0000	144.0000	1.0000	47.0000	82.0000	1.0000
42.0000	239.0000	1.0000	22.0000	150.0000	0.0000
23.0000	170.0000	1.0000	52.0000	155.0000	1.0000
50.0000	198.0000	1.0000	59.0000	239.0000	1.0000
40.0000	197.0000	1.0000	60.0000	122.0000	1.0000
44.0000	140.0000	1.0000	30.0000	64.0000	0.0000
51.0000	81.0000	1.0000	53.0000	145.0000	1.0000
27.0000	103.0000	0.0000	64.0000	114.0000	1.0000
25.0000	158.0000	0.0000	22.0000	46.0000	0.0000
54.0000	67.0000	0.0000	21.0000	134.0000	0.0000
40.0000	105.0000	1.0000	23.0000	100.0000	0.0000
43.0000	217.0000	1.0000	36.0000	111.0000	1.0000
58.0000	185.0000	1.0000	45.0000	98.0000	1.0000
41.0000	150.0000	1.0000	49.0000	139.0000	0.0000
27.0000	185.0000	0.0000	60.0000	111.0000	1.0000
24.0000	62.0000	0.0000	59.0000	178.0000	1.0000
65.0000	71.0000	1.0000	26.0000	138.0000	0.0000
63.0000	89.0000	1.0000	41.0000	137.0000	0.0000
26.0000	78.0000	0.0000	25.0000	102.0000	0.0000
47.0000	106.0000	0.0000	53.0000	244.0000	1.0000
31.0000	103.0000	1.0000	47.0000	213.0000	1.0000
50.0000	107.0000	1.0000			

Note: The variable *AGE* denotes the age of the post mortal test object, *ROSYM* the biomechanic stress at the thorax and *Y* is an indicator for injury.
Source: Härdle, Kallieris and Mattern (1988)

References

Ahmad, I. A. and Lin, P. E. (1976). Non-parametric sequential estimation of a multiple regression function. *Bulletin of Mathematical Statistics,* *17, 63-75.*

Akaike, H. (1970). Statistical predictor information. *Annals of the Institute of Statistical Mathematics, 22, 203-17.*

Akaike, H. (1974). A new look at the statistical model identification. *IEEE Transactions of Automatic Control AC, 19, 716-23.*

Allen, D. M. (1974). The relationship between variable selection and data augmentation and a method for prediction. *Technometrics, 16, 125-7.*

Altman, N. S. (1988). Kernel smoothing of data with correlated errors. *Journal of the American Statistical Association.*

Andersen, A. H., Jensen, E. B. and Schou, G. (1981). Two-way analysis of variance with autocorrelated errors. *International Statistical Review, 49, 153-7.*

Azzalini, A. (1984). Estimation and hypothesis testing of autoregressive time series. *Biometrika, 71, 85-90.*

Azzalini, A., Bowman, A. and Härdle, W. (1989). On the use of nonparametric regression for model checking. *Biometrika, 76, 1-12.*

Barlow, R. E., Bartholomew, D. J., Bremner, J. M. and Brunk, H. D. (1972). *Statistical inference under order restrictions.* London: Wiley.

Bartlett, M. S. (1963). Statistical estimation of density functions. *Sankhyā, Series A, 25, 245-54.*

Becker, R. A. and Chambers, J. C. (1984). *S - An interactive computing environment for data analysis.* Belmont, CA: Wadsworth Press.

Becker, R. A., Chambers, J. C. and Wilks, A. R. (1988). *The new S language: a programming environment for data analysis and graphics.* Pacific Grove, CA: Wadsworth and Brooks/Cole Advanced Books and Software.

Benedetti, J. K. (1977). On the nonparametric estimation of regression functions. *Journal of the Royal Statistical Society, Series B, 39, 248-53.*

Bent, S. W. and John, J. (1985). Finding the median requires $2n$ comparisons. *Proc. 17th ACM Symposium on the Theory of Computing, 213-16.*

Beran, R. (1986). Discussion to Wu, C. F. J.: Jackknife, bootstrap and other resampling methods in regression analysis. *Annals of Statistics, 14, 1295–98.*

Bickel, P. J. and Doksum, K. A. (1977). *Mathematical statistics: basic ideas and selected topics.* San Fransisco: Holden-Day.

Bickel, P. J. and Freedman, D. A. (1981). Some asymptotic theory for the bootstrap. *Annals of Statistics, 9, 1196–217.*

Bickel, P. J. and Rosenblatt, M. (1973). On some global measures of the deviations of density function estimates. *Annals of Statistics, 1, 1071–91.*

Bierens, H. J. (1983). Uniform consistency of kernel estimators of a regression function under generalized conditions. *Journal of the American Statistical Association, 77, 699–707.*

Bierens, H. J. (1987). *Kernel estimators of regression functions.* Cambridge University Press: Advances in Econometrics.

Bierens, H. J. (1988). *Model-Free Asymptotically Best Forecasting of Stationary Economic Time Series.* Unpublished manuscript.

Billingsley, P. (1968). *Convergence of probability measures.* New York: Wiley.

Boneva, L. I., Kendall, D. and Stefanov, I. (1970). Spline transformations: three new diagnostic aids for the statistical data analyst. *Journal of the Royal Statistical Society, Series B, 32, 1–71.*

Bosq, D. and Lecoutre, J. P. (1987). *Théorie de l'estimation fonctionnelle.* Paris: Economica.

Box, G. E. P. and Cox, D. R. (1964). An analysis of transformations. *Journal of the Royal Statistical Society, Series B, 26, 211–52.*

Breiman, L. and Friedman, J. (1985). Estimating optimal transformations for multiple regression and correlation. *Journal of the American Statistical Association, 80, 580–619.*

Breiman, L., Friedman, J., Olshen, R. and Stone, C. J. (1984). *Classification and regression trees.* Belmont, CA: Wadsworth.

Bril, G., Dykstra, R., Pillers, C. and Robertson, T. (1984). Isotonic regression in two independent variables. *Applied Statistics, 33, 352–7.*

Broich, T., Härdle, W. and Krause, A. (1990). *XploRe – a computing environment for eXploratory Regression.* Springer-Verlag, in print.

Bussian, B. M. and Härdle, W. (1984). Robust smoothing applied to white noise and single outlier contaminated Raman spectra. *Applied Spectroscopy, 38, 309–13.*

Carroll, R. J. (1982). Adapting for heteroscedasticity in linear models. *Annals of Statistics, 10, 1224–33.*

Carroll, R. J. and Härdle, W. (1988). Symmetrized nearest neighbor regression estimates. *Statistics and Probability Letters, 7, 315–18.*

Carroll, R. J. and Härdle, W. (1989). A note on second-order effects in a semiparametric context. *Statistics, 20, 179–86.*

Carroll, R. J. and Ruppert, D. (1988). *Transformation and weighting in regression.* New York: Chapman and Hall.

Casady, R. J. and Cryer, D. J. (1976). Monotone percentile regression. *Annals of Statistics, 4, 532-41.*

Cenzov, N. N. (1962). Evaluation of an unknown distribution density from observations. *Soviet Math. Dokl., 3, 1559-62.*

Cheng, K. F. and Cheng, P. E. (1986). *Robust nonparametric estimation of a regression function.* Unpublished manuscript.

Cheng, K. F. and Lin, P. E. (1981). Nonparametric estimation of a regression function. *Zeitschrift für Wahrscheinlichkeitstheorie und verwandte Gebiete, 57, 223-33.*

Cheng, P. E. and Cheng, K. F. (1987). *Asymptotic normality for robust R-estimators of regression function.* Unpublished manuscript.

Clark, R. M. (1975). A calibration curve for radiocarbon dates. *Antiquity, 49, 251-66.*

Clark, R. M. (1977). Nonparametric estimation of a smooth regression function. *Journal of the Royal Statistical Society, Series B, 39, 107-13.*

Clark, R. M. (1980). Calibration, cross-validation and carbon 14 II. *Journal of the Royal Statistical Society, Series A, 143, 177-94.*

Cleveland, W. S. (1979). Robust locally weighted regression and smoothing scatter plots. *Journal of the American Statistical Association, 74, 829-36.*

Cleveland, W. S. (1985). *The elements of graphing data.* Belmont, CA: Wadsworth.

Cleveland, W. S. and McGill, R. (1984). The many faces of a scatter plot. *Journal of the American Statistical Association, 79, 807-22.*

Collomb, G. (1977). Quelques propriétés de la méthode du noyau pour l'estimation non-paramétrique de la régression en un point fixé. *C. R. Acad. Sc. Paris, 285, 289-92.*

Collomb, G. (1981). Estimation non-paramétrique de la régression: Revue Bibliographique. *International Statistical Review, 49, 75-93.*

Collomb, G. (1984). Propriétés de convergence presque complète du prédicteur à noyau. *Zeitschrift für Wahrscheinlichkeitstheorie und verwandte Gebiete, 66, 441-60.*

Collomb, G. (1985a). Nonparametric time series analysis and prediction: uniform almost sure convergence of the window and k-NN autoregression estimates. *Statistics, 16, 297-307.*

Collomb, G. (1985b). Nonparametric regression: an up-to-date bibliography. *Statistics, 16, 309-24.*

Collomb, G. and Härdle, W. (1986). Strong uniform convergence rates in robust nonparametric time series analysis and prediction: kernel regression estimation from dependent observations. *Stochastic Processes and their Applications, 23, 77-89.*

Collomb, G., Härdle, W. and Hassani, S. (1987). A note on prediction via estimation of the conditional mode function. *Journal of Statistical Planning and Inference, 15, 227-36.*

Cover, T. M. and Hart, P. E. (1967). Nearest neighbor pattern classification. *IEEE Transactions on Information Theory, 13, 21-7.*

Cox, D. D. (1983). Asymptotics for M-type smoothing splines. *Annals of Statistics, 11, 530-51.*

Craven, P. and Wahba, G. (1979). Smoothing noisy data with spline functions. *Numer. Math. 31, 377-403.*

Cristóbal, C., Faraldo, R. and Manteiga, G. (1987). A class of linear regression parameter estimators constructed by nonparametric estimation. *Annals of Statistics, 15, 603-9.*

Cryer, J. D., Robertson, T., Wright F. T. and Casady, R. J. (1972). Monotone median regression. *Annals of Mathematical Statistics, 43, 1459-69.*

Deaton, A. (1988). *Agricultural pricing policies and demand patterns in Thailand.* Unpublished manuscript.

de Jong, P. (1987). A central limit theorem for generalized quadratic forms. *Probab. Th. Rel. Fields 75, 261-77.*

Devroye, L. P. (1978a). The uniform convergence of nearest neighbor regression function estimators and their application in optimization. *IEEE Transactions on Information Theory, 24, 142-51.*

Devroye, L. P. (1978b). The uniform convergence of the Nadaraya–Watson regression function estimate. *Canadian Journal of Statistics, 6, 179-91.*

Devroye, L. P. and Györfi, L. (1985). Distribution-free exponential bound for the L_1 error of partitioning estimates of a regression function. In: *Probability and statistical theory, Proceedings of the 4th Pannonian Symposium on Mathematical Statistics,* eds. F. Konecny, J. Mogyorodi and W. Wertz. Dortrecht: Reidel, 67-76.

Devroye, L. P. and Wagner, T. J. (1980a). Distribution-free consistency results in nonparametric discrimination and regression function estimation. *Annals of Statistics, 8, 231-9.*

Devroye, L. P. and Wagner, T. J. (1980b). On the L_1-convergence of kernel estimators of regression functions with applications in discrimination. *Zeitschrift für Wahrscheinlichkeitstheorie und verwandte Gebiete, 51, 15-25.*

Diaconis, P. and Shahshahani, M. (1984). On nonlinear functions of linear combinations. *SIAM J. Sci. Statist. Computing, 5, 175-91.*

Dikta, G. (1988). *Bootstrap approximations of nearest neighbor regression function estimates.* Unpublished manuscript.

Doukhan, P. and Ghindès, M. (1980). Estimation dans le processus $X_n = f(X_{n-1}) + \varepsilon_n$. *Comptes Rendus, Acad. Sci. Paris, 297, Sér A, 61-4.*

Doukhan, P. and Ghindès, M. (1983). Estimation de la transition de probabilité d'une chaîne de Markov Doëblin-Récurrente. Etude du cas du processus autorégressif général d'ordre 1. *Stochastic Processes and their Applications, 15, 271-93.*

Durbin, J. and Knott, M. (1972). Components of Cramer–von Mises Statistics I. *J.Royal Statist. Soc. (B), 34, 290-307.*

Engle, R. F., Granger, W. J., Rice, J. and Weiss, A. (1986). Semiparametric estimates of the relation between weather and electricity sales. *Journal of the American Statistical Association, 81, 310-20.*

Epanechnikov, V. (1969). Nonparametric estimates of a multivariate probability density. *Theory of Probability and its Applications, 14, 153-8.*

Eubank, R. (1988). *Spline smoothing and nonparametric regression.* New York: Dekker.

Euclid (−300). *Die Elemente.* Reprint from *Wissenschaftlische Buchgesellschaft Darmstadt,* 1980.

Family Expenditure Survey, Annual Base Tapes (1968-1983) Department of Employment, Statistics Division, Her Majesty's Stationery Office, London 1968-1983. The data utilized in this book were made available by the ESRC Data Archive at the University of Essex.

Feller, W. (1971). *An introduction to probability theory and its applications, Volume II.* New York: Wiley.

Fisher, L. and Yakowitz, S. J. (1976). Uniform convergence of the potential function algorithm. *SIAM Journal of Control and Optimization, 14, 95-103.*

Fisher, N. (1987). Graphical methods in statistics: current and prospective views. *Proceedings of the 46. ISI Session, 3, 387-400.*

Fisher, R. A. (1922). On the mathematical foundations of theoretical statistics. *Phil. Trans. of the Royal Society of London, Series A, 222, 309-68.*

Fisherkeller, M. A., Friedman, J. H. and Tukey, J. W. (1974). PRIM-9; an interactive multidimensional data display and analysis system SLAC-PUB-1408, Stanford University, Stanford, CA.

Franke, J. and Härdle, W. (1988). On bootstrapping kernel spectral estimates. *Annals of Statistics,* accepted.

Friedman, J. (1984). A Variable span smoother. Department of Statistics Technical Report LCS5, Stanford University, Stanford, CA.

Friedman, J. and Stuetzle, W. (1981). Projection pursuit regression. *Journal of the American Statistical Association, 76, 817-23.*

Friedman, J. and Tibshirani, R. (1984). The monotone smoothing of scatter plots. *Technometrics, 26, 243-50.*

Friedman, J. H. and Tukey, J. W. (1974). A projection pursuit algorithm for exploratory data analysis. *IEEE Transactions on Computers, C-23, 881-90.*

Frisén, M. and Goteborg, S. (1980). U-shaped Regression. In: *Compstat 1980.* Wien: Physica Verlag.

Gasser, T., Köhler, W., Müller, H. G., Largo, R., Molinari, L. and Prader, A. (1985). Human height growth: correlational and multivariate structure of velocity and acceleration. *Annals of Human Biology, 12, 501-15.*

Gasser, T. and Müller, H. G. (1979). Kernel estimation of regression functions. In: *Smoothing Techniques for Curve Estimation,* eds. Gasser and Rosenblatt. Heidelberg: Springer-Verlag.

Gasser, T. and Müller, H. G. (1984). Estimating regression functions and their derivatives by the kernel method. *Scandanavian Journal of Statistics*, *11, 171-85*.

Gasser, T., Müller, H. G., Köhler, W., Molinari, L. and Prader, A. (1984). Nonparametric regression analysis of growth curves. *Annals of Statistics*, *12, 210-29*.

Gasser, T., Müller, H. G. and Mammitzsch, V. (1985). Kernels for nonparametric curve estimation. *Journal of the Royal Statistical Society, Series B, 47, 238-52*.

GAUSS (1987). GAUSS is a program for PCs available from Aptech Systems, Inc., Product Development, P.O. Box 6487, Kent, WA 98064.

Georgiev, A. A. (1984a). Nonparametric system identification by kernel methods. *IEEE Transactions of Automatic Control, 29, 356-8*.

Georgiev, A. A. (1984b). Speed of convergence in nonparametric kernel estimation of a regression function and its derivatives. *Annals of the Institute of Statistical Mathematics, 36, 455-62*.

Good, I. J. and Gaskins, R. A. (1971). Nonparametric roughness penalties for probability densities. *Biometrika, 58, 255-77*.

Gordon, L. and Olshen, R. A. (1980). Consistent nonparametric regression from recursive partitioning schemes. *Journal of Multivariate Analysis, 10, 611-27*.

Gray, H. L. and Schucany, W. R. (1972). *The generalized jackknife statistic*. New York: Dekker.

Greblicki, W. (1974). *Asymptotically optimal probabilistic algorithms for pattern recognition and identification* (in Polish). *Prace Naukowe Instytutu Cybernetyki Technicznej No. 18, Seria: Monografie No. 3, Wroclaw*.

Greblicki, W. and Krzyzak, A. (1980). Asymptotic properties of kernel estimates of a regression function. *Journal of Statistical Planning and Inference, 4, 81-90*

Greblicki, W., Rutkowska, D. and Rutkowski, L. (1983). An orthogonal series estimate of time-varying regression. *Annals of the Institute of Statistical Mathematics, 35, 215-28*.

Green, P., Jennison, C. and Seheult, A. (1985). Analysis of field experiments by least squares smoothing. *Journal of the Royal Statistical Society, Series B, 47, 299-315*.

Györfi, L. (1981). The rate of convergence of k_n-NN regression estimation and classification. *IEEE Transactions of Information Theory, 27, 500-9*.

Györfi, L., Härdle, W., Sarda, P. and Vieū, Ph. (1989). Nonparametric Curve Estimation from Time Series. *Springer Lecture Notes in Statistics 60*. Springer-Verlag.

Hadley, G. and Kemp, M. C. (1971). *Variational methods in economics*. New York: North Holland.

Hall, P. (1988). *On projection pursuit regression*. Unpublished manuscript.

Hall, P. and Marron, J. S. (1987). On the amount of noise in bandwidth selection for a kernel density estimator. *Annals of Statistics, 15, 163–81.*

Hall, P. and Marron, J. S. (1988). *Lower bounds for bandwidth selection in density estimation.* Unpublished manuscript.

Hall, P. and Titterington, M. (1986a). *On the structure of smoothing techniques in regression problems.* Unpublished manuscript.

Hall, P. and Titterington, M. (1986b). *On confidence bands in nonparametric density estimation and regression.* Unpublished manuscript.

Hanson, D. L. and Pledger, G. (1976). Consistency in concave regression. *Annals of Statistics, 4, 1038–50.*

Hanson, D. L., Pledger, G. and Wright, F. T. (1973). On consistency in monotonic regression. *Annals of Statistics, 1, 401–21.*

Härdle, W. (1984a). A law of the iterated logarithm for nonparametric regression function estimators. *Annals of Statistics, 12, 624–35.*

Härdle, W. (1984b). Robust regression function estimation. *Journal of Multivariate Analysis, 14, 169–80.*

Härdle, W. (1984c). How to determine the bandwidth of nonlinear smoothers in practice? In: *Robust and Nonlinear Time Series Analysis,* eds. J. Franke, W. Härdle and D. Martin. Heidelberg: Springer-Verlag.

Härdle, W. (1986a). A note on jackknifing kernel regression function estimators. *IEEE Transactions of Information Theory, 32, 298–300.*

Härdle, W. (1986b). Approximations to the mean integrated squared error with applications to optimal bandwidth selection for nonparametric regression function estimators. *Journal of Multivariate Analysis, 18, 150-68.*

Härdle, W. (1986c). Automatic curve smoothing. In: *Proceedings of the First World Congress of the Bernoulli Society.* Tashkent: VNU Science Press.

Härdle, W. (1987a). Resistant smoothing using the Fast Fourier Transform, AS 222. *Applied Statistics, 36, 104–11.*

Härdle, W. (1987b). XploRe – a computing environment for eXploratory Regression. In: *Statistical Data Analysis Based on the L_1-norm,* ed. Y. Dodge. New York: North Holland.

Härdle, W. (1989). Asymptotic maximal deviation of M-smoothers. *Journal of Multivariate Analysis.*

Härdle, W. and Bowman, A. (1988). Bootstrapping in nonparametric regression: local adaptive smoothing and confidence bands. *Journal of the American Statistical Association, 83, 102-10.*

Härdle, W. and Carroll, R. J. (1990). Biased cross-validation for a kernel regression estimator and its derivatives. *Östereichische Zeitschrift für Statistik und Informatik, 20, 53–64.*

Härdle, W. and Gasser, T. (1984). Robust nonparametric function fitting. *Journal of the Royal Statistical Society, Series B, 46, 42–51.*

Härdle, W. and Gasser, T. (1985). On robust kernel estimation of derivatives of regression functions. *Scandanavian Journal of Statistics, 12, 233-40.*

Härdle, W., Hall, P. and Marron, J. S. (1988). How far are automatically chosen regression smoothing parameters from their optimum? (with discussion). *Journal of the American Statistical Association, 83, 86-99.*

Härdle, W., Hart, J., Marron, J. S., and Tsybakov, A. B. (1989). Bandwidth choice for average derivative estimation. *Journal of the American Statistical Association, submitted.*

Härdle, W., Hildenbrand, W. and Jerison, M. (1989). Empirical evidence for the law of demand. *Econometrica, submitted.*

Härdle, W., Janssen, P. and Serfling, R. (1988). Strong uniform consistency rates for estimators of conditional functionals. *Annals of Statistics, 16, 1428-49.*

Härdle, W. and Jerison, M. (1988). Evolution of Engel curves over time. Discussion paper No. A-178. SFB 303, University of Bonn. Talk EC 48 at the Econometric Society Meeting in Bologna 1988.

Härdle, W. and Kelly, G. (1987). Nonparametric kernel regression estimation – optimal choice of bandwidth. *Statistics, 18, 21-35.*

Härdle, W. and Luckhaus, S. (1984). Uniform consistency of a class of regression function estimators. *Annals of Statistics, 12, 612-23.*

Härdle, W. and Mammen, E. (1988). *Comparing nonparametric versus parametric regression fits.* Unpublished manuscript.

Härdle, W. and Marron, J. S. (1983). The nonexistence of moments of some kernel regression estimators. Institute of Statistics Mimeo Series 1537, Institute of Statistics, Chapel Hill, North Carolina.

Härdle, W. and Marron, J. S. (1985a). Asymptotic nonequivalence of some bandwidth selectors in nonparametric regression. *Biometrika, 72, 481-4.*

Härdle, W. and Marron, J. S. (1985b). Optimal bandwidth selection in nonparametric regression function estimation. *Annals of Statistics, 13, 1465-81.*

Härdle, W. and Marron, J. S. (1990a). Bootstrap simultaneous error bars for nonparametric regression. *Annals of Statistics, in print.*

Härdle, W. and Marron, J. S. (1990b). Semiparametric comparison of regression curves. *Annals of Statistics, in print.*

Härdle, W. and Mattern, R. (1983). Mathematische Modellierung der Eliminationsphase des Ethanols. In: *Fortschritte der Rechtsmedizin,* eds. H. Froberg, J. Barz, J. Bösche, R. Käppner and R. Mattern. Heidelberg: Springer-Verlag.

Härdle, W. and Nixdorf, R. (1987). Nonparametric sequential estimation of zeros and extrema of regression functions. *IEEE Transactions of Information Theory, IT-33, 367-72.*

Härdle, W. and Scott, D. W. (1988). *Smoothing in low and high dimensions using weighted averaging of rounded points.* Unpublished manuscript.

Härdle, W. and Steiger, W. (1988). *Efficient median smoothing.* Unpublished manuscript.

Härdle, W. and Stoker, T. (1989). Investigating smooth multiple regression by the method of average derivatives. *Journal of the American Statistical Association, 84, 986-95.*

Härdle, W. and Tsybakov, A. B. (1988). Robust nonparametric regression with simultaneous scale curve estimation. *Annals of Statistics, 16, 120-35.*

Härdle, W. and Tuan, P. D. (1986). Some theory on M-smoothing of time series. *Journal of Time Series Analysis, 7, 191-204.*

Härdle, W. and Vieu, P. (1989). Nonparametric prediction by the kernel method. Submitted to *Econometrica.*

Harrison, D. and Rubinfeld, D. C. (1978). Hedonic prices and the demand for clean air. *Journal of Environmental Economics and Management, 5, 81-102.*

Hart, D. and Wehrly, T. E. (1986). Kernel regression estimation using repeated measurements data. *Journal of the American Statistical Association, 81, 1080-8.*

Hastie, T. and Tibshirani, R. (1986). Generalized additive models (with discussion). *Statistical Science, 1, 297-318.*

Hastie, T. and Tibshirani, R. (1987). Nonparametric logistic and proportional odds regression. *Applied Statistics, 1, 260-76.*

Heckman, N. E. (1986). Spline smoothing in a partly linear model. *Journal of the Royal Statistical Society, Series B, 48, 244-8.*

Hildenbrand, W. (1985). A problem in demand aggregation: per capita demand as a function of per capita expenditure. Discussion paper A-12, SFB 303, University of Bonn.

Hildenbrand, W. (1986). Equilibrium analysis of large economies. Talk presented at the International Congress of Mathematicians, Berkeley, California, August 3-11, 1986. Discussion paper A-72, SFB 303, University of Bonn.

Hildenbrand, K. and Hildenbrand, W. (1986). On the mean income effect: a data analysis of the U.K. family expenditure survey. In: *Contributions to Mathematical Economics,* eds. W. Hildenbrand and A. Mas-Colell. New York: North Holland.

Hildreth, C. (1954). Point estimates of ordinates of concave functions. *Journal of the American Statistical Association, 49, 598-618.*

Hillig, K. and Morris, M. (1982). Raman spectra estimation. *Applied Spectroscopy, 36, 700.*

Huber, P. J. (1979). Robust smoothing. In: *Robustness in Statistics,* eds. E. Launer and G. Wilkinson. New York: Academic Press.

Huber, P. J. (1981). *Robust statistics.* New York: Wiley.

Huber, P. J. (1985). Projection pursuit. *Annals of Statistics, 13, 435-75.*

Ibgragimov, I. A. and Hasminskii, R. Z. (1980). On nonparametric estimation of regression. *Soviet Math. Dokl., 21, 810-14.*

ISP (1987). ISP is a program for PCs available from Artemis Systems Inc.

Jennen-Steinmetz, C. and Gasser, T. (1988). *A unifying approach to nonparametric regression estimation.* Unpublished manuscript.

Johnston, G. J. (1979). Smooth nonparametric regression analysis. *Institute of Statistics Mimeo Series 1253, University of North Carolina, Chapel Hill, NC.*

Johnston, G. J. (1982). Probabilities of maximal deviations for nonparametric regression function estimates. *Journal of Multivariate Analysis, 12, 402-14.*

Jones, M. C. and Sibson, R. (1987). What is projection pursuit ? (with discussion). *Journal of the Royal Statistical Society, Series A, 150, 1-38.*

Jørgensen, M., Nielsen, C. T., Keiding, N. and Skakkebaek, N. E. (1985). Parametrische und Nichtparametrische Modelle für Wachstumsdaten. In: *Neuere Verfahren der nichtparametrischen Statistik,* ed. G. Pflug. Heidelberg: Springer-Verlag. (English version available as Research Report 85/3 from the Statistical Research Unit, University of Copenhagen.)

Kallieris, D. and Mattern, R. (1984). Belastbarkeitsgrenze und Verletzungsmechanik des angegurteten Fahrzeuginsassen beim Seitenaufprall. Phase I: Kinematik und Belastungen beim Seitenaufprall im Vergleich Dummy/Leiche. *FAT Schriftenreihe 36, Forschungsvereinigung Automobiltechnik e.V. (FAT).*

Kallieris, D., Mattern, R. and Härdle, W. (1986). Belastbarkeitsgrenze und Verletzungsmechanik des angegurteten PKW–Insassen beim Seitenaufprall. Phase II: Ansätze zur Verletzungsprädiktion. *FAT Schriftenreihe 60, Forschungsvereinigung Automobiltechnik e.V. (FAT).*

Katkovnik, V. Y. (1979). Linear and nonlinear methods for nonparametric regression analysis (in Russian). *Avtomatika, 35-46.*

Katkovnik, V. Y. (1983). Convergence of the linear and nonlinear nonparametric kernel estimates (in Russian). *Avtomatika i Telemehanika, 108-20.*

Katkovnik, V. Y. (1985). *Nonparametric identification and data smoothing: local approximation approach* (in Russian). Moscow: Nauka.

Kelly, C. and Rice, J. (1988). *Monotone smoothing with application to dose response curves and the assessment of synergism.* Unpublished manuscript.

Kendall, M. and Stuart, A. (1979). *The advanced theory of statistics,* Vol 2. London: Charles Griffin.

Kiefer, J. and Wolfowitz, J. (1952). Stochastic estimation of the maximum of a regression function. *Annals of Mathematical Statistics, 23, 462-6.*

Kleiner, B., Martin, R. D. and Thomson, D. J. (1979). Robust estimation of power spectra (with discussion). *Journal of the Royal Statistical Society, Series B, 41, 313-51.*

Knafl, G., Sacks, J., Spiegelman, C. and Ylvisaker, D. (1984). Nonparametric calibration. *Technometrics, 26, 233-41.*

Knafl, G., Sacks, J. and Ylvisaker, D. (1985). Confidence bands for regression functions. *Journal of the American Statistical Association, 80, 683-91*.

Kneip, A. and Gasser, T. (1988). Convergence and consistency results for self-modeling nonlinear regression. *Annals of Statistics, 16, 82-112*.

Kruskal, J. B. (1965). Analysis of factorial experiments by estimating monotone transformations of the data. *Journal of the Royal Statistical Society, Series B, 27, 251-63*.

Kruskal, J. B. (1969). Toward a practical method which helps uncover the structure of a set of multivariate observations by finding the linear transformation which optimizes a new "index of condensation". In: *Statistical Computing*, eds. R. C. Milton and J. A. Nelder. New York: Academic Press.

Lai, S. L. (1977). Large sample properties of k-nearest neighbor procedures Ph.D. dissertation, Dept. Mathematics, UCLA, Los Angeles.

Lawton, W. H., Sylvestre, E. A. and Maggio, M. S. (1972). Self-modeling nonlinear regression. *Technometrics, 14, 513-32*.

Lecoutre, J. P. (1983). Almost complete convergence of the statistically equivalent blocks estimator of the regression function. In: *Probability and statistical theory, Proceedings of the 4th Pannonian Symposium on Mathematical Statistics*, eds. F. Konecny, J. Mogyorodi and W. Wertz. Dortrecht: Reidel.

Lecoutre, J. P. (1984). *The L_2-optimal cell width for the regressogram*. Unpublished manuscript.

Lejeune, M. (1985). Estimation non-paramétrique par noyaux: régression polynomiale mobile. *Revue Statist. App., 33, 43-67*.

Leontief, W. (1947a). A note on the interrelation of subsets of independent variables of a continuous function with continuous first derivatives. *Bulletin of the American Mathematical Society, 53, 343-50*.

Leontief, W. (1947b). Introduction to a theory of the internal structure of functional relationships. *Econometrica, 15, 361-73*.

Leser, C. E. (1963). Forms of Engel functions. *Econometrica, 31, 694-703*.

Leung, D. (1988). *Some problems in robust nonparametric regression*. Unpublished manuscript.

Li, K-C. (1985). From Stein's unbiased risk estimates to the method of generalized cross-validation. *Annals of Statistics, 13, 1352-77*.

Liero, H. (1982). On the maximal deviation of the kernel regression function estimate. *Mathematische Operationsforschung, Serie Statistics, 13, 171-82*.

Lipsey, R. G., Sparks, G. R. and Steiner, P. O. (1976). *Economics* (2nd ed). New York: Harper and Row.

Loftsgaarden, D. O. and Quesenberry, G. P. (1965). A nonparametric estimate of a multivariate density function. *Annals of Mathematical Statistics, 36, 1049-51*.

316   References

McCullagh, P. and Nelder, J. A. (1983). *Generalized linear models*. London: Chapman and Hall.

McDonald, J. A. (1982). Projection pursuit regression with the ORION I workstation. A 25 minute film, available from Jerome H. Friedman, Computation Research Group, Bin 88 SLAC, P.O. 4349, Standford, CA 94305.

McDonald, J. A. and Owen, A. B. (1986). Smoothing with split linear fits. *Technometrics, 28, 195-208.*

McDonald, J. A. and Pederson, J. (1986). Computing environments for data analysis: Part 3, programming environments. Laboratory for Computational Statistics, Technical Report, 24, University of Stanford, Stanford, CA.

Mack, Y. P. (1981). Local properties of k-NN Regression Estimates. *SIAM J. Alg. Disc. Meth., 2, 311-23.*

Mack, Y. P. and Silverman, B. W. (1982). Weak and strong uniform consistency of kernel regression estimates. *Zeitschrift für Wahrscheinlichkeitstheorie und verwandte Gebiete, 61, 405-15.*

Major, P. (1973). On a nonparametric estimation of the regression function. *Studia Scientiarum Mathematicarum Hungaria, 8, 347-61.*

Mallows, C. L. (1980). Some theory of nonlinear smoothers. *Annals of Statistics, 8, 695-715.*

Mammen, E. (1987). *Estimating a smooth monotone regression function.* Unpublished manuscript.

Mammen, E. (1988). *A short note on optimal bandwidth selection for kernel estimators.* Unpublished manuscript.

Manski, C. F. (1989). *Nonparametric estimation of expectations in the analysis of discrete choice under uncertainty.* Unpublished manuscript.

Manski, C. F. and McFadden, D. (1981). *Structural analysis of discrete data with econometric applications.* Cambridge, MA: MIT Press.

Marhoul, J. C. and Owen, A. B. (1984). Consistency of smoothing with running linear fits. Technical Report 8, Stanford University, Stanford, CA.

Maronna, R. A. (1976). Robust M-estimators of multivariate location and scatter. *Annals of Statistics, 4, 51-67.*

Marron, J. S. (1985). Will the art of smoothing ever become a science? In: *Function estimates*, ed. J. S. Marron. *Amer. Math. Soc. Contemporary Mathematics 59.*

Marron, J. S. and Härdle, W. (1986). Random approximations to an error criterion of nonparametric statistics. *Journal of Multivariate Analysis, 20, 91-113.*

Marron, J. S. and Nolan, D. (1988). Canonical kernels for density estimation. *Statistics and Probability Letters, 7, 195-9.*

Mattern, R., Bösche, J., Birk, J. and Härdle, W. (1983). Experimentelle Untersuchungen zum Verlauf der Alkoholkurve in der späteren Eliminationsphase. In: *Fortschritte der Rechtsmedizin*, eds. Froberg, Barz, Bösche, Käppner and Mattern. Heidelberg: Springer-Verlag.

Morgan, B. J. T. (1984). *Elements of simulation*. London: Chapman and Hall.

Müller, H. G. (1984a). Smooth optimum kernel estimators of densities, regression curves and modes. *Annals of Statistics, 12, 766-74.*

Müller, H. G. (1984b). Boundary effects in nonparametric curve estimation models. In: *COMPSTAT, 84-89, Physica Verlag.*

Müller, H. G. (1985). Kernel estimators of zeros and of location and size of extrema of regression functions. *Scandanavian Journal of Statistics, 12, 221-32.*

Müller, H. G. (1987). Weighted local regression and kernel methods for nonparametric curve fitting. *Journal of the American Statistical Association, 82, 231-8.*

Müller, H. G. and Stadtmüller, U. (1987). Estimation of heteroscedasticity in regression analysis. *Annals of Statistics, 12, 221-32.*

Müller, H. G., Stadtmüller, U. and Schmidt, T. (1987). Bandwidth choice and confidence intervals for derivatives of noisy data. *Biometrika, 74, 743-50.*

Nadaraya, E. A. (1964). On estimating regression. *Theory Prob. Appl. 10, 186-90.*

Nemirovskii, A. S., Polyak, B. T. and Tsybakov, A. B. (1983). Estimators of maximum likelihood type for nonparametric regression. *Soviet Math. Dokl., 28, 788-92.*

Nemirovskii, A. S., Polyak, B. T. and Tsybakov, A. B. (1985). Rate of convergence of nonparametric estimates of maximum likelihood type. *Problemy peredachi informatsii, 21, 17-33.* English translation in *Problems of information transmission, 258-72.* New York: Plenum.

Nussbaum, M. (1985). Spline smoothing in regression models and asymptotic efficiency in L_2. *Annals of Statistics, 13, 984-97.*

Oldford, R. W. and Peters, S. C. (1985). DINDE: Towards more statistically sophisticated software. Technical Report, Tr-55, MIT, Cambridge, MA.

Owen, A. (1987). Nonparametric conditional estimation. Technical Report, 25, Stanford University, Stanford, CA.

Parzen, E. (1962). On estimation of a probability density and mode. *Annals of Mathematical Statistics, 35, 1065-76.*

Pourciau, B. H. (1980). Modern multiplier rules. *American Mathematical Monthly, 6, 433-52.*

Powell, J. L., Stock, J. H. and Stoker, T. M. (1989). *Semiparametric estimation of index coefficients.* Unpublished manuscript.

Prakasa Rao, B. L. S. (1983). *Nonparametric functional estimation.* New York: Academic Press.

Priestley, M. B. and Chao, M. T. (1972). Nonparametric function fitting. *Journal of the Royal Statistical Society, Series B, 34, 385-92.*

Reinsch, H. (1967). Smoothing by spline functions. *Numerische Mathematik*, 10, 177–83.

Revesz, P. (1976). Robbins–Monro procedure in a Hilbert space and its application in the theory of learning processes I. *Studia Sci. Math. Hung.*, 391–8.

Revesz, P. (1977). How to apply the method of stochastic approximation in the nonparametric estimation of a regression function. *Mathematische Operationsforschung, Serie Statistics*, 8, 119–26.

Rice, J. A. (1984a). Bandwidth choice for nonparametric regression. *Annals of Statistics*, 12, 1215–30.

Rice, J. A. (1984b). Boundary modification for kernel regression. *Communications in Statistics, Series A*, 13, 893–900.

Rice, J. A. (1985). Bandwidth choice for differentiation. *Journal of Multivariate Analysis*, 20, 251–64.

Rice, J. A. (1986). Convergence rates for partially splined models. *Statistics and Probability Letters*, 4, 203–8.

Rice, J. A. and Rosenblatt, M. (1983). Smoothing splines: regression, derivatives and deconvolution. *Annals of Statistics*, 11, 141–56.

Robbins, H. and Monro, S. (1951). A Stochastic approximation method. *Annals of Mathematical Statistics*, 22, 400–7.

Robinson, P. M. (1983). Nonparametric estimators for time series. *J. Time Series Analysis*, 4, 185–207.

Robinson, P. M. (1984). Robust nonparametric autoregression. In: *Robust and nonlinear time series analysis*, eds. Franke, Härdle and Martin. Heidelberg: Springer-Verlag.

Robinson, P. M. (1987a). Asymptotically efficient estimation in the presence of heteroskedasticity of unknown form. *Econometrica*, 55, 875–91.

Robinson, P. M. (1987b). On the consistency and finite-sample properties of nonparametric kernel time series regression, autoregression and density estimators. *Annals of the Institute of Statistical Mathematics*.

Rosenblatt, M. (1956). Remarks on some nonparametric estimates of a density function. *Annals of Mathematical Statistics*, 27, 642–69.

Rosenblatt, M. (1969). Conditional probability density and regression estimators. In: *Multivariate Analysis II*, 25–31. New York: Academic Press.

Rousseeouw, P. and Yohai, P. (1984). Robust regression by means of S-estimators. In: *Robust and nonlinear time series analysis*, eds. Franke, Härdle and Martin. Heidelberg: Springer-Verlag.

Rutkowski, L. (1981). Sequential estimates of a regression function by orthogonal series with applications in discrimination. In: *The First Pannonian Symposium on Mathematical Statistics*, eds. Revesz, Schmetterer and Zolotarev, 236–44. Heidelberg: Springer-Verlag.

Rutkowski, L. (1982). On-line identification of time varying systems by nonparametric techniques. *IEEE Transactions of Automatic Control*, 27, 228–30.

Rutkowski, L. (1985a). Nonparametric identification of quasi-stationary systems. *System and Control Letters, 6, 33-5.* New York: North Holland.

Rutkowski, L. (1985b). Real-time identification of time-varying systems by nonparametric algorithms based on Parzen kernels. *International Journal of Systems Science, 16, 1123-30.*

S (1988). See Becker, Chambers and Wilks, (1988).

Sacks, J. and Ylvisaker, D. (1981). Asymptotically optimum kernels for density estimation at a point. *Annals of Statistics, 9, 334-46.*

Schmerling, S. and Peil, J. (1985). Verfahren der Lokalen Approximation zur Nichtparametrischen Schätzung Unbekannter Stetiger Funktionen aus Meßdaten. *Gegenbaurs morphologisches Jahrbuch Leipzig, 131, 367-81.*

Schmerling, S. and Peil, J. (1986). Improvement of the method of kernel estimation by local polynomial approximation of the empirical distribution function and its application to empirical regression. *Gegenbaurs morphologisches Jahrbuch Leipzig, 132, 29-35.*

Schmidt, G. Mattern, R. and Schüler, F. (1981). Biomechanical investigation to determine physical and traumatological differentiation criteria for the maximum load capacity of head and vertebral column with and without protective helmet under effects of impact. EEC Research Program on Biomechanics of Impacts. Final Report Phase III, Project 65, Institut für Rechtsmedizin, Universität Heidelberg, West Germany.

Schoenberg, I. J. (1964). Spline functions and the problem of graduation. *Mathematics, 52, 947-50.*

Schönfeld, P. (1969). Methoden der Ökonometrie, Band I Lineare Regressionmodelle. *Verlag Franz Vahlen GmbH Berlin und Frankfurt a.M.*

Schucany, W. R. and Sommers, J. P. (1977). Improvement of kernel-type density estimators *Journal of the American Statistical Association, 72, 420-3.*

Schuster, E. F. (1972). Joint asymptotic distribution of the estimated regression function at a finite number of distinct points. *Annals of Mathematical Statistics, 43, 84-8.*

Schuster, E. F. and Yakowitz, S. (1979). Contributions to the theory of nonparametric regression, with application to system identification. *Annals of Statistics, 7, 139-49.*

Scott, E. M., Baxter, M. S. and Aitchison, T. C. (1984). A comparison of the treatment of error in radiocarbon dating calibration methods. *Journal of Archeological Sciences, 11, 455-66.*

Serfling, R. J. (1980). *Approximation theorems of mathematical statistics.* New York: Wiley.

Shibata, R. (1981). An optimal selection of regression variables. *Biometrika, 68, 45-54.*

Silverman, B. W. (1982). Kernel density estimation using the Fast Fourier Transformation. *Applied Statistics 31, 93-7.*

Silverman, B. W. (1984). Spline smoothing: the equivalant variable kernel method. *Annals of Statistics, 12, 898–916.*

Silverman, B. W. (1985). Some aspects of the spline smoothing approach to nonparametric regression curve fitting (with discussion). *Journal of the Royal Statistical Society, Series B, 47, 1 52.*

Silverman, B. W. (1986). *Density estimation for statistics and data analysis.* London: Chapman and Hall.

Singh R. S. and Ullah, A. (1985). Nonparametric time series estimation of joint DGP, conditional DGP and vector autoregression. *Econometric Theory, 1.*

Speckman, P. (1988). Kernel smoothing in partial linear models *Journal of the Royal Statistical Society, Series B, 50, 413–46.*

Spiegelman, C. H. (1976). Two techniques for estimating treatment effects in the presence of hidden variables: adaptive regression and a solution to Reiersol's problem Unpublished Ph.D. thesis, Northwestern University, Dept. Mathematics.

Stone, C. J. (1977). Consistent nonparametric regression (with discussion). *Annals of Statistics, 5, 595–645.*

Stone, C. J. (1980). Optimal rates of convergence for nonparametric estimators. *Annals of Statistics, 8, 1348–60.*

Stone, C. J. (1982). Optimal global rates of convergence for nonparametric regression. *Annals of Statistics, 10, 1040–53.*

Stone, C. J. (1985). Additive regression and other nonparametric models. *Annals of Statistics, 13, 689–705.*

Stone, C. J. (1986). The dimensionality reduction principle for generalized additive models. *Annals of Statistics, 14, 590–606.*

Stone, C. J. and Koo, C. Y. (1985). Additive splines in statistics. In: *Function Estimates,* ed. J. S. Marron. Amer. Math. Soc. Contemporary Mathematics 59.

Stone, M. (1974). Cross-validatory choice and assessment of statistical predictions (with discussion). *Journal of the Royal Statistical Society, Series B, 36, 111–47.*

Stuetzle, W. and Mittal, Y. (1979). Some comments on the asymptotic behavior of robust smoothers. In: *Smoothing techniques for curve estimation,* eds. T. Gasser, and M. Rosenblatt. Heidelberg: Springer-Verlag.

Stuetzle, W., Gasser, T., Molinari, L., Largo, R. H., Prader, A. and Huber, P. J. (1980). Self-invariant modeling of human growth. *Ann. Human Biology, 7, 507–28.*

Stute, W. (1984). Asymptotic normality of nearest neighbor regression function estimates. *Annals of Statistics, 12, 917–26.*

Suess, H. E. (1980). A calibration table for conventionel radiocarbon dates. In: *Proc. IXth Int. Conf. UCLA, 1976, 777–84.* Los Angeles: UC Press.

Szegö, G. (1959). Orthogonal polynomials. *Amer. Math. Soc. Coll. Publ., 23.*

Tapia, D. and Thompson, J. (1978). *Nonparametric probability density estimation.* Baltimore, MD: The Johns Hopkins University Press.

Truong, Y. K. and Stone, C. J. (1987a). *Nonparametric time series prediction: kernel estimators based on local averages.* Unpublished manuscript.

Truong, Y. K. and Stone, C. J. (1987b). *Nonparametric time series prediction: kernel estimators based on local medians.* Unpublished manuscript.

Tsybakov, A. B. (1982a). Nonparametric signal estimation when there is incomplete information on the noise distribution, (in Russian). *Problemy peredachi informatsii, 18, 44–60.* English translation in: *Problems of information transmission, 116–30.* New York: Plenum.

Tsybakov, A. B. (1982b). Robust estimates of a function, (in Russian). *Problemy peredachi informatsii, 18, 39–52.* English translation in: *Problems of information transmission, 18, 190–201.* New York: Plenum.

Tsybakov, A. B. (1983). Convergence of nonparametric robust algorithms of reconstruction of functions, (in Russian). *Avtomatika i Telemakhanika, 12, 66–76.* English translation in: *Automation and Remote Control, 1582–91.* New York: Plenum.

Tsybakov, A. B. (1986). Robust reconstruction of functions by the local approximation method, (in Russian). *Problemy peredachi informatsii, 22, 69–84.* English translation in: *Problems of information transmission, 22, 133–46.* New York: Plenum.

Tsybakov, A. B. (1988). Passive stochastic approximation. University of Bonn, SFB 303 Discussion Paper.

Tufte, G. (1983). *The visual display of quantitative information.* New Haven, CT: Graphics.

Tukey, J. W. (1947). Nonparametric estimation II. Statistically equivalent blocks and tolerance regions. The continuous case. *Annals of Mathematical Statistics, 18, 529–39.*

Tukey, J. W. (1961). Curves as parameters and touch estimation. *Proc 4th Berkeley Symposium, 681–94.*

Tukey, J. W. (1977). *Exploratory data analysis.* Reading, MA; Addison-Welsley.

Tukey, J. W. (1987). Discussion of "What is projection pursuit" of Jones and Sibson. *Journal of the Royal Statistical Society, Series A, 150, 1–38.*

Ullah, A. (1987). *Nonparametric estimation of econometric functionals.* Unpublished manuscript.

Uspensky, J. V. (1937). *Introduction to mathematical probability.* New York: McGraw Hill.

Utreras, F. I. (1986). Smoothing noisy data using monotonicity constraints. *Numerische Mathematik, 47, 611–25.*

Velleman, P. F. (1977). Robust nonlinear data smoothers: definitions and recommendations. *Proc. Natl. Acad. Sci. USA, 74, 434–6.*

Velleman, P. F. (1980). Definition and comparison of robust nonlinear data smoothing algorithms. *Journal of the American Statistical Association, 75, 609–15.*

Wahba, G. (1975). Optimal convergence properties of variable knot, kernel, and orthogonal series methods for density estimation. *Annals of Statistics, 3, 15–29.*

Wahba, G. (1977). A survey of some smoothing problems and the method of generalized cross-validation for solving them. In: *Applications of Statistics,* ed. P. R. Krishnaiah. Amsterdam: North Holland.

Wahba, G. (1979). Convergence rates of "thin plate" smoothing splines when the data are noisy. In: *Smoothing techniques for curve estimation,* eds. T. Gasser and M. Rosenblatt. New York: Springer-Verlag.

Wahba, G. (1980). Automatic smoothing of the log periodogram. *Journal of the American Statistical Association, 75, 122–32.*

Wahba, G. and Wold, S. (1975). A completely automatic French curve: fitting spline functions by cross-validation. *Communications in Statistics, Series A, 4, 1–17.*

Walter, G. (1977). Properties of Hermite series estimation of probability density. *Annals of Statistics, 5, 1258–64.*

Walter, G. and Blum, J. (1979). Probability density estimation using delta sequences. *Annals of Statistics, 7, 328–40.*

Watson, G. S. and Leadbetter, M. R. (1963). On the estimation of the probability density, I. *Annals of Mathematical Statistics, 34, 480–91.*

Watson, G. S. (1964). Smooth regression analysis. *Sankhyā, Series A, 26, 359–72.*

Watson, G. S. and Leadbetter, M. R. (1964). Hazard analysis II. *Sankhyā, Series A, 26, 101–16.*

Whittaker, E. T. (1923). On a new method of graduation. *Proc. Edinburgh Math. Soc., 41, 63–75.*

Whittle, P. (1960). Bounds for the moments of linear and quadratic forms in independent variables. *Theory of Probability and Its Applications, 5, 302.*

Working, H. and Hotelling, H. (1929). Application of the theory of error to the interpretation of trends. *Journal of the American Statistical Association, Suppl. (Proc.), 24, 73–85.*

Wright, I. W. and Wegman E. J. (1980). Isotonic, convex and related splines. *Annals of Statistics, 8, 1023–35.*

Wu, C. F. J. (1986). Jackknife, bootstrap and other resampling methods in regression analysis. *Annals of Statistics, 14, 1261–343.*

Wynn, H. P. (1984). An exact confidence band for one-dimensional polynomial regression. *Biometrika, 71, 375–9.*

XploRe (1989). See Härdle (1987b) and Broich, Härdle and Krause (1989).

Yakowitz, S. (1985a). Nonparametric density estimation, prediction, and regression for Markov sequences. *Journal of the American Statistical Association, 80, 215–21.*

Yakowitz, S. (1985b). Markov flow models and the flood warning problem. *Water Resources Research, 21, 81–8.*

Yakowitz, S. (1987). Nearest neighbor methods for time series analysis. *Journal of Time Series Analysis, 18, 1-13.*

Yakowitz, S. and Szidarovsky, F. (1986). *An introduction to numerical computations.* New York: Macmillan.

Yang, S. (1981). Linear functions of concomitants of order statistics with application to nonparametric estimation of a regression function. *Journal of the American Statistical Association, 76, 658-62.*

Author index

Subject index

(Page numbers in italics indicate material in figures or tables.)

accuracy, 133–8

adaptive smoothing (local), 177

additive separable model, 270

adjusted curve, 232–3

alternating conditional expectations (ACE), 269–74

asymptotic confidence bands; *see* confidence bands

automatically chosen band widths (comparing between laboratories and parameter choice), 184–9

automatic selection, 147, 165–77

average derivative estimation (ADE), 274–81, 298–9

average squared error (ASE), 90, 172; smoothing parameter selection and, 150

bandwidth changes, optimal choice of, 213–14

bandwidth choice and derivative estimation (minimizing MISE), 160–1

bandwidths, comparing automatically chosen between laboratories and parameter choice, 184–9

bandwidth selection procedures, 148–52

bias, 213; cross validation and, 148, 149, 151; kernel smoothers and,

bias (*cont.*)

76, *77*, 141–6; trade-off between variance (k-NN estimate) and, 44

bins, 35

biomechanical experiments, 14

Bonferroni method, 119, 126, 128

bootstrap technique: confidence band construction and, 102–8; improving the smooth locally by, 177–81; naive, 246–7; variability bands for functions and, 111, 118–28; wild, 247, 249

boundary behavior: effects, 80; kernel smooth and, 130–3; weight function and smoothing parameter and, 162

Box plot, 295, 297

Box–Cox procedure, 219

canonical kernels, 135, 184–9

computing programming, 291–300

confidence bands, variability bands for functions and, 114–18

conditional intervals for kernel estimates (pointwise), 98–111

convolution smoothing, 28, 68

cross-validation, 166; bandwidth selection procedures and, 148–52; choice of global smoothing parameter and, 179; derivative estimation bandwidth choice and,

329